Thomas Erskine May

**The Constitutional History of England**

Vol. 2

Thomas Erskine May

**The Constitutional History of England**
*Vol. 2*

ISBN/EAN: 9783337338121

Printed in Europe, USA, Canada, Australia, Japan

Cover: Foto ©ninafisch / pixelio.de

More available books at **www.hansebooks.com**

# THE
# CONSTITUTIONAL HISTORY
# OF ENGLAND

*SINCE THE ACCESSION OF GEORGE THE THIRD*

## 1760–1860

BY

SIR THOMAS ERSKINE MAY, K.C.B. D.C.L.

WITH A NEW SUPPLEMENTARY CHAPTER, 1861–71

*Fifth Edition*

IN THREE VOLUMES
VOL. II.

LONDON
LONGMANS, GREEN, AND CO.
1875

*All rights reserved*

# CONTENTS

## OF

# THE SECOND VOLUME.

## CHAPTER VII.

RELATIONS OF PARLIAMENT TO THE CROWN, THE LAW, AND THE PEOPLE.

|  | PAGE |
|---|---|
| Contests of the Commons on questions of privilege | 1 |
| Proceedings of the Commons against Wilkes, 1763 | 2 |
| And of the Lords | 6 |
| Wilkes returned for Middlesex | 8 |
| His two years' imprisonment | 9 |
| His expulsion for libel on Lord Weymouth | 10 |
| His re-elections, and final exclusion | 13 |
| Lord Chatham's efforts to reverse the proceedings against Wilkes, 1770 | 16 |
| Similar proceedings in the Commons | 17 |
| The City of London addresses the king on Wilkes's expulsion | 20 |
| Motions in the Lords to reverse the proceedings against Wilkes | 22 |
| Resolutions against him expunged, 1782 | 26 |
| Exclusion of strangers from parliamentary debates | 27 |
| Members of the Commons excluded from the Lords, 1770 | 31 |
| Consequent misunderstanding between the two Houses | 32 |
| Publication of parliamentary debates | 34 |
| Commencement of the system | ib. |
| Misrepresentations of reporters | 37 |
| Their personalities | 39 |
| Contest between the Commons and the printers, 1771 | 40 |

## Contents of the Second Volume.

| | PAGE |
|---|---|
| Wilkes and the Lord Mayor interpose in behalf of the latter | 41 |
| The Commons proceed against the city magistrates | 43 |
| Reports of debates permitted | 49 |
| Progress of the system | ib. |
| Political results of reporting | 53 |
| Presence of strangers recognised, 1845 | 55 |
| The publication of the division lists, 1836 | ib. |
| And of parliamentary papers | 58 |
| Freedom of comments upon Parliament | 59 |
| Early petitions, and rights of petitioners | 60 |
| Commencement of modern system of petitioning | 63 |
| Petitioning at the beginning of the present century | 66 |
| Abuses of petitioning | 68 |
| Debates on presenting petitions restrained | 69 |
| Pledges of members to constituents considered | 70 |
| Surrender of certain parliamentary privileges | 73 |
| Conflict of privilege and law | 75 |
| Sir F. Burdett's case | 76 |
| The Stockdale cases | 78 |
| Right of Parliament to publish papers affecting character determined by statute | 82 |
| Moderation of the Commons in forwarding the admission of Jews to Parliament | 84 |
| Control of Parliament over the executive government | 85 |
| Over questions of peace and war | 86 |
| Advice of Parliament concerning a dissolution | 88 |
| Popular addresses on the same subject | 89 |
| Relations between the Commons and the ministers of the Crown | 90 |
| Votes expressing confidence or otherwise | 91 |
| Impeachments | 92 |
| Improved relations of the Crown with the Commons | 95 |
| Stability of governments, before and since reform, considered | ib. |
| Control of the Commons over supply and taxes | 98 |
| Their liberality to the Crown | 99 |
| Cases of delaying the supplies | 102 |
| Restraints upon the liberality of the Commons | 103 |
| Exclusive rights of the Commons concerning taxation | 104 |
| Power of the Lords to reject a money bill considered | 105 |
| Rejection of the Paper Duties Bill, 1860 | 108 |
| Sketch of parliamentary oratory | 112 |

| | PAGE |
|---|---|
| Orators of the age of Chatham and Pitt | 113 |
| Orators at the commencement of this century | 118 |
| Characteristics of modern oratory | 123 |
| Coarse personalities of former times | 125 |
| General standard of modern debate | 128 |

## CHAPTER VIII.

### PARTY.

| | |
|---|---|
| Influence of party on Parliamentary government | 131 |
| The principles represented by English parties | 132 |
| Origin of parties | 133 |
| The Puritans | ib. |
| Parties under the Stuarts | 134 |
| Whigs and Tories | 135 |
| Parties after the Revolution | 136 |
| Classes from which parties were mainly drawn | 138 |
| Revival of the Tory party on the accession of George III. | 141 |
| The king's efforts to break up parties | 142 |
| Alliance of the king's friends with the Tories | 143 |
| The Whigs in opposition | 144 |
| Resistance to change, a principle adopted by the Tories | 145 |
| Party principles tested by the American war | 147 |
| Secession of the Whigs from Parliament, 1776 | 148 |
| The Whigs and the American war | 149 |
| Rise of the democratic party | 151 |
| The Whigs in power, 1782 | ib. |
| Party crisis on the death of Lord Rockingham | 152 |
| The Coalition, 1783 | 153 |
| Its overthrow | 155 |
| Principles of coalition considered | 157 |
| The Tory party under Mr. Pitt | 158 |
| Character of Lord Thurlow | 160 |
| The Whigs and the Prince of Wales | 161 |
| Influence of the French Revolution upon parties | 163 |
| Disruption of the Whigs | 164 |
| Many leading Whigs coalesce with Mr. Pitt | 166 |
| The consolidation of his party | 168 |
| Ostracism of liberal opinions | 171 |
| The Tory party in Scotland | 172 |
| Secession of the Whigs from Parliament, 1798 | 173 |

|                                                                 | PAGE |
|-----------------------------------------------------------------|------|
| Disunion of the Tories, 1805                                    | 174  |
| The Whigs in office, 1806                                       | 177  |
| The Tories reinstated, 1807                                     | 179  |
| The Whig party revived                                          | 180  |
| The Tories under Lord Liverpool                                 | 182  |
| Democratic sentiments provoked by distress, 1817–1820           | 185  |
| The Whigs associated with the people                            | 186  |
| Increasing power of public opinion                              | ib.  |
| Disunion of the Tories on the death of Lord Liverpool           | 189  |
| Mr. Canning supported by the Whigs                              | 190  |
| The Duke of Wellington's administration                         | 191  |
| Effect of Catholic emancipation upon parties                    | 192  |
| The Whigs in power, 1830: their union with the people           | 195  |
| Parties after the Reform Act                                    | 198  |
| The Radicals                                                    | ib.  |
| The Irish party                                                 | 201  |
| The Tory party assume the name of Conservatives                 | 203  |
| Sir Robert Peel's short ministry, 1834–35                       | 205  |
| Parties under Lord Melbourne                                    | 206  |
| Conservative reaction                                           | 208  |
| Sir Robert Peel's second ministry                               | 209  |
| His free-trade policy                                           | 210  |
| His relations with his party                                    | 212  |
| Obligations of a party leader considered                        | 214  |
| Conservatives after Sir Robert Peel's fall                      | 215  |
| The Whigs in office, 1846–1852                                  | 216  |
| Lord Derby's ministry, 1852                                     | ib.  |
| Union of Whigs and Peelites under Lord Aberdeen, 1853           | 217  |
| Lord Palmerston as premier, 1855                                | 219  |
| Combination of parties against him                              | ib.  |
| His popularity, and sudden fall                                 | 220  |
| Lord Derby's second ministry, 1858                              | 221  |
| Lord Palmerston's second ministry, 1859                         | 222  |
| Fusion of parties                                               | 223  |
| Essential difference between Conservatives and Liberals         | ib.  |
| Changes in the character of parties                             | 225  |
| Politics formerly a profession                                  | 227  |
| Effect of reform upon parties                                   | 230  |
| Conservatism of age                                             | 232  |
| Statesmen under the old and new systems                         | ib.  |
| Patronage as an instrument of party                             | 234  |
| Effect of competition upon patronage                            | 235  |
| Review of the evils and merits of party                         | 236  |

## CHAPTER IX.

### THE PRESS, AND LIBERTY OF OPINION.

|  | PAGE |
|---|---|
| Freedom of opinion the greatest of liberties | 238 |
| The last to be recognised | ib. |
| Censorship of the press | 239 |
| The first newspapers | 240 |
| The press under the Stuarts and the Commonwealth | ib. |
| After the Restoration | 242 |
| Expiration of the Licensing Bill | 243 |
| The press in the reign of Anne | ib. |
| In the reigns of Geo. I. and II. | 245 |
| The press on the accession of Geo. III. | 246 |
| Wilkes and the 'North Briton' | 247 |
| Ex-officio informations | 251 |
| Junius's letters and the law of libel | 252 |
| Juries denied the right to judge of the offence of libel | 253 |
| Case of the Dean of St. Asaph | 258 |
| Stockdale's trial | 259 |
| Mr. Fox's Act to amend the law of libel | 262 |
| Progress of free discussion in the press | 264 |
| Public meetings and associations | 265 |
| The silk-weavers' riots, 1765 | 266 |
| Meetings and associations, 1768–70 | 268 |
| Public meetings, 1779–80 | ib. |
| Political associations considered | 270 |
| Protestant associations, their bigotry and violence | 272 |
| Lord George Gordon's riots, 1780 | 273 |
| Military action in absence of a magistrate | 276 |
| The Slave Trade Association, 1787: its means of agitation, and causes of success | 277 |
| Progress of public opinion, 1760–92 | 278 |
| Democratic publications, 1792 | 279 |
| Democratic associations | 281 |
| Exaggerated alarm of democracy | 284 |
| Repressive policy, 1792 | 285 |
| Proclamation against seditious writings | 287 |
| Prosecutions for sedition | 289 |
| Societies for suppressing sedition | 290 |

|                                                           | PAGE |
| --------------------------------------------------------- | ---- |
| Democracy in Scotland                                     | 292  |
| Trials of Muir, Palmer, and others                        | ib.  |
| These trials noticed in Parliament                        | 299  |
| Trials for sedition in England, 1794                      | 300  |
| Reports of secret committees                              | 302  |
| State trials, 1794, of Watt and Downie                    | 304  |
| And of Hardy, Horne Tooke, and others                     | 307  |
| Attack upon the king, 1795                                | 316  |
| The Treasonable Practices Bill                            | 317  |
| The Seditious Meetings Bill                               | 319  |
| Public opposition to these bills                          | 323  |
| Mr. Reeves's pamphlet                                     | 325  |
| Regulation of newspapers, 1789–98                         | 327  |
| Bill to suppress corresponding societies, 1799            | 329  |
| Repressive measures completed: their effects              | 330  |
| Trials of Mr. Wakefield and the 'Courier,' 1799           | 331  |
| Trials of Jean Peltier, 1803                              | 333  |
| Trials of Cobbett and the Messrs. Hunt, 1804–11           | 334  |
| Progress of free discussion reviewed                      | 337  |

## CHAPTER X.

### THE PRESS, AND LIBERTY OF OPINION, CONTINUED.

|                                                                       |      |
| --------------------------------------------------------------------- | ---- |
| Repressive policy of the regency                                      | 340  |
| Disturbed state of the country, 1815–16                               | 341  |
| Outrage on the prince regent, 1817                                    | 342  |
| Repressive measures                                                   | 343  |
| Trials of Watson and others, 1817                                     | 345  |
| Lord Sidmouth's circular to the magistrates                           | ib.  |
| Powers exercised against the press                                    | 348  |
| Trials of Hone, 1817                                                  | 349  |
| Agitation in the manufacturing districts, 1819                        | 351  |
| The Manchester meeting                                                | 353  |
| The Six Acts, 1819                                                    | 358  |
| The Cato Street Conspiracy, 1820                                      | 362  |
| Trials of Hunt and Sir C. Wolseley                                    | 363  |
| The contest between authority and liberty of opinion reviewed         | ib.  |
| Final domination of public opinion over authority                     | 364  |
| The Constitutional Society and the press, 1821                        | 367  |
| The Catholic Association                                              | 368  |

## Contents of the Second Volume.    xi

|  | PAGE |
|---|---|
| Suppressed by Parliament, 1825 | 371 |
| But continued in another form | ib. |
| Final suppression of the association, 1829 | 375 |
| Progress of public opinion in the reign of Geo. IV. | 376 |
| Later prosecutions of the press, 1830 | 378 |
| Complete freedom of the press established | 379 |
| Fiscal laws affecting the press | 380 |
| Repeal of 'Taxes on knowledge' | 381 |
| General freedom of opinion | 383 |
| Agitation for Parliamentary Reform, 1830-32 | ib. |
| Political unions and excited meetings | 385 |
| Riots on rejection of the second Reform Bill | 387 |
| Dangerous excitement during the Reform crisis | 391 |
| Causes of the popular triumph | 392 |
| Agitation for repeal of the Union: causes of its failure | 393 |
| Mr. O'Connell submits to the law, 1831 | 394 |
| His trial, 1844 | 398 |
| The Orange lodges suppressed | 402 |
| The Anti-Slavery Association | 404 |
| Trades' unions and Dorchester labourers | 405 |
| The Chartists, 1837-48: inevitable failure of their agitation | 407 |
| Chartist meeting, April 10th, 1848 | 410 |
| The Anti-Corn Law League: its organisation, and causes of success | 413 |
| Political agitation reviewed | 417 |
| Altered relations of government to the people | 419 |

# CHAPTER VII.

RELATIONS OF PARLIAMENT TO THE CROWN, THE LAW, AND THE PEOPLE.—ABUSES OF PRIVILEGE IN PROCEEDINGS AGAINST WILKES. —EXCLUSION OF STRANGERS:—PUBLICATION OF DEBATES RESTRAINED:—CONTEST WITH THE PRINTERS, 1771:—FREEDOM OF REPORTING ESTABLISHED:—ITS POLITICAL RESULTS:—ENTIRE PUBLICITY OF PROCEEDINGS IN PARLIAMENT:—PETITIONS:—PLEDGES OF MEMBERS.—CONFLICT OF PRIVILEGE AND LAW.—INCREASED POWER, AND MODERATION OF THE COMMONS.—CONTROL OF PARLIAMENT OVER THE EXECUTIVE:— IMPEACHMENTS:— CONTROL OF THE COMMONS OVER TAXES AND EXPENDITURE.—SKETCH OF PARLIAMENTARY ORATORY.

WE have traced, in the last chapter, the changes which were successively introduced into the constitution of the House of Commons,—the efforts made to reduce the influence of the crown, the ministers, and the aristocracy over its members,—to restrain corruption, and encourage an honest and independent discharge of its duties to the public. We have now to regard Parliament,—and mainly the House of Commons,— under another aspect: to observe how it has wielded the great powers entrusted to it,—in what manner it has respected the prerogatives of the crown, the authority of the law, and other jurisdictions,—and how far it has acknowledged its own responsibilities to the people.

Throughout its history, the House of Commons has had struggles with the crown, the House of Lords, the courts of law, the press, and the people. At one time straining *Contests of the Commons on questions of privilege.*

its own powers, at another resisting encroachments upon its just authority: successful in asserting its rights, but failing in its usurpations; it has gradually assumed its proper position in the state,— controlling all other powers, but itself controlled and responsible. The worst period of its dependence and corruption, was also marked by the most flagrant abuses of its power. And the more it has been brought under the control of public opinion,—the greater have been its moderation and forbearance.

The reign of George III. witnessed many remarkable changes in the relations of Parliament to the people, which all contributed to increase its responsibility. Moral causes also extended the control of the people over their rulers, even more than amendments of the law, by which constitutional abuses were corrected. Events occurred early in this reign, which brought to a decisive issue, important questions affecting the privileges of Parliament, and the rights of the subject.

*Proceedings of the Commons against Wilkes, 1763.*
The liberty of the subject had already been outraged by the imprisonment of Wilkes, under a general warrant, for the publication of the celebrated No. 45 of the 'North Briton;'[1] when Parliament thrust itself forward, as if to prove how privilege could still be abused, as well as prerogative. Being a member of the House of Commons, Wilkes had been released from his imprisonment, by the Court of Common Pleas, on a writ of *habeas corpus*, on the ground of his privilege.[2]

[1] See Chap. XI.   [2] Wilson's Reports, ii 150. St. Tr., xix. 539.

The only exceptions to the privilege of freedom from arrest, which had ever been recognised by Parliament, were 'treason, felony, and breach of the peace,' 'or refusing to give surety of the peace.' The court properly acknowledged the privilege, as defined by Parliament itself; and discharged Wilkes from his imprisonment. He was afterwards served with a subpœna, on an information against him in the Court of King's Bench, to which, on the ground of privilege, he had not entered an appearance. On the meeting of Parliament, however, in November, 1763, he lost no time in stating that if his privilege should be affirmed, he was ready to waive it, 'and to put himself upon a jury of his countrymen.'[1] Parliament,—which had ordinarily been too prone to enlarge its privileges,—was now the first to abridge and surrender them. Eager to second the vengeance of the king, the Commons commenced by voting that the 'North Briton,' No. 45, was 'a false, scandalous, and malicious libel,' and ordering it to be burned by the hands of the common hangman. Then, in defiance of their own previous resolutions, they resolved 'that privilege of Parliament does not extend to the case of writing and publishing seditious libels, nor ought to be allowed to obstruct the ordinary course of law, in the speedy and effectual prosecution of so heinous and dangerous an offence.'[2]

*Wilkes denied his privilege.*

To the principle of the latter part of this resolution there can be little exception; but here it was

[1] Parl. Hist., xv. 1361.
[2] Com. Journ., xxix. 689; Parl. Hist., xv. 1362-1378.

applied *ex post facto* to a particular case, and used to justify a judicial decision, contrary to law and usage. Mr. Pitt, while he denounced the libel and the libeller, remonstrated against the abandonment of the privilege. These resolutions being communicated to the Lords, were agreed to; but not without a most able protest, signed by seventeen peers, against the surrender of the privilege of Parliament 'to serve a particular purpose, *ex post facto, et pendente lite,* in the courts below.'[1]

Such a libel as that of Wilkes, a few years later, would have attracted little notice: but at that time it is not surprising that it provoked a legal prosecution. It was, however, a libel upon the king's ministers, rather than upon the king himself. Upon Parliament it contained nothing but an obscure innuendo,[2] which alone brought the matter legitimately within the limits of privilege. There were, doubtless, many precedents,—to be avoided, rather than followed,—for pronouncing writings to be seditious: but sedition is properly an offence cognisable by law. So far as the libel affected the character of either House, it was within the scope of privilege: but its seditious character could only be determined by the courts, where a prosecution had already been commenced. To condemn the libel as seditious was, therefore, to anticipate the decision of the proper

---

[1] Parl. Hist., xv. 1371; Ann. Reg., 1763, 135. Horace Walpole says it was drawn up by Chief Justice Pratt.
[2] The passage reflecting upon Parliament was as follows: 'As to the entire approbation of Parliament [of the peace] which is so vainly boasted of, the world knows how that was obtained. The large debt on the civil list, already above half a year in arrear, shows pretty clearly the transactions of the winter.'

tribunal: and to order it to be burned by the hands of the common hangman,—if no great punishment to the libeller,—yet branded him as a criminal before his trial. The mob took part with Wilkes, —assailed the Sheriffs who were executing the orders of Parliament; and having rescued part of the obnoxious 'North Briton' from the flames, bore it in triumph to Temple Bar, beyond the limits of the city jurisdiction. Here they made another bonfire, and burned a jack-boot and a petticoat, the favourite emblems of the late unpopular minister Lord Bute, and the Princess.[1] This outrage was resented by both Houses; an address being voted for a prosecution of all persons concerned in it.[2]

The severities of Parliament were still pursuing Wilkes. He had been ordered by the Commons to attend in his place, with a view to further proceedings; but having been wounded in a duel,—provoked and forced upon him by Mr. Martin, one of their own members,[3]—his attendance was necessarily deferred. Meanwhile, expecting no mercy either from the crown or from Parliament,—tracked by spies, and beset with petty persecutions,[4]— he prudently withdrew to Paris. Being absent, in contempt of the orders of the House, the proceedings were no longer stayed; and evidence having been taken at the bar, of his being the author and publisher of the 'North Briton,' No. 45, he was expelled the House. In expelling a

*Wilkes absconds, and is expelled.*

---

[1] Walpole's Mem., i. 330.   [2] Parl. Hist., xv. 1380.
[3] See Corresp., Parl. Hist., xv. 1356, n.
[4] Grenville Papers, ii. 155.

member, whom they had adjudged to have committed the offence of writing and publishing a seditious libel, the Commons acted within their powers: but the vote was precipitate and vindictive. He was about to be tried for his offence; and they might at least have waited for his conviction, instead of prejudging his cause, and anticipating his legal punishment.

But the Lords far outstripped the other House, in this race of persecution. On the first day of the session, while the Commons were dealing with the 'North Briton,' Lord Sandwich complained to the Lords of an 'Essay on Woman,' with notes, to which the name of Bishop Warburton was affixed; and of another printed paper called 'The *Veni Creator* paraphrased.' Of the 'Essay on Woman,' thirteen copies only had been printed, in Wilkes' private printing-press: there was no evidence of publication; and a proof-copy of the work had been obtained through the treachery of one of his printers. If these writings were obscene and blasphemous, their author had exposed himself to the law: but the only pretence for noticing them in Parliament, was the absurd use of the name of a bishop,— a member of their Lordships' House. Hence it became a breach of privilege! This ingenious device was suggested by the chancellor, Lord Henley; and Mr. Grenville obtained the bishop's consent to complain of the outrage, in his name.[1] But it was beneath the dignity of the House to notice such writings, obtained in such a manner; and it was notorious that the politics of

*Proceedings of the Lords.*

---
[1] Grenville Papers, ii. 154.

the author were the true ground of offence, and not his blasphemy, or his irreverence to the bishop. The proceeding was the more ridiculous, from the complaint of obscenity having been made by the most profligate of peers,—' Satan rebuking sin.'[1] Nevertheless the Lords were not ashamed to examine the printers, from whom the proof-sheets had been obtained, in order to prove that Wilkes was the author. They at once addressed the king to order a prosecution of Wilkes : but as he was, at this time, laid up with his wounds, proceedings against him for the breach of privilege were postponed. On the 24th January, when he had escaped from their jurisdiction, they ordered him into custody.[2] They were at least spared the opprobrium of further oppression: but their proceedings had not escaped the indignation and ridicule which they deserved.

Leaving Wilkes, for a time, as a popular martyr, —and passing over his further contests with the government in the courts of law,—we shall find him, a few years later, again coming into collision with Parliament, and becoming the successful champion of popular rights.

The discussions on his case were scarcely concluded, when a complaint was made to the Lords, by Lord Lyttelton, of a book with the title of 'Droit Le Roi.' It was the *'Droit Le Roi' ordered to be burned.*

---

[1] '"The Beggar's Opera" being performed at Covent-Garden Theatre soon after this event, the whole audience, when Macheath says, "That Jemmy Twitcher should peach me, I own surprises me," burst out into an applause of application; and the nick-name of Jemmy Twitcher stuck by the earl so as almost to occasion the disuse of his title.'—*Walpole's Mem.*, i. 314.
[2] Parl. Hist., xv. 1346.

very opposite of Wilkes' writings,—being a high prerogative treatise, founded upon statutes, precedents, and the dicta of lawyers before the Revolution. It was too monstrous to be defended by any one; and, like the 'North Briton,' it was ordered by both Houses to be burned by the hands of the common hangman.[1] There was no pretence for dealing with this case as a breach of privilege: but as the popular cause had suffered from the straining of privilege, in the person of Wilkes, no one attempted to save this ultra-loyal treatise from the flames.

<small>Wilkes returned for Middlesex, 1768.</small>

At the dissolution of Parliament in 1768, Wilkes, who had, in the meantime, resided abroad, —an exile and an outlaw,—offered himself as a candidate for the city of London. He was defeated: but the memory of his wrongs was revived; and with no other claim to popular favour, he found himself the idol of the people. He now became a candidate for Middlesex, and was returned by a large majority. His triumph was celebrated by his partisans, who forced the inhabitants of London to illuminate, and join in their cry of 'Wilkes and liberty,'—marking every door, as they passed along, with the popular number '45.'

<small>His imprisonment by the Court of King's Bench.</small>

But he was soon to suffer the penalties of his past offences. On the first day of the ensuing session, having appeared before the Court of King's Bench on his outlawry, he was committed on a *capias utlagatum*. Rescued by the mob, he again surrendered himself;

---

[1] Parl. Hist., xv. 1418; Lords' Journ., xxx. 477, &c.; Walpole's Mem., i. 383.

and his imprisonment was the unhappy occasion of riots, and of a collision between the military and the people. His outlawry was soon afterwards reversed: but he was sentenced to two years' imprisonment for his libels.

During the first session of this Parliament, therefore, Wilkes was unable to take his seat; and as yet no proceedings were commenced against him in the House of Commons. At the opening of the second session, in November, he brought himself into notice by accusing Lord Mansfield,—in a petition to the House,—of having altered the record on his trial; and Mr. Webb, the Solicitor of the Treasury, of having bribed Curry, the printer, with public money, to appear as a witness against him. His charges were voted to be groundless: but they served the purpose of exciting popular sympathy. He was brought down to Westminster to prove them, attended by a large concourse of people;[1] and for a moment he perplexed the House by submitting whether, being a member, he could stand at the bar, without having taken the oaths, and delivered in his qualification. But he soon received the obvious answer that being in custody at the bar, the acts affecting members sitting in the House, did not apply to his case.[2] *Wilkes' charges against Lord Mansfield and Mr. Webb, 1768.*

But a graver matter in which Wilkes had involved himself, was now to be considered. He had published a letter from Lord Weymouth *Libel upon Lord Weymouth.*

[1] Walpole's Mem., iii. 314; Wraxall's Mem., ii. 303.
[2] Com. Journ., Nov. 14th, 1768, to Feb. 1st, 1769; Cavendish Deb., i. 46-131.

to the magistrates of Surrey, advising them to call in the military for the suppression of riots, with a prefatory letter of his own, in which he had applied the strongest language to the secretary of state; and had designated the late collision between the troops and the populace in St. George's Fields, as a bloody massacre. Here again, a strange and irregular proceeding was resorted to. The letter was a libel upon a secretary of state, as an officer of the crown; who, being also a peer, complained of it as a breach of privilege. But instead of proceeding against the author in the House of Lords, the paper was voted an insolent, scandalous, and seditious libel; and a conference was held with the Commons on the conduct of Wilkes, as a member of their House.[1] They immediately took the matter up; and rushing headlong into a quarrel which did not concern them, called upon Wilkes for his defence. He boldly confessed himself the author of the prefatory letter; and gloried in having brought 'to light that bloody scroll' of Lord Weymouth. The letter was voted to be an insolent, scandalous, and seditious libel. A motion was then made for the expulsion of Wilkes, founded upon several distinct grounds: first, this last seditious libel, which, if a breach of privilege, was cognisable by the Lords, and not by the Commons, and, if a seditious libel, was punishable by law: secondly, the publication of the 'North Briton,' five years before, for which Wilkes was already under sentence,

*Resolutions for his expulsion.*

[1] Lords' Journ., xxxii. 213.

and had suffered expulsion from a former Parliament: thirdly, his impious and obscene libels, for which he was already suffering punishment, by the judgment of a criminal court; and, fourthly, that he was under sentence of the court to suffer twenty-two months' imprisonment.

Such were the cumulative charges, upon which it was now proposed to expel him. Nothing can be more undoubted than the right of the House of Commons to expel one of its own members, for any offence which, in its judgment, deserves such punishment,—whether it be a breach of privilege or not. But here the exercise of this right was unjust and oppressive. It was forcibly argued, that for all the offences enumerated, but one, Wilkes had already suffered, and was still suffering. For his remaining offence,—the libel on a secretary of state,—it was not the province of the House to condemn and punish him by this summary process. It should be left to the courts to try him,—and, if found guilty, to inflict the punishment prescribed by law. For his old offences he could scarcely be expelled. During a whole session he had been a member; and yet they had not been held to justify his expulsion. Then why should they now call for such severity? Clearly on the ground of his libel on Lord Weymouth. The very enumeration of so many grounds of expulsion, implied their separate weakness and insufficiency; while it was designed to attract the support of members, influenced by different reasons for their votes. These arguments were urged by Mr. Burke, Mr. Pitt, Mr. Dowdeswell, Mr. Beckford,

Mr. Cornwall, and, above all, by Mr. George Grenville.[1] The masterly speech of the latter does great credit to his judgment and foresight. When a minister, he had been the first to bring the House of Commons into collision with Wilkes: but he now recoiled from the struggle which was impending. Having shown the injustice of the proposed punishment, he proceeded to show its impolicy and danger. He predicted that Wilkes would be re-elected, and that the House would have but two alternatives,—both objectionable; either to expel him again, and suspend the issue of the writ for the entire Parliament; or to declare another candidate,—with a minority of votes,—to be elected, on the ground of Wilkes' legal disqualification. In both cases the law would be violated, and the rights of the electors invaded. And in warning them of the dangerous contest they were about to commence, he predicted that the power and popularity of the demagogue would suddenly be reduced, if he were relieved from his martyrdom, and admitted to the legislature, where his true character would be discovered.

But all these arguments and cautions were proffered in vain. The House,—making common cause with the court,—had resolved to scourge the insolent libeller who had intruded himself into their councils; and, regardless of future consequences, they voted his expulsion by a large majority. According to Burke, 'the point to be gained by the cabal was this: that a precedent should be established, tending to show that the favour of the

---

[1] Parl. Hist., xvi. 546; Cavendish Deb., i. 151.

people was not so sure a road as the favour of the court, even to popular honours and popular trusts.' 'Popularity was to be rendered, if not directly penal, at least highly dangerous.'[1] This view, however, is too deep and philosophical, to have been the true one. The court party, having been defied and insulted by a political opponent, were determined to crush him; and scarcely stopped to consider whether the laws were outraged or not.

Up to this time, whatever may have been the injustice and impolicy of their proceedings, the Commons had not exceeded their legal powers. The grounds on which they had expelled a member may have been insufficient; but of their sufficiency, they alone were competent to judge.

They were now, however, about to commit unwarrantable excesses of jurisdiction, and to violate the clearest principles of law. As Mr. Grenville had predicted, Wilkes was immediately re-elected without opposition.[2] The next day, on the motion of Lord Strange, the House resolved that Mr. Wilkes 'having been, in this session of Parliament, expelled the House, was and is incapable of being elected a member, to serve in this present Parliament.' The election was accordingly declared void, and a new writ issued.[3] There were precedents for this course;[4] for this was not the first time the Commons

*Wilkes re-elected.*

*His election declared void.*

---

[1] Present Discontents; Works, ii. 294.
[2] So stated by a member who was present; Parl. Hist., xvi. 580.
[3] Feb. 17th, 1769; Cavendish Deb., i. 345.
[4] See May's Law of Parliament (6th Ed.), 58; Townsend's Mem., ii. 100.

had exceeded their jurisdiction; but it could not be defended upon any sound principles of law. If by a vote of the House, a disability, unknown to the law, could be created,—any man who became obnoxious might, on some ground or other, be declared incapable. Incapacity would then be declared,—not by the law of the land, but by the arbitrary will of the House of Commons. On the other hand, the House felt strongly that their power of expulsion was almost futile, if their judgment could be immediately set aside by the electors; or, as it was put by General Conway, 'if a gentleman who returns himself for any particular borough, were to stand up and say that he would, in opposition to the powers of the House, insist upon being a member of Parliament.'[1]

*Again re-elected, and election declared void.* Again, with still increasing popularity, Wilkes was re-elected without opposition; and again a new writ was issued. In order to prevent a repetition of these fruitless proceedings, an alternative,—already pointed out by Mr. Grenville,—was now adopted. *Opposed by Colonel Luttrell.* Colonel Luttrell, a member, vacated his seat, and offered himself as a candidate. Wilkes was, of course, returned by a large majority. He received one thousand one hundred and forty-three votes: Colonel Luttrell only two hundred and ninety-six. There were also two other candidates, Mr. Serjeant *Again returned; but Colonel Luttrell seated.* Whitaker and Mr. Roache, the former of whom had five votes, and the latter none. The Commons immediately pronounced the

[1] Cavendish Deb., i. 352.

return of Wilkes to be null and void; and, having called for the poll-books, proceeded to vote,—though not without a strenuous opposition,—that Henry Lawes Luttrell ought to have been returned.[1] To declare a candidate, supported by so small a number of votes, the legal representative of Middlesex, was a startling step in the progress of this painful contest; but the ultimate seating of another candidate, notwithstanding Wilkes' majorities, was the inevitable result of the decision which affirmed his incapacity.

Leave was given to petition the House against Colonel Luttrell's election, within fourteen days. Of this permission the electors soon availed themselves; and, on the 8th May, they were heard by counsel, at the bar of the House. Their arguments were chiefly founded upon the original illegality of the vote, by which Wilkes' incapacity had been declared; and were ably supported in debate, particularly by Mr. Wedderburn, Mr. Burke, and Mr. George Grenville:[2] but the election of Colonel Luttrell was confirmed by a majority of sixty-nine.

Wilkes was now effectually excluded from Parliament; but his popularity had been increased, while the House, and all concerned in his oppression, were the objects of popular indignation. As some compensation for his exclusion from the House of Commons, Wilkes was elected an alderman of the city of London. A liberal subscription was also raised, for the payment of his debts.

*Popularity of Wilkes.*

[1] April 14th, 1769; Cavendish Deb., i. 360–386. Ayes, 197; Noes. 143—Majority, 54.
[2] Cavendish Deb., i. 406; Ann. Reg., 1769, p. 68*.

So dangerous a precedent was not suffered to rest unquestioned. Not only the partisans of Wilkes, but the statesmen and lawyers opposed to the government, continued to protest against it, until it was condemned.

*Efforts to reverse the proceedings against him.*

On the 9th January, 1770, Lord Chatham,—reappearing in the House of Lords after his long prostration,—moved an amendment to the address, denouncing the late proceedings in the House of Commons, as 'refusing, by a resolution of one branch of the legislature, to the subject his common right, and depriving the electors of Middlesex of their free choice of a representative.'[1] Lord Camden, the chancellor, now astonished the Lords by a statement 'that for some time he had beheld· with silent indignation, the arbitrary measures which were pursuing by the ministry;' and, 'that as to the incapacitating vote, he considered it as a direct attack upon the first principles of the constitution.'[2] Lord Mansfield, while he said that his opinion upon the legality of the proceedings of the House of Commons was 'locked up in his own breast, and should die with him,' (though for what reason it is not easy to explain,) argued that in matters of election the Commons had a complete jurisdiction, without appeal; that their decisions could only be reversed by themselves, or by Act of Parliament; and that except in discussing a bill, the Lords could not inquire into the question, without violating the privileges of the other House.

*By Lord Chatham, Jan., 1770.*

---

[1] Parl. Hist., xvi. 653.

[2] This speech is not reported in the Parl. Hist., but is printed from the Gentleman's Mag. of Jan., 1770, in a note; Parl. Hist., xvi. 644, *n*.

Lord Chatham replied in his finest manner. Lord Mansfield's remarks on the invasion of the privileges of the other House, called forth this comment: 'What is this mysterious power,—undefined by law, unknown to the subject, which we must not approach without awe, nor speak of without reverence,—which no man may question, and to which all men must submit? My Lords, I thought the slavish doctrine of passive obedience had long since been exploded; and when our kings were obliged to confess that their title to the crown, and the rule of their government, had no other foundation than the known laws of the land, I never expected to hear a divine right, or a divine infallibility attributed to any other branch of the legislature.' He then proceeded to affirm that the Commons 'have betrayed their constituents, and violated the constitution. Under pretence of declaring the law, they have made a law, and united in the same persons, the office of legislator and of judge.'[1] His amendment was negatived; but the stirring eloquence and constitutional reasoning of so eminent a statesman, added weight to Wilkes' cause.

In the Commons also, very strong opinions were expressed on the injustice of Wilkes' exclusion. Sir George Savile especially distinguished himself by the warmth of his language; and accused the House of having betrayed the rights of its constituents. Being threatened with the Tower, he twice repeated his opinion; and,—declining the friendly intervention

*Proceedings in the Commons, 1770.*

[1] Parl. Hist., xvi. 647.

of Colonel Conway and Lord North, who attributed his language to the heat of debate,—he assured the House that if he was in a rage, 'he had been so ever since the fatal vote was passed, and should be so till it is rescinded.'[1] Mr. Sergeant Glynn thought 'his declaration not only innocent, but laudable.' A formidable opposition showed itself throughout the debate; and while in the Lords, the Chancellor had pronounced his opinion against the incapacitating vote,—in the Commons, the Solicitor-General, Mr. Dunning, also spoke and voted against the government. The question had thus assumed a formidable aspect, and led to changes which speedily ended in the breaking up of the Duke of Grafton's administration.

On the 25th January, 1770, Mr. Dowdeswell moved a resolution in a committee of the whole House, 'That this House in its judicature in matters of election, is bound to judge according to the law of the land, and the known and established law and custom of Parliament, which is part thereof.' This premiss could neither be denied nor assented to by the government without embarrassment; but Lord North adroitly followed it out by a conclusion, 'that the judgment of this House was agreeable to the said law of the land, and fully authorised by the law and custom of Parliament.'[2] On the 31st January, Mr. Dowdeswell repeated his attack in another form, but with no better success.[3]

*Mr. Dowdeswell's resolutions.*

---

[1] Parl. Hist., xvi. 699.  [2] Ibid., 797.
[3] Ibid., 800.

The matter was now again taken up in the House of Lords. On the 2nd February, in com- *Lord Rockingham's motion, 2nd Feb., 1770.* mittee on the state of the nation, Lord Rockingham moved a resolution similar to that of Mr. Dowdeswell.[1] Though unsuccessful, it called forth another powerful speech from Lord Chatham, and a protest signed by forty-two peers. The rejection of this motion was immediately followed,—without notice, and after twelve o'clock at night,—by a motion of Lord Marchmont, that to impeach a judgment of the House of Commons would be a breach of the constitutional right of that House. Lord Camden, being accused by Lord Sandwich of duplicity, in having concealed his opinion as to the illegality of the incapacitating vote, while a member of the cabinet, asserted that he had frequently declared it to be both illegal and imprudent. On the other hand, the Duke of Grafton and Lord Weymouth complained that he had always withdrawn from the Council Board to avoid giving his opinion,—a circumstance explained by Lord Camden on the ground that as his advice had been already rejected, and the cabinet had resolved upon its measures, he declined giving any further opinion.[2] In either case, it seems, there could have been no doubt of his disapproval of the course adopted by ministers.

The next effort made in Parliament, in reference to Wilkes' case, was a motion by Mr. Herbert for a bill to regulate the consequences of the expulsion of members. But as this bill did not reverse, or

---

[1] Parl. Hist., xvi. 814.     [2] *Ibid.*, 823.

directly condemn the proceedings in the case of Wilkes, it was not very warmly supported by the opposition; and numerous amendments having been made by the supporters of the government, by which its character became wholly changed, the bill was withdrawn.[1]

The scene of this protracted contest was now varied for a time. Appeals to Parliament had been made in vain; and the city of London resolved to carry up their complaints to the throne. A petition had been presented to the king in the previous year, to which no answer had been returned. And now the Lord Mayor, aldermen, and livery, in Common Hall assembled, agreed to an 'address, remonstrance, and petition' to the king, which, whatever the force of its statements, was conceived in a tone of unexampled boldness. 'The majority of the House of Commons,' they said, 'have deprived your people of their dearest rights. They have done a deed more ruinous in its consequences than the levying of ship-money by Charles I., or the dispensing power assumed by James II.' They concluded by praying the king 'to restore the constitutional government and quiet of his people, by dissolving the Parliament and removing his evil ministers for ever from his councils.'[2]

*The city address to the king, 1770.*

In his answer, his Majesty expressed his concern that any of his subjects 'should have been so far misled as to offer him an address and remonstrance,

---

[1] Parl. Hist., xvi. 830-833; Cavendish Deb., i. 435.
[2] The address is printed at length, Cavendish Deb., i. 576.

the contents of which he could not but consider as disrespectful to himself, injurious to Parliament, and irreconcilable to the principles of the constitution.'[1]

The Commons, whose acts had been assailed by the remonstrance, were prompt in rebuking the city, and pressing forward in support of the king. They declared the conduct of the city 'highly unwarrantable,' and tending 'to disturb the peace of the kingdom;' and having obtained the concurrence of the Lords, a joint address of both Houses, conveying this opinion, was presented to the king. In their zeal, they had overlooked the unseemliness of lowering both Houses of Parliament to a level with the corporation of the city of London, and of wrangling with that body, at the foot of the throne. The city was ready with a rejoinder, in the form of a further address and remonstrance to the king. *Joint address of both Houses to the king.*

Lord Chatham, meanwhile, and many of the leaders of the Whig party, saw, in the king's answer, consequences dangerous to the right of petitioning. Writing to Lord Rockingham, April 29th, Lord Chatham said: 'A more unconstitutional piece never came from the throne, nor any more dangerous, if left unnoticed.'[2] And on the 4th of May, not deterred by the joint address already agreed to by both Houses, he moved a resolution in the House of Lords, that the advice *Lord Chatham condemns the king's answer.*

---

· Having returned this answer, the king is said to have turned round to his courtiers, and burst out laughing.—*Public Advertiser*, cited in Lord Rockingham's Mem., ii. 174.

[2] Rockingham Mem., ii. 177; Woodfall's Junius, ii. 104.

inducing his Majesty to give that answer 'is of the most dangerous tendency,' as 'the exercise of the clearest rights of the subject to petition the king for redress of grievances, had been checked by reprimand.' He maintained the constitutional right of the subject to petition for redress of all grievances; and the justice of the complaints which the city of London had laid at the foot of the throne. But the motion provoked little discussion, and was rejected.[1] And again, on the 14th May, Lord Chatham moved an address for a dissolution of Parliament. But all strangers, except peers' sons and members of the House of Commons, having been excluded from this debate, no record of it has been preserved. The question was called for at nine o'clock, and negatived.[2]

On the 1st of May, Lord Chatham presented a bill for reversing the several adjudications of the House of Commons, in Wilkes' case. The bill, after reciting all these resolutions, declared them to be 'arbitrary and illegal;' and they were 'reversed, annulled, and made void.' Lord Camden said, 'The judgment passed upon the Middlesex election has given the constitution a more dangerous wound than any which were given during the twelve years' absence of Parliament in the reign of Charles I.;' and he trusted that its reversal would be demanded, session after session, until the people had obtained redress. Lord Mansfield deprecated any interference with the

*Lord Chatham's bill to reverse the judgment of the Commons.*

---

[1] Parl. Hist., xvi. 666.  [2] Ibid., 979.

privileges of the Commons, and the bill was rejected by a large majority.[1]

The next session witnessed a renewal of discussions upon this popular question. On the 5th December, Lord Chatham moved another resolution; which met the same fate as his previous motions on the subject.[2] On the 30th April, the Duke of Richmond moved to expunge from the journals of the House the resolution of the 2nd of February, 1770, in which they had deprecated any interference with the jurisdiction of the Commons, as unconstitutional. He contended that if such a resolution were suffered to remain on record, the Commons might alter the whole law of elections, and change the franchise by an arbitrary declaration; and yet the Lords would be precluded from remonstrance. Lord Chatham repeated his opinion, that the Commons 'had daringly violated the laws of the land;' and declared that it became not the Lords to remain 'tame spectators of such a deed, if they would not be deemed accessory to their guilt, and branded with treason to their country.' The ministers made no reply, and the question was negatived.[3]

*Lord Chatham's resolution, 5th Dec., 1770.*

*Duke of Richmond's motion, April, 1771.*

A few days afterwards, Lord Chatham moved an address for a dissolution, on the ground of the violations of law by the Commons in the Middlesex election, and the contest which had lately arisen

---

[1] Parl. Hist., xvi. 955; Walpole's Mem., iv. 121; Rockingham Mem., ii. 177.
[2] Parl. Hist., xvi. 1302. It was superseded by adjournment.
[3] Parl. Hist., xvii. 214.

between them and the city magistracy;[1] but found no more than twenty-three supporters.[2]

The concluding incidents of the Middlesex election may now be briefly told, before we advert to a still more important conflict which was raging at this time, with the privileges of the Commons; and the new embarrassments which Wilkes had raised.

*Sir George Savile's motion, 1772.*  In the next session, Sir George Savile, in order to renew the annual protest against the Middlesex election, moved for a bill to secure the rights of electors, with respect to the eligibility of persons to serve in Parliament. Lord North here declared, that the proceedings of the Commons had 'been highly consistent with justice, and the law of the land; and that to his dying day he should continue to approve of them.' The motion was defeated by a majority of forty-six.[3]

*Mr. Wilkes complains of the Deputy-Clerk of the Crown.*  In 1773, Mr. Wilkes brought his case before the House, in the shape of a frivolous complaint against the Deputy-Clerk of the Crown, who had refused to give him a certificate, as one of the members for Middlesex. Sir G. Savile, also, renewed his motion for a bill to secure the rights of electors, and found one hundred and fifty supporters.[4] Mr. Burke took this occasion to predict that, 'there would come a time when those now in office would be reduced to their penitentials, for having turned a deaf ear to the voice of the people.' In 1774, Sir G. Savile renewed his

---

[1] See *infra*, p. 41. [2] May 1st, 1771; Parl. Hist., xvii. 224.
[3] Feb. 27th, 1772; *Ibid.*, 318. [4] Parl. Hist., xvii. 838.

motion for a bill to secure the rights of electors, with the usual result.[1]

The Parliament, which had been in continual conflict with Wilkes for five years, was now dissolved; and Wilkes was again returned for Middlesex. According to the resolution of the Commons, his incapacity had been limited to the late Parliament; and he now took his seat without further molestation. Before the meeting of Parliament, Wilkes had also attained the highest civic honour,—being elected Lord Mayor of London. *Wilkes elected in the new Parliament, 1774.*

He did not fail to take advantage of his new privileges; and on the 22nd February, 1775, he moved that the resolution which had declared his incapacity, be expunged from the journals, 'as subversive of the rights of the whole body of electors.' He said, 'the people had made his cause their own, for they saw the powers of the government exerted against the constitution, which was wounded through his sides.' He recapitulated the circumstances of his case; referred very cleverly to the various authorities and precedents; and showed the dangerous consequences of allowing a resolution to remain upon the journals, which was a violation of the law. He was ably supported by Mr. Sergeant Glynn, Sir George Savile, and Mr. Wedderburn; and in the division secured one hundred and seventy-one votes.[2] *Moves to expunge the resolution.*

He renewed this motion in 1776,[3] in 1777,[4] in

---

[1] Parl. Hist., xvii. 1057.
[3] Parl. Hist., xviii. 1336.
[2] 171 to 239; *Ibid.*, xviii. 358.
[4] *Ibid.*, xix. 193.

1779,[1] and in 1781.[2]  At length, on the 3rd of May, 1782, he proposed it for the last time, and with signal success.  The Rockingham ministry was in office, and had resolved to condemn the proceedings of the Commons, which its leading members had always disapproved.  Mr. Fox was now the only statesman, of any eminence, by whom Wilkes' motion was opposed.  He had always maintained that the Commons had not exceeded their powers; and he still consistently supported that opinion, in opposition to the premier and the leaders of his party.  Wilkes' motion was now carried by a triumphant majority of sixty-eight; and by order of the House, all the declarations, orders, and resolutions, respecting the Middlesex election, were expunged from the journals, as being subversive of the rights of the whole body of electors in this kingdom.[3]

*Resolution expunged, 1782.*

Thus at length, this weary contest was brought to a close.  A former House of Commons, too eager in its vengeance, had exceeded its powers; and now a succeeding Parliament reversed its judgment.  This decision of 1782 stands out as a warning to both Houses, to act within the limits of their jurisdiction, and in strict conformity with the laws.  An abuse of privilege is even more dangerous than an abuse of prerogative.  In the one case, the wrong is done by an irresponsible body: in the other the ministers who advised it, are open to censure and punishment.  The judgment of

*Abuses of privilege; their danger.*

---

[1] Parl. Hist., xx. 144.        [2] *Ibid.*, xxii. 99.
[3] Ayes, 115; Noes, 47; Parl. Hist., xxii. 1407.

offences especially, should be guided by the severest principles of law. Mr. Burke applied to the judicature of privilege, in such cases, Lord Bacon's description of the Star Chamber,—'a court of criminal equity:" saying, 'a large and liberal construction in ascertaining offences, and a discretionary power in punishing them, is the idea of criminal equity, which is in truth a monster in jurisprudence.'[1] The vindictive exercise of privilege,—once as frequent as it was lawless,—was now discredited and condemned.

But before Wilkes had obtained this crowning triumph over the Commons, he had contrived to raise another storm against their privileges, which produced consequences of greater constitutional importance; and again this bold and artful demagogue became the instrument, by which popular liberties were extended.

*Exclusion of strangers from debates.*

Among the privileges of Parliament, none had been more frequently exercised by both Houses, than the exclusion of strangers from their deliberations; and restraints upon the publication of debates. The first of these privileges is very ancient; and probably originated in convenience, rather than in any theory of secrecy in their proceedings. The members met not so much for debate, as for deliberation: they were summoned for some particular business, which was soon disposed of; and as none but those summoned were expected to attend; the chambers in which they assembled, were simply adapted for their own accommodation. Hence the

---

[1] Present Discontents; Works, ii. 297.

occasional intrusion of a stranger was an inconvenience, and a disturbance to the House. He was in the midst of the members,—standing with them in the gangway,—or taking his place, where none but members had the privilege of sitting. Such intrusion resembled that of a man who, in the present day, should force his way into Brookes's or the Carlton, and mingle with the members of the club. Some strangers even entered the House, pretending to be members.[1] Precautions were necessary to prevent confusion; for even so late as 1771 a stranger was counted in a division.[2] Hence, from early times, the intrusion of a stranger was generally punished by his immediate commitment, or reprimand.[3] The custom afterwards served as an auxiliary to the most valuable of all privileges,—the freedom of speech. What a member said in his place, might indeed be reported to the king, or given in evidence against him in the Court of King's Bench, or the Stannary Court, by another member of the House: but strangers might be there, for the very purpose of noting his words, for future condemnation. So long, therefore, as the Commons were obliged to protect themselves against the rough hand of prerogative, they strictly enforced the exclusion of strangers.

Long after that danger had passed away, the privilege was maintained as a matter of custom, rather than of policy. At length appre-

*Relaxation of the privilege.*

---

[1] Mr. Perne, March 5th, 1557; Mr. Bukeley, May 14th, 1614.
[2] Com. Journ., xxxiii. 212.
[3] *Ibid.*, i. 105, 118, 417, 484; *Ibid.*, ii. 74, 433.

hensions arose from another quarter; and the privilege was asserted as a protection to Parliament, against the clamours and intimidation of the people. But the enforcement of this privilege was gradually relaxed. When the debates in Parliament began to excite the interest of the public, and to attract an eager audience, the presence of strangers was connived at. They could be dismissed in a moment, at the instance of any member: but the Speaker was not often called upon to enforce the orders of the House.

Towards the middle of last century, attendance upon the debates of both Houses of Parliament had become a fashionable amusement. On the 9th of December, 1761, the interest excited by a debate in the Commons, on the renewal of the Prussian Treaties, was so great, that Lord Royston, writing to Lord Hardwicke, said, 'The house was hot and crowded,—as full of ladies as the House of Lords when the king goes to make a speech. The members were standing above half way up the floor.' It became necessary on this occasion to enforce the standing order for the exclusion of strangers.[1] And in this way, for several years the presence of strangers, with rare exceptions, was freely admitted. *Exclusion of strangers, 1770.* But the same Parliament which had persecuted Wilkes, was destined to bring to an issue other great questions, affecting the relations of Parliament to the people. It is not surprising that the worst of Parliaments should have been the most resolute in enforcing the rule for excluding

[1] Rockingham Mem., i. 71.

strangers.[1] It was at war with the public liberties; and its evil deeds were best performed in secret. The exclusion of strangers was generally more strict than had been customary; and whenever a popular member of opposition endeavoured to make himself heard by the people, the ready expedient was adopted of closing the doors. Burke, describing the position of an opposition member at this period, wrote, 'In the House he votes for ever in a dispirited minority; if he speaks, the doors are locked.'[2] Could any abuse of privilege be more monstrous than this? Was any misrepresentation of reporters half so mischievous?

Lord Chatham's repeated motions impugning the proceedings of the Commons upon the Middlesex election, were naturally distasteful to ministers, and to the majority of the House of Lords; who, being unable to repress his impetuous eloquence, determined that, at least, it should not be heard beyond their walls. Accordingly on the 14th May, 1770, on his motion for a dissolution of Parliament, the Lords ordered the exclusion of all but members of the House of Commons, and the sons of peers; and no reports of the debates reached the public.

*Proceedings in the Lords.*

---

[1] This Parliament, assembled May 10th, 1768, and dissolved June 22nd, 1774, was commonly called the unreported Parliament, in consequence of the strict enforcement of the standing order for the exclusion of strangers. Pref. to Cavendish's Deb. Sir Henry Cavendish has supplied a great *hiatus* in the debates of this period, and it is much to be regretted that the publication of his valuable work has never been completed. The reports consist of forty-nine small 4to. volumes, amongst the Egerton MSS. at the British Museum, of which less than half were edited by Mr. Wright, and published in two volumes.

[2] Present Discontents; Works, ii. 301.

In the next session, the same tactics were resumed. On the 10th December, the Duke of Manchester rose, to make a motion relative to preparations for the war with Spain, then believed to be impending; when he was interrupted by Lord Gower, who desired that the House might be cleared. He urged, as reasons for excluding strangers, that the motion had been brought on without notice; that matters might be stated which ought not to be divulged; that, from the crowded state of the House, emissaries from Spain might be present; and lastly, that notes were taken of their debates. The Duke of Richmond attempted to arrest the execution of the order; but his voice was drowned in clamour. Lord Chatham rose to order, but failed to obtain a hearing. The Lord Chancellor attempted to address the House and restore order; but even his voice could not be heard. Lord Chatham, and eighteen other peers,—indignant at the disorderly uproar, by which every effort to address the House had been put down,—withdrew from their places. The messengers were already proceeding to clear the House, when several members of the House of Commons, who had been waiting at the bar to bring up a bill, desired to stay for that purpose: but were turned out with the crowd,—several peers having gone down to the bar, to hasten their withdrawal. They were presently called in again: but the moment they had delivered their message,—and before time had been allowed them to withdraw from the bar,—an outcry

*Lord Gower desires the House to be cleared.*

*Members of the Commons excluded from the Lords.*

arose, and they were literally hooted out of the House.[1]

Furious at this indecent treatment, the members hastened back to their own House. The first result of their anger was sufficiently ridiculous. Mr. George Onslow desired the House to be cleared, 'peers and all.' The only peers below the bar were the very lords who had in vain resisted the exclusion of strangers from their own House, which they had just left in indignation; and now the resentment of the Commons,—provoked by others,—was first expended upon them.

<small>Misunderstanding between the two Houses.</small>

In debate, the insult to the Commons was warmly resented. Various motions were made:—for inspecting the Lords' journals; for demanding a conference upon the subject; for sending messages by the eldest sons of peers and masters in Chancery, who alone, it was said, would not be insulted; and for restraining members from going to the Lords without leave. But none of them were accepted.[2] The only retaliation that could be agreed upon, was the exclusion of peers, which involved a consequence by no means desired,—the continued exclusion of the public.

In the Lords, sixteen peers signed a strong protest against the riotous proceedings of their House, and deprecating the exclusion of strangers. An order, however, was made that none but persons having a right to be present, should be admitted

---

[1] Parl. Hist., xvi. 1318–1320; Walpole's Mem., iv. 217; Chatham Corr., iv. 51.

[2] Dec. 10th and 13th, 1770; Parl. Hist., xvi. 1322; Cavendish Deb., ii. 149, 160; Walpole's Mem., iv. 228.

during the sitting of the House; and instructions were given to the officers, that members of the House of Commons should not be allowed to come to the bar, except when announced as bringing messages; and should then immediately withdraw.[1] To this rule the Lords continued strictly to adhere for the remainder of the session; and none of their debates were reported, unless notes were communicated by the peers themselves. The Commons were less tenacious, or their officers less strict; and strangers gradually crept back to the gallery. Lord Chatham happily expressed his contempt for a senate debating with closed doors. Writing to Colonel Barré on the 22nd January, 1771, he says, 'I take it for granted that the same declaration will be laid before the tapestry on Friday, which will be offered to the live figures in St. Stephen's;'[2] and again on the 25th he writes to Lady Chatham, 'Just returned from the tapestry.'[3] The mutual exclusion of the members of the two Houses, continued to be enforced, in a spirit of vindictive retaliation, for several years.[4]

In the Commons, however, this system of exclusion took a new turn; and, having commenced in a quarrel with the Peers, it ended in a collision with the press. Colonel George Onslow complained of the debates which still appeared in the newspapers; and insinuating that they must have been supplied by members

*Contest with the printers, 1771.*

---

[1] Parl. Hist., xvi. 1319–1321.
[2] Chatham Corr., iv. 73.  [3] Ibid., 86.
[4] Debate in the Commons, Dec. 12th, 1774; Parl. Hist., xviii. 52; Burke's Speeches, i. 250.

themselves, insisted upon testing this view, by excluding all but members.[1] The reports continued; and now he fell upon the printers.

But before this new contest is entered upon, it will be necessary to review the position which the press occupied at this time, in its relation to the debates of Parliament. The prohibition to print and publish the debates, naturally dates from a later period than the exclusion of strangers. It was not until the press had made great advances, that such a privilege was declared. Parliament, in order to protect its freedom of speech, had guarded its proceedings by a strong fence of privilege: but the printing of its debates was an event beyond its prevision.

*Publication of debates.*

In 1641, the Long Parliament permitted the publication of its proceedings, which appeared under the title of 'Diurnal Occurrences in Parliament.' The printing of speeches, however, without leave of the House, was, for the first time, prohibited.[2] In particular cases, indeed, where a speech was acceptable to the Parliament, it was ordered to be printed: but if any speech was published obnoxious to the dominant party, the vengeance of the House was speedily provoked. Sir E. Dering was expelled and imprisoned in the Tower, for printing a collection of his speeches; and the book was ordered to be burned by the common hangman.[3]

*Progress of reporting.*

---

[1] Feb. 7th, 1771; Parl. Hist., xvi. 1355, *n.*; Cavendish Deb., ii. 244.

[2] July 13th and 22nd; Com. Journ., ii. 209, 220.

[3] Feb. 2nd, 1641; Com. Journ., ii. 411.

The prohibition to print debates was continued after the Restoration; but, in order to prevent inaccurate accounts of the business transacted, the House of Commons, in 1680, directed its 'votes and proceedings,' without any reference to debates, to be printed under the direction of the Speaker.[1] Debates were also frequently published, notwithstanding the prohibition. When it served the purpose of men like Lord Shaftesbury, that any debate should be circulated, it made its appearance in the form of a letter or pamphlet.[2] Andrew Marvell reported the proceedings of the Commons, to his constituents at Hull, from 1660 to 1678;[3] and Grey, for thirty years member for Derby, took notes of the debates from 1667 to 1694, which are a valuable contribution to the history of that time.[4]

After the Revolution, Parliament was more jealous than ever of the publication of its proceedings, or of any allusion to its debates. By frequent resolutions,[5] and by the punishment of offenders, both Houses endeavoured to restrain 'news-letter writers' from 'intermeddling with their debates or other proceedings,' or 'giving any account or minute of the debates.' But privilege could not prevail against the press, nor against the taste for political news, which is natural to a free country.

---

[1] Com. Journ., ix. 74; Grey's Deb., viii. 292.
[2] 'Letter from a Person of Quality to a Friend in the Country,' 1675, by Locke. 'Letter from a Parliament-man to his Friend, concerning the Proceedings of the House of Commons, 1675.'
[3] Letters to the Corporation of Hull; Marvell's Works, i. 1–400.
[4] They were published in ten volumes 8vo. 1769.
[5] Commons, Dec. 22nd, 1694, Feb. 11th, 1695, Jan. 18th, 1697, &c.; Lords, Feb. 27th, 1698.

Towards the close of the reign of Anne, regular but imperfect accounts of all the principal debates were published by Boyer.[1] From that time, reports continued to appear in Boyer's 'Political State of Great Britain,' the 'London Magazine,' and the 'Gentleman's Magazine,' the authors of which were frequently assisted with notes from members of Parliament. In the latter, Dr. Johnson wrote the Parliamentary reports, from the 19th of Nov., 1740, till the 23rd of Feb., 1743, from the notes of Cave and his assistants. The names of the speakers, however, were omitted.[2] Until 1738, it had been the practice to give their initials only, and, in order to escape the censure of Parliament, to withhold the publication of the debates, until after the session. In that year, the Commons prohibited the publication of debates, or proceedings, 'as well during the recess, as the sitting of Parliament;' and resolved to 'proceed with the utmost severity against offenders.'[3] After this period, the reporters, being in fear of parliamentary privilege, were still more careful in their disguises. In the 'Gentleman's Magazine,' the debates were assigned to 'the Senate of Great Lilliput;' and in the 'London Magazine' to the Political Club, where the speeches were attributed to Mark Anthony, Brutus, and other Roman worthies. This caution was not superfluous; for both Houses were quick to punish the publication of their proceedings, in any form; and printers

---

[1] Boyer's Political State of Great Britain was commenced in 1711.
[2] Prefaces to Cobbett's Parl. Hist., vols. ix.—xiii.
[3] April 13th, 1738. Parl. Hist., x. 800.

and publishers became familiar with the Black Rod, the Sergeant-at-Arms, and Newgate.[1] At length, in 1771, at the instigation of Wilkes,[2] notes of the speeches, with the names of the speakers, were published in several journals.[3]

These papers had rarely attempted to give a correct and impartial account of the debates: but had misrepresented them to suit the views of different parties. Dr. Johnson is said to have confessed that 'he took care that the Whig dogs should not have the best of it;' and, in the same spirit, the arguments of all parties were in turn perverted or suppressed. Galling as was this practice, it had been less offensive while the names of the speakers were withheld: but when these were added, members were personally affronted by the misconstruction of their opinions and arguments, and by the ludicrous form in which they were often presented. The chief complaints against reporting had arisen from the misrepresentations to which it was made subservient. In the debate upon this subject in 1738, nearly all the speakers, including Sir W. Wyndham, Sir W. Yonge, and Mr. Winnington, agreed in these complaints, and rested their objections to reporting, on that ground. The case

*Misrepresentations of reporters.*

---

[1] Woodfall, Baldwin, Jay, Millar, Oxlade, Randall, Egglesham, Owen, and Knight, are amongst the names of publishers committed or censured for publishing debates or proceedings in Parliament. Such was the extravagance with which the Lords enforced their privilege, that in 1729, a part of their Journal having been printed in Rymer's Fœdera, they ordered it to be taken out and destroyed.—*Lords' Journ.*, xxiii. 422.

[2] Walpole's Mem., iv. 278.

[3] The London Evening Post, the St. James' Chronicle, the Gazetteer, and others.

was well and humorously stated, by Sir R. Walpole. 'I have read some debates of this House, in which I have been made to speak the very reverse of what I meant. I have read others, wherein all the wit, the learning, and the argument has been thrown into one side, and on the other, nothing but what was low, mean, and ridiculous; and yet, when it comes to the question, the division has gone against the side which, upon the face of the debate, had reason and justice to support it. So that, had I been a stranger to the proceedings, and to the nature of the arguments themselves, I must have thought this to have been one of the most contemptible assemblies on the face of the earth.' In this debate, Mr. Pulteney was the only speaker who distinctly objected to the publication of the speeches of members, on the ground 'that it looks very like making them accountable without doors, for what they say within.'[1]

Indeed, it is probable that the early jealousies of Parliament would soon have been overcome, if the reports had been impartial. The development of the liberty of the press was checked by its own excesses; and the publication of debates was retarded by the unfairness of reporters. Nor were the complaints of members confined to mere misrepresentation. The reports were frequently given in the form of narratives, in which the speakers were distinguished by nicknames, and described in opprobrious terms. Thus, Colonel George Onslow was called 'little *cocking* George,'[2] 'the little

*Offensive adjuncts to reporting.*

---

[1] Parl. Hist., x. 300.     [2] Cavendish Deb., ii. 257.

scoundrel,'[1] and 'that little paltry, insignificant insect.'[2] The Colonel and his cousin were also spoken of in scurrilous comments, as being like 'the constellations of the two bears in the heavens, one being called the *great*, and the other the *little* scoundrel.'[3]

To report the debates in such a spirit, was at once to violate the orders of the House, and to publish libellous insults upon its members. Parliament had erred in persisting in the prohibition of reporting, long after its occasion had passed away; and the reporters had sacrificed a great public privilege, to the base uses of a scurrilous press. The events of the first ten years of this reign had increased the violence of public writers, and embittered the temper of the people. The 'North Briton' and 'Junius' had assailed the highest personages, and the most august assemblies, with unexampled license and audacity. Wilkes had defied the House of Commons, and the ministers. The city had bearded the king upon his throne. Yet this was the time chosen by an unpopular House of Commons, to insist too rigorously upon its privileges, and to seek a contest with the press.

On the 8th February, 1771, Colonel George Onslow made a complaint of 'The Gazetteer and New Daily Advertiser,' printed for R. Thompson, and of the 'Middlesex Journal,' printed by R. Wheble, 'as misrepresenting the speeches, and reflecting on several of the members

*Complaints against Thompson and Wheble, 1771.*

---

[1] Cavendish Deb., 258.  [2] *Ibid.*, 377, *n.*
[3] *Ibid.*, 379.

of this House.' The printers were ordered to attend, —but not without serious warnings and remonstrances from those who foresaw the entanglements, into which the House was likely to be drawn.[1] They kept out of the way, and were ordered to be taken into custody. The Sergeant proceeded to execute the order, and was laughed at by their servants.[2] Thus thwarted, the House addressed the king to issue a proclamation, offering a reward for their apprehension.

Meanwhile, the offences for which the House was pursuing Thompson and Wheble, were practised by several other printers; and on the 12th March, Colonel Onslow made a complaint against the printers of six other newspapers. The House had not yet succeeded in apprehending the first offenders, and now another host was arraigned before them. In some of these papers, the old disguises were retained. In the 'St. James's Chronicle' the speeches were entitled 'Debates of the representatives of Utopia;'[3] Mr. Dyson was described as 'Jeremiah Weymouth, Esq., the d——n of this country,' and Mr. Constantine Phipps as 'Mr. Constantine Lincoln.'[4] None of the errors of Parliament have been committed, without the warnings and protests of some of its enlightened members; and this further onslaught upon the printers was vigorously resisted. The minority availed themselves of motions for adjournment, amendments, and

*Complaints against other printers.*

---

[1] Cavendish Deb., ii. 257.   [2] Ibid., 324.
[3] Ibid., 383.
[4] One represented Weymouth, and the other Lincoln.

other parliamentary forms, well adapted for delay, until past four in the morning. During this discussion there were no less than twenty-three divisions,—an unprecedented number.[1] 'Posterity,' said Burke, 'will bless the pertinaciousness of that day.'[2]

All the six printers were ordered to attend at the bar; and on the day appointed, four of the number appeared, and a fifth,—Mr. Woodfall,—being already in the custody of the Black Rod, by order of the Lords, was prevented from attending. Two of them, Baldwin and Wright, were reprimanded on their knees and discharged; and Bladon, having made a very humble submission, was discharged without a reprimand. Evans, who had also attended the order of the House, went home before he was called in, in consequence, it was said, of an accident to his wife. He was ordered to attend on another day: but wrote a letter to the Speaker, in which he questioned the authority of the House, and declined to obey its order. Lastly, Miller did not attend, and was ordered into custody for his offence.[3]

On the 14th March, Wheble, who was still at large, addressed a letter to the Speaker, inclosing the opinion of counsel on his case, and declaring his determination 'to yield no obedience but to the laws of the land.' The next day, he was collusively apprehended by Carpenter, a printer,—by virtue of the proclamation,—and taken before Alderman Wilkes! This dexterous and cunning agitator had encouraged the printers to resist

*Wheble taken before Alderman Wilkes.*

---

[1] Cavendish Deb., ii. 377.   [2] Ibid., 395.
[3] Parl. Hist., xvii. 90, n.; Com. Journ., xxxiii. 250-259.

the authority of the House, and had concerted measures for defying its jurisdiction, and insulting its officers. He immediately discharged the prisoner, and bound him over to prosecute Carpenter, for an assault and false imprisonment. He further wrote a letter to Lord Halifax, the Secretary of State, acquainting him that Wheble had been apprehended by a person who 'was neither a constable nor peace-officer of the city,' and for no legal offence, but merely in consequence of the proclamation,—'in direct violation of the rights of an Englishman, and of the chartered privileges of a citizen of this metropolis,'—and that he had discharged him.[1]

On the same day, Thompson was apprehended by another printer, and carried before Alderman Oliver at the Mansion House; but 'not being accused of having committed any crime,' was discharged. In both cases, the captors applied for a certificate that they had apprehended the prisoners, in order to obtain the rewards offered by the proclamation: but the collusion was too obvious, and the Treasury refused to pay them.

*And Thompson before Alderman Oliver.*

On the following day, a graver business arose. Hitherto the legality of apprehending persons under the proclamation, had alone been questioned; but now the authority of the House was directly contemned. In obedience to the Speaker's warrant for taking Miller into custody, Whittam, a messenger of the House, succeeded in apprehending him, in his shop. But Miller, instead

*Commitment of the messenger.*

[1] Parl. Hist., xvii. 95.

of submitting, sent for a constable,—accused the messenger of having assaulted him in his own house, —and gave him into custody. They were both taken to the Mansion House, and appeared before the Lord Mayor, Mr. Alderman Oliver, and Mr. Alderman Wilkes. Miller charged the messenger with an assault and false imprisonment. The messenger justified himself by the production of the Speaker's warrant; and the Deputy Sergeant-at-Arms claimed both the messenger and his prisoner. But the Lord Mayor inquired if the messenger was a peace-officer or constable, and if the warrant was backed by a city magistrate; and being answered in the negative, discharged Miller out of custody. The charge of the latter against the messenger was then proved; and Whittam, by direction of the Sergeant, having declined to give bail, was committed under a warrant, signed by the three magistrates. After his commitment, he was admitted to bail on his own application.

The artful contrivances of Wilkes were completely successful. The contumacious printers were still at large; and he had brought the city into open conflict with the House of Commons. The House was in a ferment. Many members who had resisted the prosecution of the printers, admitted that the privileges of the House had now been violated; but they were anxious to avert any further collision between the House,—already too much discredited by recent proceedings,—and the popular magistracy of the city. The Lord Mayor, Mr. Brass Crosby, being a member of the House, was first ordered to attend in his place, on the following day;[1] and afterwards Mr. Oliver, also a member, was ordered to attend in his place, and Mr. Wilkes at the bar, on other days.

At the appointed time, the Lord Mayor, though he had been confined for several days by the gout, obeyed the order of the House. His carriage was escorted by a prodigious crowd, —whose attendance had been invited by a handbill; and he was received with such acclamations in the lobby, that the Speaker desired it to be cleared of strangers.[2] The Lord Mayor,—who was so ill as to be obliged to speak sitting,—justified himself by his oath of office, which bound him to protect the citizens in their rights and franchises. He stated that by the charters of the city, confirmed by Act of Parliament, no warrant, process, or attachment could be executed within the city but by its own magistrates, and that he should have been guilty of perjury, if he had not discharged the prisoner. He then desired to be heard by counsel, in support of the jurisdiction of the city. The Speaker intimated that the House could not hear counsel against its privileges; and while this matter was under discussion, the Lord Mayor, being too ill to remain in the House, was allowed to go home. It was at length decided to hear counsel on such points as did not controvert the privileges of the House;[3] and the same right was afterwards conceded to Alderman Oliver.[4] The scene was enlivened by Mr. Wilkes,

*The Lord Mayor (Brass Crosby) attends the House.*

---

[1] March 19th; Parl. Hist., xvii. 98; Cavendish Deb., ii. 400.
[2] Cavendish Deb., ii. 422. [3] Ibid., ii. 436.
[4] Ibid., 442; Parl. Hist., xvii. 119.

who having been ordered to attend at the bar, wrote to the Speaker, with his usual effrontery, claiming to attend in his place, as member for Middlesex.[1]

So far the House had stood upon its unassailable privilege of commitment: but now it proceeded to a violation of the law, at once arbitrary and ridiculous. The clerk to the Lord Mayor had been ordered to attend with the book containing the recognizance of Whittam the messenger; and on its production by that officer, he was ordered to expunge the entry at the table, which he accordingly did.[2] While this scene was being enacted, most of the opposition members left the House, in order to mark their reprobation of an act, by which a record was effaced,—over which the House had no authority,—and the course of justice violently stayed.[3] According to Lord Chatham, it was the 'act of a mob, and not of a Parliament.'[4] *Record of recognizances erased.*

The House then ordered that no prosecution should be commenced against the messenger, for his pretended assault. He was nevertheless indicted; and a true bill being found against him, he was only saved by the Attorney-General, who entered a *nolle prosequi*. *Messenger saved from prosecution.*

Some delay ensued in the proceedings, in consequence of the continued indisposition of the Lord Mayor: but on the 25th March, he and Mr. Alderman Oliver attended in their places. They were accompanied to *The Lord Mayor and Alderman Oliver heard in their places.*

---

[1] Parl. Hist., xvii. 113, n.
[2] Cavendish Deb., ii. 438; Parl. Hist., xvii. 117; Com. Journ., xxxiii. 275.
[3] Ann. Reg., 1771, p. 66; Walpole's Mem., iv. 294.
[4] May 1st, 1771 : Parl. Hist., xvii. 221.

the House by immense crowds, who cheered them on their way. Before their case was proceeded with, the order for the attendance of Alderman Wilkes,—the prime mover of all this mischief,—was discharged; the court and ministers being fairly afraid of another contest with so dangerous an antagonist. The Lord Mayor now declined being heard by counsel; and after the reading of the city charters, and the oaths of office, he briefly urged that he had acted in obedience to the laws and constitution, and appealed to the justice of the House. An endeavour was made to evade any further proceedings, by the previous question : but after an exciting debate,—interrupted by the shouts and uproar of the crowd, by which the House was surrounded,[1]—resolutions were agreed to, declaring that the privileges of the House had been violated.[2] The Lord Mayor had been allowed to go home early in the evening; when the crowd took the horses from his carriage, and bore him triumphantly to the Mansion House. Alderman Oliver being still in the House, was now called upon for his defence. In a few words he said that he gloried in what he had done; that he was unconcerned at the punishment intended for him, and which nothing he could say would avert; 'and as he expected little from their justice, he defied their power.'[3] Motions were immediately made that he had been guilty of a breach of privilege, and should be committed to the Tower; and after a debate, protracted by earnest protests and

Alderman Oliver committed to the Tower.

---

[1] Parl. Hist.. xvii. 125; Cavendish Deb., ii. 452, 454.
[2] Cavendish Deb., ii. 461.    [3] Parl. Hist., xvii. 125.

remonstrances against this proceeding, till half-past three in the morning, an order for his commitment was agreed to.[1]

At the next sitting of the House, the Lord Mayor attended in his place. Again he was accompanied by a crowd, larger and more tumultuous than before. The members *The Lord Mayor committed to the Tower.* with difficulty made their way through Palace Yard and Westminster Hall. Lord North's carriage was broken to pieces, and he himself escaped,—not without injury,—with the assistance of Sir W. Meredith. Mr. Charles Fox,—a violent champion of privilege,—and his brother Stephen, had their carriages injured; and several members were insulted and pelted with stones and mud. For some time, the House was unable to proceed to business. The magistrates tried in vain to disperse or tranquillise the mob: but the Sheriffs,—who both happened to be members,—being sent by the Speaker, at length succeeded in restoring order. In consideration of the Lord Mayor's state of health, it was at first proposed merely to commit him to the custody of the Sergeant-at-Arms: but as he boldly declined to accept this favour from the House, and desired to bear his friend Oliver company, he was committed to the Tower.[2] Meanwhile Wilkes, the chief offender, was still at large. He had been again ordered to attend on the 8th April: but ministers discreetly moved the adjournment for the Easter Holidays until the 9th;

---

[1] He was allowed to sleep at his house that night, and early the next morning the Sergeant took him to the Tower. (Gentleman's Mag., cited in Parl. Hist., xvii. 155, *n.*)

[2] March 27th; Parl. Hist., xvii. 157.

and thus the dreaded culprit was eluded. This subterfuge may have been prudent: but it was not magnanimous.

<small>Ovation of the prisoners.</small> The authority of the House of Commons had clearly been defied; and however ill-advised the proceedings which had led to the contest with the city magistrates, the House could scarcely have flinched from the vindication of its privileges.[1] But Parliament has no means of punishing a popular offender. The Lord Mayor, on leaving the House, accompanied by the Sergeant-at-Arms, was surrounded by the crowd, who took the horses from his carriage, and bore him to Temple Bar. Here they shut the city gates, and would have rescued him from custody, but for the adroitness of the Lord Mayor, who assured them he was going home, accompanied by his friends. He slept that night at the Mansion House, and early the following morning reached the Tower, without observation. Here the prisoners received every mark of public attention and sympathy. Visited by the most distinguished leaders of the opposition,—attended by deputations,—flattered in addresses,—complimented by the free-

---

[1] Lord Chatham condemned all the parties to this contest. 'Nothing appears to me more distinct than declaring their right to jurisdiction, with regard to printers of their proceedings, and debates, and punishing their member, and in him his constituents, for what he has done in discharge of his oath and conscience as a magistrate.' Lord Chatham to Colonel Barré, March 26th, 1771.—*Chatham Corresp.*, iv. 136. Again, writing to Earl Temple, April 17th, 1771, he said, 'Great is the absurdity of the city in putting the quarrel on the exercise of the most tenable privilege the House is possessed of,—a right to summon before them printers printing their debates during the session. Incomparable is the wrong-headedness and folly of the Court, ignorant how to be twenty-four hours on good ground; for they have most ingeniously contrived to be guilty of the rankest tyranny, in every step taken to assert the right.'—*Grenville Papers*, iv. 533. See also Junius, Letter xliv.

dom of many cities,—and overloaded with presents, —their imprisonment, instead of being a punishment, was a long-continued ovation. They failed to obtain their release under writs of *habeas corpus*, as the legality of their commitment could not be impeached: but on the 8th May, after six weeks' confinement, the prorogation of Parliament set them at liberty. Attended by a triumphal procession, they proceeded from the Tower to the Mansion House; and the people exulted at the liberation of their popular magistrates.[1]

Thus ended this painful and embarrassing conflict. Its results were decisive. The publication of debates was still asserted to be a breach of privilege: but the offence was committed with impunity. Another contest with the press, supported by a powerful opposition and popular sympathies, was out of the question; and henceforth the proceedings of both Houses were freely reported. Parliament as well as the public has since profited by every facility which has been afforded to reporting. The suppression of the names of the speakers, and the adoption of fictitious designations, had encouraged reporters to introduce other fictions into their narratives; and to impute arguments and language, which had never been used, to characters of their own creation. *Reporting henceforth permitted.*

But reporters were still beset with too many difficulties, to be able to collect accurate accounts of the debates. Prohibited from *Its difficulties.*

---

[1] Memoirs of Brass Crosby, 1829; Almon's Life of Wilkes; Ann. Reg., 1771, 59, *et seq.*; Adolphus, Hist., chap. xix.

taking notes, they were obliged to write mainly from memory. If notes were taken at all, they were written surreptitiously, and in fear of the Sergeant-at-Arms. Nor was this the only impediment to reporting. The accommodation for strangers was very limited; and as no places were reserved for reporters, they were obliged to wait upon the stairs, — sometimes for hours, — before the doors were opened, in order to secure admission. Under such restraints, imperfections in the reports were to be expected. However faithfully the substance of the debates may have been rendered, it is not conceivable that the language of the speakers could have been preserved. It had probably been no vain boast of Dr. Johnson, when, to a company lost in admiration at one of Mr. Pitt's most eloquent speeches, he exclaimed, 'That speech *I* wrote in a garret, in Exeter Street.'[1] And long after his time, much was left to the memory or invention of reporters.

Nor were any further facilities conceded to the press, after the struggle of 1771. Lord Malmesbury, speaking of Mr. Pitt's speech, 23rd May, 1803, on the renewal of hostilities with France, said: 'By a new arrangement of the Speaker's, strangers were excluded till so late an hour, that the newspaper printers could not get in, and of course, no part of

---

[1] Sir J. Hawkins' Life of Dr. Johnson. The editor of Cobbett's Parliamentary History bears testimony to the general accuracy of Dr. Johnson's reports, and discredits the statements of Sir John Hawkins and others, who had regarded them as the works of his own imagination; but there can be little doubt that the language of the composition was often that of the reporter.—*Prefs.* to vols. xi. and xii.

Pitt's speech can be printed.'[1] A sketch of this speech, however, has been preserved: but the whole debate was very imperfectly reported.[2] Even so late as 1807, it was noticed in the House of Lords, that a person was taking notes in the gallery.[3]

Another interruption to which reporting was still exposed, was the frequent and capricious exclusion of strangers, at the desire of a single member. During the discussions upon the American War in 1775 and 1776, the galleries were repeatedly closed.[4] On the 29th January, 1778, seven years after the contest with the printers, Colonel Luttrell complained of misrepresentation in a newspaper; and said he should move the exclusion of strangers, in order to prevent the recurrence of such a practice: upon which Mr. Fox made this remarkable observation: 'He was convinced the true and only method of preventing misrepresentation was by throwing open the gallery, and making the debates and decisions of the House as public as possible. There was less danger of misrepresentation

*Reports interrupted by exclusion of strangers.*

---

[1] Corr., iv. 262; and see Lord Colchester's Diary, i. 421.
[2] Parl. Hist., xxxvi. 1386.
[3] Court and Cabinets of Geo. III., iv. 150; not mentioned in the Parl. Debates.
[4] Feb. 2nd, March 22nd, Nov. 16th, 1775. *Parl. Hist.*, xviii. 221, 540, 963. Cooke's Hist. of Party, iii. 224. In the debate on the budget, 24th April, 1776, Governor Johnstone observed that ' it was a little extraordinary that the gallery should be open on that day and shut up upon almost every other, since the commencement of the session, on which matters of importance came under discussion.'— *Parl. Hist.*, xviii. 1322. Mr. Fox said : ' As strangers were admitted here for one day, it was necessary for him to repeat what he had often urged.'—*Ibid.*, 1325. The Speaker said : 'An hon. gentleman had, at an early period of the session, desired the standing order to be read, and he had ever since punctiliously kept to it.'—*Ibid.*, 1327. See also Walpole's Journ., ii. 194.

in a full company than a thin one, as there would be a greater number of persons to give evidence against the misrepresentation.'[1]

In 1798, the debate on Mr. Sheridan's motion for a committee on the state of Ireland, was lost to the public, by the exclusion of strangers.[2] The Lords also discussed the same important subject with closed doors.[3] In 1810, Mr. Yorke enforced the exclusion of strangers during the inquiries, at the bar, into the expedition to the Scheldt; when Mr. Sheridan vainly attempted to obtain a modification of the rule, which vested in a single member the power of excluding the public.[4] And on several later occasions, the reports of the debates in both houses have been interrupted from the same cause.[5]

But when the fear of punishment was abated, the reports became more systematic; and were improved in character and copiousness. There were still de-

[1] Parl. Hist., xix. 647. A few days afterwards, strangers were ordered to withdraw. This order was enforced against the gentlemen; but the ladies, who were present in unusual numbers, were permitted to remain. Governor Johnstone, however, remonstrated upon the indulgence shown to them, and they were also directed to withdraw. But they showed no disposition to obey this ungracious order, and business was interrupted for nearly two hours, before their exclusion was accomplished. Among the number were the Duchess of Devonshire and Lady Norton. The contumacy of the ladies on this occasion unhappily led to the withdrawal of the privilege, which they had long enjoyed, of being present at the debates of the House of Commons. Feb. 2nd, 1778. London Chronicle, cited in note to Parl. Hist., vol. xix. p. 673. Hatsell, Prec., ii. 181, n. See also Grey's Deb., iii. 222. Parl. Hist., xix. 674, n.
[2] 4th June. Parl. Hist., xxxiii. 1487.
[3] Ibid., 1489; Stanhope's Life of Pitt, iii. 135.
[4] Hans. Deb., xv. 325.
[5] E.g., 4th and 5th March, 1813, during debate concerning the Princess of Wales. Lord Colchester's Diary, ii. 430. In 1849, the doors of the House of Commons were closed against strangers for nearly two hours; and no report of the debate during that time was published. In 1870, strangers were twice excluded.

lays, and other shortcomings: but mainly by the enterprise and ability of Almon, Woodfall, and Perry, the system of reporting and printing the debates gradually attained its present marvellous rapidity and completeness. And what a revolution has it accomplished!

The entire people are now present, as it were, and assist in the deliberations of Parliament. An orator addresses not only the assembly of which he is a member; but, through them, the civilised world. His influence and his responsibilities are alike extended. Publicity has become one of the most important instruments of parliamentary government. The people are taken into counsel by Parliament, and concur in approving or condemning the laws, which are there proposed; and thus the doctrine of Hooker is verified to the very letter: 'Laws they are not, which public approbation hath not made so.' While publicity secures the ready acceptance of good laws by the people, the passing of bad laws, of which the people disapprove, is beyond the power of any minister. Long before a measure can be adopted by the legislature, it has been approved or condemned by the public voice; and living and acting in public, Parliament, under a free representation, has become as sensitive to public opinion, as a barometer to atmospheric pressure. Such being the direct influence of the people over the deliberations of Parliament, they must share, with that body, the responsibility of legislation. They have permitted laws to be passed,—they have accepted and approved them; and they will not

*Political results of reporting.*

afterwards allow them to be disturbed. Hence the remarkable permanence of every legislative settlement. There has been no retrogression in our laws or policy. The people,—if slow to perceive the value of new principles,—hold fast to them when once acknowledged, as to a national faith.[1] No circumstance in the history of our country,—not even parliamentary reform,—has done more for freedom and good government, than the unfettered liberty of reporting. And of all the services which the press has rendered to free institutions, none has been greater than its bold defiance of parliamentary privilege, while labouring for the interests of the people.

Reporting, instead of being resented by Parliament, is now encouraged as one of the main sources of its influence; while the people justly esteem it, as the surest safeguard of liberty. Yet such is the tenacity with which ancient customs are observed,—long after their uses have ceased to be recognised,—that the privilege itself has never been relinquished. Its maintenance, however, is little more than a harmless anomaly. Though it is still a breach of privilege to publish the debates, parliamentary censure is reserved for wilful misrepresentation; and even this offence is now scarcely known. The extraordinary ability, candour, and good faith of the modern school

*Reporting still a breach of privilege.*

[1] Though equal publicity prevails in the United States, their legislation is more sudden and impulsive, and remarkable, therefore, for its instability.—*De Tocqueville, Démocratie en Amérique,* i. 242, 301 (13th ed.). See also an interesting essay of Sismondi, 'De la Délibération Nationale:' *Études sur les Constitutions des Peuples Libres,* 131.

of reporters, have left nothing for Parliament or the public to desire.

The fire which destroyed both Houses of Parliament in 1834, introduced a new era in reporting. Though, for many years past, the reporters of the daily press had enjoyed facilities unknown to their predecessors, they still carried on their difficult labours in the strangers' gallery. In the temporary houses, separate galleries, for the accommodation of reporters, were first introduced; and this significant change has been perpetuated in the present buildings. Galleries for the accommodation of reporters.

In 1845, the presence of strangers in the galleries and other parts of the House, not appropriated to members, was for the first time recognised by the orders of the House of Commons; yet this tardy recognition of their presence did not supersede the ancient rule by which they could be excluded on the word of a single member. Presence of strangers recognised.

A further change was still wanting to complete the publicity of parliamentary proceedings, and the responsibility of members. The conduct of members who took part in the debates,—until recently a very small number,—was now known: but the conduct of the great majority who were silent, was still a secret. Who were present,—how they voted,—and what members composed the majority,—and therefore the ruling body,—could not be ascertained. On questions of unusual interest, it was customary for the minority to secure the publication of their own names; but it was on very rare occasions indeed, that a list of the Publication of division lists.

majority could also be obtained.[1] In either case the publication was due to the exertions of individual members. The House itself took no cognisance of names: but concerned itself merely with the numbers. The grave constitutional objections to this form of voting, had not escaped the notice of parliamentary reformers. Lord John Russell, in his speech on parliamentary reform in 1819, said:—
'We are often told that the publication of the debates is a corrective for any defect in the composition of this House. But to these men, such an argument can by no means apply: the only part they take in the affairs of this House, is to vote in the majority; and it is well known that the names of the majority are scarcely ever published. Such members are unlimited kings,—bound by no rule in the exercise of their power,—fearing nothing from public censure, in the pursuit of selfish objects,—not even influenced by the love of praise and historical fame, which affects the most despotic sovereigns: but making laws, voting money, imposing taxes, sanctioning wars, with all the plenitude of

---

[1] At the dissolution of 1689, division lists were first published by the Whigs and Tories, to influence the elections.—*Macaulay's Hist.*, iii. 535. In 1696, the Commons declared the printing the names of the minority a breach of privilege, as 'destructive of the freedom and liberties of Parliament.'—*Com. Journ.*, xi. 572. Mr. Burke wrote, in 1770: 'Frequent and correct lists of voters on all important questions ought to be procured.'—*Present Discontents*, Works, ii. 325. In 1782, the opposition published division lists, the ministerial members appearing in red letters, and the minority in black.—*Wraxall Mem.*, ii. 591. In Ireland, before the Union, 'the divisions were public, and red and black lists were immediately published of the voters on every public occasion.'—*Sir Joseph Barrington's Personal Sketches*, i. 195.

power, and all the protection of obscurity: having nothing to deter them but the reproach of conscience, and everything to tempt the indulgence of avarice and ambition.'[1]

It was not, however, until 1836,—four years after the passing of the reform act,—that the House of Commons adopted the wise and popular plan of recording the votes of every member; and publishing them, day by day, as part of the proceedings of the House. So stringent a test had never been applied to the conduct of members; and if free constituencies have since failed in their duty of sending able and conscientious representatives, the fault has been entirely their own.

The Commons have since extended the principle of publicity still further. The admission of strangers to debates had been highly prized: but the necessity of clearing them during a division had never been doubted.[2] Yet in 1853, it was shown by Mr. Muntz that they might be permitted to remain in the galleries, without any embarrassment to the tellers;[3] and they have since looked down upon the busy scene, and shared in the excitement of the declaration of the numbers. *Strangers present at divisions.*

In these important changes, the Commons have also been followed by the Lords. Since 1857, their Lordships have published their division lists daily; and during a division, strangers *Divisions in the Lords.*

[1] Hans. Deb., 3rd Ser., xli. 1097.
[2] In 1849 a committee reported that their exclusion was necessary.
[3] Report of Select Committee on Divisions, 1853.

are permitted to remain in the galleries and in the space within the rails of the throne.¹

*Names of members on committees.*
In a minor, yet not unimportant change, the personal responsibility of members, as well to the House as to the public, has been extended. In the Commons, since 1839, the name of every member addressing questions to witnesses before select committees, has been published with the minutes of evidence; and in 1852, the same practice was adopted by the Lords. It displays the intelligence, the knowledge, and the candour of the questioners; or their obtuseness, ignorance, and prejudice. It exhibits them seeking for truth, or obstinately persisting in error. Their presence at each sitting of the committee, and their votes upon every question, are also recorded and published in the minutes of proceedings.

*Publication of parliamentary reports and papers.*
One other concession to the principle of unrestricted publicity, must not be overlooked. One of the results of increasing activity and vigilance in the Legislature, has been the collection of information, from all sources, on which to found its laws. Financial and statistical accounts,—reports and papers upon every question of foreign and domestic policy,—have been multiplied in so remarkable a manner, since the union with Ireland, that it excites surprise how Parliament affected to legislate, in earlier times, without such information. These documents were distributed to all members of the Legislature; and, by their favour, were also accessible to the public.

---

[1] Resolutions, March 10th, 1857.

In 1835, the Commons took a further step in the encouragement of publicity, by directing all their papers to be freely sold, at a cheap rate.[1] The public have since had the same means of information, upon all legislative questions, as the House itself. Community of knowledge, as well as community of discussion, has been established. If comments are justly made upon the extravagance of parliamentary printing,—if voluminous 'blue books' are too often a fair object of ridicule,—yet the information they afford is for the public; and the extent and variety of the documents printed, attest at once the activity of members, and the keen interest taken by the people in the business of legislation.

While the utmost publicity has thus been gradually extended to all parliamentary proceedings, a greater freedom has been permitted to the press, in criticising the conduct of Parliament. *Freedom of comments upon Parliament.* Relying upon the candour of public opinion for a justification of its conduct, Parliament has been superior to that irritable sensitiveness, which formerly resented a free discussion of its proceedings. Rarely has either House thought fit, of late years, to restrain by punishment, even the severest censures upon its own debates and proceedings. When gross libels have been published upon the House itself, or any of its members, the House has occasionally thought it necessary to vindicate its honour, by the commitment of the offenders to custody. But it has rightly distinguished between libels upon character and motives,—and comments,

[1] Reports on Printed Papers, 1835.

however severe, upon political conduct. In 1810, Mr. Gale Jones was committed to Newgate, for publishing an offensive placard announcing for discussion, in a debating society, the conduct of two members, Mr. G. Yorke and Mr. Windham. Sir Francis Burdett was sent to the Tower, for publishing an address to his constituents, denouncing this act of the House, and denying its right of commitment. Twenty years later, both these offences would probably have been disregarded, or visited with censure only. Again, in 1819, Mr. Hobhouse was committed to Newgate for violent, if not seditious, language in a pamphlet. A few years afterwards, such an offence, if noticed at all, would have been remitted to the Attorney-General, and the Court of Queen's Bench. In 1838, Mr. O'Connell, for a much grosser libel than any of these, was only reprimanded in his place, by the Speaker. The forbearance of both Houses has not compromised their dignity, while it has commanded public respect. Nor has it been without other good results; for, however free the commentaries of newspapers,— they have rarely been disgraced by the vulgar scurrilities which marked the age of Wilkes and Junius, when Parliament was still wielding the rod of privilege over the press. Universal freedom of discussion has become the law of our political system; and the familiar use of the privilege has gradually corrected its abuses.

The relations of Parliament with the people have also been drawn closer, by the extended use of the popular right of petitioning for re-

*Early petitions to Parliament.*

dress of grievances. Though this right has existed from the earliest times, it had been, practically, restricted for many centuries, to petitions for the redress of personal and local grievances; and the remedies sought by petitioners were such as Courts of Equity, and private Acts of Parliament have since been accustomed to provide. The civil war of Charles I. encouraged a more active exercise of the right of petitioning. Numerous petitions of a political character, and signed by large bodies of people, were addressed to the Long Parliament.[1] Freedom of opinion, however, was little tolerated by that assembly. The supporters of their cause were thanked and encouraged: its incautious opponents, if they ventured to petition, were punished as delinquents.[2] Still it was during this period of revolution, that the practice of addressing Parliament upon general political questions had its rise. After the Restoration, petitions were again discouraged. For long periods, indeed, during the reign of Charles II., the discontinuance of Parliaments effectually suppressed them; and the collecting of signatures to petitions and addresses to the king, or either House of Parliament, for alteration of matters established by law, in church or state, was restrained by Act of Parliament.[3]

Nor does the Revolution appear to have extended

[1] Clarendon Hist. (Oxford Ed., 1826), i. 357; ii. 166, 206, 207, 222; v. 460; vi. 406.
[2] Ibid., ii. 221, 348; Com. Journ., v. 354, 367, 368; Rushworth Coll., v. 462, 487.
[3] 13 Chas. II. c. 5. Petitions to the king for the assembling of Parliament were discountenanced in 1679 by proclamation (Dec. 12th).

the free use of petitions. In the next ten years, petitions in some numbers were presented,—chiefly from persons interested,—relative to the African Company,—the scarcity and depreciation of the coinage,—the duties on leather,—and the woollen trade: but very few of a general political character. Freedom of opinion was not tolerated. In 1690, a petition from the city of London, hinting at a repeal of the Test Act, so far as it affected Protestant dissenters, could hardly obtain a reading;[1] and in 1701, the Commons imprisoned five of the Kentish petitioners, until the end of the session, for praying that the loyal addresses of the House might be turned into bills of supply.[2] During the reigns of Queen Anne, and the first two Georges, petitions continued to pray for special relief; but rarely interposed in questions of general legislation. Even the ten first turbulent years of George III.'s reign failed to develope the agency of petitions, among other devices of agitation. So little indulgence did Parliament then show to petitions, that if they expressed opinions of which the majority disapproved, the right of the subject did not protect them from summary rejection. In 1772, a most temperate petition, praying for relief from subscription to the Thirty-nine Articles, was rejected by the Commons, by a large majority.[3]

*Rarely political.*

It was not until 1779, that an extensive organi-

[1] Parl. Hist., v. 359.
[2] Somers' Tracts, xi. 242; Parl. Hist., v. 1255; *ibid.*, App., xvii. xviii.
[3] By 217 to 71.

sation to promote measures of economical and parliamentary reform, called into activity a general system of petitioning,—commencing with the freeholders of Yorkshire, and extending to many of the most important counties and cities in the kingdom.[1] This may be regarded as the origin of the modern system of petitioning, by which public measures, and matters of general policy, have been pressed upon the attention of Parliament. Corresponding committees being established in various parts of the country, were associated for the purpose of effecting a common object, by means of petitions, to be followed by concerted motions made in Parliament. An organisation which has since been so often used with success, was now first introduced into our political system.[2] But as yet the number of petitions was comparatively small; and bore little proportion to the vast accumulations of later times. Notwithstanding the elaborate system of association and correspondence established, there do not appear to have been more than forty petitions;[3] but many of these were very numerously signed. The Yorkshire

*Commencement of the modern system of petitioning.*

---

[1] Adolphus, iii. 94, 113; Remembrancer, vol. ix.; Wyvill's Political Papers, i. 1–296; Wraxall's Mem., iii. 292; Ann. Reg., 1789, p. 85; Parl. Hist., xx. 1378.

[2] Mr. Hallam, in a valuable note to his Constitutional History, vol. ii. p. 434, to which I am much indebted, says that 'the great multiplication of petitions wholly unconnected with particular interests, cannot, I believe, be traced higher than those for the abolition of the slave trade in 1787; though a few were presented for reform about the end of the American War, which would undoubtedly have been rejected with indignation at any earlier stage of our constitution.' I have assigned the somewhat earlier period of 1779, as the origin of the modern system of petitioning.

[3] Parl. Hist., xxi. 339; Ann. Reg., 1780, p. 165.

petition was subscribed by upwards of eight thousand freeholders;[1] the Westminster petition, by five thousand electors.[2] The meetings at which they were agreed to, awakened the public interest in questions of reform, to an extraordinary degree, which was still further increased by the debates in Parliament, on their presentation. At the same time, Lord George Gordon and his fanatical associates were engaged in preparing petitions against the Roman Catholics. To one of these, no less than one hundred and twenty thousand signatures were annexed.[3] But not satisfied with the influence of petitions so numerously signed, the dangerous fanatic who had collected them, sought to intimidate Parliament by the personal attendance of the petitioners; and his ill-advised conduct resulted in riots, conflagrations, and bloodshed, which nearly cost their mischievous originator his head.

In 1782, there were about fifty petitions praying *Its development.* for reform in the representation of the Commons in Parliament; and also a considerable number in subsequent years. The great movement for the abolition of the slave trade soon followed. The first petition against that infamous traffic was presented from the Quakers, in 1782;[4] and was not supported by other petitions for some years. But in the meantime, an extensive association had instructed the people in the enormities of

[1] Speech of Sir George Savile; Parl. Hist., xx. 1374.
[2] Speech of Mr. Fox; *Ibid.*, xxi. 287.
[3] Ann. Reg., 1780, p. 259.
[4] June 17th, 1782; Com. Journ., xxxix. 487; Adolphus Hist., iv. 301.

the slave trade, and aroused the popular sympathies in favour of the African negro. In 1787 and 1788, a greater number of petitions were presented for this benevolent object, than had ever been addressed to Parliament, upon any other political question. There were upwards of a hundred petitions, numerously signed, and from influential places.[1] Never yet had the direct influence of petitions upon the deliberations of Parliament been so remarkably exemplified. The question of the slave trade was immediately considered by the government, by the Privy Council, and by Parliament; and remedial measures were passed, which ultimately led to its prohibition. This consummation was indeed postponed for several years, and was not accomplished without many struggles: but the influence of petitions, and of the organisation by which they were produced, was marked throughout the contest.[2] The king and Mr. Pitt appear, from the first, to have regarded with disfavour this agitation for the abolition of the slave trade, by means of addresses and petitions, as being likely to establish a precedent for forcing the adoption of other measures, less unobjectionable.[3]

Notwithstanding this recognition of the constitutional right of addressing Parliament upon public questions, the growth of petitions was not yet

---

[1] Com. Journ., xliii. 159, *et seq.*; Adolphus, Hist., iv. 306.

[2] Mr. Fox, writing to Dr. Wakefield, April 28th, 1801, said: 'With regard to the slave trade, I conceive the great numbers which have voted with us, sometimes amounting to a majority, have been principally owing to petitions.'—*Fox Mem.*, iv. 429.

[3] Malmesbury Corr., ii. 430. See also Bancroft's Amer. Rev., iii. 469. Lord Holland's Mem., ii. 157, &c.

materially advanced. Throughout the reign of George III. their numbers, upon the most interesting questions, were still to be reckoned by hundreds.[1] As yet, it was sought to express the sentiments of influential classes only; and a few select petitions from the principal counties and cities,—drawn with great ability, and signed by leading men,—characterised this period of the history of petitions. Even in 1816 there were little more than four hundred petitions against the continuance of the Property Tax, notwithstanding the strong public feeling against it.

It was not until the latter part of the succeeding reign, that petitioning attained that development, by which it has since been distinguished. From that period it has been the custom to influence the judgment of Parliament, not so much by the weight and political consideration of the petitioners, as by their numbers. Religious bodies,—especially of Dissenting communions,—had already contributed the greatest number of petitions; and they have since been foremost in availing themselves of the rights of petitioners. In 1824, an agitation was commenced, mainly by means of petitions, for the abolition of slavery; and from that period until 1833, when the Emancipation Act was passed, little less than twenty thousand petitions were presented: in 1833 alone, nearly seven thou-

*Petitions from religious bodies.*

---

[1] In 1813, there were 200 in favour of Roman Catholic claims, and about 700 for promulgating the Christian religion in India: in 1814, about 150 on the corn laws, and nearly 1,000 for the abolition of the slave trade: in 1817 and 1818, upwards of 500 petitions for reform in Parliament.

sand were laid before the House of Commons. Upon many other subjects, petitions were now numbered by thousands, instead of hundreds. In 1827 and 1828, the repeal of the Corporation and Test Acts was urged by upwards of five thousand petitions. Between 1825 and 1829, there were about six thousand petitions in favour of the Roman Catholic claims, and nearly nine thousand against them. Other questions affecting the Church and Dissenters, —the Maynooth grant, church rates, and the observance of the Sabbath, have since called them forth, in still greater numbers.[1] On a single day, in 1860, nearly four thousand petitions were presented, on the question of church rates.[2]

The people have also expressed their opinions upon all the great political measures of the last thirty years, by prodigious numbers of petitions;[3] and these petitions *Extraordinary increase of petitions.*

---

[1] In 1834 there were upwards of 2,000 petitions in support of the Church Establishment, and 2,400 for relief of Dissenters. In 1837 there were about 10,000 petitions relating to church rates. Between 1833 and 1837, 5,000 petitions were presented for the better observance of the Lord's Day. In 1845, 10,253 petitions, with 1,288,742 signatures, were presented against the grant to Maynooth College. In 1850, 4,475 petitions, with 656,919 signatures, were presented against Sunday labour in the Post-office. In 1851, 4,144 petitions, with 1,016,657 signatures, were presented for repelling encroachments of the Church of Rome; and 2,151 petitions, with 948,081 signatures, against the Ecclesiastical Titles Bill. In 1856, 4,999 petitions, with 629,926 signatures, were presented against opening the British Museum on Sundays; and in 1860, there were 5,575 petitions, with 197,687 signatures, against the abolition of church rates; and 5,538 petitions, with 610,877 signatures, in favour of their abolition.

[2] March 28th, 1860.

[3] In 1846 there were 1,958 petitions, with 145,855 signatures, against the repeal of the corn laws; and 467 petitions, with 1,414,303 signatures, in favour of repeal. In 1848 there were 577 petitions, with 2,018,080 signatures, praying for universal suffrage. In the

have been freely received, however distasteful their opinions,—however strong their language. Disrespect and menace have not been suffered: but the wise and tolerant spirit of the age has recognised unbounded liberty of opinion.

This general use of petitions had been originally developed by associations; and in its progress, active organisation has ever since been resorted to, for bringing its great influence to bear upon Parliament. Sometimes, indeed, the manner in which petitioning has been systematised, has discredited the right on which it is founded, and the questions it has sought to advance. Petitions in thousands,—using the same language,—inscribed in the same handwriting, and on the same description of paper,—and signed by fabulous numbers,—have marked the activity of agents, rather than the unanimity of petitioners; and, instead of being received as the expression of public opinion, have been reprobated as an abuse of a popular privilege. In some cases, the unscrupulous zeal of agents has even led them to resort to forgery and other frauds, for the multiplication of signatures.[1]

*Abuses of petitioning.*

While the number of petitions was thus increas-

five years ending 1843, 94,000 petitions were received by the House of Commons; in the five years ending 1848, 66,501; in the five years ending 1853, 54,908; and in the five years ending 1858, 47,669. In 1860, 24,279 petitions were received, being a greater number than in any previous year except 1843.

[1] Such practices appear to have been coeval with agitation by means of petitions. Lord Clarendon states that in 1640, 'when a multitude of hands was procured, the petition itself was cut off, and a new one framed suitable to the design in hand, and annexed to the long list of names, which were subscribed to the former. By this means many men found their hands subscribed to petitions of which they before had never heard.'—*Hist. of Rebellion*, ii. 357.

ing, their influence was further extended, by the discussions to which their presentation gave rise. The arguments of the petitioners were repeated and enforced in debate. Debates on presenting petitions restrained. Whatever the business appointed for consideration, the claims of petitioners to a prior hearing were paramount. Again and again, were the same questions thus forced upon the attention of Parliament. A popular question absorbed all others: it was for ever under discussion. This free access of petitioners to the inner deliberations of Parliament, was a great privilege. It had long been enjoyed and appreciated: but when it was too often claimed, its continuance became incompatible with good government. After the reform act, the debating of petitions threatened to become the sole business of the House of Commons. For a time, expedients were tried to obtain partial relief from this serious embarrassment: but at length, in 1839, the House was forced to take the bold but necessary step, of prohibiting all debate upon the presentation of petitions.[1] The reformed Parliament could venture upon so startling an invasion of the right of petitioning; and its fearless decision was not misconstrued by the people. Nor has the just influence of petitions been diminished by this change; for while the House restrained desultory and intrusive discussion, it devised other means for giving publicity, and extended circulation to the opinions of petitioners.[2] Their voice is still heard and respected in

---

[1] Com. Journ., xciv. 16; Hans. Deb., 3rd Ser., xlv. 156, 197.
[2] About a thousand petitions are annually printed *in extenso*; and

the consideration of every public measure: but it is no longer suffered unduly to impede the toilsome work of legislation.

*Pledges of members.* To these various modes of subjecting Parliament to the direct control of public opinion, must be added the modern custom of exacting pledges from candidates at elections. The general election of 1774 appears to have been the first occasion, on which it prevailed so far as to attract public notice.[1] Many popular questions, especially our differences with America, were then under discussion; and in many places, tests were proposed to candidates, by which they were required to support or oppose the leading measures of the time. Wilkes was forward in encouraging a practice so consonant with his own political principles; and volunteered a test for himself and his colleague, Sergeant Glynn, at the Middlesex election. Many candidates indignantly refused the proposed test, even when they were favourable to the views to which it was sought to pledge them. At this period, Mr. Burke explained to the electors of Bristol,—with that philosophy and breadth of constitutional principle, which distinguished him,—the relations of a representative to his constituents. 'His unbiassed opinion, his mature judgment, his enlightened conscience, he ought not to sacrifice to you, to any man, or to any set of men living. . . . . Your representative owes you, not his industry only,

---

all petitions are classified, so as to exhibit the number of petitions, with the signatures, relating to every subject.

[1] Adolphus, Hist., ii. 143.

but his judgment; and he betrays, instead of serving you, if he sacrifices it to your opinion. . . . Government and legislation are matters of reason and judgment, and not of inclination; and what sort of reason is that in which the determination precedes the discussion,—in which one set of men deliberate, and another decide? . . . Parliament is not a congress of ambassadors from different and hostile interests; . . . but Parliament is a deliberative assembly of one nation, with one interest,—that of the whole; where not local purposes, not local prejudices, ought to guide, but the general good, resulting from the general reason of the whole.'[1]

Since that time, however, the relations between representatives and their constituents have become more intimate; and the constitutional theory of pledges has been somewhat modified. According to the true principles of representation, the constituents elect a man in whose character and general political views they have confidence; and their representative enters the Legislature a free agent, to assist in its deliberations, and to form his own independent judgment upon all public measures. If the contrary were universally the rule, representatives would become delegates; and government, by the entire body of the people, would be substituted for representative institutions.[2] But the political

[1] Burke's Works, iii. 18-20.
[2] There is force, but at the same time exaggeration, in the opinions of an able reviewer upon this subject. 'For a long time past we have, unconsciously, been burning the candle of the constitution at both ends; our electors have been usurping the functions of the House of Commons, while the House of Commons has been monopolising those of the Parliament.'—*Ed. Rev.*, Oct. 1852, No. 196,

conditions of our own time have brought occasional pledges more into harmony with the spirit of the constitution. The political education of the people, —the publicity of all parliamentary proceedings,— and the free discussions of the press, have combined to force upon constituencies the estimation of measures as well as of men. Hence candidates have sought to recommend themselves by the advocacy of popular measures; and constituents have expected explicit declarations of the political faith of candidates. And how can it be contended that upon such measures as catholic emancipation, parliamentary reform, and the repeal of the corn laws, constituencies were not entitled to know the opinions of their members? Unless the electors are to be deprived of their voice in legislation, such occasions as these were surely fit for their peculiar vigilance. At a dissolution, the crown has often appealed directly to the sense of the people, on the policy of great public measures;[1] and how could they respond to that appeal without satisfying themselves regarding the opinions and intentions of the candidates? Their response was found in the majority returned to the new Parliament, directly or indirectly pledged to support their decision.

p. 469. Again, p. 470: 'In place of selecting men, constituencies pronounce upon measures; in place of choosing representatives to discuss questions and decide on proposals in one of three co-ordinate and co-equal bodies, the aggregate of which decree what shall be enacted or done, electors consider and decree what shall be done themselves. It is a reaction towards the old Athenian plan of direct government by the people, practised before the principle of representation was discovered.'

[1] Speeches from the throne, 24th March, 1784; 27th April, 1807; 22nd April, 1831; 21st March, 1857.

But while the right of electors to be assured of the political opinions of candidates has been generally admitted, the first principles of representative government are ever to be kept in view. A member, once elected, is free to act upon his own convictions and conscience. As a man of honour, he will violate no engagement which he may have thought it becoming to accept: but if he has a due respect for his own character, and for the dignity of his office, he will not yield himself to the petty meddling and dictation of busy knots of his constituents, who may assume to sway his judgment.

Such being the multiplied relations of Parliament to the people, let us inquire how, since its early excesses in the reign of George III., it has deferred to the law, and respected other jurisdictions besides its own. *Servants' privilege discontinued.* The period signalised by the ill-advised attempts of the House of Commons to enlarge its powers, and assert too tenaciously its own privileges,—was yet marked by the abandonment of some of its ancient customs and immunities. From the earliest times, the members of both Houses had enjoyed the privilege of freedom from arrest in all civil suits; and this immunity,— useful and necessary as regarded themselves,— had also extended to their servants. The abuses of this privilege had long been notorious; and repeated attempts had already been made to discontinue it. For that purpose bills were several times passed by the Lords, but miscarried in the Commons.[1] At length, in 1770, a bill was agreed to by the Com-

[1] Lord Mansfield's speech, May 9th, 1770; Parl. Hist., xvi. 974.

mons,[1] and sent up to the House of Lords. There it encountered unexpected opposition from several peers: but was carried by the powerful advocacy of Lord Mansfield.[2] Nor was this the only privilege restrained by this useful act. Members and their servants had formerly enjoyed immunity from the distress of their goods, and from all civil suits, during the periods of privilege. Such monstrous privileges had been flagitiously abused; and few passages in parliamentary history are more discreditable than the frivolous pretexts under which protections were claimed by members of both Houses, and their servants. These abuses had already been partially restrained by several statutes:[3] but it was reserved for this act, to leave the course of justice entirely free, and to afford no protection to members, but that of their persons from arrest.

This same period witnessed the renunciation of an offensive custom, by which prisoners appeared before either House to receive judgment, kneeling at the bar. Submission so abject, while it degraded the prisoner, exhibited privilege as odious, rather than awful, in the eyes of a free people. In the late reign, the proud spirit of Mr. Murray had revolted against this indignity; and his contumacy had been punished by close confinement

*Prisoners kneeling at the bar.*

---

[1] Walpole says: 'The bill passed easily through the Commons, many of the members who were inclined to oppose it, trusting it would be rejected in the other House.'—*Mem.*, iv. 147. But this is scarcely to be reconciled with the fact that similar bills had previously been passed by the Lords.

[2] 10 Geo. III. c. 50.

[3] 12 & 13 Will. III. c. 3; 2 & 3 Anne, c. 18; 11 Geo. II. c. 24.

in Newgate.¹ But in 1772, when privilege was most unpopular, the Commons formally renounced this opprobrious usage, by standing order.² The Lords, less candid in their proceedings, silently discontinued the practice, in cases of privilege: but, by continuing the accustomed entries in their journal, still affected to maintain it.³

Parliament, having relinquished every invidious privilege, has not been without embarrass- *Privilege and the* ments in exercising the powers necessary *Courts.* for maintaining its own authority and independence, and which,—if rightly used,—are no restraint upon public liberty. Each House has exercised a large jurisdiction, in declaring and enforcing its own privileges. It administers the law of Parliament: the courts administer the law of the land; and where subjects have considered themselves aggrieved by one jurisdiction, they have appealed to the other.⁴ In such cases the appeal has been to inferior courts,

---

¹ Parl. Hist., xiv. 894; Walpole's Mem. of Geo. II., i. 15. In 1647, David Jenkins, a Royalist Welsh judge, had refused to kneel before the Commons; and Sir John Maynard, Sir John Gayre, and others, before the Lords.—Com. Journ., v. 469; Parl. Hist., iii. 844, 880.

² March 16th, 1772; Com. Journ., xxvi. 48.

³ In 1787, Mr. Warren Hastings, on being admitted to bail, on his impeachment, was obliged to kneel at the bar; and again, at the opening of his trial, in the following year, he appeared kneeling until desired by the Chancellor to rise. Of this ceremony he thus wrote: 'I can with truth affirm that I have borne with indifference all the base treatment I have had dealt to me—all except the ignominious ceremonial of kneeling before the House.'—*Trial of Hastings : Lord Stanhope's Life of Pitt*, i. 356. The same humiliating ceremony was repeated eight years afterwards, when he was called to the bar to hear his acquittal announced by the Chancellor.—*Ibid.*, ii. 319.

⁴ All the principles and authorities upon this matter are collected in Chap. VI. of the author's Treatise on the Law and Usage of Parliament.

—to courts whose judgments may again be reviewed by the High Court of Parliament. The courts,—without assuming the right to limit the privileges of Parliament,—have yet firmly maintained their own unfettered jurisdiction to try all causes legally brought before them; and to adjudge them according to the law, whether their judgment may conflict with privilege, as declared elsewhere, or not. A court of equity or common law can stay actions, by injunction or prohibition: but neither House is able to interdict a suit, by any legal process. Hence embarrassing contests have arisen between Parliament and the courts.

The right of both Houses to imprison for contempt, had been so often recognised by the courts, on writs of *habeas corpus*, that it appeared scarcely open to further question. Yet, in 1810, Sir Francis Burdett denied the authority of the Commons, in his place in Parliament. He enforced his denial in a letter to his constituents; and having himself been adjudged guilty of contempt, he determined to defy and resist their power. By direction of the House, the Speaker issued his warrant for the commitment of Sir Francis to the Tower. He disputed its legality, and resisted and turned out the Sergeant, who came to execute it: he barred up his house; and appealed for protection to the Sheriffs of Middlesex. The mob took his part, and being riotous, were dispersed in the streets, by the military. For three days he defended himself in his house, while the authorities were consulting as to the legality of breaking into it, by force. It was

*Case of Sir Francis Burdett.*

held that the Sergeant, in executing the Speaker's warrant, would be armed with all the powers of the law; and accordingly, on the third day, that officer having obtained the aid of a sufficient number of constables, and a military force, broke into the beleaguered house, and conveyed his prisoner to the Tower.[1] The commitment of a popular opponent of privilege was followed by its usual consequences. The martyred prisoner was an object of sympathy and adulation,—the Commons were denounced as tyrants and oppressors.

Overcome by force, Sir Francis brought actions against the Speaker and the Sergeant, in the Court of King's Bench, for redress. The House would have been justified by precedents and ancient usage, in resisting the prosecution of these actions, as a contempt of its authority: but instead of standing upon its privilege it directed its officers to plead, and the Attorney-General to defend them. The authority of the House was fully vindicated by the court; but Sir Francis prosecuted an appeal to the Exchequer Chamber, and to the House of Lords. The judgment of the court below being affirmed, all conflict between law and privilege was averted. The authority of the House had indeed been questioned: but the courts declared it to have been exercised in conformity with the law.

Where the courts uphold the authority of the House, all is well: but what if they deny and repudiate it? Since the memorable cases of Ashby and

[1] Ann. Reg., 1810, p. 344; Hans. Deb., xvi. 257, 454, &c. Lord Colchester's Diary, ii. 245-260.

White, and the electors of Aylesbury in 1704, no such case had arisen until 1837: when the cause of dispute was characteristic of the times. In the last century, we have seen the Commons contending for the inviolable secrecy of all their proceedings: now they are found declaring their inherent right of publishing all their own papers, for the information of the public.

The circumstances of this case may be briefly told. In 1836, Messrs. Hansard, the printers of the House of Commons, had printed, by order of that House, the reports of the Inspectors of Prisons,—in one of which a book published by Stockdale, and found among the prisoners in Newgate, was described as obscene and indecent. After the session, Stockdale brought an action against the printers, for libel. The character of the book being proved, a verdict was given against him, upon a plea of justification: but Lord Chief Justice Denman, who tried the cause, took occasion to say that 'the fact of the House of Commons having directed Messrs. Hansard to publish all their parliamentary reports, is no justification for them, or for any bookseller who publishes a parliamentary report, containing a libel against any man.' The assertion of such a doctrine was naturally startling to the House of Commons; and at the next meeting of Parliament, after an inquiry by a committee, the House declared 'That the power of publishing such of its reports, votes, and proceedings as it shall deem necessary, or conducive to the public interests, is an essential inci-

*Right of Commons to publish papers affecting character.*

dent to the constitutional functions of Parliament, more especially of this House, as the representative portion of it.' It was further resolved, that for any person to institute a suit in order to call its privileges in question, or for any court to decide upon matters of privilege, inconsistent with the determination of either House, was a breach of privilege.[1]

Stockdale, however, immediately brought another action, to which the House,—instead of acting upon its own recent resolutions,— directed Messrs. Hansard to plead. The case was tried upon this single issue,—whether the printers were justified by the privilege and order of the House; and the Court of Queen's Bench unanimously decided against them. *Case of Stockdale.*

The position of the Commons was surrounded with difficulties. Believing the judgment of the court to be erroneous, they might have sought its reversal by a writ of error. But such a course was not compatible with their dignity. It was not the conduct of their officer that was impugned: but their own authority, which they had solemnly asserted. In pursuing a writ of error, they might be obliged, in the last resort, to seek justice from the House of Lords,—a tribunal of equal but not superior, authority in matters of privilege; and having already pronounced their own judgment, such an appeal would be derogatory to their proper position in the state. They were equally unwilling

---

[1] Com. Journ., xcii. 418; May's Law and Usage of Parliament, 6th Ed., 167, *et seq.*

to precipitate a conflict with the courts. Their resolutions had been set at defiance; yet the damages and costs were directed to be paid! Their forbearance was not without humiliation. It was resolved, however, that in case of any future action, Messrs. Hansard should not plead at all; and that the authority of the House should be vindicated by the exercise of its privileges.

During the recess of 1839, another action was brought; and judgment having gone against Messrs. Hansard by default, the damages were assessed in the Sheriff's Court at 600*l.*, and levied by the Sheriffs. On the meeting of Parliament in 1840, the Sheriffs had not yet paid over the money to the plaintiff. The House now proceeded with the rigour which it had previously threatened,—but had forborne to exercise. Stockdale was immediately committed to the custody of the Sergeant-at-Arms, while Mr. Howard, his solicitor, escaped with a reprimand. The Sheriffs were directed to restore the money, which they had levied upon Messrs. Hansard. Being bound by their duty to the Court of Queen's Bench, they refused to obey this order; and were also committed to the custody of the Sergeant. In the hope of some settlement of the difficulty, they retained possession of the money, until compelled by an attachment from the Court of Queen's Bench to pay it over to Stockdale. Much sympathy was justly excited by the imprisonment of these gentlemen,—who, acting in strict obedience to the law and the judgment of the court, had nevertheless endeavoured to avoid a contempt of the

House of Commons, which, in the execution of their duty, they were constrained to commit. Punished with reluctance,—and without the least feeling of resentment,—they were the innocent victims of conflicting jurisdictions.

In an earlier age the Commons, relying upon their own paramount authority, might even have proceeded to commit the Judges of the Court of Queen's Bench,—for which a precedent was not wanting:[1] but happily, the wise moderation of this age revolted from so violent and unseemly an exercise of power. Confident in the justice and legality of their own proceedings,—defied by a low plaintiff in an unworthy cause,—and their deliberate judgment overruled by an inferior court,—they yet acted with as much temper and forbearance, as the inextricable difficulties of their position would allow.

Stockdale, while in custody, repeated his offence by bringing another action. He and his attorney were committed to Newgate; and Messrs. Hansard were again ordered not to plead. Judgment was once more entered up against them, and another writ of inquiry issued; when Mr. France, the Under-Sheriff, anxious to avoid offence to the House, obtained leave to show cause before the court, why the writ should not be executed. Meanwhile, the indefatigable Stockdale solaced his imprisonment, by bringing another action; for which his attorney's son, and his clerk, Mr. Pearce, were committed.

At length these vexatious proceedings were brought to a close, by the passing of an act, providing that all

[1] Jay v. Topham, 1689; Com. Journ., x. 227.

such actions should be stayed on the production of a certificate or affidavit, that any paper, the subject of an action, was printed by order of either House of Parliament.[1] Such an intervention of the supreme authority of Parliament, two years before, would have averted differences between concurrent jurisdictions, which no other power was competent to reconcile. No course was open to the Commons,—befitting their high jurisdiction and dignity,—by which the obedience of courts and plaintiffs could be ensured: their power of commitment was at once impotent, and oppressive: yet they could not suffer their authority to be wholly defied and contemned. Hence their proceedings were inevitably marked by hesitation and inconsistency. In a case, for which the constitution has made no provision,—even the wisdom of Sir Robert Peel, and the solid learning of Mr. Sergeant Wilde, were unequal to devise expedients less open to objection.[2]

<small>Actions stayed by statute.</small>

Another occasion immediately arose for further forbearance. Howard commenced an action of trespass against the officers of the House, who had taken him into custody. As it was possible that, in executing the Speaker's warrant, they might have exceeded their authority, the action was suffered to take its course. On the trial, it appeared that they had remained some time in the plaintiff's house, after they had ascertained that he was from home; and on that ground, a verdict was obtained against them for 100*l*. Howard brought a second action

<small>Case of Howard *v.* Gosset.</small>

---

[1] 3 & 4 Vict. c. 9. Papers reflecting upon private character are sometimes printed for the use of members only.
[2] Proceedings printed by the Commons, 1839 (283); Report of Precedents, 1837; Hans. Deb., 1847–1849.

against Sir W. Gosset, the Sergeant-at-Arms, in which he was also successful, on the ground of the informality of the Speaker's warrant. The Judges, however, took pains to show that their decision in no way impugned the authority of the House itself. The House, while it regarded this judgment as erroneous, could not but feel that its authority had been trifled with, in the spirit of narrow technicality, by an inferior court. Still moderation prevailed in its counsels; and, as the act of an officer, and not the authority of the House itself, was questioned, it was determined not to resist the execution of the judgment: but to test its legality by a writ of error. The judgment was reversed by the unanimous decision of the Court of Exchequer Chamber. As this last judgment was founded upon broader principles of law than those adopted by the court below, it is probable that, in Stockdale's case, a Court of Error would have shown greater respect to the privileges of the Commons, than the Court of Queen's Bench had thought fit to pay; and it is to be regretted that the circumstances were not such as to justify an appeal to a higher jurisdiction.

The increased power of the House of Commons, under an improved representation, has been patent and indisputable. Responsible to the people, it has, at the same time, wielded the people's strength. No longer subservient to the crown, the ministers, and the peerage, it has become the predominant authority in the state. But it is characteristic of the British constitution, and a proof of its freedom from *Increased power of the Commons.*

*Their moderation since the increase of their power.*

the spirit of democracy, that the more dominant the power of the House of Commons,—the greater has been its respect for the law, and the more carefully have its acts been restrained within the proper limits of its own jurisdiction. While its authority was uncertain and ill-defined,—while it was struggling against the crown,—jealous of the House of Lords,—distrustful of the press,—and irresponsible to the people,—it was tempted to exceed its constitutional powers: but since its political position has been established, it has been less provoked to strain its jurisdiction; and deference to public opinion, and the experience of past errors, have taught it wisdom and moderation.

The proceedings of the House in regard to Wilkes, *Conduct of the Commons in regard to Baron Rothschild, 1850.* present an instructive contrast to its recent conduct in forwarding the admission of Jews to Parliament. In the former case, its own privileges were strained or abandoned at pleasure, and the laws of the land outraged, in order to exclude and persecute an obnoxious member.[1] How did this same powerful body act in the case of Baron de Rothschild and Mr. Salomons? Here the House,—faithful to the principles of religious liberty, which it had long upheld,—was earnest in its desire to admit these members to their place in the legislature. They had been lawfully chosen: they laboured under no legal disability; and they claimed the privileges of members. A few words in the oath of abjuration, alone prevented them from taking their seats. A large majority of the House was favourable to their claims: the law was doubtful;

[1] See *supra*, p. 3, &c.

and the precedent of Mr. Pease, a Quaker,—who had been allowed to omit these words,—was urged by considerable authorities, as a valid ground for their admission. Yet the House, dealing with the seats of its own members,—over which it has always had exclusive jurisdiction,—and with every inducement to accept a broad and liberal interpretation of the law,—nevertheless administered it strictly, and to the letter.[1] For several years, the House had endeavoured to solve the difficulty by legislation. Its failures, however, did not tempt it to usurp legislative power, under the semblance of judicial interpretation. But it persevered in passing bills, in various forms, until it ultimately forced upon the other House an amendment of the law.

The limits within which Parliament, or either House, may constitutionally exercise a control over the executive government, have been defined by usage, upon principles consistent with a true distribution of powers, in a free state and limited monarchy. Parliament has no direct control over any single department of the state. It may order the production of papers, for its information:[2] it may investigate the conduct of public officers; and may pronounce its opinion upon the manner in which every function of the government has been, or ought to be, discharged. But it cannot convey its orders or directions to the meanest executive officer, in relation to the performance of his duty. Its power over the executive is exercised

*Control of either House over the executive.*

---

[1] Hans. Deb., July 29th and 30th, and Aug. 5th, 1850; July 18th and 21st, 1851. See also Chap. XIII.

[2] Many papers, however, can only be obtained by address to the Crown.

indirectly,—but not the less effectively,—through the responsible ministers of the crown. These ministers regulate the duties of every department of the state; and are responsible for their proper performance, to Parliament, as well as to the crown. If Parliament disapprove of any act, or policy of the government,—ministers must conform to its opinion, or forfeit its confidence. In this manner, the House of Commons, having become the dominant body in the legislature, has been able to direct the conduct of the government, and control its executive administration of public affairs, without exceeding its constitutional powers. It has a right to advise the crown,—even as to the exercise of prerogative itself; and should its advice be disregarded, it wields the power of impeachment, and holds the purse-strings of the state.

History abounds with examples, in which the exercise of prerogative has been controlled by Parliament. Even questions of peace and war, which are peculiarly within the province of prerogative, have been resolved, again and again, by the interposition of Parliament. From the reign of Edward III., Parliament has been consulted by the crown; and has freely offered its advice on questions of peace and war.[1] The exercise of this right,—so far from being a modern invasion of the royal prerogative,—is an ancient constitutional usage. It was not, however, until the power of Parliament had

*It has controlled the exercise of prerogative.*

*Questions of peace and war.*

[1] *E.g.* Edw. III., Parl. Hist., i. 122; Henry VII., *Ibid.*, 452; James I., *Ibid.*, 1293; Queen Anne, *Ibid.*, vi. 609.

prevailed over prerogative, that it had the means of enforcing its advice.

At a time when the influence of the crown had attained its highest point under George III., the House of Commons was able to bring to a close the disastrous American war, against the personal will of the king himself. Having presented an address against the further prosecution of offensive war,— to which they had received an evasive answer,—the House proceeded to declare, that it would ' consider as enemies to his Majesty and this country all who should advise, or by any means attempt the further prosecution of offensive war on the continent of America, for the purpose of reducing the revolted colonies to obedience by force.'[1] Nor did the House rest until it had driven Lord North, the king's war minister, from power.

During the long war with France, the government was pressed with repeated motions, in both Houses, for opening negotiations for peace.[2] Ministers were strong enough to resist them: but,—at a period remarkable for assertions of prerogative,— objections to such motions, on constitutional grounds, were rarely heard. Indeed the crown, by communicating to Parliament the breaking out of hostilities[3] or the commencement of negotiations for peace,[4]

---

[1] Feb. 27th and March 4th, 1782; Parl. Hist., xxii. 1064, 1086, 1087.

[2] Lord Stanhope, the Marquess of Lansdowne, &c.; Dec. 15th, 1792; June 17th, 1793, &c.; Mr. Grey, Feb. 21st, 1794, &c.; Mr. Whitbread, March 6th, 1794; Mr. Wilberforce, May 27, 1795; Mr. Sheridan, Dec. 8th, 1795.

[3] Feb. 11th, 1793; May 22nd, 1815; March 27th, 1854, &c.

[4] Dec. 8th, 1795; Oct. 29th, 1801; Jan. 31st, 1856, &c.

has invited its advice and assistance. That advice may be unfavourable to the policy of ministers; and the indispensable assistance of Parliament may be withheld. If the crown be dissatisfied with the judgment of Parliament, an appeal may still be made to the final decision of the people. In 1857, the House of Commons condemned the policy of the war with China: but ministers, instead of submitting to its censure, appealed to the country, and obtained its decisive approval.

<small>War with China, 1857.</small>

Upon the same principles, Parliament has assumed the right of advising the crown, in regard to the exercise of the prerogative of dissolution. In 1675, an address was moved in the House of Lords, praying Charles II. to dissolve the Parliament; and on the rejection of the motion, several Lords entered their protest.[1] Lord Chatham's repeated attempts to induce the House of Lords to address the crown to dissolve the Parliament which had declared the incapacity of Wilkes, have been lately noticed.[2] The address of the Commons, after the dismissal of the coalition ministry, praying the king not to dissolve Parliament, has been described elsewhere.[3] Lord Wharncliffe's vain effort to arrest the dissolution of Parliament in 1831, has also been adverted to.[4]

<small>Advice of Parliament concerning dissolution.</small>

But though the right of Parliament to address the crown, on such occasions, is unquestionable,—its exercise has been restrained by considerations of

---

[1] Lords' Journ., xiii. 33; Rockingham Mem., ii. 139.
[2] *Supra*, p. 23, &c. [3] *Supra*, Vol. I. 73. [4] *Supra*, Vol. I. 141.

policy, and party tactics. The leaders of parties,—profiting by the experience of Mr. Fox and Lord North,—have since been too wise to risk the forfeiture of public esteem, by factiously opposing the right of ministers to appeal from the House of Commons to the people. Unless that right has been already exercised, the alternatives of resigning office or dissolving Parliament have been left,—by general consent,—to the judgment of ministers who cannot command the confidence of the House of Commons. In the exercise of their discretion, ministers have been met with remonstrances: but sullen acquiescence on the part of their opponents, has succeeded to violent addresses, and measures for stopping the supplies.

As Parliament may tender its advice to the crown, regarding its own dissolution, so the people, praying the crown to exercise its prerogative, in order to give them the means of condemning the conduct of Parliament. In 1701, during a fierce contest between the Whig and Tory parties, numerous petitions and addresses were presented to William III. at the instance of the Whigs, praying for the dissolution of the Parliament, which was soon afterwards dissolved.[1] The constitutional character of these addresses having been questioned, it was upheld by a vote of the House of Commons, which affirmed 'that it is the undoubted right of the people of England to petition or address the king, for the calling, sitting, and dissolving Parlia-

*Popular addresses concerning prerogative.*

[1] Burnet's Own Time, iv. 543. Rockingham Mem., ii. 105.

ments, and for the redressing of grievances.'[1] In 1710, smilar tactics were resorted to by the Tories, when addresses were presented to Queen Anne, praying for a dissolution, and assuring her Majesty that the people would choose none but such as were faithful to the crown, and zealous for the church.[2]

In 1769, Lord Chatham sought public support of the same kind, in his efforts to obtain a dissolution of Parliament. Lord Rockingham and some of the leading Whigs, who doubted at first, were convinced of the constitutional propriety of such a course; and Lord Camden expressed a decisive opinion, affirming the right of the subject.[3] The people were justly dissatisfied with the recent proceedings of the House of Commons; and were encouraged by the opposition to lay their complaints at the foot of the throne, and to pray for a dissolution.

The contest between Mr. Pitt and the coalition was characterised by similar proceedings. While the Commons were protesting against a dissolution, the supporters of Mr. Pitt were actively engaged in obtaining addresses to his Majesty, to assure him of the support of the people, in the constitutional exercise of his prerogative.[4]

The House of Commons in the first instance,—

*Votes of want of confidence.* and the people in the last resort,—have become arbiters of the fate of the ministers

---

[1] Parl. Hist., v. 1339; Grenville Papers, iv. 446.
[2] Somerville's Reign of Queen Anne, 409: Smollett's Hist., ii. 191; Grenville Papers, iv. 453.
[3] 'His answer was full and manly, that the right is absolute, and unquestionable for the exercise.' Lord Chatham to Lord Temple, Nov. 8th, 1769; Grenville Papers, iv. 479.
[4] See Address of the City, Ann. Reg., 1784, p. 4, &c.

of the crown. Ministers may have the entire confidence of their sovereign, and be all-powerful in the House of Lords: but without a majority of the House of Commons, they are unable, for any considerable time, to administer the affairs of the country. The fall of ministries has more often been the result of their failure to carry measures which they have proposed, or of adverse votes on general questions of public policy: but frequently it has been due,—particularly in modern times,—to express representations to the crown, that its ministers have not the confidence of the House of Commons. Where such votes have been agreed to by an old Parliament,—as in 1784,—ministers have still had before them the alternative of a dissolution: but when they have already appealed to the country for support,—as in 1841, and again in 1859,—a vote affirming that they have not the confidence of the House of Commons, has been conclusive.

The disapprobation of ministers by the House of Commons being decisive, the expression of its confidence has, at other times, arrested their impending fall. Thus in 1831, Lord Grey's ministry, embarrassed by an adverse vote of the House, on the second reform bill,[1] was supported by a declaration of the continued confidence of the House of Commons.  *Votes of confidence.*

And at other times, the House has interposed its advice to the crown, on the formation of administrations, with a view to favour or obstruct political arrangements, then in progress. Thus, in 1784,

[1] *Supra*, Vol. I. p. 142.

when negotiations had been commenced for a fusion of parties, resolutions were laid before his Majesty expressing the opinion of the House of Commons, that the situation of public affairs required a 'firm, efficient, extended, and united administration, entitled to the confidence of the people, and such as may have a tendency to put an end to the divisions and distractions of the country.'[1] Similar advice was tendered to the Prince Regent in 1812, after the death of Mr. Perceval; and to William IV., in 1832, on the resignation of Earl Grey.[2]

But this constant responsibility of ministers, while it has made their position dependent upon the pleasure of Parliament, has protected fallen ministers from its vengeance. When the acts and policy of statesmen had been dictated by their duty to the crown alone, without regard to the approval of Parliament, they were in danger of being crushed by vindictive impeachments, and attainders. Strafford had died on the scaffold: Clarendon had been driven into exile:[3] Danby had suffered a long imprisonment in the Tower;[4] Oxford, Bolingbroke, and Ormond had been disgraced and ruined,[5] at the suit of the Commons. But parliamentary responsibility has prevented the commission of those political crimes, which had provoked the indignation of the

*Impeachments.*

---

[1] Parl. Hist., xxiv. 450; Ann. Reg., 1784, p. 265.
[2] *Supra*, Vol. I. p. 125, 143; Hans. Deb., 1st Ser., xxiii. 249.
[3] Having gone abroad pending his impeachment, an Act of banishment and incapacity was passed by Parliament.
[4] Not being brought to trial, he was admitted to bail by the Court of King's Bench, after an imprisonment of five years. St. Tr., xi. 871.
[5] Oxford was imprisoned for two years in the Tower. Bolingbroke and Ormond, having escaped, were attainted.

Commons; and when the conduct or policy of ministers has been condemned, loss of power has been their only punishment. Hence the rarity of impeachment in later times. The last hundred years present but two cases of impeachment,—the one against Mr. Warren Hastings, on charges of misgovernment in India,—the other against Lord Melville, for alleged malversation in his office. The former was not a minister of the crown, and he was accused of offences committed beyond the reach of parliamentary control; and the offences charged against the latter, had no relation to his political duties as a responsible minister.

The case of Mr. Warren Hastings finally established the constitutional doctrine, that an impeachment by the Commons is not terminated by any prorogation or dissolution of Parliament. It had been affirmed by the Lords in 1678, after an examination of precedents:[1] when Lord Stafford fell a victim to its assertion; and six years afterwards, it had been denied, in order to secure the escape of the 'popish lords,' then under impeachment.[2] Lord Danby's lingering impeachment had been continued by the first decision, and annulled by the last. The same question having arisen after the lapse of a century, Parliament was called upon to review the precedents of former impeachments, and to pass its judgment upon the contradictory decisions of the Lords. Many of the precedents were so obscure as to furnish arguments

*Impeachments not abated by a dissolution.*

---

March 18th, 19th, 1678. Lords' Journ., xiii. 464, 466.
[2] May 22nd, 1685. Lords' Journ., xiv. 11. This decision was reversed, in the case of the Earl of Oxford, May 25th, 1717; Ibid. xx. 475.

on both sides of the question: conflicting opinions were to be found amongst text-writers; and the most eminent lawyers of the day were not agreed.[1] But the masterly and conclusive speech of Mr. Pitt was alone sufficient to settle the controversy, even on the grounds of law and precedent. On broad constitutional principles, the first statesmen of all parties concurred in upholding the inviolable right of the Commons to pursue an impeachment, without interruption from any act of the crown. It could not be suffered that offenders should be snatched from punishment, by ministers who might be themselves concerned in their guilt. Nor was it just to the accused, that one impeachment should be arrested before a judgment had been obtained; and another preferred,—on the same or different grounds, perhaps after his defence had suggested new evidence to condemn him. Had not the law already provided for the continuance of impeachments, it would have been necessary to declare it. But it was agreed in both Houses, by large majorities, that by the law and custom of Parliament, an impeachment pending in the House of Lords continued *in statu quo*, from one Session and from one Parliament to another, until a judgment had been given.[2]

[1] Lord Thurlow, Lord Kenyon, Sir Richard Arden, Sir Archibald Macdonald, Sir John Scott, Mr. Mitford, and Mr. Erskine contended for the abatement: Lord Mansfield, Lord Camden, Lord Loughborough, and Sir William Grant, maintained its continuance.

[2] Com. Deb.; Parl. Hist., xxviii. 1018, *et seq.*; Lords' Deb.; *Ibid.*, xxix. 514; Report of Precedents; Lords' Journ., xxxix. 125; Tomline's Life of Pitt, iii. 161.

As parliamentary responsibility has spared ministers the extreme penalties of impeachments,—so it has protected the crown from those dangerous and harassing contests with the Commons, with which the earlier history of this country abounds. What the crown has lost in power, it has gained in security and peace. Until the Commons had fully established their constitutional rights, they had been provoked to assert them with violence, and to press them to extreme conclusions: but they have exercised them, when acknowledged, with moderation and forbearance. *Improved relations of the crown with the Commons.*

At the same time, ministers of the crown have encountered greater difficulties, from the increased power and independence of the Commons, and the more direct action of public opinion upon measures of legislation and policy. They are no longer able to fall back upon the crown for support: their patronage is reduced, and their influence diminished. They are left to secure a majority, not so much by party connexions, as by good measures and popular principles. Any error of judgment,—any failure in policy or administration, is liable to be visited with instant censure. Defeated in the Commons, they have no resource but an appeal to the country, unaided by those means of influence, upon which ministers formerly relied. *Strong and weak governments.*

Their responsibility is great and perilous: but it has at least protected them from other embarrassments, of nearly equal danger. When the crown was more powerful, what was the fate of ministries?

The first ten years of the reign of George III. witnessed the fall of five feeble administrations; and their instability was mainly due to the restless energies of the king. Until Mr. Pitt came into power, there had not been one strong administration during this reign. It was the king himself who overthrew the coalition ministry, the absolute government of Mr. Pitt, and the administration of 'All the Talents.'

For more than ten years after Mr. Pitt's fall, there was again a succession of weak administrations, of short duration. If the king could uphold a ministry,—he could also weaken or destroy it. From this danger, governments under the new parliamentary system, have been comparatively free. More responsible to Parliament, they have become less dependent upon the crown. The confidence of the one has guarded them from the displeasure of the other.

No cause of ministerial weakness has been more frequent than disunion. It is the common lot of men acting together; and is not peculiar to any time, or political conditions. Yet when ministers looked to the crown for support, and relied upon the great territorial lords for a parliamentary majority,—what causes were so fruitful of jealousies and dissensions, as the intrigues of the court, and the rivalries of the proprietors of boroughs? Here, again, governments deriving their strength and union from Parliament and the people, have been less exposed to danger in this form. Governments have, indeed, been weakened, as in former times, by divisions among their own party: but they have been, in some measure, protected from faction, by the greater responsibility of all parties to public opinion. This protection will be more assured, when the old system of government, by influence and patronage, shall have given place to the recognition of national interests, as the sole basis of party.

The responsibility of ministers has been further simplified, by the dominant power of the Commons. The Lords may sometimes thwart a ministry, reject or mutilate its measures, and even condemn its policy: but they are powerless to overthrow a ministry supported by the Commons, or to uphold a ministry which the Commons have condemned. Instead of many masters, a government has only one. Nor can it be justly said, that this master has been severe, exacting, or capricious.

It can neither be affirmed that strong governments were characteristic of the parliamentary system, subverted by the reform act; nor that weak governments have been characteristic of the new system, and the result of it. In both periods, the stability of administrations has been due to other causes. If in the latter period, ministers have been overthrown, who, at another time might have been upheld by the influence of the crown; there have yet been governments supported by a parliamentary majority and public approbation, stronger in moral force,—and more capable of overpowering interests adverse to the national welfare,—than any ministries deriving their power from less popular sources.

After the reform act, Earl Grey's ministry was all-powerful, until it was dissolved by disunion in the cabinet. No government was ever stronger than that of Sir Robert Peel, until it was broken up by the repeal of the corn laws. Lord Aberdeen's cabinet was scarcely less strong, until it fell by disunion and military failures. What government was more powerful than Lord Palmerston's first administration, until it split upon the sunken rock of the Orsini conspiracy?

On the other hand, the ministry of Lord Melbourne was enfeebled by the disunion of the Liberal party. The first ministry of Sir Robert Peel, and the ministries of Lord Derby, in 1852 and 1858, were inevitably weak,—being formed upon a hopeless minority in the House of Commons. Such causes would have produced weakness at any time; and are not chargeable upon the caprices, or ungovernable temper, of a reformed Parliament. And throughout this period, all administrations,—whether strong or weak, and of whatever political party,—relying mainly upon public confidence, have laboured successfully in the cause of good government; and have secured to the people more sound laws, prosperity, and contentment, than have been enjoyed at any previous epoch, in the history of this country.

*Control of the Commons over supplies and taxes.* One of the most ancient and valued rights of the Commons, is that of voting money and granting taxes to the crown, for the public service. From the earliest times, they have made this right the means of extorting concessions from the crown, and advancing the liberties of the people. They upheld it with a bold spirit against the most arbitrary kings; and the Bill of Rights crowned their final triumph over prerogative. They upheld it with equal firmness against the Lords. For centuries they had resented any 'meddling' of the other House 'with matter of supply;' and in the reign of Charles II., they successfully maintained their exclusive right to determine 'as to the matter, the measure and the time' of every tax imposed upon the people.

In the same reign, they began to scrutinise the public expenditure; and introduced the salutary practice of appropriating their grants to particular purposes. But they had not yet learned the value of a constant control over the revenue and expenditure of the crown; and their liberality to Charles, and afterwards to James II., enabled those monarchs to violate the public liberties.

The experience of these reigns prevented a repetition of the error; and since the Revolution, the grants of the Commons have been founded on annual estimates,—laid before them on the responsibility of ministers of the crown, —and strictly appropriated to the service of the year. This constant control over the public expenditure has, more than any other cause, vested in the Commons the supreme power of the state; yet the results have been favourable to the crown. When the Commons had neither information as to the necessities of the state, nor securities for the proper application of their grants,—they had often failed to respond to the solicitation of the king for subsidies, *Their liberality to the crown.*

—or their liberality had fallen short of his demands.[1] But not once since the reign of William III. have the demands of the crown, for the public service, been refused.[2] Whatever sums ministers have stated to be necessary, for all the essential services of the state, the Commons have freely granted.[3] Not a soldier has been struck from the rank and file of the army: not a sailor or a ship from the fleet, by any vote of the Commons.[4] So far from opposing the demands of the crown, they have rather laid themselves open to the charge of too facile an acquiescence in a constantly-increasing expenditure. Since they have assumed the control of the finances, the expenditure has increased about fifty-fold; and a stupendous national debt has been created. Doubt-

[1] In 1625, the Commons postponed the supplies demanded by Charles I. for carrying on the war with Spain.—*Parl. Hist.*, ii. 35. In 1675, they refused a supply to Charles II. to take off the anticipations upon his revenue.—*Ibid.*, iv. 757. In 1677, they declined a further supply till his Majesty's alliances were made known.—*Ibid.*, 879. And in the next year they refused him an additional revenue. —*Ibid.*, 1000. In 1685, James II. required 1,400,000*l.*; the Commons granted one half only.—*Ibid.*, 1379.

[2] The reductions in the army insisted upon by the Commons, in 1697 and 1698, were due to their constitutional jealousy of a standing army, and their aversion to the Dutch Guards, rather than to a niggardly disposition towards the public service.—See Lord Macaulay's Hist., v. 18, 24, 151, 177.

[3] With a few exceptions, so trifling as sometimes to be almost ridiculous, it will be found that, of late years, the annual estimates have generally been voted without deduction. In 1857, the Committee of Supply refused a vote for the purchase of a British chapel in Paris: in 1858, the only result of the vigilance of Parliament was a disallowance of 300*l.* as the salary of the travelling agent of the National Gallery! In 1859, the salary of the Register of Sasines was refused; but on the recommitment of the resolution, was restored!

[4] On the 27th Feb., 1786, Mr. Pitt's motion for fortifying the dockyards was lost by the casting vote of the Speaker; and no grant for that purpose was therefore proposed.—*Parl. Hist.*, xxv. 1096.

less their control has been a check upon ministers. The fear of their remonstrances has restrained the prodigality of the executive: but parsimony cannot be justly laid to their charge. The people may have some grounds for complaining of their stewardship: but assuredly the crown and its ministers have none.

While voting the estimates, however, the Commons have sometimes dissented from the financial arrangements proposed by ministers. Responding to the pecuniary demands of the crown, they have disapproved the policy by which it was sought to meet them. In 1767, Mr. Charles Townshend, the Chancellor of the Exchequer, proposed to continue, for one year, the land tax of four shillings in the pound: but on the motion of Mr. Grenville, the tax was reduced to three shillings, by which the budget sustained a loss of half-a-million. This was the first occasion, since the Revolution, on which a minister had been defeated upon any financial measure.[1]

<small>Ministers defeated on financial measures.</small>

Throughout the French war, the Commons agreed to every grant of money, and to nearly every new tax, and loan, proposed by successive administrations.[2] But on the termination of the war, when the ministers desired to continue one-half of the war property tax, amounting to about seven millions

---

[1] Parl. Hist., xvi. 362.
[2] On the 12th May, 1796, the numbers being equal on the third reading of the Succession Duty to Real Estates Bill, the Speaker voted for it: but Mr. Pitt said he should abandon it.—*Parl. Hist.*, xxxii. 1041. Lord Colchester's Diary, i. 57. Lord Stanhope's Life of Pitt, ii. 369. On the 12th March, 1805, the Agricultural Horse Duty Bill was lost on the second reading.—*Hans. Deb.*, 1st Ser., iii. 861.

and a half,—such was the national repugnance to that tax, that they sustained a signal defeat.¹ Again in 1852, Lord Derby's ministry were out-voted on their proposal for doubling the house tax.² But when the Commons have thus differed from the ministry, the questions at issue have involved the form and incidence of taxation, and not the necessities of the state; and their votes have neither diminished the public expenditure, nor reduced the ultimate burthens upon the people.

Nor have the Commons, by postponing grants, or in other words, by 'stopping the supplies,' endeavoured to coerce the other powers in the state. No more formidable instrument could have been placed in the hands of a popular assembly, for bending the executive to its will. It had been wielded with effect, when the prerogative of kings was high, and the influence of the Commons low: but now the weapon lies rusty in the armoury of constitutional warfare. In 1781, Mr. Thomas Pitt proposed to delay the granting of the supplies for a few days, in order to extort from Lord North a pledge regarding the war in America. It was then admitted that no such proposal had been made since the Revolution; and the House resolved to proceed with the committee of supply, by a large majority.³ In the same session Lord Rockingham moved, in the House

*Stopping the supplies.*

[1] Ayes, 201; Noes, 238: Hans. Deb., 1st Ser., xxxiii. 451; Lord Brougham's Speeches, i. 495; Lord Dudley's Letters, 136; Horner's Mem., ii. 318.
[2] Hans. Deb., 3rd Ser., cxxiii. 1693.
[3] Nov. 30, 1781; Parl. Hist., xxii. 751; Ayes, 172; Noes, 77. Mr. T. Pitt had merely opposed the motion for the Speaker to leave the Chair.

of Lords, to postpone the third reading of a land tax bill, until explanations had been given regarding the causes of Admiral Kempenfeldt's retreat: but did not press it to a division.[1]

The precedent of 1784, is the solitary instance in which the Commons have exercised their power of delaying the supplies. They were provoked to use it, by the unconstitutional exercise of the influence of the crown: but it failed them at their utmost need,[2]—and the experiment has not been repeated. Their responsibility, indeed, has become too great for so perilous a proceeding. The establishments and public credit of the country are dependent on their votes; and are not to be lightly thrown into disorder. Nor are they driven to this expedient for coercing the executive; as they have other means, not less effectual, for directing the policy of the state.

While the Commons have promptly responded to the demands of the crown, they have endeavoured to guard themselves against importunities from other quarters, and from the unwise liberality of their own members. *Restraints upon the liberality of the Commons.* They will not listen to any petition or motion which involves a grant of public money, until it has received the recommendation of the crown;[3] and they have further protected the public purse, by delays and other forms, against hasty and inconsiderate resolutions.[4] Such precautions have been the more neces-

---

[1] Nov. 19; Parl. Hist., xxii. 865.  [2] See *supra*, Vol. I. p. 80.
[3] Standing Order, Dec. 11th, 1706.
[4] See May's Law and Usage of Parliament, 6th ed., 549.

sary, as there are no checks upon the liberality of the Commons, but such as they impose upon themselves. The Lords have no voice in questions of expenditure, save that of a formal assent to the Appropriation Acts. They are excluded from it by the spirit, and by the forms of the constitution.

Not less exclusive has been the right of the Commons to grant taxes for meeting the public expenditure. These rights are indeed inseparable; and are founded on the same principles. 'Taxation,' said Lord Chatham, 'is no part of the governing, or legislative power. The taxes are a voluntary gift and grant of the Commons alone. In legislation the three estates of the realm are alike concerned: but the concurrence of the peers and the crown to a tax, is only necessary to clothe it with the form of a law. The gift and grant is of the Commons alone.'[1] On these principles, the Commons had declared that a money bill was sacred from amendment. In their gifts and grants they would brook no meddling. Such a position was not established without hot controversies.[2] Nor was it ever expressly admitted by the Lords:[3] but as they were unable to shake the strong determination of the Commons, they tacitly acquiesced, and submitted. For one hundred and fifty years, there was scarcely a

*Exclusive rights of the Commons concerning taxation.*

---

[1] Parl. Hist., xvi. 99.

[2] The Reports of the conferences between the two Houses (1640–1703), containing many able arguments on either side, are collected in the Appendix to the third volume of Hatsell's Precedents, and in the Report of the Committee on Tax Bills, 1860.

[3] To the claim, as very broadly asserted by the Commons in 1700, at a conference upon the Bill for the sale of Irish Forfeited Estates, the Lords replied: 'If the said assertions were exactly true, which their Lordships cannot allow.'

dispute upon this privilege. The Lords, knowing how any amendment affecting a charge upon the people, would be received by the Commons, either abstained from making it, or averted misunderstanding, by not returning the amended bill. And when an amendment was made, to which the Commons could not agree, on the ground of privilege alone, it was their custom to save their privilege, by sending up a new bill, embracing the Lords' amendment.

But if the Lords might not amend money bills, could not they reject them? This very question was discussed in 1671. The Commons had then denied the right of amendment on the broadest grounds. In reply, the Lords argued thus:—'If this right should be denied, the Lords have not a negative voice allowed them, in bills of this nature; for if the Lords, who have the power of treating, advising, giving counsel, and applying remedies, cannot amend, abate, or refuse a bill in part, by what consequence of reason can they enjoy a liberty to reject the whole? When the Commons shall think fit to question it, they may pretend the same grounds for it.' The Commons, however, admitted the right of rejection. 'Your Lordships,' they said, 'have a negative to the whole.' 'The king must deny the whole of every bill, or pass it; yet this takes not away his negative voice. The Lords and Commons must accept the whole general pardon or deny it; yet this takes not away their negative.'[1] And again in 1689, it was stated by a committee of the Commons, that the Lords are 'to

*Power of the Lords to reject a money bill.*

[1] Hatsell, iii. 405, 422, 423.

pass all or reject all, without diminution or alteration.'[1] But these admissions cost the Commons nothing, at that time. To reject a money bill, was to withhold supplies from the crown,—an act of which the Lords were not to be suspected. .The Lords themselves were fully alive to this difficulty, and complained that 'a hard and ignoble choice was left to them, either to refuse the crown supplies when they are most necessary, or to consent to ways and proportions of aid, which neither their own judgment or interest, nor the good of the government or people, can admit.'[2] In argument, the Commons were content to recognise this barren right; yet so broad were the grounds on which they rested their own claims of privilege,—and so stubborn was their temper in maintaining them,—that it may well be questioned whether they would have submitted to its practical exercise. If the Lords had rejected a bill for granting a tax,—would the Commons have immediately granted another? Would they not rather have sat with folded arms, rejoicing that the people were spared a new impost; while the king's treasury was beggared by the interference of the Lords?

Taxes were then of a temporary character. They were granted for one year, or for a longer period, according to the exigencies of the occasion. Hearth money was the first per-

*Temporary and permanent taxes.*

---

[1] Hatsell, iii. 452. This admission, however, is not of equal authority, as it formed part of the reasons reported from a committee, which were re-committed, and not adopted by the House.

[2] Conference, 1671 ; Hatsell, iii. 405.

manent tax, imposed in 1663.¹ No other tax of that character appears to have been granted, until after the Revolution; when permanent duties were raised on beer,² on salt,³ on vellum and paper,⁴ on houses,⁵ and on coffee.⁶ These duties were generally granted as a security for loans; and the financial policy of permanent taxes increased with the national debt, and the extension of public credit. This policy somewhat altered the position of the Lords, in relation to tax bills. Taxes were from time to time varied and repealed; and to such alterations of the law, the Lords, might have refused their assent, without withholding supplies from the crown. But such opportunities were not sought by the Lords. They had given up the contest upon privilege; and wisely left to the Commons the responsibility and the odium, of constantly increasing the public burthens. Taxes and loans were multiplied: but the Lords accepted them, without question. They rarely even discussed financial measures; and when, in 1763, they opposed the third reading of the Wines and Cider Duties Bill, it was observed that this was the first occasion, on which they had been known to divide upon a money bill.⁷

But while they abstained from interference with the supplies and ways and means, granted by the Commons for the public service, they occasionally rejected or postponed other bills, *Tax bills rejected by the Lords.*

---

[1] 13 and 14 Charles II. c. 10.
[2] 1 Will. and Mary, Sess. 1, c. 24.
[3] 5 & 6 Will. and Mary, c. 31.
[4] 9 & 10 Will. III. c. 25.  [5] 5 Anne, c. 13.  [6] 7 Anne, c. 7.
[7] March 30th, 1763; Parl. Hist., xv. 1316.

incidentally affecting supply and taxation: bills imposing or repealing protective duties: bills for the regulation of trade; and bills embracing other disputable matters of legislation, irrespective of taxation. Of these, the greater part were measures of legislative policy, rather than measures of revenue; and with the single exception of the Corn Bill of 1827, their fate does not appear to have excited any jealousy, in the sensitive minds of the Commons.

At length, in 1860, the Lords exercised their power, in a novel and startling form. The Commons had resolved, among other financial arrangements for the year, to increase the property tax and stamp duties, and to repeal the duties on paper. The Property Tax and Stamp Duties Bills had already received the royal assent, when the Paper Duties Repeal Bill was received by the Lords. It had encountered strong opposition in the Commons, where its third reading was agreed to, by the small majority of nine. And now the Lords determined, by a majority of eighty-nine, to postpone the second reading for six months. Having assented to the increased taxation of the annual budget, they refused the relief by which it had been accompanied.

*Paper Duties Repeal Bill, 1860.*

Never until now, had the Lords rejected a bill for imposing or repealing a tax, raised solely for the purpose of revenue,—and involving the supplies and ways and means, for the service of the year. Never had they assumed the right of reviewing the calculations of the Commons, regarding revenue and expenditure. In principle, all previous invasions of the cherished rights of the Commons,

*Relative rights of the two Houses.*

had been trifling compared with this. What was a mere amendment in a money bill, compared with its irrevocable rejection? But on the other hand, the legal right of the Lords to reject any bill whatever, could not be disputed. Even their constitutional right to 'negative the whole' of a money bill, had been admitted by the Commons themselves. Nor was this strictly, and in technical form, a money bill. It neither granted any tax to the crown, nor recited that the paper duty was repealed, in consideration of other taxes imposed. It simply repealed the existing law, under which the duty was levied. Technically, no privilege of the Commons, as previously declared, had been infringed. Yet it was contended, with great force, that to undertake the office of revising the balances of supplies and ways and means,—which had never been assumed by the Lords, during two hundred years,—was a breach of constitutional usage, and a violation of the first principles, upon which the privileges of the House are founded. If the letter of the law was with the Lords, its spirit was clearly with the Commons.

Had the position of parties, and the temper of the times been such as to encourage a violent collision between the two Houses, there *Proceedings of the Commons.* had rarely been an occasion more likely to provoke it. But this embarrassment the government was anxious to avert; and many causes concurred to favour moderate councils. A committee was therefore appointed in the Commons, to search for precedents. The search was long and intricate: the report copious and elaborate: but no opinion was given upon the grave question at issue. The lapse of six weeks had already moderated the heat and excitement of the controversy; when on the 5th July, Lord Palmerston, on the part of the government, explained the course which he counselled the House to adopt. Having stated what were the acknowledged privileges of the House, and referred to the precedents collected by the committee, he expressed his opinion that the Lords, in rejecting the Paper Duties Bill, had no desire to invade the constitutional rights of the Commons: but had been actuated, as on former occasions, by motives of public policy. He could not believe that they were commencing a deliberate course of interference with the peculiar functions of the Commons. But should that appear to be their intention, the latter would know how to vindicate their privileges, if invaded, and would be supported by the people. He deprecated a collision between the two Houses. Any one who should provoke it, would incur a grave responsibility. With these views, he proposed three resolutions. The first asserted generally, 'that the right of granting aids and supplies to the crown, is in the Commons alone.' The second affirmed, that although the Lords had sometimes exercised the power of rejecting bills of several descriptions, relating to taxation, yet the exercise of that power was 'justly regarded by this House with peculiar jealousy, as affecting the right of the Commons to grant supplies, and to provide the ways and means for the service of the year.' The third stated, 'that to guard for the future, against an undue exercise of that power by the Lords, and to secure to the Commons their rightful control over taxation and supply, this House has, in its own hands, the power so to impose and remit taxes, and to frame bills of supply, that the right of the Commons as to the matter, manner, measure, and time, may be maintained inviolate.'

The aim of these resolutions was briefly this:—to assert broadly the constitutional rights of the Commons: to qualify former admissions, by declaring their jealousy of the power exercised by the Lords of rejecting bills relating to taxation; and to convey a warning that the Commons had the means of resisting that power, if unduly exercised, and were prepared to use them. They were a protest against future encroachments, rather than a remonstrance on the past. They hinted—not obscurely—that the Commons could guard their own privileges by reverting to the simpler forms of earlier times, and embracing all the financial arrangements of the year, in a single bill, which the Lords must accept or reject, as a whole. The resolutions, though exposed to severe criticism, as not sufficiently vindicating the privileges of the House, or condemning the recent conduct of the Lords, were yet accepted,—it may be said, unanimously.[1] The soundest friends of the House of Lords, and of constitutional government, trusted that a course so temperate and conciliatory, would prevent future differences of the same kind. It was clear that the Commons had the means of protecting their own rights, without invading any

[1] Debates, July 5th and 6th, 1860; Hans. Deb., 3rd Ser., clix. 1383; Report of Committee on Tax Bills, June 29th, 1860.

privilege claimed by the Lords; and having shown an example of forbearance,—which might have been vainly sought, in an assembly less conscious of its strength,—they awaited another occasion for the exercise of their unquestionable powers. Having gained moral force, by their previous moderation, they knew that they would not appeal in vain for popular support.[1]

One of the proud results of our free constitution has been the development of Parliamentary oratory,—an honour and ornament to our history,—a source of public enlightenment,—and an effective instrument of popular government. Its excellence has varied, like our literature, with the genius of the men, and the events of the periods, which have called it forth: but from the accession of George III. may be dated the Augustan era of Parliamentary eloquence.

*Parliamentary oratory.*

The great struggles of the Parliament with Charles I. had stirred the eloquence of Pym, Hampden, Wentworth, and Falkland; the Revolution had developed the oratory of Somers; and the Parliaments of Anne, and the two first Georges, had given scope to the various talents of Bolingbroke, Pulteney, Wyndham, and Walpole. The reputation of these men has reached posterity: but their speeches,—if they survived the memory of their own generations,

---

[1] In the following year,—after the date of this history,—the Commons effectually repelled this encroachment, and vindicated their authority in the repeal and imposition of taxes, by including the repeal of the paper duty in a general financial measure, granting the property tax, the tea and sugar duties, and other ways and means for the service of the year, which the Lords were constrained to accept. —24 & 25 Vict. c. 20. Hans. Deb., clxii. 594; clxiii. 68, &c.

—have come down to us in fragments,—as much the composition of the historian or reporter, as of the orators to whom they are assigned.[1] Happily the very period distinguished by our most eloquent statesmen was that in which they had the privilege of addressing posterity, as well as their own contemporaries. The expansion of their audience gave a new impulse to their eloquence, which was worthy of being preserved for all ages.

Lord Chatham had attained the first place among statesmen in the late reign, but his fame as an orator mainly rests upon his later speeches, in the reign of George III. Lofty and impassioned in his style, and dramatic in his manner, his oratory abounded in grand ideas and noble sentiments, expressed in language simple, bold and vigorous. The finest examples of his eloquence stand alone, and unrivalled: but he flourished too early, to enjoy the privilege of transmitting the full fruits of his genius to posterity.[2] *Lord Chatham.*

He was surrounded and followed by a group of orators, who have made their time the classic age of Parliamentary history. Foremost among them was his extraordinary son, William Pitt. Inferior to his father in the highest qualities of an orator,—he surpassed him in argument, in knowledge, in intellectual force, and mastery. Magnilo- *Mr. Pitt.*

---

[1] Of the speeches of Somers and Bolingbroke there are no remains whatever. Mr. Pitt said he would rather recover a speech of Bolingbroke than the lost books of Livy, or other writings of antiquity.

[2] Some of his earlier speeches were composed by Dr. Johnson from the notes of others; and even his later speeches were delivered when reporting was still very imperfect.

quent in his style, his oratory sometimes attained the elevation of eloquence: but rarely rose above the level of debate. His composition was felicitously described by Windham, as a 'State paper style.' He may be called the founder of the modern school of Parliamentary debaters. His speeches were argumentative, admirably clear in statement, skilfully arranged, vigorous and practical. Always marked by rare ability, they yet lacked the higher inspirations of genius. In sarcasm he had few equals. No one held so absolute a sway over the House of Commons. In voice and manner, he was dignified and commanding. The minister was declared in every word he uttered; and the consciousness of power, while it sustained the dignity of his oratory, increased its effect upon his audience.

The eloquence of his great rival, Mr. Fox, was as
Mr. Fox. different, as were his political opinions and position. His success was due to his natural genius, and to the great principles of liberty which he advocated. Familiar with the best classical models, he yet too often disdained the studied art of the orator; and was negligent and unequal in his efforts. But when his genius was aroused within him, he was matchless, in demonstrative argument, in force, in wit, in animation, and spontaneous eloquence. More than any orator of his time, he carried with him the feelings and conviction of his audience; and the spirit and reality of the man, charm us scarcely less in his printed speeches. Wanting in discretion,— he was frequently betrayed into intemperance of language and opinion: but his generous ardour in the cause of liberty still appeals to our sympathies;

and his broad constitutional principles are lessons of political wisdom.

Mr. Fox had been from his earliest youth, the friend and disciple of Mr. Burke,—and *Mr. Burke.* vast was the intellect of his master. In genius, learning, and accomplishments, Mr. Burke had no equal either among the statesmen, or writers of his time; yet he was inferior, as an orator, to the three great men who have been already noticed. His speeches, like his writings, bear witness to his deep philosophy, his inexhaustible stores of knowledge, and redundant imagination. They are more studied and more often quoted than the speeches of any other statesman. His metaphors and aphorisms are as familiar to our ears as those of Lord Bacon. But transcendent as were his gifts, they were too often disfigured by extravagance. He knew not how to restrain them within the bounds of time and place; or to adapt them to the taste of a popular assembly, which loves directness and simplicity. His addresses were dissertations rather than speeches. To influence men, an orator must appeal directly to their reason, their feelings, and present temper: but Mr. Burke, while he astonished them with his prodigious faculties, wearied them with refinements and imagery, in which they often lost the thread of his argument.

Mr. Sheridan is entitled to the next place in this group of orators. His brilliancy and *Mr. Sheridan.* pointed wit,—his spirited declamation and effective delivery,—astonished and delighted his audience. Such was the effect of his celebrated speech on the fourth, or 'Begum charge' against Warren Hastings, that the peers and strangers joined with the House in a 'tumult of applause;' and could not be restrained from clapping their hands in ecstasy. The House adjourned, in order to recover its self-possession. Mr. Pitt declared that this speech 'surpassed all the eloquence of ancient or modern times, and possessed everything that genius or art could furnish, to agitate or control the human mind.' Mr. Fox said, 'eloquent indeed it was; so much so, that all he had ever heard,—all he had ever read, dwindled into nothing, and vanished like vapour before the sun.' Mr. Sheridan afterwards addressed the Lords, in Westminster Hall, on the same charge, for four days; and Mr. Burke said of his address, 'that no species of oratory,—no kind of eloquence which had been heard in ancient or modern times; nothing which the acuteness of the bar, the dignity of the senate, or the morality of the pulpit could furnish, was equal to what they had that day heard in Westminster Hall.' But while particular efforts of this accomplished speaker met with extraordinary success, he was restrained by want of statesmanship and character, from commanding a position in the House of Commons, equal to his great talents as an orator.[1]

The qualities of Mr. Windham were of another class. Superior to the last in education and at-

[1] Lord Byron said of him: 'Whatever Sheridan has done, or chosen to do, has been, *par excellence*, always the best of its kind. He has written the best comedy, the best opera, the best farce (it is only too good for a farce), and the best address (the monologue on Garrick), and to crown all, delivered the very best oration, the famous Begum speech, ever conceived or heard in this country.'

tainments, and little inferior in wit, he never achieved successes so dazzling; yet he maintained a higher place among the debaters of his age. Though his pretensions to the higher qualities of a statesman were inconsiderable, and his want of temper and discretion too often impaired his unquestionable merits in debate, his numerous talents and virtues graced a long and distinguished public life.

*Mr. Windham.*

Lord Erskine was not inferior, as an orator, to the greatest of his contemporaries: but the senate was not the scene of his most remarkable triumphs. His speeches at the bar combined the highest characteristics of eloquence,—fire, —force,—courage,—earnestness,—the closest argument,—imagery,—noble sentiments,—great truths finely conceived and applied,—a diction pure and simple,—action the most graceful and dignified. But none of these great qualities were used for display. They were all held, by the severity of his taste, and the mastery of his logic, in due subordination to the single design of persuading and convincing his audience. The natural graces of his person completed the orator. Lord Brougham has finely pourtrayed 'that noble figure, every look of whose countenance is expressive, every motion of whose form graceful; an eye that sparkles and pierces, and almost assures victory, while it "speaks audience ere the tongue."' Had his triumphs been as signal in the senate, he would have been the first orator of his age. In that arena there were men greater than himself: but he was admitted to an eminent place amongst them. He fought for many

*Lord Erskine.*

years, side by side, with Mr. Fox; and his rare gifts were ever exerted in the cause of freedom.

<small>Other great orators.</small> To complete the glittering assemblage of orators who adorned the age of Chatham and of Pitt, many remarkable figures yet stand in the foreground. We are struck with the happy wit and resources of Lord North,—the finished precision of Wedderburn,—the rude force of Lord Thurlow,—the bold readiness of Dundas,—the refinement and dignity of Lord Mansfield,—the constitutional wisdom of Lord Camden,—the logical subtlety of Dunning,—the severe reason of Sir William Grant,—the impassioned gentleness of Wilberforce,—and the statesmanlike vigour of Lord Grenville.

<small>Mr. Grattan.</small> The succession of orators has still been maintained. Some of Mr. Pitt's contemporaries continued to flourish many years after he had passed from the scene of his glory; and others were but commencing their career, when his own was drawing to its close. He lived to hear the eloquence of Mr. Grattan, which had long been the pride of his own country. It was rich in imagination, in vehemence, in metaphor, and pointed epigram. Though a stranger to the British Parliament, his genius and patriotism at once commanded a position, scarcely less distinguished than that which he had won in the Parliament of Ireland. Englishmen, familiar with the eloquence of their own countrymen, hailed his accession to their ranks, as one of the most auspicious results of the Union.

<small>Mr. Canning.</small> Mr. Canning's brilliant talents, which had been matured under Mr. Pitt, shone forth in full splendour, after the death of that states-

man. In wit and sarcasm, in elegant scholarship, in lively fancy, and in the graces of a finished composition, he was without a rival. His imagery,—if less original than that of Chatham, Burke, and Erskine,—was wrought up with consummate skill, and expressed in language of extraordinary beauty. For more than twenty years, he was the most successful and accomplished debater in the House of Commons,—delighting his friends with his dazzling wit,—and confounding his opponents with inexhaustible repartee.

Earl Grey had also risen to distinction in the days of Mr. Pitt: but the memorable achievements of his riper age, associate him with a later generation. In dignity and high purpose,—in breadth of principle,—in earnest gravity of argument and exposition, he was the very model of a statesman. His oratory bespoke his inflexible virtues, and consistency. While his proud bearing would have pronounced him the leader of an aristocracy, and the mouthpiece of his order,—he devoted a long life to the service of the people. *Earl Grey.*

Lord Eldon exercised so important an influence upon political affairs, that he cannot be omitted from this group of orators, though his claims to oratory alone, would not have entitled him to a place amongst them. From the time when he had been Mr. Pitt's Solicitor-General, until he left the woolsack,—a period of nearly forty years,—his high offices gave authority to his parliamentary efforts. For twenty years he led captive the judgment of the House of Lords: but assuredly neither by eloquence, nor argument in debate. Tears and *Lord Eldon.*

appeals to his conscience were his most moving eloquence,—a dread of innovation his standing argument. Even upon legal questions, the legislature obtained little light from his discourses. The main service which posterity can derive from his speeches, is to note how recently prejudice and errors were maintained in high places, and how trivial the reasons urged in their defence.

Lord Plunket, like his great countryman, Mr. Grattan, had gained a high reputation for eloquence in the Parliament of Ireland, which he not only sustained, but advanced in the British House of Commons. He had risen to eminence at the bar of Ireland, where his style of speaking is said to have resembled that of Erskine. In debate,—if displaying less originality and genius than Mr. Grattan, and less brilliancy than Mr. Canning,—he was as powerful in sustained argument, as felicitous in illustration, and as forcible and pointed in language, as any orator of his time.

<small>Lord Plunket.</small>

Sir Robert Peel was a striking counterpart of Mr. Pitt. At first his extraordinary abilities in debate had been outshone by the dazzling lustre of Mr. Canning, and subdued by the fiery vehemence of Mr. Brougham: but his great powers, always improving and expanding, could not fail to be acknowledged. His oratory, like that of Mr. Pitt, was the perfection of debate. He rarely aspired to eloquence: but in effective declamation,—in close argument,—in rapid appreciation of the points to be assailed or defended,—in dexterity,—in tact,—and in official and Parliamentary know-

<small>Sir Robert Peel.</small>

ledge, he excelled every debater of his time. Even when his talents were exercised in maintaining the political errors of his age and party, it is impossible not to admire the consummate skill with which he defended his untenable positions, against assailants who had truth on their side. Arguments which provoke a smile, when we read them in the words of Lord Eldon, surprise us with their force and semblance of truth, when urged by Sir Robert Peel.

The oratory of a man so great as the Duke of Wellington, was the least of all of his claims to renown. First in war, in diplomacy, and in the councils of his sovereign,—his speeches in Parliament were but the natural expression of his experience, opinions, and purposes. His mind being clear,—his views practical and sagacious,—and his objects singularly direct,—his speaking was plain, and to the point. Without fluency or art, and without skill in argument, he spoke out what his strong sense and judgment prompted. He addressed an audience, whom there was no need to convince. They hung upon his words, and waited upon his opinions; and followed as he led. The reasons of such a man could not fail to be weighty: but they were reasons which had determined his own course, and might justify it to others, rather than arguments to prove it right, or to combat opponents. The Duke of Wellington.

The House of Commons was not the field for the best examples of Mr. O'Connell's oratory. He stood there at a disadvantage,—with a course to uphold which all but a small band of fol- Mr. O'Connell.

lowers condemned as false and unpatriotic,—and with strong feelings against him, which his own conduct had provoked; yet even there, the massive powers of the man were not unfrequently displayed. A perfect master of every form of argument,—potent in ridicule, sarcasm, and invective,—rich in imagination and humour,—bold and impassioned, or gentle, persuasive and pathetic,—he combined all the powers of a consummate orator. His language was simple and forcible, as became his thoughts:[1] his voice extraordinary for compass and flexibility. But his great powers were disfigured by coarseness, by violence, by cunning, and audacious license. At the bar, and on the platform, he exhibited the greatest, but the most opposite endowments. When he had thrown open the doors of the legislature to himself and his Roman Catholic brethren, the great work of his life was done; yet he wanted nothing but the moral influence of a good cause, and honest patriotism, to have taken one of the highest places in the senate.

His countryman, Mr. Sheil, displayed powers singularly unlike those of his great master. He was an orator of extraordinary brilliancy,—imaginative, witty, and epigrammatic. Many parts of his speeches were exquisite compositions,—clothing his fancy in the artistic language of the poet. Such passages may be compared with many similar examples in the speeches of Mr. Canning. He was equally happy in antithesis and epigram. He ex-

---

[1] It was happily said of him by Mr. Sheil, 'He brings forth a brood of lusty thoughts, without a rag to cover them.'

celled, indeed, in the art and graces of oratorical composition. But his thoughts were wanting in depth and reality: his manner was extravagant in its vehemence: his action melodramatic; and his voice, always shrill, was raised in his impassioned efforts, to a harsh and discordant shriek.

This second group of contemporary orators would be incomplete, without some other striking characters who played their part amongst them. We would point to the classical elegance of Lord Wellesley,—the readiness and dexterity of Perceval,—the high bearing and courage of Lord Castlereagh,—the practical vigour of Tierney,—the manly force and earnestness of Whitbread, —the severe virtues and high intellect of Romilly, —the learned philosophy of Francis Horner,—the didactic fulness of Mackintosh,—the fruitful science of Huskisson,—the lucid argument of Follett, and the brilliant declamation of Macaulay. Other contemporary orators.

All these have passed away: but there are orators still living, who have contended in the same debates, and have won an equal fame. Their portraiture will adorn future histories: but who is there that will not at once fill up this picture of the past, with the transparent clearness and masterly force of Lord Lyndhurst, and the matchless powers and accomplishments of Lord Brougham. Living orators.

Progressive excellence in so divine an art as oratory, is no more to be achieved than in poetry or painting,—in sculpture or architecture. Genius is of all ages. But if orators of our own time have been unable to excel Improved knowledge and taste in debate.

their great models, a candid criticism will scarcely assign them an inferior place. Their style has changed,—as the conditions under which they speak are altered. They address themselves more to the reason, and less to the imagination, the feelings and the passions of their audience, than the orators of a former age. They confront, not only the members of their own body, but the whole people,—who are rather to be convinced by argument, than persuaded by the fascination of the orator. In their language, there is less of study and artistic finish, than in the oratory of an earlier period. Their perorations are not composed, after frequent recitals of Demosthenes:[1] but give direct and forcible expression to their own opinions and sentiments. Their speaking is suited to the subjects of debate,—to the stir and pressure of public affairs,—and to the taste and temper of their audience. The first principles of government are no longer in dispute: the liberties of the people are safe: the oppression of the law is unknown. Accordingly, the councils of the state encourage elevated reason, rather than impassioned oratory. Every age has its own type of excellence; and if the Nestors of our own time insist upon the degeneracy of living orators, perhaps a more cultivated taste may now condemn as rant, some passages from the speeches of Burke and Chat-

---

[1] 'I composed the peroration of my speech for the Queen, in the Lords, after reading and repeating Demosthenes for three or four weeks, and I composed it twenty times over at least, and it certainly succeeded in a very extraordinary degree, and far above any merits of its own.'—Lord Brougham to Zachary Macaulay, as advice to his celebrated son, March 10th, 1823.

ham, which their contemporaries accepted as eloquence.

But whatever may be the claims of different generations to the highest examples of oratory, the men of our own age have advanced in political knowledge, and statesmanship; and their deliberations have produced results more beneficial to the people. They have also improved in temper and moderation. In the earlier years of George III., party spirit and personal animosities,—not yet restrained by the courtesies of private society, or refined by good taste,—too often gave rise to scenes discreditable to the British senate. The debates were as coarse and scurrilous as the press.

In these excesses, Lord Chatham was both sinned against, and sinning. In the debate upon the indemnity Bill in 1766, the Duke of Richmond 'hoped the nobility would not be browbeaten by an insolent minister'[1]—a speech which Horace Walpole alleges to have driven the Earl from the House of Lords, during the remainder of his unfortunate administration.[2] Some years later, we find Lord Chatham himself using language repugnant to order, and decency of debate. On the 1st February, 1775, he thus addressed the ministers : ' Who can wonder that you should put a negative upon any measure which must annihilate your power, deprive you of your emoluments, and at once reduce you to that state of insignificance, for which God and nature designed you.'[3] A few days later,

<small>Coarse personalities of former times.</small>

---

[1] Dec. 10th, 1766.     [2] Walpole's Mem., ii. 410, 411.
[3] Parl. Hist., xviii. 211.

the House of Lords became the scene of personalities still more disorderly. Lord Shelburne having insinuated that Lord Mansfield had been concerned in drawing up the bills of the previous session relating to America, Lord Mansfield rising in a passion, 'charged the last noble Lord with uttering the most gross falsehoods,' and said that 'the charge was as unjust, as it was maliciously and indecently urged.' In the same debate Lord Lyttelton imputed to Lord Camden 'professional subtlety and low cunning.'[1] Again on the 5th December, 1777, we find Lord Chatham accusing Earl Gower of 'petulance and malignant misrepresentation.'[2]

No man so often outraged propriety and good taste as Edmund Burke. His excessive love of imagery and illustration, often displayed itself in the grossest forms. Who is not familiar with his coarse portrait of Lord North, 'extending his right leg a full yard before his left, rolling his flaming eyes, and moving his ponderous frame'? or with the offensive indecency with which he likened Lord North's Ministry to a party of courtesans?[3] Of Lord Shelburne he ventured to say, 'if he was not a Cataline or Borgia in morals, it must not be ascribed to anything but his understanding.'[4]

We find Colonel Barré denouncing the conduct of Lord North as 'most indecent and scandalous;' and Lord North complaining of this language as 'extremely uncivil, brutal, and insolent,' until he was

---

[1] Feb. 7th, 1775; Parl. Hist., xviii. 276, 282.
[2] Parl. Hist., xix. 507.
[3] Feb. 5th, 1770; Cavendish Deb., i. 441.
[4] Lord J. Russell's Life of Fox, i. 326.

called to order, and obliged to apologise.¹ We find Mr. Fox threatening that Lord North's ministry should expiate their crimes upon the scaffold, and insinuating that they were in the pay of France.² Nay, transgressing the bounds of political discussion, and assailing private character, he went so far as to declare that he should consider it unsafe to be alone with Lord North, in a room;³ and would not believe his word.⁴ Even of the king, he spoke with indecorous violence.⁵

There have since been altercations of equal bitterness. The deepest wounds which sarcasm and invective could inflict, have been unsparingly dealt to political opponents. Combatants 'have sharpened their tongues like a serpent; adder's poison is under their lips.' But good taste and a stricter order in debate, have restrained the grosser outrages to decency. The weapons of debate have been as keen and trenchant as ever: but they have been wielded according to the laws of a more civilised warfare. The first years of the Reformed Parliament threatened the revival of scenes as violent and disorderly as any in the last century:⁶ but as the host of new members became

*Rarer outrages of decorum in recent times.*

---

¹ Feb. 22nd, 1852; Parl. Hist., xxii. 1050. Wraxall Mem., ii. 134.
² Nov. 27th, 1781.
³ Lord Brougham's Life of Lord North; Works, iii. 56.
⁴ 20th March, 1782; Parl. Hist., xxii. 1216.
⁵ Wraxall's Mem., ii. 255–258, 517.
⁶ Mr. Sheil and Lord Althorp, 5th Feb., 1834.—Hans. Deb., 3rd Ser., xxi. 146. Mr. Rigby Wason and Lord Sandon, 12th March, 1834.—*Ibid.*, xxii. 116. Mr. Romayne and Mr. O'Connell, 6th May, 1834. *Ibid.*, xxiii. 614. Mr. Hume and Mr. Charlton, 3rd June, 1835.—*Ibid.*, xxvii. 485, 22nd July, 1835.—*Ibid.*, 879.

disciplined by experience, and the fierce passions of that period subsided, the accustomed decorum of the House of Commons was restored.

Indeed, as the Commons have advanced in power and freedom, they have shown greater self-restraint, and a more ready obedience to the authority of the Speaker. They have always been more orderly in their proceedings than the Lords; and the contrast which the scenes of the first twenty years of George III. present to those of later times, can scarcely fail to strike an attentive student of Parliamentary history.

*Increased authority of the Chair.*

What would now be thought of such scenes as those enacted in the time of Sir John Cust, Sir Fletcher Norton, and Mr. Cornwall,—of rebukes and interruptions,[1]—of unseemly altercations with the Chair,—of the words of the Speaker himself being taken down,—and of a motion that they were disorderly and dangerous to the freedom of debate?[2]

In concluding this sketch of Parliamentary oratory, a few words may be added concerning the general standard of debate in the House of Commons. If that standard be measured by the

*General standard of debate.*

---

[1] Scenes between Mr. Rigby and the Speaker, Sir John Cust, in 1762. *Cavendish Deb.*, i. 342. And between Sir J. Cavendish and the same Speaker, March 9th, 1769.—*Ibid.*, 567. Mr. Burke and the same, April 15th, 1769.—*Ibid.*, 878. Scenes with Sir Fletcher Norton, Dec. 14th, 1770.—*Ibid.*, ii. 168.—March 12th and 27th, 1771.—*Ibid.*, ii. 390, 476. General Tarleton and Mr. Speaker Addington, 16th Nov., 1795.—Lord Colchester's Diary, i. 7. Even so late as March 16th, 1808, there was an altercation between the Chair and Mr. Tierney, which ended in a resolution affirming the impartiality of Mr. Speaker Abbot.—Lord Colchester's Diary, ii. 142.

[2] Feb. 16th, 1770; Parl. Hist., xvi. 807.

excellence of the best speakers at different periods, we have no cause to be ashamed of the age in which our living orators and statesmen have flourished. But judged by another test, this age has been exposed to disparaging criticisms. When few save the ablest men contended in debate, and the rank and file were content to cheer and vote, a certain elevation of thought and language was, perhaps, more generally sustained. But, of late years, independent members,—active, informed, and business-like, representing large interests,—more responsible to constituents, and less devoted to party chiefs,—living in the public eye, and ambitious of distinction,—have eagerly pressed forward, and claimed a hearing. Excellence in debate has suffered from the multiplied demands of public affairs. Yet in speeches without pretensions to oratory, are found strong common sense, practical knowledge, and an honesty of purpose that was wanting in the silent legions of former times. The debates mark the activity and earnest spirit of a representative assembly. At all times there have been some speakers of a lower grade,—without instruction, taste, or elevation. Formerly their common-place effusions were not reported: now they are freely read, and scornfully criticised. They are put to shame by the writers of the daily press, who discuss the same subjects with superior knowledge and ability. Falling below the educated mind of the country, they bring discredit upon the House of Commons, while they impair its legislative efficiency. But worse evils than these have been overcome; and we may hope to see this abuse of free discussion eventually corrected, by a less tolerant endurance on the part of the House, and by public reprobation and contempt.

## CHAPTER VIII.

INFLUENCE OF PARTY ON PARLIAMENTARY GOVERNMENT:—PRINCIPLES AND ORIGIN OF ENGLISH PARTIES:—WHIGS AND TORIES:—SKETCH OF PARTIES FROM THE ACCESSION OF GEORGE III. UNTIL THE CLOSE OF THE AMERICAN WAR:—THE COALITION:—TORY PARTY UNDER MR. PITT:—EFFECT OF FRENCH REVOLUTION UPON PARTIES:—STATE OF PARTIES FROM 1801 TO 1830; AND THENCE TO 1860:—CHANGES IN THE CHARACTER AND ORGANISATION OF PARTIES.

WE have surveyed the great political institutions by which the state is governed; and examined the influence which each has exercised, and their combined operation. That a form of government so composite, and combining so many conflicting forces, has generally been maintained in harmonious action, is mainly due to the organisation of parties,—an agency hardly recognised by the constitution, yet inseparable from parliamentary government, and exercising the greatest influence, for good or evil, upon the political destinies of the country. Party has guided and controlled, and often dominated over the more ostensible authorities of the state: it has supported the crown and aristocracy against the people: it has trampled upon public liberty: it has dethroned and coerced kings, overthrown ministers and Parliaments, humbled the nobles, and established popular rights. But it has protected the fabric of the government from shocks which threatened its very foundations.

*Influence of party in Parliamentary government.*

Parties have risen and fallen: but institutions have remained unshaken. The annals of party embrace a large portion of the history of England:[1] but passing lightly over its meaner incidents,—the ambition, intrigues, and jealousies of statesmen,—the greed of place-hunters, and the sinister aims of faction,—we will endeavour to trace its influence in advancing or retarding the progress of constitutional liberty, and enlightened legislation.

The parties in which Englishmen have associated, at different times, and under various names, have represented cardinal principles of government,[2]—authority on the one side,—popular rights and privileges on the other. The former principle, pressed to extremes, would tend to absolutism,—the latter to a republic: but, controlled within proper limits, they are both necessary for the safe working of a balanced constitution. When parties have lost sight of these principles, in pursuit of objects less worthy, they have degenerated into factions.[3]

*Principles represented by English parties.*

The divisions, conspiracies, and civil wars by which England was convulsed until late in the six-

[1] Mr. Wingrove Cooke, in his spirited 'History of Party,' to which I desire to acknowledge many obligations, related the most instructive incidents of general history.

[2] 'Party is a body of men united, for promoting by their joint endeavours the national interest, upon some particular principle in which they are all agreed.'—*Burke's Present Discontents, Works,* ii. 335.

[3] 'National interests' . . . 'would be sometimes sacrificed, and always made subordinate to, personal interests; and that, I think, is the true characteristic of faction.'—*Bolingbroke's Dissert. upon Parties, Works,* iii. 15.

'Of such a nature are connections in politics; essentially necessary to the full performance of our public duty: accidentally liable to degenerate into faction.'—*Ibid., Works,* ii. 332.

teenth century, must not be confounded with the development of parties. Rarely founded on distinctive principles, their ends were sought by arms, or deeds of violence and treason. Neither can we trace the origin of parties in those earlier contentions,—sometimes of nobles, sometimes of Commons, with the crown, to which we owe many of our most valued liberties. They marked, indeed, the spirit of freedom which animated our forefathers: but they subsided with the occasions which had incited them. Classes asserted their rights: but parliamentary parties, habitually maintaining opposite principles, were unknown.

Origin of parties.

The germs of party, in the councils and Parliament of England,—generated by the Reformation,—were first discernible in the reign of Elizabeth. The bold spirit of the Puritans then spoke out in the House of Commons, in support of the rights of Parliament, and against her prerogatives, in matters of Church and State.[1] In their efforts to obtain toleration for their brethren, and modifications of the new ritual, they were countenanced by Cecil and Walsingham, and other eminent councillors of the queen. In matters of state, they could expect no sympathy from the court; but perceiving their power, as an organised party, they spared no efforts to gain admission into the House of Commons, until, joined by other opponents of prerogative, they at length acquired a majority.

The Puritans.

[1] D'Ewes' Journ., 156–175. Hume's Hist., iii. 497, 511. This author goes too far, when he says, 'It was to this sect, whose principles appear so frivolous, and habits so ridiculous, that the English owe the whole freedom of their constitution.'—*Ibid.*, 520.

In 1601, they showed their strength by a successful resistance to the queen's prerogative of granting monopolies in trade, by royal patent. Under her weak successor, James I., ill-judged assertions of prerogative were met with bolder remonstrances. His doctrine of the divine right of kings, and the excesses of the High Church party, widened the breach between the crown and the great body of the Puritans,[1] and strengthened the popular party. Foremost among them were Sandys, Coke, Eliot, Selden, and Pym, who may be regarded as the first leaders of a regular parliamentary opposition.

*Conflict of parties under the Stuarts.*

The arbitrary measures of Charles I., the bold schemes of Strafford, and the intolerant bigotry of Laud, precipitated a collision between the opposite principles of government; and divided the whole country into Cavaliers and Roundheads. On one side, the king's prerogative had been pushed to extremes: on the other, the defence of popular rights was inflamed by ambition and fanaticism, into a fierce republican sentiment. The principles and the parties then arrayed against one another long retained their vitality, under other names and different circumstances.

Charles II., profiting little by the experience of the last reign,—nay, rather encouraged by the excesses of the Commonwealth to cherish kingly

---

[1] 'The principles by which King James and King Charles I. governed, and the excesses of hierarchical and monarchical power exercised in consequence of them, gave great advantage to the opposite opinions, and entirely occasioned the miseries which followed.'—*Bolingbroke, Works,* iii. 50.

power,[1]—pursued the reckless course of the Stuarts: his measures being supported by the Court party, and opposed by the Country party.

The contest of these parties upon the Exclusion Bill, in 1680, at length gave rise to the well-known names of Whig and Tory. Originally intended as terms of reproach and ridicule, they afterwards became the distinctive titles of two great parties, representing principles essential to the freedom and safety of the State.[2] The Whigs espoused the principles of liberty,—the independent rights of Parliament and the people,—and the lawfulness of resistance to a king who violated the laws. The Tories maintained the divine and indefeasible right of the king, the supremacy of prerogative, and the duty of passive obedience on the part of the subject.[3] Both parties alike upheld the monarchy: but the Whigs contended for the limitation of its authority within the bounds of law: the principles of the Tories favoured absolutism in Church and State.[4]

<sub>Whigs and Tories.</sub>

[1] Bolingbroke's Dissertation on Parties, Works, iii. 52.

[2] Nothing can be more silly or pointless than these names. The supporters of the Duke of York, as Catholics, were assumed to be Irishmen, and were called by the Country party 'Tories,'—a term hitherto applied to a set of lawless bog-trotters, resembling the modern 'Whiteboys.' The Country party were called 'Whigs,' according to some, 'a vernacular in Scotland, for corrupt and sour whey;' and, according to others, from the Scottish Covenanters of the South-western counties of Scotland, who had received the appellation of Whiggamores, or Whigs, when they made an inroad upon Edinburgh in 1648, under the Marquess of Argyll.—Roger North's Examen, 320-324; Burnet's Own Times, i. 78; Cooke's Hist. of Party, i. 137; Macaulay's Hist., i. 256.

[3] Bolingbroke's Dissertation on Parties, Works, iii. 39; Roger North's Examen, 325-342; Macaulay's Hist., i. 473; ii. 391-400.

[4] Brady's Hist. of the Crown, 1684, Tracts, 339; Preface to Hist. of England, &c.; and Declaration of University of Oxford,

The infatuated assaults of James II. upon the religion and liberties of the people united, for a time, the Whigs and Tories in a common cause; and the latter, in opposition to their own principles, concurred in the necessity of expelling a dangerous tyrant from his throne.[1] The Revolution was the triumph and conclusive recognition of Whig principles, as the foundation of a limited monarchy. Yet the principles of the two parties, modified by the conditions of this constitutional settlement, were still distinct and antagonistic. The Whigs continued to promote every necessary limitation of the royal authority, and to favour religious toleration: the Tories generally leaned to prerogative, to High-church doctrines, and hostility to Dissenters; while the extreme members of that party betrayed their original principles, as Nonjurors and Jacobites.[2]

*Parties after the Revolution of 1688.*

The two parties contended and intrigued, with varying success, during the reigns of William and of Anne; when the final victory of the Whigs secured constitutional government. But the stubborn principles, disappointed ambition, and factious violence of Tories disturbed the reigns of the two first kings of the House of Hanover, with disaf-

---

July 21st, 1683; Cooke's Hist. of Party, i. 346; Macaulay's Hist., i. 270. Filmer, representing the extreme views of this party, says: 'A man is bound to obey the king's command against law; nay, in some cases, against divine laws.'—*Patriarchia*, 100.

[1] Bolingbroke's Works, iii. 124, 126; Macaulay's Hist., ii. 398, et seq.

[2] See *infra*, Chap. XII.; Swift's Four Last Years of Queen Anne, 45; Bolingbroke's Works, iii. 132; Macaulay's Hist., iii. 7–11, 71, 440–464, 489, 586, &c.; Macknight's Life of Bolingbroke p. 400.

fection, treason, and civil wars.[1] The final overthrow of the Pretender, in 1745, being fatal to the Jacobite cause, the Tories became a national party; and, still preserving their principles, at length transferred their hearty loyalty to the reigning king. Meanwhile the principles of both parties had naturally been modified by the political circumstances of the times. The Whigs, installed as rulers, had been engaged for more than forty years after the death of Anne, in consolidating the power and influence of the crown, in connection with parliamentary government. The Tories, in opposition, had been constrained to renounce the untenable doctrines of their party, and to recognise the lawful rights of Parliament and the people.[2] Nay, at times they had adroitly paraded the popular principles of the Whig school against ministers, who in the practical administration of the government, and in furtherance of the interests of their party, had been too prone to forget them. Bolingbroke, Wyndham, and Shippen had maintained the constitutional virtues of short parliaments, and denounced the dangers of parliamentary corruption, the undue influence of the crown, and a standing army.[3]

[1] Parl. Hist., xiii. 568; Coxe's Life of Walpole, i. 66, 199, &c.
[2] 'Toryism,' says Mr. Wingrove Cooke, 'was formed for government: it is only a creed for rulers.'—*Hist. of Party*, ii. 49.
[3] Bolingbroke's Dissertation on Parties, Works, iii. 133; The Craftsman, No. 40, &c.; Parl. Hist., vii. 311; Ib., ix. 426, *et seq.*; Ib., x. 375, 479; Coxe's Life of Walpole, ii. 62; Tindal's Hist., iii. 722, iv. 423. 'Your right Jacobite,' said Sir R. Walpole in 1738, 'disguises his true sentiments: he roars for revolution principles: he pretends to be a great friend to liberty, and a great admirer of our ancient constitution.'—*Parl. Hist.*, x. 401.

Through all vicissitudes of time and circumstance, however, the distinctive principles of the two great parties were generally maintained;[1] and the social classes from which they derived their strength were equally defined. The loyal adherents of Charles I. were drawn from the territorial nobles, the country gentlemen, the higher yeomanry, the Church, and the universities: the Parliament was mainly supported by the smaller freeholders, the inhabitants of towns, and Protestant nonconformists. Seventy years afterwards, on the accession of George I., the same classes were distinguished by similar principles. The feudal relations of the proprietors of the soil to their tenantry and the rural population,—their close connection with the Church,—and their traditional loyalty, assured their adherence to the politics of their forefathers. The rustics, who looked to the squire for bounty, and to the rector for the consolations of religion and charity, were not a class to inspire sentiments favourable to the sovereignty of the people. Poor, ignorant, dependent, and submissive, they seemed born to be ruled as children, rather than to share in the government of their country.

*Classes from which parties mainly drawn.*

On the other hand, the commercial and manufacturing towns,—the scenes of active enterprise

---

[1] Mr. Wingrove Cooke says, that after Bolingbroke renounced the Jacobite cause on the accession of Geo. II., 'henceforward we never find the Tory party struggling to extend the prerogative of the Crown.' 'The principle of that party has been rather aristocratical than monarchical,'—a remark which is, probably, as applicable to one party as to the other until the period of the Reform Bill.—*Hist. of Party*, ii. 105.

and skilled handicraft,—comprised classes who naturally leaned to self-government, and embraced Whig principles. Merchants and manufacturers, themselves springing from the people, had no feelings or interests in common with the county families, from whose society they were repelled with haughty exclusiveness: they were familiarised, by municipal administration, with the practice of self-government: their pursuits were congenial to political activity and progress. Even their traditions were associated with the cause of the Parliament and the people against the crown. The stout burghers among whom they dwelt were spirited and intelligent. Congregated within the narrow bounds of a city, they canvassed, and argued, and formed a public opinion concerning affairs of state, naturally inclining to popular rights. The stern nonconformist spirit,—as yet scarcely known in country villages,—animated large bodies of townsmen with an hereditary distrust of authority in church and state.

It was to such communities as these that the Whig ministers of the House of Hanover, and the great territorial families of that party, looked for popular support. As landowners, they commanded the representation of several counties and nomination boroughs. But the greater number of the smaller boroughs being under the influence of Tory squires, the Whigs would have been unequal to their opponents in parliamentary following, had not new allies been found in the moneyed classes, who were rapidly increasing in numbers and importance. The superior wealth and influence of these men enabled them to wrest borough after borough from the local squires, until they secured a parliamentary majority for the Whigs. It was a natural and appropriate circumstance, that the preservation and growth of English liberties should have been associated with the progress of the country in commercial wealth and greatness. The social improvement of the people won for them privileges which it fitted them to enjoy.

Meanwhile, long-continued possession of power by the Whigs, and the growing discredit of the Jacobite party, attracted to the side of the government many Tory patrons of boroughs. These causes, aided by the corrupt parliamentary organisation of that period,[1] maintained the ascendency of the Whig party until the fall of Sir Robert Walpole; and of the same party, with other alliances, until the death of George II.[2] Their rule, if signalised by few measures which serve as landmarks in the history of our liberties, was yet distinguished by its moderation, and by respect for the theory of constitutional government, which was fairly worked out, as far as it was compatible with the political abuses and corruptions of their times. The Tories were a dispirited and helpless minority; and in 1751, their hopes of better times were extinguished by the death of the Prince of Wales and Bolingbroke.[3] Some were gained over by the government; and others cherished,

*Ruin of the Tories prior to the accession of George III.*

---

[1] *Supra*, Vol. I. 333 *et seq.*
[2] Dodington's Diary, 386; Coxe's Pelham Administration, ii. 166.
[3] Coxe's Life of Walpole, 379.

in sullen silence, the principles and sympathies of their ruined party. But the new reign rapidly revived their hopes. The young king, brought up at Leicester House, had ac- quired, by instruction and early association, the principles in favour at that little court.[1] His political faith, his ambition, his domestic affections, and his friendships alike attracted him towards the Tories; and his friends were, accordingly, transferred from Leicester House to St. James's. He at once became the regenerator and leader of the Tory party. If their cause had suffered discouragement and disgrace in the two last reigns, all the circumstances of this period were favourable to the revival of their principles, and the triumph of their traditional policy. To rally round the throne had ever been their watchword: respect for prerogative and loyal devotion to the person of the sovereign had been their characteristic pretensions. That the source of all power was from above, was their distinctive creed. And now a young king had arisen among them who claimed for himself their faith and loyalty. The royal authority was once more to be supreme in the government of the state: the statesmen and parties who withstood it, were to be cast down and trampled upon. Who so fit as men of Tory principles and traditions to aid him in the recovery of regal power? The party which had clung with most fidelity to the Stuarts, and had defended government by prerogative, were the

*Their revival in the new reign.*

[1] *Supra*, Vol. I. 10; Lord Waldegrave's Mem., 63; Lord Hervey's Mem., ii. 443, &c.; Coxe's Life of Walpole, 703-707.

natural instruments for increasing,—under another dynasty and different political conditions,—the influence of the crown.

We have seen how early in his reign the king began to put aside his Whig councillors; and with what precipitation he installed his Tory favourite, Lord Bute, as first minister.[1] With singular steadiness of purpose, address, and artful management, he seized upon every occasion for disuniting and weakening the Whigs, and extending the influence of the Tories. It was his policy to bring men of every political connection into his service; but he specially favoured Tories, and Whigs alienated from their own party. All the early administrations of his reign were coalitions. The Whigs could not be suddenly supplanted: but they were gradually displaced by men more willing to do the bidding of the court. Restored for a short time to power, under Lord Rockingham, they were easily overthrown, and replaced by the strangely composite ministry of the Duke of Grafton, consisting, according to Burke, 'of patriots and courtiers, king's friends and Republicans, Whigs and Tories, treacherous friends and open enemies.'[2] On the retirement of Lord Chatham, the Tories acquired a preponderance in the cabinet; and when Lord Camden withdrew, it became wholly Tory. The king could now dispense with the services of Whig statesmen; and accordingly Lord North was placed at the head of the first ministry of this

*The king's efforts to overthrow the Whigs.*

[1] *Supra*, Vol. I. pp. 18-22.
[2] Speech on American Taxation, Works, ii. 420.

reign, which was originally composed of Tories. But he seized the first opportunity of strengthening it, by a coalition with the Grenvilles and Bedfords.[1]

Meanwhile, it was the fashion of the court to decry all party connections as factions. Personal capacity was held up as the sole qualification for the service of the crown. *'Men, not measures.'* This doctrine was well calculated to increase the king's own power, and to disarm parliamentary opposition. It served also to justify the gradual exclusion of the Whigs from the highest offices, and the substitution of Tories. When the Whigs had been entirely supplanted, and the Tories safely established in their place, the doctrine was heard of no more, except to discredit an opposition.

The rapid reconstruction of the Tory party was facilitated by the organisation of the king's friends.[2] Most of these men originally belonged to that party; and none could be enrolled amongst them, without speedily becoming converts to its principles.[3] Country gentlemen who had been out of favour nearly fifty years, found themselves courted and caressed; and faithful to their principles, could now renew their activity in public life, encouraged by the smiles of their sovereign. This party was also recruited from another class of auxiliaries. Hitherto the new men, unconnected with county families, had generally enrolled themselves on the opposite side. Even where their

*The king's friends allied to the Tories.*

---

[1] Lord Mahon's Hist., v. 442.
[2] *Supra,* Vol. I. p. 12, 38.
[3] Walp. Mem., i. 15; Butler's Rem., i. 74, &c.

preference to Whig principles was not decided, they had been led to that connection by jealousy of the landowners, by the attractions of a winning cause, and government favours: but now they were won over, by similar allurements, to the court. And, henceforth, much of the electoral corruption which had once contributed to the parliamentary majority of the Whigs, was turned against them by their Tory rivals and the king's friends.

Meanwhile, the Whigs, gradually excluded from power, were driven back upon those popular principles which had been too long in abeyance.

*The Whigs in opposition.*

They were still, indeed, an aristocratic body: but no longer able to rely upon family connections, they offered themselves as leaders of the people. At the same time, the revival and activity of Tory principles, in the government of the state, re-animated the spirit of freedom, represented by their party. They resisted the dangerous influence of the crown, and the scarcely less dangerous extension of the privileges of Parliament: they opposed the taxation of America: they favoured the publication of debates, and the liberty of the press: they exposed and denounced parliamentary corruption. Their strength and character as a party were impaired by the jealousies and dissensions of rival families. Pelhams, Rockinghams, Bedfords, Grenvilles, and the followers of Lord Chatham too often lost sight of the popular cause, in their contentions for mastery. But in the main, the least favourable critic of the Whigs will scarcely venture to deny their services in the cause of liberty, from the commencement of this reign, until the death of Lord Rockingham. Such was the vigour of their opposition, and such the genius and eloquence of their leaders,—Lord Chatham, Mr. Fox, Lord Camden, Mr. Burke, and Mr. Sheridan,—that they exercised a strong influence upon public opinion, and checked and moderated the arbitrary spirit of the court party. The haughty pretensions to irresponsibility which marked the first ministers of this reign, became much lowered in the latter years of Lord North's administration. Free discussion prevailed over doctrines opposed to liberty. Nor was the publication of debates already without its good results upon the conduct of both parties.

But while the Tories were renouncing doctrines repugnant to public liberty, they were initiating a new principle not hitherto characteristic of their party. *Tories opposed to change.* Respect for authority, nay, even absolute power, is compatible with enlightened progress in legislation. Great emperors, from Justinian to Napoleon, have gloried in the fame of lawgivers. But the Tory party were learning to view the amendment of our laws with distrust and aversion. In their eyes change was a political evil. Many causes concurred to favour a doctrine wholly unworthy of any school of statesmen. Tory sympathies were with the past. Men who in the last generation would have restored the Stuarts, and annulled the Revolution, had little, in their creed, congenial to enlightened progress. The power which they had recovered, was associated with the influence of the crown, and the existing polity of the state. Changes in the laws urged by opponents, and designed to restrain their own authority, were naturally resisted. Nor must the character of the men who constituted this party be forgotten. Foremost among them was the king himself,—a man of narrow intellect and intractable prejudices,—without philosophy or statesmanship,—and whose science of government was ever to carry out, by force or management, his own strong will. The main body of the party whom he had raised to power and taken into his confidence, consisted of country gentlemen,—types of immobility,—of the clergy, trained by their trust and calling to reverence the past, —and of lawyers, guided by prescription and precedent,—venerating laws which they had studied and expounded, but not aspiring to the higher philosophy of legislation. Such men were content '*stare super antiquas vias*;' and dreaded every change as fraught with danger. In this spirit the king warned the people, in 1780, against 'the hazard of innovation.'[1] In the same spirit the king's friend Mr. Rigby, in opposing Mr. Pitt's first motion for reform, 'treated all innovations as dangerous theoretical experiments.'[2] This doctrine was first preached during the ministry of Lord North. It was never accepted by Mr. Pitt and his more enlightened disciples: but it became an article of faith with the majority of the Tory party.

The American War involved principles which rallied the two parties, and displayed their natural antagonism. It was the duty of the government

[1] *Supra*, Vol. I. 395.   [2] Wraxall's Hist. Mem., iii. 85.

to repress revolt, and to maintain the national honour. Had the Whigs been in power, they would have acknowledged this obligation. But the Tories,—led by the king himself,—were animated by a spirit of resentment against the colonists, which marked the characteristic principles of that party. In their eyes resistance was a crime: no violation of rights could justify or palliate rebellion. Tories of all classes were united in a cause so congenial to their common sentiments. The court, the landed gentry, and the clergy insisted, with one voice, that rebellion must be crushed, at whatever cost of blood and treasure. They were supported by a great majority of the House of Commons, and by the most influential classes in the country. The Whigs, on the other hand, asserted the first principles of their party in maintaining the rights of all British subjects to tax themselves, by their representatives, and to resist oppression and injustice. But in their vain efforts to effect a reconciliation with America, they had a slender following in Parliament; and in the country had little support but that of the working classes,— then wholly without influence,—and of the traders, who generally supported that party, and whose interests were naturally concerned in the restoration of peace.[1]

*Principles tested by the American War.*

---

[1] Lord Camden, writing to Lord Chatham, February, 1775, said: 'I am grieved to observe that the landed interest is almost altogether anti-American, though the common people hold the war in abhorrence, and the merchants and tradesmen, for obvious reasons, are altogether against it.'—*Chatham Corr.*, iv. 401.—' Parties were divided nearly as they had been at the end of the reign of Queen Anne; the Court and the landed gentry, with a majority in the

Such were the sentiments, and such the temper of the ruling party, that the leading Whigs were not without apprehension that, if America should be subdued, English liberty would be endangered.[1]

Having vainly opposed and protested against the measures of the government, in November, 1776, they seceded from Parliament on American questions,—desiring to leave the entire responsibility of coercion with ministers and their majority. It can scarcely be denied that their secession—like earlier examples of the same policy[2] —was a political error, if not a dereliction of duty. It is true that an impotent minority, constantly overborne by power and numbers, may encourage and fortify, instead of restraining, their victorious opponents. Their continued resistance may be denounced as factious, and the smallness of their numbers pointed at as evidence of the weakness of their cause. But secession is flight. The enemy is left in possession of the field. The minority confess themselves vanquished. They even abandon the hope of retrieving their fallen cause, by rallying the people to their side. Nor do they escape imputations more injurious than any which persistence, under every discouragement, could bring upon them.

*Secession of the Whigs in 1776.*

House of Commons, were with the Tories: the trading interest and popular feeling with the Whigs.'—*Lord J. Russell's Life of Fox*, i. 83; Belsham's Hist., vi. 194.

[1] Debates on Amendments to Address, 31st Oct. 1776, &c.; Fox's Mem., i. 143; Lord J. Russell's Life of Fox, i. 136; Lord Rockingham's Corr., ii. 276; Walpole's Mem., iv. 125; Grenville Papers, iv. 573; Burke's Works, ii. 399; Walpole's Journ., ii. 107, 241, 511.

[2] The Tory opposition had seceded in 1722, and again in 1738.— Parl. Hist., x. 1323; Tindal's Hist., iv. 668; Smollett's Hist., ii. 219, 364; Coxe's Walpole, iii. 519; Marchmont Papers, ii. 190.

They may be accused of sullen ill-temper,—of bearing defeat with a bad grace,—and of the sacrifice of public duty to private pique.

The latter charge, indeed, they could proudly disregard, if convinced that a course, conscientiously adopted, was favourable to their principles. Yet it is difficult to justify the renunciation of a public duty, in times of peril, and the absolute surrender of a cause believed to be just. The Whigs escaped none of these charges; and even the dignity of a proud retirement before irresistible force was sacrificed by want of concert and united action. Mr. Fox and others returned after Christmas, to oppose the suspension of the Habeas Corpus Act,[1] while many of his friends continued their secession. Hence his small party was further weakened and divided,[2] and the sole object of secession lost.[3]

The fortunes of the Whig party were now at their lowest point; and, for the present, the Tories were completely in the ascendant.[4] But the disastrous incidents of the *The Whigs and the American war.*

---

[1] This Act applied to persons suspected of high treason in America, or on the high seas.

[2] He mustered no more than forty-three followers on the second reading, and thirty-three on the third reading.

[3] The Duke of Richmond, writing to Lord Rockingham, said:—'The worst, I see, has happened,—that is, the plan that was adopted has not been steadily pursued.'—*Rockingham Corr.*, ii. 308; Parl. Hist., xvi. 1229.

[4] Burke, writing to Fox, 8th Oct. 1777, says:—'The Tories universally think their power and consequence involved in the success of this American business. The clergy are astonishingly warm in it, and what the Tories are when embodied and united with their natural head the Crown, and animated by the clergy, no man knows better than yourself. As to the Whigs, I think them far from extinct. They are, what they always were (except by the able use of opportunities) by far the weakest party in this country. They have

American war, followed by hostilities with France, could not fail to increase the influence of one party, while it discredited and humbled the other. The government was shaken to its centre; and in the summer of 1778, overtures were made to the Whigs, which would have given them the majority in a new cabinet under Lord Weymouth, on the basis of a withdrawal of the troops from America, and a vigorous prosecution of the war with France. Contrary to the advice of Mr. Fox, these overtures were rejected; and the Whigs continued their opposition to the fruitless contest with our revolted colonists.[b] A war at once so costly, and so dishonourable to our arms, disgusted its former supporters; and the Whigs pressed Lord North with extraordinary energy and resolution, until they finally drove him from power. Their position throughout this contest,— the generous principles which they maintained, and the eloquence and courage with which they resisted the united force of the king, the ministers, and a large majority of both Houses of Parliament,—went far to restore their strength and character as a party. But, on the other hand, they too often laid themselves open to the charge of upholding rebels, and encouraging the foreign enemies of their country,— a charge not soon forgotten, and successfully used to their prejudice.[2]

not yet learned the application of their principles to the present state of things; and as to the Dissenters, the main effective part of the Whig strength, they are, to use a favourite expression of our American campaign style, "not all in force."'—*Burke's Works*, ix. 148.

[1] Lord J. Russell's Life of Fox, i. 193; Sir G. C. Lewis's Administrations, 13.

[2] They were accused of adopting the colours of the American army,

In watching the struggles of the two great parties, another incident must not be overlooked. The American contest fanned the latent embers of democracy throughout Europe; and in England a democratic party was formed,[1] which, a few years later, exercised an important influence upon the relations of Whigs and Tories.

*The democratic party.*

The Whigs, restored to power under their firm and honest leader, Lord Rockingham, appeared, once more, in the ascendant. The king, however, had taken care that their power should be illusory, and their position insecure. Lord Rockingham was placed at the head of another coalition ministry, of which one part consisted of Whigs, and the other of the Court party,—Lord Shelburne, Lord Thurlow, Lord Ashburton, and the Duke of Grafton. In such a cabinet, divisions and distrust were unavoidable. The Whig policy, however, prevailed, and does honour to the memory of that short-lived administration.[2]

*The restoration of the Whigs to power.*

The death of Lord Rockingham again overthrew his party. The king selected Lord Shelburne to succeed him; and Mr. Fox, objecting to that minister as the head of the rival party in the Coalition, in whom he had no confidence, and whose good faith towards himself he

*Death of Lord Rockingham, July 1st, 1782.*

---

—'blue and buff,'—as the insignia of their party. It appears, however, that the Americans, in fact, borrowed the Whig colours.— *Wraxall's Mem.*, ii. 229; Rockingham Corr., ii. 276; Lord Stanhope's Miscellanies, 116–122.

[1] Stephen's Life of Horne Tooke, i. 162–175; ii. 28; Cooke's Hist. of Party, iii. 188; Wyvill's Pol. Papers, ii. 463.

[2] *Supra*, Vol. I. 60.

had strong reasons to doubt, refused to serve under him, and retired with most of his friends.[1]

This was a crisis in the history of parties, whose future destinies were deeply affected by two eminent men. Had Mr. Fox arranged his differences with Lord Shelburne, his commanding talents might soon have won for himself and his party a dominant influence in the councils of the state. His retirement left Lord Shelburne master of the situation, and again disunited his own inconsiderable party. Mr. William Pitt, on his entrance into Parliament, had joined the Whigs in their opposition to Lord North.[2] He was of Whig connections and principles, and concurred with that party in all liberal measures. His extraordinary talents and ambition at once marked him, in his early youth, as a leader of men. His sympathies were all with Lord Rockingham: he supported his government;[3] and there can be little doubt that he might have been won as a member of his party. But he was passed over when the Rockingham ministry was formed;[4] and was now secured by Lord Shelburne as his Chancellor of the Exchequer. Henceforth the young statesman, instead of co-operating with Mr. Fox, became his successful rival; and as his fortunes were identified with the king's

*Crisis in the history of parties.*

---

[1] Fox's Mem., i. 304–430; Lord J. Russell's Life of Fox, i. 321–325; Sir G. C. Lewis's Administrations, 31.
[2] Lord Stanhope's Life of Pitt, i. 50, 52.
[3] Lord Stanhope's Life of Pitt, i. 72.
[4] In an article in the Law Magazine, Feb. 1861, attributed to Lord Brougham,—on the Auckland Correspondence,—it is said, 'What mischief might have been spared, both to the party and the country, had not this error been committed!'

friends and the Tories, he was permanently alienated from the Whig connection. Who can tell what two such men, acting in concert, might have accomplished for the good of their country and the popular cause![1] Their altered relations proved a severe discomfiture to the Whigs, and a source of hope and strength to the Tories.

There were now three parties,—Lord Shelburne and the Court,—Lord North and his Tory adherents,—and Mr. Fox and his Whig followers. *The Coalition.* It was plain that the first could not stand alone; and overtures were therefore made, separately, to Lord North and to Mr. Fox, to strengthen the administration. The former was still to be excluded himself, but his friends were to be admitted,—a proposal not very conciliatory to the leader of a party. The latter declined to join the ministry, unless Lord Shelburne resigned in favour of the Duke of Portland,[2]—a suggestion not likely to be agreeable to the premier. These overtures, consequently, failed: but Lord North, fearing a junction between Mr. Fox and Mr. Pitt, and the

---

[1] Wraxall's Mem., iii. 152, 158, 176.—' I am indeed persuaded, that if Fox had been once confirmed in office, and acceptable to the sovereign, he would have steadily repressed all democratic innovations; as, on the other hand, had Pitt passed his whole life on the opposition bench, poor, and excluded from power, I believe he would have endeavoured to throw his weight into the scale of the popular representation. . . . It appeared to me, that Pitt had received from nature a greater mixture of republican spirit than animated his rival: but royal favour and employment softened its asperity.'—*Wraxall's Mem.*, iii. 98.

[2] Wraxall's Mem., iii. 252; Tomline's Life of Pitt, i. 88; Fox's Mem., ii. 12, 21, 30; Lord J. Russell's Life of Fox, i. 346; Court and Cabinets of Geo. III., i. 301; Sir G. C. Lewis's Administrations, 57.

destruction of his own party, was inclined to listen favourably to suggestions for uniting with Mr. Fox, and overpowering the party of Lord Shelburne, to whom both were opposed. The singular coalition of these two statesmen, so long opposed in principles, in connections, and in party strife, was brought about by the arts of Lord Loughborough, Mr. Eden, Mr. Adam, Colonel Fitzpatrick, and Mr. George North.[1]

The immediate occasion of their alliance was a coincidence of opinion, adverse to the preliminaries of peace. The concessions made by Lord Shelburne to the enemy were such as fairly to provoke objections; and a casual agreement between parties, otherwise opposed, was natural and legitimate. To restrain the influence of the crown was another object which Mr. Fox had much at heart; and in this also he found his facile and compliant ally not indisposed to co-operate. The main cause of their previous differences, the American war, was at an end; and both were of too generous a temper to cherish personal animosities with sullen tenacity. What Mr. Fox said finely of himself, could be affirmed with equal truth of his former rival, '*Amicitiæ sempiternæ, inimicitiæ placabiles.*' But the principles of the two parties were irreconcilable; and their sudden union could not be effected without imputations injurious to the credit of both. Nor could it be disguised that personal ambition

<small>Feb. 17th–21st, 1783.</small>

---

[1] Wraxall's Mem., iii. 261; Lord Auckland's Corr., chap. i., ii.; Fox's Mem., ii. 15; Lord J. Russell's Life of Fox, i. 345; Lord Stanhope's Life of Pitt, i. 94, &c.

dictated this bold stroke for power, in which principles were made to yield to interest. It was the alliance of factions, rather than of parties; and on either side it was a grave political error. Viewed with disfavour by the most earnest of both parties, it alienated from the two leaders many of their best followers. Either party could have united with Lord Shelburne, more properly than with one another. The Whigs forfeited the popularity which they had acquired in opposition. Even Wilkes and the democratic party denounced them. Courtiers and mob-orators vied with one another in execrating the 'infamous coalition.' So long as coalitions had served to repress the Whigs, advance the Tories, and increase the personal authority of the king, they had been favoured at court: but the first coalition which threatened the influence of the crown was discovered to be unprincipled and corrupt, and condemned as a political crime.[1]

How the coalition, having triumphed for a time, was trampled under foot by the king and Mr. Pitt, has been already told.[2] It fell amidst groans and hisses; and has since been scourged, with unsparing severity, by writers of all parties. Its failure left it few friends: Lord North's followers were soon lost in the general body of Tories who supported Mr. Pitt; and Mr. Fox's party was again reduced to a powerless minority. But the errors and ruin of its leaders have, perhaps, brought

*Opinions concerning the coalition.*

---

[1] Wraxall gives an entertaining narrative of all the proceedings connected with the coalition.—*Mem.*, iii. 254-277.
[2] Vol. I. 63.

down upon them too harsh a judgment. The confusion and intermixture of parties, which the king himself had favoured, must not be forgotten. Every administration of his reign, but that of Lord North, had been a coalition; and the principles and connections of statesmen had been strangely shifting and changing. Mr. Fox, having commenced his career as a Tory, was now leader of the Whigs: Mr. Pitt, having entered Parliament as a Whig, had become leader of the Tories. The Grenvilles had coalesced with Lord Rockingham. Lord Temple had, at one time, consorted with Wilkes, and braved the king; at another, he was a stout champion of his Majesty's prerogative. Lord Shelburne and Mr. Dunning, having combined with Lord Rockingham to restrain the influence of the crown, had been converted to the policy of the court. Lord Thurlow was the inevitable chancellor of Whigs and Tories alike. Wilkes was tamed, and denied that he had ever been a Wilkite. Such being the unsettled condition of principles and parties, why was the indignation of the country reserved for Mr. Fox and Lord North alone? Courtiers were indignant because the influence of the crown was threatened: the people, scandalised by the suspicious union of two men whose invectives were still resounding in their ears, followed too readily the cry of the court. The king and his advisers gained their end; and the overthrow of the coalition ensured its general condemnation. The consequent ruin of the Whigs secured the undisputed domination of the crown for the next fifty years.[1]

[1] Mr. Fox, writing in 1804, said: 'I know this coalition is always

That the prejudices raised against coalitions were, in a great measure, a pretence, was shown by the composition of Mr. Pitt's own ministry, which was scarcely less a coalition than that which he had overthrown and covered with opprobrium, for their supposed sacrifice of principle and consistency. He had himself contended against Lord North, yet his government was composed of friends and associates of that minister, and of Whigs who had recently agreed with himself and Mr. Fox. Having deserted his own party to lead their opponents, he was willing to accept support from every quarter. And when it became doubtful whether he could hold his ground against the opposition, negotiations were entered into, by the king's authority, for the reconstruction of the government, on the basis of a new coalition.[1] Yet Mr. Pitt escaped the censure of those who were loudest in condemning the late coalition. Both arrangements, however, were the natural consequence of the condition of parties at that period. No one party being able to rule singly, a fusion of parties was inevitable. Lord Shelburne, unable to stand alone, had sought the alliance of each of the other parties. They had rejected his offers and

*Mr. Pitt's ministry a coalition.*

*Principles of coalition.*

quoted against us, because we were ultimately unsuccessful: but after all that can be said, it will be difficult to show when the power of the Whigs ever made so strong a struggle against the crown, the crown being thoroughly in earnest and exerting all its resources.'— *Fox's Mem.*, iv. 40. Again, in 1805, he wrote: 'Without coalitions nothing can be done against the crown; with them, God knows how little!'—*Ibid.*, 102.

[1] Nicholls' Recoll., ii. 113; Adolphus' Hist., iv. 85; Tomline's Life of Pitt, i. 294; Ann. Reg., 1784, ch. vi.; Parl. Hist., xxiv. 472; Lord Stanhope's Life of Pitt, i. 184; *Supra*, Vol. I. 78.

united against him; and Mr. Pitt, in his weakness, was driven to the same expedient, to secure a majority. A strong party may despise coalitions: but parties divided and broken up, are naturally impelled to unite; and to reprobate such unions, unconditionally, is to condemn the principles upon which the organisation of parties is founded. Members of the same party cannot agree upon all points: but their concurrence in great leading principles, and general sympathy, induce them to compromise extreme opinions, and disregard minor differences. A coalition of parties is founded upon the same basis. Men who have been opposed at another time, and upon different questions of policy, discover an agreement upon some important measures, and a common object in resisting a third party. Hence they forget former differences, and unite for the purpose of carrying out the particular policy in which they agree.

*Enlarged basis of the Tory party under Mr. Pitt.* Mr. Pitt's popularity and success, at the elections of 1784, widened the basis of the Tory party. He was supported by squires and traders, churchmen and dissenters. He had gained over the natural allies of the Whigs; and he governed with the united power of the crown, the aristocracy, and the people.[1] He had no natural connection with the party which he led, except as the king's minister. He had been born and educated a Whig. He had striven to confine the in-

---

[1] Adolphus' Hist., iv. 115; Tomline's Life of Pitt, i. 468; Lord Stanhope's Life of Pitt, i. 211, &c.; Lord Macaulay's Biography of Pitt; Lord J. Russell's Life of Fox, ii. 92.

fluence of the crown, and enlarge the liberties of the people. But before his principles had time to ripen, he found himself the first minister of a Tory king, and the leader of the triumphant Tory party. The doctrines of that party he never accepted or avowed. If he carried them into effect, it was on the ground of expediency rather than of principle.[1] In advocating the rights of Parliament in regard to the Regency, and the abatement of impeachments, he spoke the sentiments and language of the Whig school. In favouring freedom of commerce, and restoring the finances, he stands out in favourable contrast with his great Whig rival, Mr. Fox, who slighted political economy, and the fruitful philosophy of Adam Smith.[2] But called, at twenty-four years of age, to the practical administration of the government,—possessing unbounded power,—of a haughty and imperious temper,—and surrounded by influences congenial to authority,—who can wonder that he became alienated from popular principles? Even the growth and expansion of his powerful intellect were affected by too early an absorption in the cares of office, and the practical details of business. A few more years of opposition

[1] 'His education and original connections must have given him some predilection for popular notions; and although he too often promoted measures of an opposite tendency, he was at great pains to do so on the ground of immediate expediency rather than of principle.'—*Lord Holland's Mem.*, ii. 35.

[2] Butler's Reminiscences, i. 176; Massey's Hist., iii. 281; Lord Stanhope's Life of Pitt, i. 263-273; Debates on Commercial Intercourse with Ireland in 1785, Parl. Hist., xxv. 311, 575; Pitt's Budget Speech, 1792, Parl. Hist., xxix. 816; Debates on Commercial Treaty with France, 1787, Parl. Hist., xxvi. 342, &c.; Tomline's Life of Pitt, ii. 227; Lord Stanhope's Life of Pitt, i. 315, 317, 323, ii. 141; Fox's Mem., ii. 276.

and study,—even the training of a less eminent office in the government, would have matured his powers, and enlarged his philosophy. Yet, notwithstanding these early trammels, he surpassed every statesman of his party in enlightenment and liberality.

Widely different was the character of Lord Thurlow. Long in the king's most secret counsels,—his chancellor in every administration, except the coalition, from Lord North's to Mr. Pitt's—he had directed the movements of the king's friends, encouraged his Majesty's love of power, and supported those principles of government which found most favour in the royal mind. He was in theory, in sympathy, and in temper, the very impersonation of a Tory of that period. For some years he exercised a sway,—less potential, indeed, than that of Mr. Pitt, in the general policy of the state, but—scarcely inferior to that of the minister in influence with the king, in patronage, in court favours, and party allegiance. If Mr. Pitt was absolute master of the House of Commons, the House of Lords was the plaything of Lord Thurlow. It was not until Mr. Pitt resolved to endure no longer the intrigues, treachery, and insolent opposition of his chancellor, that he freely enjoyed all the powers of a responsible minister.[1]

*Lord Thurlow.*

The Whigs, proscribed at court, and despairing of royal favour, cultivated the friendship of the Prince

---

[1] Moore's Life of Sheridan, i. 406; Campbell's Lives of the Chancellors, v. 532, 555, 602, &c.; Lord Stanhope's Life of Pitt, ii. 148.

of Wales, who, in his first youth, warmly encouraged their personal intimacy, and espoused their cause. The social charms of such men as Fox, Sheridan, and Erskine, made their society most attractive to a young prince of ability and many accomplishments; and his early estrangement from the king and his ministers naturally threw him into the arms of the opposition. Even his vices received little reproof or discouragement from the gay members of the Whig party, who shared in the fashionable indulgences of that period. Young men of fashion drank deeply; and many wasted their health and fortunes at the gaming-table. Some of his Whig associates,—Fox and Sheridan among the number,—did not affect to be the most moral or prudent men of their age; and their association with the prince aggravated the king's repugnance to their party. How could he forgive the men whom he believed to be perverting the politics, alienating the affections, and corrupting the morals of the heir to his throne?

It was no new political phenomenon to see the court of the heir-apparent the nucleus of the opposition. It had been the unhappy lot of the Hanoverian family that every Prince of Wales had been alienated from the reigning sovereign. George I. hated his son with unnatural malignity; and the prince, repelled from court, became the hope of the opposition.[1] Again, in the next reign, Frederick Prince of Wales, estranged from his father in domestic life, espoused the opinions and cultivated

[1] Coxe's Walpole, i. 78, 93.

the friendship of Bolingbroke, Chesterfield, Wyndham, Carteret, Pulteney, and other statesmen most vehemently opposed to the king's government.[1]

The Whigs being in office throughout both these reigns, the court of the heir-apparent fell naturally under the influence of the Tories. And now the first-born son of George III. was in open opposition to his father, and his father's chosen ministers; and the Tories being in the ascendant at court, the Whigs took possession of Carlton House. The prince wore the buff-and-blue uniform, and everywhere paraded his adherence to the Whig party. In 1784, after the Westminster election, he joined Mr. Fox's procession, gave fêtes at Carlton House in celebration of his victory, attended public dinners, and shared in other social gatherings of the party.[2]

Their alliance was still more ostensible during the king's illness, in 1788. They openly espoused the cause of the prince, and boasted of their approaching restoration to power;[3] while the prince was actively canvassing for votes to support them in Parliament. To the Earl of Lonsdale he wrote to solicit his support as a personal favour; and all his nominees in the House of Commons, though ordinarily stanch supporters of Mr. Pitt, were found voting with Mr. Fox and the opposition.[4]

[1] Walpole's Mem. of Geo. II., i. 47; Lord Hervey's Mem., i. 235, 236, 271, 277. Hearing of their meeting at Kew, in September, 1737, the king said, 'They will all soon be tired of the puppy, for besides his being a scoundrel, he is such a fool that he will talk more fiddle-faddle to them in a day than any old woman talks in a week.' —*Ibid.*, 442.
[2] Lord J. Russell's Life of Fox, i. 337, &c.
[3] *Supra*, Vol. I. 193.
[4] Court and Cabinets of George III., ii. 64.

The Whigs were still a considerable party. However inferior, in numbers, to the ministerial phalanx, they were led by men of commanding talents, high rank, and social influence: their principles were popular, and they were generally united in sentiment and policy. But events were impending which were destined to subvert the relations of parties. The momentous incidents of the French Revolution,—new and unexampled in the history of the world,—could not fail to affect deeply the minds of every class of politicians. In their early development, the democrats hailed them with enthusiasm,—the Whigs with hopeful sympathy,—the king and the Tories with indignation and alarm.[1] Mr. Fox foresaw the spread of liberty throughout Europe.[2] Mr. Pitt, sympathising with freedom more than any of his party, watched the progress of events with friendly interest.[3] Mr. Burke was the first statesman who was overcome with terror. Foreseeing nothing but evil and dangers, he brought the whole force of his genius, with characteristic earnestness, to the denunciation of the French Revolution, its principles, its actors, and its consequences.[4] In his excitement

*Effects of the French Revolution upon parties.*

---

[1] Tomline's Life of Pitt, iii. 104; Stanhope's Life of Pitt, ii. App. xvii.

[2] Mem. of Fox, ii. 361.

[3] Tomline's Life of Pitt, iii. 118; Lord Stanhope's Life of Pitt, ii. 48, 49.

[4] Prior's Life of Burke, ii. 42; MacKnight's Life of Burke, iii. 274, *et seq.*; Burke's Correspondence, iii. 102, 183, 267, 286.—'He loved to exaggerate everything: when exasperated by the slightest opposition, even on accidental topics of conversation, he always pushed his principles, his opinions, and even his impressions of the moment, to the extreme.'—*Lord Holland's Mem.*, i. 7.

against democracy, he publicly renounced the generous and manly friendship of Mr. Fox, and repudiated the old associations of his party.[1]

<small>Divisions among the Whigs.</small> Society was becoming separated into two opposite parties,—the friends and the foes of democracy. For a time, the Whigs were able to stand between them,—maintaining liberty, without either encouraging or fearing democracy. But their position was not long tenable. Democrats espoused parliamentary reform: their opponents confounded it with revolution. Never had there been a time so inopportune for the discussion of that question, when the Society of the Friends of the People was founded. Mr. Fox, foreseeing the misconstructions to which it would be exposed, prudently withheld his support: but it was joined by Mr. Sheridan, Mr. Erskine, Mr. Grey, Mr. Tierney, and other leading Whigs, who, for the sake of the cause they had espoused, were willing to co-operate with men of democratic opinions, and even with members of the Corresponding Society, who had enrolled themselves among the Friends of the <small>April 30th, 1792.</small> People.[2] When Mr. Grey gave notice of his motion for reform, the tone of the debate disclosed the revulsion of feeling that was arising against popular questions, and the widening schism

---

[1] Parl. Hist., Feb. 9, 1790, xxviii. 363, xxix. 249; Fox's Speeches, iv. 51–200; Burke's Appeal from the new to the old Whigs, *Works*, vi. 110; Lord J. Russell's Life of Fox, ii. 241–252, 273, 283, 318; Annual Register, 1791, p. 114; Lord Holland's Mem., i. 10; Lord Stanhope's Life of Pitt, ii. 91, *et seq.*; Moore's Life of Sheridan, ii. 125; MacKnight's Life of Burke, iii, 383–411.

[2] Lord Holland's Mem., i. 13; Lord J. Russell's Life of Fox, ii. 218; Life and Opinions of Earl Grey, 9–13.

of the Whig party. While some of its members were not diverted from their purpose by the contact of democracy, others were repelled by it, even from their traditional love of liberty. A further breach in the ranks of the opposition was soon afterwards caused by the proclamation against seditious writings. Mr. Fox, Mr. Whitbread, and Mr. Grey condemned the proclamation, as designed to discredit the Friends of the People, and to disunite the opposition.¹ On the other hand, Lord North, Lord Tichfield, Mr. Windham, and Mr. Powys thought the proclamation necessary, and supported the government. Whether Mr. Pitt designed it or not, no measure could have been more effectual for dividing the Whig party.

<small>May 21st, 1792.</small>

An attempt was now made, through Mr. Dundas, Lord Loughborough, Lord Malmesbury, and the Duke of Portland, to arrange a coalition between Mr. Pitt and Mr. Fox. Both were, at this time, agreed in viewing the revolutionary excesses of France with disgust, and both were alike anxious for neutrality and peace: but the difficulties of satisfying the claims of the different parties,—the violent opposition of Mr. Burke, the disunion of the Whigs, and little earnestness on either side,—ensured the failure of these overtures.² Their mis-

---

¹ Lord Holland's Mem., i. 15; Parl. Hist., xxix. 1476, 1514. Before the proclamation was issued, 'Mr. Pitt sent copies of it to several members of the opposition in both Houses, requesting their advice.'—*Lord Malmesbury's Diary*, June 13, 1792; Tomline's Life of Pitt, iii. 347; Lord Stanhope's Life of Pitt, ii. 156.

² Lord Malmesbury's Corr., ii. 425-440. Lord Colchester's Diary and Corr., i. 13. '"It was the object of Mr. Pitt to separate Mr. Fox from some of his friends, and particularly from Sheridan. He wished

carriage had a serious influence upon the future policy of the state. The union of two such men as Mr. Pitt and Mr. Fox would have ensured temperate and enlightened counsels, at the most critical period in the history of Europe. But Mr. Fox, in opposition, was encouraged to coquet with democracy, and proclaim, out of season, the sovereignty of the people; while the alarmist section of the Whigs were naturally drawn closer to Mr. Pitt.

Coalition of leading Whigs with Mr. Pitt.
The advancing events of the French Revolution, —the decree of fraternity issued by the French Convention,—the execution of the king,—the breaking out of the revolutionary war,—and the extravagance of the English democrats, completed the ruin of the Whig party. In Jan. 28th, 1793. January, 1793, Lord Loughborough passed from the opposition benches to the woolsack. He was afterwards followed, in the House of Lords, by the Duke of Portland,—the acknowledged leader of the Whigs,—Lord Spencer, Lord Fitzwilliam, and Lord Carlisle; and in the Commons, by Mr. Windham, Mr. Thomas Grenville, Sir Gilbert Elliot, many of the old Whigs, and all the adherents of Lord North, who were henceforth the colleagues or firm supporters of Mr. Pitt.[1] Even Mr. Grattan and the Irish patriots sided with the government.[2]

to make him a party to a coalition between the ministry and the aristocratical branches of the Whigs. Mr. Fox, with his usual generosity, declined the offer.'—*Lord Holland's Mem.*, ii. 46. Lord Campbell's Life of Lord Loughborough—Lives of Chancellors, vi. 221, et seq.

[1] Lord Malmesbury's Corr., ii. 452; Mem. of Fox, iii. 24; Lord Holland's Mem. of the Whig Party, i. 5, 22-25; Lord Stanhope's Life of Pitt, ii. 242; Lord J. Russell's Life of Fox, ii. 309.

[2] Lord Holland's Mem., i. 73-77.

The small party which still clung to Mr. Fox numbered scarcely sixty members; and rarely mustered more than forty in a division.[1] In the Lords, Lord Derby, Lord Lansdowne, Lord Stanhope, and Lord Lauderdale constituted nearly the entire opposition.[2] Mr. Burke, having commenced the ruin of his party, retired from Parliament when it was consummated, to close his days in sorrow and dejection.[3]

The great Whig party was indeed reduced in numbers and influence: but all their ablest men, except Mr. Burke and Mr. Windham, were still true to their principles. Mr. Fox was supported by Mr. Sheridan, Mr. Erskine, Mr. Grey, Mr. Whitbread, Mr. Coke of Norfolk, Mr. Lambton, Lord John and Lord William Russell;[4] and soon received a valuable auxiliary in the person of Mr. Tierney.[5] They were powerless against ministers in divisions: but in debate, their eloquence, their manly defence of constitutional liberty, and their courageous resistance to the arbitrary measures of the government, kept alive a spirit of freedom which the disastrous events of the time had nearly

*The remains of the opposition.*

[1] Feb. 18, 1792, 44 to 270; 43 to 284 on Parl. Reform; 40 on the breaking out of the war.—*Lord Holland's Mem.*, i. 30; Parl. Hist., xxx. 59, 453, 925. They mustered 53 against the third reading of the Seditious Assembly Bill, Dec. 3, 1795; and 50 in support of Mr. Grey's motion in favour of treating for peace, Feb. 15, 1796.—*Lord Colchester's Diary*, i. 12, 33: 42 on Mr. Fox's motion on the state of the nation with regard to the war, May 10, 1796.—*Ibid.*, 57.

[2] Lord Holland's Mem., i. 32.—They were soon joined by the Duke of Bedford.—*Ibid.*, 78.

[3] Prior's Life of Burke, 489; MacKnight's Life of Burke, iii. 582, 604; Lord Stanhope's Life of Pitt, ii. 243, 320, &c.; Burke's Corr., iv. 430.

[4] Lord Holland's Mem., 30; Lord J. Russell's Life of Fox, ii. 324, &c.

[5] Mr. Tierney entered Parliament in 1796.

extinguished. And the desertion of lukewarm and timid supporters of their cause left them without restraint in expressing their own liberal sentiments.[1] They received little support from the people. Standing between democracy on the one side, and the classes whom democracy had scared, and patriotism or interest attracted to the government on the other, they had nothing to lean upon but the great principles and faith of their party.[2] Even the Prince of Wales abandoned them. His sympathies were naturally with kings and rulers, and against revolution; and, renouncing his friends, he became a fickle and capricious supporter of the minister.[3] The great body of the people, whom the democrats failed to gain over, recoiled from the bloodthirsty Jacobins, and took part with the government, in the repression of democracy.

If such was the prostration of the Whigs, what was the towering strength of Mr. Pitt? Never had any minister been so absolute

*Consolidation of Mr. Pitt's party.*

[1] Lord Holland's Mem., i. 25.
[2] Fox's Mem., iii. 35; Lord J. Russell's Life of Fox, ii. 253–324; Cooke's Hist. of Party, iii. 366–452; Life and Opinions of Earl Grey, 22.
[3] 'In 1795 the Prince was offended by Mr. Pitt's arrangement for the payment of his debts out of his increased income, upon his marriage, and his support of the government was weakened.'—*Lord Holland's Mem.*, i. 81.
March 28, 1797. 'The Prince of Wales sat under the gallery during the whole debate (on the Bank Committee), and his friends voted in the opposition.'—*Lord Colchester's Diary*, i. 88.
April 3, 1797. The Prince of Wales, not being permitted to undertake a mission to Ireland, which he had proposed, 'wrote to Lord Fitzwilliam, and also to Mr. Fox, offering to put himself at the head of their party at home, and to oppose openly all measures of the present administration. They all dissuaded him from that line of conduct: but on Saturday, 25th March, Mr. Fox, Erskine, the Duke of Norfolk, &c., dined at Carlton House.'—*Ibid.*, i. 94.

since England had been a constitutional state, governed by the instrumentality of parties. Never had a minister united among his supporters so many different classes and parties of men. Democracy abroad had threatened religion; and the clergy,—almost to a man,—were with the defenders of 'Church and King.' The laws and institutions of the realm were believed to be in danger; and the lawyers pressed forward to support the firm champion of order. Property and public credit were menaced; and proprietors of the soil, capitalists, fund-holders, confided in the strong-handed minister. And above all, the patriotism of the nation was aroused in support of a statesman who was wielding all the resources of the state in a deadly war.

Such were the political causes which attracted men of all parties to the side of the minister, whose policy was accepted as national. Motives less patriotic, but equally natural, contributed to the consolidation of his power.

Many of the largest proprietors of boroughs were now detached from the Whig party, and carried over their parliamentary interest to the other side. Their defection was not met by the minister with ingratitude. They shared his influence, and were overloaded with honours, which he himself despised. Boroughs in the market also rapidly fell into the hands of the dominant party. To supporters of the government, the purchase of a borough was a promising investment: to opponents it offered nothing but disappointment. The close corporations were filled with Tories, who secured the representation of their cities for their own party. None but zealous adherents of the government could hope for the least share of the patronage of the crown. The piety of a churchman brought him no preferment, unless his political orthodoxy was well attested. All who aspired to be prebendaries, deans, and bishops sought Tory patrons, and professed the Tory creed. At the bar, an advocate might be learned and eloquent, beyond all rivalry,—eagerly sought out by clients,—persuasive with juries,—and overmastering judges by his intellect and erudition; but all the prizes of his noble profession were beyond his reach, unless he enrolled himself a member of the dominant party. An ambitious man was offered the choice of the fashionable opinions of the majority, with a career of honour and distinction,— or the proscribed sentiments of a routed party, with discouragement, failure, and obscurity. Who can wonder that the bar soon made their choice, and followed the minister?

The country gentlemen formed the natural strength of the Tory party. They joined it heartily, without any inducement save their own strong convictions: but their fidelity was rewarded by a generous monarch and a grateful minister. If a man's ambition was not entirely satisfied by the paternal acres,—let him display zeal at the elections. If he would not see his rivals outstrip him in the race of life,—let him beware of lukewarmness in the Tory cause. A Whig country gentleman could rarely aspire even to the commission of the peace: a dissenter could not hope for such a trust. Ambition quickened the enthusiasm of Tories, and converted many an undecided and hesitating Whig. The moneyed classes, as we have already seen, had been gradually detached from the Whig interest, and brought over to the king and the Tories; and now they were, heart and soul, with Mr. Pitt. If the people were impoverished by his loans and war-taxes, —they, at least, prospered and grew rich. Such a minister was far too 'good for trade' not to command their willing allegiance. A vast expenditure bound them to him; and posterity is still paying, and will long continue to pay, the price of their support.

Another cause contributed to the depression of the Whigs. There was a social ostracism of liberal opinions, which continued far into the present century. It was not enough that every man who ventured to profess them should be debarred from ambition in public and professional life: he was also frowned upon and shunned in the social circle. It was whispered that he was not only a malcontent in politics, but a freethinker or infidel in religion. Loud talkers at dinner-tables, emboldened by the zeal of the company, decried his opinions, his party, and his friends. If he kept his temper, he was supposed to be overcome in argument: if he lost it, his warmth was taken as evidence of the violence of his political sentiments.[1] <small>Ostracism of liberal opinions.</small>

In Scotland, the organisation of the Tory party was stronger, and its principles more arbitrary and violent, than in England. All <small>Tory party in Scotland.</small>

[1] Sydney Smith's Mem., i. 65, &c.

men of rank, wealth, and power, and three-fourths of the people, were united in a compact body, under Mr. Dundas, the dictator of that kingdom. Power, thus concentrated, was unchecked by any popular institutions. In a country without freedom of election,[1]—without independent municipalities,—without a free press,—without public meetings,—an intolerant majority proscribed the opposite party, in a spirit of savage persecution. All Whigs were denounced as Jacobins,—shunned in society,—intimidated at the bar, and ruthlessly punished for every indiscretion as public speakers or writers in the press.[2] Their leaders were found at the bar, where several eminent men, at great sacrifice and risk, still ventured to avow their opinions, and rally the failing hopes of their party. Of these, the most remarkable in wit, in eloquence, and political courage, was the renowned advocate, Henry Erskine.[3] Let all honour be paid to the memory of men who, by their talents and personal character, were able to keep alive the spirit and sentiment of liberty, in the midst of a reign of terror!

Lord Cockburn thus sums up a spirited account of the state of parties under the administration of Mr. Dundas: 'With the people put down and the Whigs powerless, government was the master of nearly every individual in Scotland, but especially in Edinburgh,

---

[1] *Supra*, Vol. I. 355.
[2] Lord Cockburn's Memorials of his Time, p. 80, 147, *et seq.*; Lord Holland's Mem., i. 240.
[3] He was removed from the office of Dean of the Faculty of Advocates 12th January, 1796, for presiding at a public meeting, to petition against the war with France.

which was the chief seat of its influence. The infidelity of the French gave it almost all the pious; their atrocities all the timid; rapidly increasing taxation and establishments, all the venal: the higher and middle ranks were at its command, and the people at its feet. The pulpit, the bench, the bar,. the colleges, the parliamentary electors, the press, the magistracies, the local institutions, were so completely at the service of the party in power, that the idea of independence, besides being monstrous and absurd, was suppressed by a feeling of conscious ingratitude.'[1]

It is one of the first uses of party to divide the governing classes, and leave one section to support the authority of the state, and the other to protect the rights of the people. But Mr. Pitt united all these classes in one irresistible phalanx of power. Loyalty and patriotism, fears and interests, welded together such a party as had never yet been created; and which, for the sake of public liberty, it is to be hoped will never be known again. Mr. Pitt's power dangerous to liberty.

Under these discouragements, the remnant of the Whig party resisted the repressive measures of Mr. Pitt,[2] and strove earnestly to promote the restoration of peace. But it was vain to contend against the government. Arguments and remonstrances were unavailing: divisions merely exposed the numerical weakness of the minority; and at length, in 1798, Mr. Fox and many of his friends resolved to protest against the minister, and absolve themselves from the re- The Whigs in opposition. Their secession in 1798.

---

[1] Lord Cockburn's Memorials of his Time, 86.   [2] See Chap. IX.

sponsibility of his measures, by withdrawing from the debates, and seceding from Parliament. The tactics of 1776 were renewed, and with the same results. The opposition was weakened and divided, and, in the absence of its chiefs, was less formidable to ministers, and less capable of appealing, with effect, to public opinion. Mr. Tierney was the only man who profited by the secession. Coming to the front, he assumed the position of leader; and with great readiness and vigour, and unceasing activity, assailed every measure of the government. The secession was continued during three sessions.* As a protest against the minister, it availed nothing: he was more absolute, and his opponents more insignificant, than ever.[1]

Mr. Pitt needed no further accession of strength; but the union with Ireland recruited his majority with an overwhelming force of Tories from the sister country. Yet, at the moment of his highest prosperity, this very union cast down the minister, and shook his party to its centre. It was far too powerful to be overthrown by the loss of such a leader; but it was

Disunion of the Tory party in 1801: its effects.

[1] Lord Holland's Mem., i. 84, 101; Lord Sidmouth's Life, i. 203; Memorials of Fox, iii. 136, 137, 249. 'During the whole of this Session (1799) the powerful leaders of opposition continued to secede. Mr. Fox did not come once. Grey came and spoke once against the Union, and Sheridan opposed it in several stages. Tierney never acted with them, but maintained his own line of opposition, especially on questions of finance.'—*Lord Colchester's Diary*, i. 192.

' 1800. In February, Fox came upon the question of treating for peace with Bonaparte, and upon no other occasion during the session. Grey came upon the union only. Tierney attended throughout, and moved his annual finance propositions. Upon the opening of the session in November, all the opposition came and attended regularly, except Fox.'—*Ibid.*, i. 216; Lord Stanhope's Life of Pitt, iii. 41, 76–77; Life and Opinions of Earl Grey, 49.

divided by conflicting counsels and personal rivalries; and its relations to other parties were materially changed. Mr. Pitt's liberal views upon the Catholic question and the government of Ireland were shared by his ablest colleagues, and by nearly all the Whigs; while the majority of his party, siding with the king, condemned them as dangerous to church and state. The schism was never wholly cured, and was destined, in another generation, to cause the disruption of the party. The personal differences consequent upon Mr. Pitt's retirement introduced disunion and estrangement among several of the leading men, and weakened the ties which had hitherto held the party together in a compact confederacy. Mr. Canning,—brilliant, ambitious, and intriguing,—despised the decorous mediocrity of Mr. Addington,—derided 'the Doctor' with merciless wit,—ridiculed his speeches, decried his measures, and disparaged his friends.[1] With restless activity he fomented jealousies and misunderstandings between Mr. Pitt and his successor, which other circumstances concurred to aggravate,—until the great Tory leader and his adherents were found making common cause with the Whigs, against the Tory minister.[2] The Tory party was thus seriously

[1] Lord Stanhope's Life of Pitt, ii. 297, 306, 320, 363, 405, 428.—*Ibid.*, iv. 58; Lord Malmesbury's Corr., iv. 375; Lord Sidmouth's Life, ii. 145, &c., 298; Stapleton's Canning and his Times, 66, *et seq.*; Rose's Mem., ii. 466, &c. 'Old Lord Liverpool justly observed that Mr. Addington was laughed out of power and place in 1803 by the *beau monde*, or, as that grave old politician pronounced it, the *biu mond*.'—*Lord Holland's Mem.*, ii. 211.

[2] Pellew's Life of Lord Sidmouth, ii. 254, *et seq.*, 298, 301. Sir William Scott, speaking of the state of parties in 1803, said: 'There could be no adjustment between the parties, from the numbers of their

disunited, while friendly relations were encouraged between the friends of Mr. Pitt and the Whig members of the opposition. Lord Grenville and his party now separated from Mr. Pitt, and associated themselves with the Whigs; and this accession of strength promised a revival of the influence of their party. When Mr. Pitt was recalled to power in 1804, being estranged from the king's friends and the followers of Mr. Addington, he naturally sought an alliance with Lord Grenville and the Whig leaders, whose parliamentary talents were far more important than the number of their adherents. Such an alliance was favoured by the position of Lord Grenville, who, once a colleague of Mr. Pitt, and now a friend of Mr. Fox, might fitly become the mediator between two parties, which, after a protracted contest, had at length found points of agreement and sympathy. The king's personal repugnance to Mr. Fox, however, frustrated an arrangement which, by uniting the more liberal section of the Tories with the Whigs, would have constituted an enlightened party,—progressive in its policy, and directed by the ablest statesmen of the age.[1] Lord Grenville, loyal to his new friends, declined to accept office without them, and allied himself more closely with the Whigs.[2] Mr. Pitt, thus weakened, was

respective adherents; there was not pasture enough for all.' Lord Malmesbury's Corr., iv. 77, 101, &c.; Lord Stanhope's Life of Pitt, iv. 21, 88, 116, 117, 139; Lord Colchester's Diary, ii. 403.

[1] *Supra*, Vol. I. 100; Lord Malmesbury's Corr., iv. 309; Rose's Corr., ii. 100; Life and Opinions of Earl Grey, 91-97, 107; Lord Holland's Mem., i. 191; Lord Stanhope's Life of Pitt, 177, *et seq.*: Pellew's Life of Lord Sidmouth, ii. 370, &c.

[2] Lord Malmesbury, speaking of this secession, says:—'The

soon obliged to make peace with Mr. Addington,[1] and to combine, once more, the scattered forces of his party. The reunion was of brief duration; and so wide was the second breach, that on the death of Mr. Pitt, the Addington party were prepared to coalesce with the Whigs.[2]

This disruption of the Tory party restored the Whigs to office, for a short time,—not indeed as an independent party, for which they were far too weak,—but united with the Grenvilles, Lord Sidmouth, and the king's friends. A coalition with the liberal followers of Mr. Pitt would have been the more natural and congenial arrangement:[3] but the peculiar relations of Lord Sidmouth to the late administration,—the number of his friends,—his supposed anxiety for peace,—and his personal influence with the king, suggested the necessity of such an alliance. No single party could stand alone,—a coalition was inevitable; and Lord Sidmouth, being estranged personally from Mr. Pitt's followers, was naturally led to associate himself with Lord Grenville and Mr. Fox; while the latter, being himself distasteful to the king, was glad to co-operate with the leader of the king's

*The Whigs restored to office in 1806.*

---

French proverb is here verified, " Un bon ami vaut mieux que trois mauvais parents." '—*Corr.*, iv. 309.

[1] He was created Viscount Sidmouth in January, 1805.

[2] Lord Holland's Mem., i. 203; Pellew's Life of Lord Sidmouth, ii. 371; Rose's Corr., ii. 368.

[3] Lord Holland says: 'The disunited rump of Mr. Pitt's ministry were no party, whereas Lord Sidmouth's friends, though few, formed a compact body; and if the leaders were inferior in talents to those of other political parties, their subalterns were more respectable than the clerks and secretaries of Mr. Pitt's and Lord Melville's school.' —*Mem. of Whig Party*, i. 209.

friends.[1] It was a coalition between men as widely opposed in political sentiments and connections as Mr. Fox and Lord North had been three-and-twenty years before: but it escaped the reproaches to which that more celebrated coalition had fallen a victim.

The signal failures of Mr. Pitt's war administration, and the weariness of the nation under constantly increasing taxation, afforded to the Whigs,—who had consistently urged a more pacific policy,—an opportunity of recovering some portion of their former influence and popularity. Their brief reign was signalised by the abolition of the slave trade, and other wise and useful measures. But they had not the confidence of the king:[2] they failed even to conciliate the Prince of Wales:[3] they mismanaged the elections:[4] they were weakened by the death of Mr. Fox:[5] they were unsuccessful in their nego-

---

[1] Pellew's Life of Lord Sidmouth, ii. 423.

[2] 'The king and his household were, from the beginning and throughout, hostile to the ministry.'—*Lord Holland's Mem.*, ii. 68.

[3] The prince, in a letter to Lord Moira, March 30th, 1807, said: 'From the hour of Fox's death,—that friend, towards whom and in whom my attachment was unbounded,—it is known that my earnest wish was to retire from further concern and interference in public affairs.' At the same time he complained of neglect on the part of the Grenville ministry,—'having been neither consulted nor considered in any one important instance;' and on the fall of that ministry, whom he had generally desired to support, he 'determined to resume his original purpose, sincerely prepared, in his own mind, on the death of poor Fox, to cease to be a party man.' This resolution he communicated to the king.'—*Lord Colchester's Diary*, ii. 115; Lord Holland's Mem., ii. 68-72, 244.—'In his letters to Earl Grey, immediately after the death of Mr. Fox, there is no trace of such feelings.'—*Life and Opinions of Earl Grey*, 116.

[4] Lord Holland's Mem., ii. 93.—'The king, who throughout his reign had furnished every treasury with 12,000*l.* to defray election expenses on a dissolution, withheld that unconstitutional assistance from the administration of 1806.'—*Ibid.*, 94.

[5] Lord Holland says: 'Had Lord Grenville, in the new arrangements (after Mr. Fox's death), sought for strength in the opposite

tiations for peace;[1] and fell easily before the king's displeasure, and the intrigues of their opponents.[2]

It was now evident that the party which Mr. Pitt had raised to such greatness, was not to be cast down by his death. It had been disorganised by the loss of its eminent leader, and by the estrangement of his immediate followers from Lord Sidmouth and the king's friends. It possessed no statesman of commanding talents to inspire its disheartened members with confidence; and there were jealousies and rivalries among its ablest statesmen. But the king was its active and vigilant patron, and aided it with all the influence of the crown; while the war-cries of 'The church in danger,' and 'No popery,' were sufficient to rally all the forces of the party. Even those ministers who favoured the Catholic claims were content to profit by the appeals of Mr. Perceval and his friends to the fanaticism of the people. Such appeals had, on other occasions, been a favourite device of the Tories They had even assumed the Church to be in danger on the accession of George I., as a pretence for inviting a popish pretender to the throne.[3] Mr. Pitt had fallen before the same prejudice in 1801; and

*The Tories reinstated, 1807.*

---

party,—had he consulted the wishes of the court, rather than his own principles and consistency, he would have conciliated the king, fixed himself permanently in office, and divested every party in the state of the means of annoying him in Parliament.'—*Mem. of Whig Party*, ii. 50.

[1] Ann. Reg., 1806, ch. ix., stated by Lord Holland to have been written by Mr. Allen; Parl. Papers relating to the negotiation with France, 1806; Hans. Deb., 1st Ser., viii. 305, Jan. 5, 1807, &c.; Life and Opinions of Earl Grey, 126-138.

[2] *Supra*, Vol. I. 105, *et seq*.

[3] King's Speech, 1715, Parl. Hist., vii. 222; Romilly's Life, ii. 192.

in 1807, the Duke of Portland and Mr. Perceval proved its efficacy in restoring strength and union to their party.

Even the Dissenters, swayed by their intolerant sentiments against the Catholics, often preferred the Court and High-church candidates to the friends of religious liberty. Nor did the Whigs generally gain popular support: the crown and the great Tory nobles prevailed against them in the counties, and more democratic candidates found favour in the populous towns.[1]

The Whigs were again routed: but they had gained strength, as an opposition, by their brief restoration to power. They were no longer a proscribed party, without hope of royal favour and public confidence. If not yet formidable in divisions against the government, their opinions were received with tolerance; and much popular support, hitherto latent, was gradually disclosed. This was especially apparent in Scotland. The impeachment of Lord Melville, the idol of the Scottish Tories, had been a severe blow to that party; and the unwonted spectacle of their opponents actually wielding, once more, the power and patronage of the state, 'convinced them,'—to use the words of Lord Cockburn,—'that they were not absolutely immortal.'[2] Their political power, indeed, was not materially diminished: but their spirit was tempered, and they learned to respect, with decent moderation, the rights of the minority.

*The Whigs in opposition, 1807-1811.*

[1] Lord Holland's Mem., ii. 227-230.
[2] Lord Cockburn's Mem., 215, 229.

Lord Melville was replaced in the administration of the affairs of Scotland by his son, Mr. Robert Dundas, who, with less talents than his father, brought to the office of leader of a dominant party much good sense and moderation.[1]

Younger men of the Whig party were now rising into notice, in literature and at the Scottish bar. Brougham, Francis Horner, Jeffrey, Sydney Smith, Cockburn, and Murray were destined to play a conspicuous part in the politics and literature of their age; and were already beginning to exercise an important influence upon the hopes and interests of their party. Among their most signal services was the establishment of the Edinburgh Review,[2]—a journal distinguished for the combination of the highest literary merit, with enlarged views of political philosophy far in advance of its age,—and an earnest but temperate zeal for public liberty, which had been nearly trodden out of the literature of the country.[3]

The Whigs had become, once more, a great and powerful party. Abandoned a few years before by many men of the highest rank and influence, they had gradually recovered the principal Whig families. They were represented by several statesmen of commanding talents; and their numbers had been largely recruited since 1793. But they were not well led or organised; and were without concert and discipline. When Lord Howick was removed to the House of

[1] Lord Cockburn's Mem., 229, 230.
[2] The first number of this journal was published in October, 1802.
[3] Cockburn's Mem. of Jeffrey, i. 286; Lady Holland's Life of Sydney Smith, i. 59, *et seq.*; Cockburn's Mem., 166; Lord Brougham's Autobiography, i. 245-270.

Lords, by the death of his father, the rival claims of Mr. Whitbread and Lord Henry Petty brought forward Mr. Ponsonby, an Irishman, as leader of a party with whom he had little acquaintance or connection.[1] In 1809, they were further divided by the embarrassing inquiry into the conduct of the Duke of York.[2] And for several years, there was little agreement between the aristocratic Whigs who followed Earl Grey, and members who acted with Mr. Whitbread or Sir Francis Burdett.[3]

The administrations of the Duke of Portland and Mr. Perceval were formed upon the narrowest Tory principles. They were the governments of the king and his friends. Concessions to Catholics were resisted as dangerous to the church.[4] Repression and coercion were their specifics for ensuring the safety of the state: the correction of abuses and the amendment of the laws were resisted as innovations.[5]

*Tory administrations, 1807-1812.*

On the death of Mr. Perceval, the last hopes of the Whigs, founded upon the favour of the Prince Regent, were extinguished;[6] and the Tory rule was continued, as securely as

*Lord Liverpool's administration, 1812.*

---

[1] Lord Holland's Mem., 236-242. Lord H. says: 'Mr. Windham, Mr. Sheridan, Mr. Tierney, and Mr. T. Grenville were, from very different but obvious causes, disqualified' for the lead.—*Ibid.*, 237.—Life and Opinions of Earl Grey, 174-189.

[2] *Ibid.*, 223-227, 239.

[3] *Ibid.*, 336-388; Court and Cabinets of Geo. IV., i. 131.

[4] Mr. Perceval said: 'I could not conceive a time or any change of circumstances which could render further concession to the Catholics consistent with the safety of the state.'—*Hans. Deb.*, 1st Ser., xxi. 663.

[5] e.g. Mr. Bankes' Offices in Reversion bills, 1809 and 1810; Sir S. Romilly's Criminal Law bills, 1810, 1811; Earl Grey's Life and Opinions, 202-206.

[6] *Supra*, Vol. I. 125.

ever, under Lord Liverpool : but the basis of this administration was wider and more liberal. The removal of Catholic disabilities was henceforth to be an open question. Every member of the government was free to speak and vote independently upon this important measure;[1] and the divisions to which such a constitution of the cabinet gave rise, eventually led to the dissolution of the Tory party. The domestic policy of this administration was hard and repressive.[2] They carried out, as far as was practicable in a free state, the doctrines of absolutism. But victories and glory crowned their efforts, and increased their strength; while the Whigs, by condemning their foreign and military policy, exposed themselves to the reproach of unpatriotic sentiments, which went far to impair their popularity.[3]

But, notwithstanding the power of ministers, the great force of the Tory party was being gradually undermined. The king, indeed, was on their side: the House of Lords was theirs, by connection and creations: the House of Commons was theirs, by nomination and influence: the church was wholly theirs, by sentiment, interest, and gratitude. But the fidelity of their followers could not always be relied on;[4] and great changes

*Growing weakness of the Tory party: its causes.*

---

[1] It was announced by Lord Castlereagh, 'that the present government would not, as a government, resist discussion or concession,' . . . 'and that every member of the government would be free to act upon his own individual sentiments.'—*Lord Colchester's Diary*, 10th June, 1812, ii. 387. 'Lord Sidmouth, Lord Liverpool, and Lord Eldon would resist inquiry, meaning to resist concession; but Lord Harrowby, Lord Melville, Lord Bathurst, and Lord Mulgrave, would concede all. Vansittart would go *pedetentim*.'—*Ibid.*, 403.
[2] See Chap. X. [3] Lord Dudley's Letters, 127, 145.
[4] See Letter of the Duke of Wellington to the Duke of Bucking

of sentiment and social conditions were being developed in the country. The old squires were, perhaps, as faithful as ever: but their estates were being rapidly bought by wealthy capitalists, whom the war, commerce, manufactures, and the stock-exchange had enriched.[1] The rising generation of country gentlemen were, at the same time, more open to the convictions and sympathies of an age which was gradually emancipating itself from the narrow political creed of their fathers.

Meanwhile commercial and manufacturing industry was rapidly accumulating large populations, drawn from the agricultural counties. Towns were continually encroaching upon the country; and everywhere the same uniform law prevailed, which associates activity and enterprise with a spirit of political progress,—and social inertness with sentiments opposed to political change. The great industrial communities were forcing the latent seeds of democracy: the counties were still the congenial soil of Toryism. But the former were ever growing and multiplying: the latter were stationary or retrograde. Hence liberal opinions were constantly gaining ground among the people.[2]

---

ham, March 6th, 1822.—*Court and Cabinets of Geo. IV.*, i. 292; Lord Dudley's Letters, 218, *et seq.*

[1] Lord Redesdale, writing to Lord Sidmouth, Dec. 11th, 1816, said: 'Many of the old country gentlemen's families are gone, and I have no doubt that the destruction of their hereditary influence has greatly contributed to the present insubordination. . . . We are rapidly becoming,—if we are not already,—a nation of shopkeepers.'—*Pellew's Life of Lord Sidmouth*, iii. 162.

[2] 'Depuis que les travaux de l'intelligence furent devenus des sources de force et de richesses, on dut considérer chaque développement de la science, chaque connaissance nouvelle, chaque idée neuve,

A Tory government was slow to understand the spirit of the times, and to adapt its policy to the temper and condition of the people. The heavy burthens of the war, and the sudden cessation of the war expenditure, caused serious distress and discontent, resulting in clamours against the government, and the revival of a democratic spirit among the people. These symptoms were harshly checked by severe repressive measures, which still further alienated the people from the government; while the Whigs, by opposing the coercive policy of ministers, associated themselves with the popular cause.[1] There had generally been distrust and alienation between the democrats, or Radicals,[2] and the aristocratic Whigs. The latter had steadily maintained the principles of constitutional liberty, but had shown no favour to demagogues and visionaries.[3] But the events of 1817 and 1819 served to unite the Whigs with the democratic party—if not in general sympathy, yet in a common cause; and they gained in weight and influence by the accession of a more popular following. Cobbett, Hunt, and other demagogues denounced them for their moderation, and scoffed at them as aristocratic place-hunters;[4] mobs scouted their

*Democratic sentiments provoked by distress.*

*1817-20.*

comme un germe de puissance, mis à la portée du peuple.'—*De Tocqueville*, Démocratie en Amér., i. 4.
 [1] See Chap. X.
 [2] In 1819, Hunt and his followers, for the first time, assumed the name of Radical Reformers.—*Pellew's Life of Lord Sidmouth*, iii. 247; Cooke's Hist. of Party, iii. 511.
 [3] Earl Grey's Life and Opinions, 242-254.
 [4] See Cobbett's Register, 1818, 1819, 1820, *passim*; Edinburgh Review, June 1818, p. 198. Mr. Tierney said, Nov. 23rd, 1819: 'It was impossible to conceive any set of men under less obligations to

pretensions to liberality ;[1] but the middle classes, and large numbers of reflecting people, not led by mob-orators or democratic newspapers, perceived that the position of the Whigs was favourable to the advancement of constitutional liberty, and supported them.

*Separation of the Grenvilles from the Whigs, 1817.*   In leaning to the popular cause, however, they were again separated from Lord Grenville and his friends, who renewed their ancient connection with the Tories.[2] Meanwhile, on the death of Mr. Ponsonby, the leadership of the opposition had at length fallen upon Mr. Tierney.[3]

The popular sentiments which were aroused by *The Whigs and Queen Caroline.* the proceedings against Queen Caroline again brought the Whigs into united action with the Radicals, and the great body of the people. The leading Whigs espoused her cause; and their parliamentary eminence and conspicuous talents placed them in the front of the popular movement.

While the Whigs were thus becoming more closely *Increasing enlightenment of the people.* associated with popular sentiments, a permanent change in the condition of the people was gradually increasing their influence in public affairs. Education was being

---

the Radicals than the Whigs were. True it was that ministers came in for a share of abuse and disapprobation; but it was mild and merciful compared with the castigation which their opponents received.'—*Hans. Deb.*, 1st Ser., xli. 74; Remains of Mrs. Trench, 44.

[1] See Canning's Speech on the State of the Nation,—Hans. Deb., 1st Ser, xxxvi. 1423.

[2] Court and Cabinets of the Regency, ii. 347-366; Lord Sidmouth's Life, iii. 297; Lord Dudley's Letters, 150; Life and Opinions of Earl Grey, 125, 351-384; Lord Colchester's Diary, iii. 94, 99, &c.

[3] Lord Colchester's Diary, iii. 69, &c.

rapidly extended, and all classes were growing more enlightened. The severities of successive governments had wholly failed in repressing the activity of the press: the fear of democracy had died out: the opposition speakers and writers had widely disseminated liberal principles: and public opinion was again beginning to assert its right to be heard in the councils of the state. The Tory party could not fail to respond, in some measure, to this spirit; and the last few years of Lord Liverpool's administration were signalised by many wise and liberal measures, which marked the commencement of a new era in the annals of legislation.[1] In domestic and economical policy, Mr. Peel and Mr. Huskisson were far in advance of their party: in foreign policy, Mr. Canning burst the strait bands of an effete diplomacy, and recognised the just claims of nations, as well as the rights of sovereigns. But the political creed of the dominant party was daily becoming less in harmony with the sentiments of an enlightened people, whom the constitution was supposed to invest with the privileges of self-government. Men like Lord Eldon were out of date: but they still ruled the country. Sentiments which, in the time of Mr. Perceval, had been accepted as wise and statesmanlike, were beginning to be ridiculed by younger men, as the drivellings of dotards: but they prevailed over the arguments of the ablest debaters and public writers of the day.

And looking beyond the immediate causes which

[1] See Chap. XVIII.

contributed to the growth of democratic sentiment in England, we must embrace in our more distant view the general upheaving of society, throughout Europe and America, during the last fifty years. The people of the United States had established a great republic. The revolutionary spirit of France,—itself, again, the result of deeper causes,—had spread with epidemic subtilty over the civilised world. Ancient monarchies had been overthrown, and kings discrowned, as in a drama. The traditional reverence of the people for authority had been shaken: their idols had been cast down. Men were now taught to respect their rulers less, and themselves more: to assert their own rights, and to feel their own power. In every country,—whatever its form of government, —democracy was gaining strength in society, in the press, and in the sentiments of the people. Wise governments responded to its expansive spirit; blind and bigoted rulers endeavoured to repress it as sedition. Sometimes trampled down by despotism, it lay smouldering in dangerous discontent: sometimes confronted with fear and hesitation, it burst forth in revolution. But in England, harmonising with free institutions, it merely gave strength to the popular cause, and ultimately secured the triumph of constitutional liberty. Society was at the same time acquiring a degree of freedom hitherto unknown in England. Every class had felt the weight of authority. Parents had exercised a severe discipline over their children: masters a hard rule over their workpeople: everyone armed

*General spread of democratic sentiments.*

with power, from the magistrate to the beadle, had wielded it sternly. But society was gradually asserting its claims to gentler usage and higher consideration. And this social change gave a further impulse to the political sentiments of the people.

While these changes were silently at work, the illness and death of Lord Liverpool suddenly dissolved the union of the great Tory party. He had represented the policy and political system of the late king, and of a past generation; and his adherents in the cabinet outnumbered the advocates of more advanced principles. Mr. Canning, the member of the cabinet most eminent for his talents, and long the foremost champion of the Catholics, was now called to the head of affairs. The king did not entrust him with the power of carrying the Catholic question:[1] but his promotion was the signal for the immediate retirement of the Duke of Wellington, Lord Eldon, Mr. Peel, Lord Bathurst, Lord Melville,[2] and their high Tory followers. Lord Palmerston, Mr. Huskisson, and Mr. Wynn remained faithful to Mr. Canning; and the accomplished Master of the Rolls, Sir John Copley, succeeded Lord Eldon, who, at length, had ceased to be one of the permanent institutions of the country. Differences of opinion on the Catholic question were the avowed ground of this schism in the Tory party; and whatever personal considerations of ambition or jealousy may have contributed

*Disunion of the Tories on the death of Lord Liverpool.*

---

[1] Stapleton's Canning and his Times, 582.
[2] Lord Melville concurred with Mr. Canning upon the Catholic question. Lord Bexley also resigned, but withdrew his resignation.

to this result, there can be no doubt that the open Catholic question, which had been the principle of Lord Liverpool's ministry, contained the seeds of disunion, rivalry, and conflict. Mr. Canning and his friends had contended in debates and divisions against their own colleagues, and had obtained the warmest support from the opposition. And now the personal pretensions and the cause of the first minister, alike repelled that section of his colleagues who had adopted a narrower policy than his own.[1]

The same causes naturally attracted to Mr. Canning the friendly support of the Whigs. They differed with him upon the subject of parliamentary reform, and the repeal of the Test Act; but had long fought by his side on behalf of the Catholics: they approved his liberal foreign policy, and hailed his separation from the high Tory connection as a happy augury of good government, upon enlarged and generous principles. An immediate coalition was not desirable, and was discountenanced by Earl Grey and other Whig leaders: but the cabinet was soon joined by Lord Lansdowne, Lord Carlisle, and Mr. Tierney; while the Whigs, as a body, waited to defend him against the acrimonious attacks of the Tory seceders.[2] Such was the commencement of that union between the liberal Tories and the Whigs, which was destined to lead to the most important political consequences.

*Mr. Canning supported by the Whigs.*

---

[1] Stapleton's Political Life of Canning, iii. 324; George Canning and his Times, 590; Twiss's Life of Lord Eldon, ii. 586; Hans. Deb., May 2nd, 1827, 2nd Ser., xvii. 448–498; Lord Colchester's Diary, iii. 484, 493, &c. Plumer Ward's Mem., ii. 167.

[2] Stapleton's Political Life of Canning, iii. 337–345, 348, *et seq.*, 388, *et seq.*; Torrens' Life of Sir J. Graham, i. 209–216.

In a few months, Mr. Canning was snatched from the scene of his glory and his trials.[1] His old friends and associates had become his bitterest foes: his new allies, however sincere, were estranged from him by their connections, by a life-long parliamentary opposition, and by fundamental differences of opinion. His broken health succumbed to the harassing difficulties of his position. Had he lived, he might have surmounted them: mutual concessions might have consolidated a powerful and enlightened party, under his guidance. But what his commanding talents might possibly have accomplished, was beyond the reach of his successor, Lord Goderich. That nobleman,—after a provisional rule of five months,—unable to reconcile the claims and pretensions of the two parties, resigned his hopeless office.[2] The complete union of the Whigs with the friends of Mr. Canning was soon to be accomplished: but was reserved for a more auspicious period.

<small>Divisions of parties after Mr. Canning's death.</small>

The resignation of Lord Goderich was followed by the immediate revival of the old Tory party, under the Duke of Wellington. The formation of such a ministry was a startling retrogression. A military premier, surrounded by his companions in arms, and by the narrowest school of Tory politicians, could not fail to disappoint those who had seen with hope the dawn of better days, under Mr. Canning.[3] At first, indeed, the

<small>Duke of Wellington Premier.</small>

---

[1] August 8th, 1827.
[2] Lord Colchester's Diary, iii. 527.
[3] Mr. T. Grenville, writing to the Duke of Buckingham, Sept. 9, 1828, says: 'My original objections to the formation of a govern-

Duke had the aid of Lord Palmerston, Mr. Huskisson, and other friends of Mr. Canning:[1] but the general character of the ministry was ultra-Tory; and within a few months, all the Liberal members seceded.[2] It was too late, however, for an effete school to prevail over principles of liberty and justice; and its temporary revival served to precipitate its final overthrow.

The first assault upon the stronghold of the Tory party was led by Lord John Russell, who carried against the government his motion for a bill to repeal the corporation and test acts. The Duke, once fairly overcome, retreated from his position, and suffered the bill to pass through both houses, amid the execrations of Lord Eldon, Lord Winchilsea, and the ultra-Tories.[3]

*Repeal of Corporation and Test Acts, Feb. 26th, 1828.*

Ireland was the Duke's next difficulty. Affairs in that country had, at length, reached a crisis which demanded present concessions, or a resort to the sword.[4] The narrow policy of ministers could no longer be maintained; and they preferred their duty to the state, to the

*Catholic emancipation viewed in reference to party.*

---

ment concocted out of the Army List and the ultra-Tories, are quite insuperable on constitutional principles alone; neither is there any instance since the Revolution of any government so adverse, in its formation, to all the free principles and practice of our Constitution.'
—*Court and Cabinets of Geo. IV.*, ii. 380.

[1] As first constituted, the administration comprised a majority favourable to the Catholic claims, viz., seven for and six against them.—*Lord Colchester's Diary*, iii. 535. Lord Palmerston, writing Jan. 18, 1828, said: 'I like them (the Whigs), much better than the Tories, and agree with them much more; but still we, the Canningites, if we may be so termed, did not join their government, but they came and joined ours.'—*Bulwer's Life*, i. 220.

[2] See *supra*, Vol. I. 415, and Bulwer's Life of Lord Palmerston, i. 252, *et seq.*

[3] See Chap. XIII.  [4] See Chap. XIII.

obligations of party. To the consternation of the Tories, the leaders whom they trusted suddenly resolved upon the immediate removal of the civil disabilities of the Catholics. The Duke and Mr. Peel were, doubtless, induced to renounce the faith which had gained them the confidence of their party, by a patriotic desire to avert civil war : but how could they hope to be judged by their followers, their opponents, and the people ? Tories who conscientiously believed that the church, and the Protestant constitution of their ancestors were about to be sacrificed to political expediency, loudly complained that they had been betrayed, and their citadel treacherously surrendered to the enemy. Never had party spirit been inflamed to a higher pitch of bitterness and exasperation. The great body of the Tories,—sullen, indignant, and revengeful,—were wholly alienated from their leaders. Men who had no sympathy with that party could not deny that their complaints were well founded. According to all the ethics of party, they had been wronged, and were absolved from further allegiance.[1]

Ministers were charged with sinning against political morality, in another form. The Whigs and followers of Mr. Canning, allowing their tardy resolution to be wise and statesmanlike, asked if they were the men to carry it into execution. If they were convinced that the position they had held so stubbornly could no longer be defended, should they

---

[1] Hans. Deb., Sess. 1829, *passim* ; Ann. Reg., 1829, ch. i.-iv.; Letter of Duke of Wellington to Duke of Buckingham, April 21, 1829 ; Court and Cab. of Geo. IV., ii. 397.

not have capitulated, and surrendered the fortress to the besieging force? If a just and conciliatory policy was, at length, to be adopted, the principles of the opposition had prevailed; and to that party should be confided the honourable privilege of consummating the labours of a political life. Men who had maintained power for thirty years, by deferring to the prejudices of their party, were not entitled to its continuance when they had accepted the policy of the opposition. If the Catholics were to be emancipated, they should owe their privileges to their own steady friends, and not to their oppressors.[1] Nor was this opinion confined to the opposition. The Tories themselves,—fiercely as they condemned the conversion of their leaders,—condemned no less fiercely their retention of office.[2] Had ministers resigned, the united body of Tories might have shown a formidable front against a Whig government, though aided by the Tory supporters of the Catholic cause: but they were powerless against their own leaders, who retained the entire influence of the government, and could further rely upon the support of the opposition.

The friends of Mr. Canning observed that, two years ago, the Duke of Wellington and Mr. Peel had refused to serve with that eminent man, lest they

[1] Mr. Peel freely acknowledged that the measure was due to the efforts of the opposition. He said: 'The credit belongs to others, and not to me: it belongs to Mr. Fox, to Mr. Grattan, to Mr. Plunket, —to the gentlemen opposite, and to an illustrious and right hon. friend of mine, who is now no more. By their efforts, in spite of every opposition, it has proved victorious.'—*Hans. Deb.*, 2nd Ser., xx. 1289; Guizot's Life of Peel, 39.

[2] Hans. Deb., 2nd Ser., xx. 1119, 1163, 1263; Twiss's Life of Lord Eldon, iii. 73.

should give countenance to the Catholic claims; and had pursued him with relentless hostility. And now these very men were engaged in carrying a measure which Mr. Canning himself would have been restrained, by the conditions under which he took office, from promoting.[1]

Men of all parties looked with astonishment at the sudden abandonment, by ministers, of the distinctive principles of their party. Some doubted the honesty of their former professions: others deplored an inconsistency which had shaken the confidence of the people in the character and statesmanship of public men. All saw plainly that the Tory party could not long survive the shock. The question which had first broken the consolidated strength of that party in 1801, and had continued to divide and weaken it, throughout the regency and the reign of George IV., had at length shattered it to pieces. The Catholic Relief Bill was passed: but time did not abate the resentment of the Tories. Henceforth the government were kept in power by the friendly support of the opposition, who at the same time, prepared the way for their own eventual accession, by the advocacy of economic and parliamentary reform, the exposure of abuses, and the assertion of popular principles.

In 1830, the ministers, thus weakened and discredited, were forced, by the death of George IV., to appeal to the people;— when their own unpopularity,—the resent-

*The Whigs restored to power in 1830.*

---

[1] Hans. Deb., 2nd Ser., xxi. 221; Stapleton's Political Life of Canning, iii. 460; Quarterly Review, vol. xliv. 286.

ment or coolness of their friends,—the increased activity and spirit of the Whigs and Radical reformers,—popular discontents at home, and revolutions abroad, — combined further to disturb the ministerial majority at the elections.[1] The Duke of Wellington's imprudent handling of the question of parliamentary reform speedily completed his ruin.[2] He fell; and at length the Whigs were restored to power, at a time most favourable to the triumph of their principles, and the consolidation of their strength. The ministry of Earl Grey comprised the most eminent Whigs, together with the adherents of Mr. Canning who had separated from the Duke of Wellington, and were now united with the reformers. This union was natural; and it was permanent. Its seeds had been sown in 1801, when differences first arose amongst the Tories; it had grown throughout the administration of Lord Liverpool; it had ripened under Mr. Canning; and had been forced into maturity by the new impulse of reform.

*Union of the Whigs with the people.*
The time was also propitious for enlisting, on the side of the Whigs, the general support of the people. Hitherto they had fallen, as an aristocratic party, between the dominant Tories on one side, and the clamorous Radicals on the other. Notwithstanding the popularity of their principles, they had derived little support from democracy. On the contrary, democracy had too often weakened their natural influence, and dis-

---

[1] *Supra*, Vol. I. 417; Edinb. Rev., vol. li. 574; Courts and Cabinets of Will. IV. and Queen Victoria, i. 45, 47, 77, 85, 143.
[2] *Supra*, Vol. I. 418.

credited their efforts in the cause of liberty. But now the popular voice demanded a measure of parliamentary reform; and the reform ministry became at once the leaders of the people. Even democracy, —hitherto the terror of every government,—was now the turbulent and dangerous, but irresistible ally of the king's ministers. Such was the popular ferment, that it was even able to overcome the close electoral system of the unreformed Parliament. The Tories, indeed, forgetting their recent differences, were suddenly re-united by the sense of a common danger. The utter annihilation of their power was threatened; and they boldly strove to maintain their ground. But they were routed and overthrown. The ascendency of landlords in counties,—the local influence of patrons in boroughs, were overborne by the determined cry for reform; and the dissolution of 1831, when none of the old electoral abuses had yet been corrected, secured a large majority for ministers, in the House of Commons. The dissolution of 1832, under the new franchises of the Reform Acts, completed their triumph. Sad was the present downfall of the Tories. In the first reformed Parliament they numbered less than one hundred and fifty.[1] The condition of the Whigs, in 1793, had scarcely been more hopeless. Their majority in the House of Lords was, indeed, unshaken; but it served merely to harass and hold in check their opponents.

[1] In 1834, Sir R. Peel said one hundred and thirty only.—*Hans. Deb.*, 3rd Ser., xxvi. 293. It appears, however, from statistics of the old and new Parliaments, in 'Courts and Cabinets of Will. IV. and Queen Victoria,' that there were 149 Conservatives against 509 Reformers of all descriptions, ii. 26.

To conquer with such a force alone was out of the question.

The two first years after the Reform Act formed the most glorious period in the annals of the Whig party. Their principles had prevailed; they were once more paramount in the councils of the state; and they used their newly-acquired power in forwarding the noblest legislative measures which had ever done honour to the British Parliament. Slavery was abolished; the commerce of the East thrown open: the church in Ireland reformed: the social peril of the poor-laws averted.

*Ascendency of the Whigs after the Reform Act.*

But already, in the midst of their successes, their influence and popularity were subsiding; and new embarrassments were arising out of the altered relations of parties. While they were still fighting the battle of reform, all sections of reformers united to support them. Their differences were sunk in that great contest. But when the first enthusiasm of victory was over, they displayed themselves in stronger relief than ever. The alliance of the Whigs with democracy could not be permanent; and, for the first time, democracy was now represented in Parliament. The radical reformers, or Radicals, long known as an active party in the country, had at length gained a footing in the House of Commons, where they had about fifty representatives.[1] Without organisation or unity of purpose, and with little confidence in one another, they were often found in combination against the

*State of parties after the Reform Act.*

---

[1] Edinb. Rev., July 1837, p. 270; Bulwer's England and the English, ii. 261; Guizot's Life of Peel, 67.

government. And in addition to this body, the great towns recently enfranchised, and places suddenly released from the thraldom of patrons and close corporations, had returned a new class of reformers, having little sympathy with the old Whigs. These men had sprung from a different source: they had no connection with the aristocracy, and no respect for the traditions of the constitutional Whig party. Their political views were founded upon principles more democratic; and experience of the difficulties, restraints, and compromises of public affairs had not yet taught them moderation. They expected to gather, at once, all the fruits of an improved representation; and were intolerant of delay. They ignored the obstacles to practical legislation. The nonconformist element was strong amongst them; and they were eager for the immediate redress of every grievance which dissenters had suffered from the polity of a dominant church. On the other hand, Earl Grey and his older aristocratic associates recoiled from any contact with democracy. The great object of their lives had been accomplished. They had perfected the constitution, according to their own conceptions: they looked back with trembling, upon the perils through which it had recently passed; and dreaded the rough spirit of their restless allies, who,—without veneration for the past, or misgivings as to the future,—were already clamouring for further changes in church and state. His younger and more hopeful colleagues had faith in the vital energies of the constitution, and in its power of self-adaptation to every political and social change. They were prepared to take the lead, as statesmen, in furthering a comprehensive policy, in harmony with the spirit of the times: but they desired to consummate it on safe principles, with a prudent regard to public opinion, the means at their disposal, and the opposition to be overcome.[1] Such has ever been the policy of wise statesmen, in our balanced constitution. None but despots or democrats expect instant submission to their will. Liberty not only tolerates, but respects the independent judgment of all free citizens.

The social pretensions of these two sections of the Liberal party were not less distinct than their political sentiments. The Whigs formed an aristocracy of great families, exclusive in their habits and associations, and representing the tastes of the old *régime*. The new men, speaking the dialect of Lancashire and the West Riding,—with the rough manners of the mill and the counting-house,—and wearing the unfashionable garb of the provinces,—were no congenial associates for the high-bred politicians, who sought their votes, but not their company. These men, and their families,—even less presentable

---

[1] The policy of the Whigs, as distinguished from the impatient tactics of the Radicals, was well expressed by Lord Durham, an advanced member of their party, in a letter to the electors of North Durham, in 1837. He announced his determination never to force his measures ' peremptorily and dogmatically on the consideration of the government or the Parliament. If they are (as in my conscience I believe them to be) useful and salutary measures,—for they are based on the most implicit confidence in the loyalty and good feeling of the people,—the course of events and the experience of every day will remove the objections and prejudices which may now exist, and ensure their adoption whenever they are recommended by the deliberate and determined voice of the people.'—*Edinb. Rev.*, July 1837, p. 282.

than themselves,—found no welcome to the gay saloons of the courtly Whigs: but were severed, by an impassable gulf, from the real rulers of the people, whose ambition they promoted, but could not hope to share. The Whigs held all the offices, and engrossed every distinction which public service and aristocratic connections confer. The Radicals, while supporting the government against the Tories, were in no better position than that of a despised opposition. A hearty union between men with sentiments, habits, and fortunes so diverse, was not to be expected; and jealousies and distrust were soon apparent in every debate, and disagreement in every division.[1]

A further element of discord among the ministerial ranks was found in the Irish party, under the leadership of Mr. O'Connell. They were reformers, indeed, and opposed to the persons and policy of the Tories: but no sooner did the government adopt coercive measures for the maintenance of peace in Ireland, than Mr. O'Connell denounced them as 'bloody and brutal;' and scourged the Whigs more fiercely than he had assailed the opponents of Catholic emancipation.[2]

*The Irish party.*

After the union, the members representing Ireland had generally ranged themselves on either side, according to their several political divisions. Some were returned by the influence of great Whig land-

[1] Ann. Reg., 1833, p. 32, 70, 111; Roebuck's Hist. of the Whig Ministry, ii. 407–409; Courts and Cabinets of Geo. IV. and Vict., ii. 45–47.
[2] Debate on the Address, Feb. 5th, 1833; Hans. Deb., 3rd Ser., xv. 148.

owners: but the large majority belonged to the Protestant and Orange connection, and supported successive Tory administrations. The priests and the Catholic Association wrested, for a time, from the Protestant landlords their accustomed domination, in some of the counties: but the disfranchisement of the 40s. freeholders in 1829 restored it. Soon, however, the Catholic relief act, followed by an enlarged representation, overthrew the Tory party in Ireland, and secured a majority for the Whigs and reformers.

But these men represented another country, and distinct interests, sympathies, and passions. They could not be reckoned upon, as members of the Liberal party. Upon several measures affecting Ireland, they were hotly opposed to government: on other questions they were in close alliance with the Radicals. In the struggles of the English parties, they sometimes voted with the reformers; were often absent from divisions, or forthcoming only in answer to pressing solicitations: on some occasions, they even voted with the Tories. The attitude and tactics of this party were fraught with embarrassment to Earl Grey, and succeeding ministers; and when parties became more evenly balanced, were a serious obstacle to parliamentary government. When they opposed ministers, their hostility was often dangerous: when they were appeased and satisfied, ministers were accused of truckling to Mr. O'Connell.

While the Liberal party were thus divided, their opponents were united and full of hope. A few old Tories still distrusted their leaders:

*Revival of the Tory party.*

but the promise of future triumphs to their party, hatred of the Whigs, and fear of the Radicals, went far to efface the memory of their wrongs. However small the numbers of the Tory party in the House of Commons, they were rapidly recovering their local influence, which the reform crisis had overcome. Their nomination boroughs, indeed, were lost: the close and corrupt organisation by which they had formerly maintained their supremacy was broken up: but the great confederation of rank, property, influence, and numbers was in full vigour. The land, the church, the law, were still the strongholds of the party: but having lost the means of controlling the representation, they were forced to appeal to the people for support. They readily responded to the spirit of the times. It was now too late to rely upon the distinctive principles of their party, which had been renounced by themselves, or repudiated by the people. It was a period of intelligence and progress; and they were prepared to contend with their rivals, in the race of improvement.

But to secure popular support, it was necessary to divest themselves of the discredited name of Tories. It was a name of reproach, as it had been 150 years before; and they renounced it. Henceforth they adroitly adopted the title of 'Conservatives;' and proclaimed their mission to be the maintenance of the constitution against the inroads of democracy. Accepting recent changes as the irrevocable will of Parliament and the country, they were prepared to rule in the spirit of a more popular

*They become Conservatives.*

constitution. They were ready to improve institutions, but not to destroy or reconstruct them.[1]

The position which they now assumed was well suited to the temper of the times. Assured of the support of the old Tory party, they gained new recruits through a dread of democracy, which the activity of the Radicals encouraged. At the same time, by yielding to the impulses of a progressive age, they conciliated earnest and ardent minds, which would have recoiled from the narrow principles of the old Tory school.

*Breaking up of Earl Grey's ministry.* Meanwhile the difficulties of the Whigs were increasing. In May, 1834, the cabinet was nearly broken up by the retirement of Mr. Stanley, Sir J. Graham, the Duke of Richmond, and the Earl of Ripon, on the question of dealing with the revenues of the Church in Ireland. The causes of this disunion favoured the approach of the seceding members of the cabinet to the Conservative party. Mr. Stanley and Sir J. Graham retired to the benches below the gangway; and though accompanied by a very small body of adherents, their eminent talents and character promised much future advantage to the Conservative party.[2] In July the government was dissolved by the resig-

---

[1] In his Address to the Electors of Tamworth, Sir Robert Peel stated that he 'considered the Reform Bill a final and irrevocable settlement of a great constitutional question,—a settlement which no friend to the peace and welfare of this country would attempt to disturb, either by direct or by insidious means.'—*Ann. Reg.*, 1834, p. 341; Guizot's Life of Peel, 60-66. See also Sir R. Peel's published speech at Merchant Taylors' Hall, May 11th, 1835.

[2] Torrens' Life of Sir James Graham, i. 486-504.

nation of Earl Grey; and the Reform ministry was no more.

Lord Melbourne's ministry, still further estranged from the Radicals, were losing ground and public confidence, when they were suddenly dismissed by William IV.[1] This precipitate and ill-advised measure reunited the various sections of the liberal party into an overwhelming opposition. Sir Robert Peel vainly endeavoured to disarm them, and to propitiate the good will of the people, by promising ample measures of reform.[2] He went so far in this direction, that the old school of Tories began to foresee alarming consequences from his policy:[3] but his opponents recognised the old Tory party in disguise,— the same persons, the same instincts, and the same traditions. They would not suffer the fruits of their recent victory to be wrested from them by the king, and by the men who had resisted, to the utmost, the extension of parliamentary representation. His ministry was even distrusted by Lord Stanley[4] and Sir James Graham,

*Sir Robert Peel's short ministry, 1834-35.*

[1] *Supra*, Vol. I. 146.
[2] In his Address to the Electors of Tamworth, he said that he was prepared to adopt the spirit of the Reform Act by a 'careful review of institutions, civil and ecclesiastical, undertaken in a friendly temper, combining with the firm maintenance of established rights, the correction of proved abuses and the redress of real grievances.' He also promised a fair consideration to municipal reform, the question of church rates, and other measures affecting the Church and Dissenters.—*Ann. Reg.*, 1834, p. 339.
[3] Lord Eldon wrote, in March, 1835, the new ministers, 'if they do not at present go to the full length to which the others were going, will at least make so many important changes in Church and State that nobody can guess how far the precedents they establish may lead to changes of a very formidable kind hereafter.'—*Twiss's Life of Lord Eldon*, iii. 244.
[4] By the death of his grandfather in Oct., 1834, he had become Lord Stanley.

who, though separated from the reformers, were not yet prepared to unite their fortunes with the untried Conservatives.[1]

<small>State of parties under Lord Melbourne.</small> Sir Robert Peel strengthened his minority by a dissolution:[2] but was speedily crushed by the united forces of the opposition; and Lord Melbourne was restored to power. His second administration was again exclusively Whig, with the single exception of Mr. Poulett Thomson, who, holding opinions somewhat more advanced, was supposed to represent the Radical party in the cabinet. The Whigs and Radicals were as far asunder as ever: but their differences were veiled under the comprehensive title of the 'Liberal Party,' which served at once to contrast them with the Conservatives, and to unite under one standard, the forces of Lord Melbourne, the English Radicals, and the Irish followers of Mr. O'Connell.

During the next six years, the two latter sections of the party continued to urge organic changes, which were resisted alike by Whigs and Conservatives. Meanwhile, Chartism in England, and the repeal agitation in Ireland, increased that instinctive

---

[1] Hans. Deb., 3rd Ser., xxvi. 387–398; Torrens' Life of Sir J. Graham, ii. 17–36.

[2] Before the dissolution, his followers in the House of Commons numbered less than 150; in the new Parliament, they exceeded 250; and the support he received from others, who desired to give him a fair trial, swelled this minority to very formidable dimensions. On the election of Speaker, he was beaten by ten votes only; on the Address, by seven; and on the decisive division, upon the appropriation of the surplus revenues of the Irish Church, by thirty-three.—*Hans. Deb.*, 3rd Ser., xxvi. 224, 425, &c.; *Ibid.*, xxvii. 770; Courts and Cab. of Will. IV. and Vict., ii. 161; Guizot's Life of Peel, 72; Peel's Speech at Merchant Taylors' Hall, 12th May, 1838.—*Times*, 14th May, 1838.

dread of democracy which, for the last fifty years, had strengthened the hands of the Tory party. Ministers laboured earnestly to reform political and social abuses. They strengthened the Church, both in England and Ireland, by the commutation of tithes: they conciliated the Dissenters by a liberal settlement of their claims to religious liberty: they established municipal self-government throughout the United Kingdom. But, placed between the Radicals on one side, and the Conservatives on the other, their position was one of continual embarrassment.[1] When they inclined towards the Radicals, they were accused of favouring democracy: when they resisted assaults upon the House of Lords, the Bishops, the Church, and the Constitution, they were denounced by their own extreme followers, as Tories. Nay, so much was their resistance to further constitutional changes resented, that sometimes Radicals were found joining the opposition forces in a division;[2] and the Conservative candidates were preferred to Whigs, by Radical and Chartist electors. The liberal measures of the government were accepted without grace, or fair acknowledgment; and when they fell short of the extreme Radical standard, were reviled as worthless.[3] It was their useful but thankless office to act as mediators between extreme opinions and parties, which would otherwise have

---

[1] The relative numbers of the different parties, in 1837, have been thus computed:—Whigs, 152; Liberals, 100; Radicals, 80 = 332. Tories, 139; Ultra-Tories, 100; Conservatives, 80 = 319.—*Courts and Cabinets of Will. IV. and Vict.*, ii. 253.

[2] Edinb. Rev., April, 1840, p. 283.

[3] *Ibid.*, p. 284.

been brought into perilous conflict.[1] But however important to the interests of the state, it sacrificed the popularity and influence of the party.

*Conservative reaction.* Meanwhile the Conservatives, throughout the country, were busy in reconstructing their party. Their organisation was excellent: their agents were zealous and active; and the registration courts attested their growing numbers and confidence.[2]

There were diversities of opinion among different sections of this party,—scarcely less marked than those which characterised the ministerial ranks,—but they were lost sight of, for a time, in the activity of a combined opposition to the government. There were ultra-Tories, ultra-Protestants, and Orangemen, who had not forgiven the leaders by whom they had been betrayed in 1829. There were unyielding politicians who remembered, with distrust, the liberal policy of Sir Robert Peel in 1835, and disapproved the tolerant spirit in which he had since met the Whig measures affecting the Established Church and Dissenters.[3] The leaders were appealing to the judgment and sentiments of the people, while many of their adherents were still true to the ancient traditions of their party.

But these diversities, so far from weakening the Conservatives while in opposition, served to increase

[1] Bulwer says: 'They clumsily attempted what Machiavel has termed the finest masterpiece in political science,—"to content the people and manage the nobles."'—*England and the English*, ii. 271. But, in truth, their principles and their position alike dictated a middle course.
[2] Sir Robert Peel's advice to his party was, 'Register, register register.'—*Speech at Tamworth*, August 7, 1837.
[3] Edinb. Rev., April, 1840, p. 288; Ann. Reg., 1860, p. 64, 71.

their strength, by favouring the interests, prejudices, and hopes of various classes. Men who would have repealed the Catholic Relief Act, and withheld the grant for Maynooth; who deemed the Church in danger from the aggressions of Dissenters; who regarded protection to native industry as the cardinal maxim of political economy; who saw in progress nothing but democracy,—were united with men who believed that the safety of the Church was compatible with the widest toleration of Catholics and Dissenters,—that liberty would ward off democracy, —and that native industry would flourish under free trade. All these men, having a common enemy, were, as yet, united: but their divergences of opinion were soon to be made manifest.[1]

Before the dissolution of 1841, they had become more than a match for the ministry; and Sir Robert Peel having gained a considerable majority at the elections, they were again restored to power, under the masterly leadership of Sir Robert Peel. Such were the disrepute and unpopularity into which the Whigs had fallen, that Sir Robert Peel commenced his labours with prospects more hopeful than those of any minister since Mr. Pitt. He was now joined by Lord Stanley, Sir James Graham, and the Earl of Ripon,—seceders from the reform ministry of Earl Grey. He combined in his cabinet men who retained the confidence of the old Tory school, and men who gave promise of a policy

*Sir Robert Peel's second ministry, 1841.*

---

[1] A reviewer treating in April, 1840, of Sir Robert Peel and his party, said: 'His ostracism may be distant, but to us it appears to be certain.'—*Edinb. Rev.*, April, 1840, p. 313.

as liberal and progressive as the Whigs had ever professed. He was himself prepared for measures of wisdom, and the highest statesmanship: but such was the constitution of his party, and such the state of the country, that his policy was soon destined to destroy his own power, and annihilate his party.

During the late elections, a fixed duty on corn had been advocated by the Whigs, and free-trade, on a more extended scale, by the Anti-corn-law League, and many liberal supporters of Lord Melbourne's government. The Conservatives, as a body, had denounced the impolicy of these measures, and claimed protection for native industry.[1] Their main strength was derived from the agricultural classes, who regarded any relaxation of the protective system as fatal to their interests. The Conservatives had taken issue with the Liberal party, on the policy of protection, and had triumphed. But the necessities of the country, and more advanced political science, were demanding increased supplies of food, and an enlarged field for commerce and the employment of labour. These were wants which no class or party, however powerful, could long withstand; and Sir Robert Peel, with the foresight of a statesman, perceived that by

*His free-trade policy.*

---

[1] 'Sir Robert Peel solicited and obtained the confidence of the country in the general election of 1841, as against the whole free-trade policy embodied in the Whig budget of that year.' . . . 'This budget, so scorned, so vilified, that it became the death-warrant of its authors, was destined, as it turned out, to be not the trophy, but the equipment of its conquerors,—as the Indian, after a victory, dresses himself in the bloody scalp of his adversary.'— *Quarterly Rev.*, Sept. 1846, p. 564.

gradually adopting the principles of commercial freedom, he could retrieve the finances, and develope the wealth and industry of his country. Such a policy being repugnant to the feelings and supposed interests of his party, and not yet fully accepted by public opinion,—he was obliged to initiate it with caution. The dangers of his path were shown by the resignation of the Duke of Buckingham,—the representative of the agricultural interest,—before the new policy had been announced. In 1842, the minister maintained the sliding scale of duties upon corn: but relaxed its prohibitory operation. His bold revision of the customs' tariff, in the same year, and the passing of the Canada Corn Bill in 1843, showed how little his views were in harmony with the sentiments of his party. They already distrusted his fidelity to protectionist principles; while they viewed with alarm the rapid progress of the Anti-corn-law League and the successful agitation for the repeal of the corn laws, to which he offered a dubious resistance.[1] In 1845, the policy of free trade was again advanced by a further revision of the tariff. The suspicions of the protectionists were then expressed more loudly. Mr. Disraeli declared protection to be in 'the same condition that Protestantism was in 1828;' and expressed his belief 'that a Conservative government was an organised hypocrisy.'[2]

[1] Lord Palmerston's speech, Aug. 10th, 1842; Hans. Deb., 3rd Ser., lxv. 1230; Lord Stanhope; *Ibid.*, lxx. 578; Guizot's Life of Peel, 107, 125, 226.
[2] Hans. Deb., 3rd Ser., lxxviii. 1028; Disraeli's Lord G. Bentinck, 7; Guizot's Life of Peel, 235–240.

The bad harvest of this year, and the failure of the potato crop, precipitated a crisis which the Anti-corn-law League and public opinion must ere long have brought about; and, in December, Sir Robert Peel proposed to his colleagues the immediate repeal of the corn laws. It was not to be expected that a ministry, representing the landed interest, should at once adopt a policy repugnant to their pledges and party faith. They dissented from the advice of their leader, and he resigned.[1] Lord John Russell, who had recently declared himself a convert to the repeal of the corn laws,[2] was commissioned by Her Majesty to form a government: but failed in the attempt; when Sir Robert Peel, supported by all his colleagues except Lord Stanley,[3] resumed office; and ventured, in the face of a protectionist Parliament, wholly to abandon the policy of protection.[4]

*Repeal of the Corn Laws.*

As a statesman, Sir Robert Peel was entitled to the gratitude of his country. No other man could then have passed this vital measure, for which he sacrificed the confidence of followers, and the attachment of friends. But as the leader of a party, he was unfaithful and disloyal. The events of 1829 were repeated in 1846.

*Sir Robert Peel's relations with his party.*

---

[1] Hans. Deb., 3rd Ser., lxxxiii. 39; Peel's Mem., ii. 182–226; Disraeli's Lord G. Bentinck, 21–31.
[2] Letter to the Electors of London, Nov. 22nd, 1845: Peel's Mem., ii. 175.
[3] Peel's Mem., ii. 226–251; Disraeli's Lord G. Bentinck, 30. Lord Wharncliffe died the day before Sir R. Peel's return to office. Ann. Reg., 1845, Chron. 320.
[4] Peel's Mem., ii. 259; Disraeli's Lord G. Bentinck, 49–57; 108, 204–207; Torrens' Life of Sir J. Graham, ii. 422–427.

The parallel between 'Protestantism' and 'protection' was complete. A second time he yielded to political necessity, and a sense of paramount duty to the state; and found himself committed to a measure, which he had gained the confidence of his party by opposing. Again was he constrained to rely upon political opponents to support him against his own friends.[1] He passed this last measure of his political life, amid the reproaches and execrations of his party. He had assigned the credit of the Catholic Relief Act to Mr. Canning, whom he had constantly opposed; and he acknowledged that the credit of this measure was due to 'the unadorned eloquence of Richard Cobden,'—the apostle of free trade,—whom he had hitherto resisted.[2] As he had braved the hostility of his friends for the public good, the people applauded his courage and self-sacrifice,—felt for him as he writhed under the scourging of his merciless foes,—and pitied him when he fell, buried under the ruins of the great political fabric which his own genius had reconstructed, and his own hands had twice destroyed.[3] But every one was sensible that so long as party ties and obligations should continue to form an essential part of parliamentary government, the first statesman of his age had forfeited all future claim to govern.[4]

[1] See his own memorandum on the position of ministers, June 21st, 1846; Mem., ii. 288; Disraeli's Lord G. Bentinck, 119, &c.
[2] Hans. Deb., 3rd Ser., lxxxvii. 1054; Disraeli's Lord G. Bentinck, 307-310.
[3] Guizot's Life of Peel, 270, 289-298, 368; Disraeli's Lord G. Bentinck, 259, 262, 288.
[4] On quitting office he said: 'In relinquishing power I shall leave a name, severely censured, I fear, by many who, on public

The fallen minister, accompanied by a few faithful friends,—the first and foremost men of his party,—were separated for ever from the main body of the Conservatives.

> 'They stood aloof, the scars remaining,
> Like cliffs which had been rent asunder;
> A dreary sea now flows between;—
> But neither heat, nor frost, nor thunder,
> Shall wholly do away, I ween,
> The marks of that which once hath been.

Men of all parties, whether approving or condemning the measures of 1829 and 1846, agreed that Sir Robert Peel's conduct could not be justified upon any of the conventional principles of party ethics. The relations between a leader and his followers are those of mutual confidence. His talents give them union and force: their numbers invest him with political power. They tender, and he accepts the trust, because he shares and represents their sentiments. Viewing affairs from higher ground, he may persuade them to modify or renounce their opinions, in the interests of the state: but, without their concurrence, he has no right to use for one purpose, that power which they have entrusted to him for another. He has re-

*Obligations of a party leader.*

grounds, deeply regret the severance of party ties,—deeply regret that severance, not from interested or personal motives, but from the firm conviction that fidelity to party engagements, the existence and maintenance of a great party, constitutes a powerful instrument of government.'—*Hans. Deb.*, 3rd Ser., lxxxvii. 1054.

So complete was the alienation of the Tory party from Sir R. Peel that even the Duke of Wellington, who co-operated with him in the repeal of the corn laws, concurred with Lord Derby in opinion, that it was impossible that he should ever place himself at the head of his party again, with any prospect of success.—*Speech of Lord Derby at Liverpool*, Oct. 29th, 1859.

ceived a limited authority, which he may not exceed without further instructions. If, contrary to the judgment of his party, he believes the public welfare to demand an entire change of policy, it is not for him to carry it out. He cannot, indeed, be called upon to conceal or disavow his own opinions: but he is no longer entitled to lead the forces entrusted to his command,—still less to seek the aid of the enemy. Elected chief of a free republic,— not its dictator,—it becomes his duty, honourably and in good faith, to retire from his position, with as little injury as may be to the cause he abandons, and to leave to others a task which his own party allegiance forbids him to attempt.[1]

This disruption of the Conservative party exercised an important influence upon the political history of the succeeding period. The Whigs were restored to power under Lord John Russell,—not by reason of any increase of their own strength, but by the disunion of their opponents. The Conservatives, suddenly deprived of their leaders, and committed to the hopeless cause of protection, were, for the present, powerless. They were now led by Lord Stanley, one of the greatest orators of his time, who had been the first to separate from Earl Grey, and the first to renounce Sir Robert Peel. In the Commons, their cause was maintained by the chivalrous devotion of Lord George Bentinck, and the powerful, versatile, and caustic eloquence of Mr. Disraeli,—the two fore-

*The Conservatives after the fall of Sir R. Peel.*

---

[1] See his own justification, Mem., ii. 163, 229, 311–325; Disraeli's Lord George Bentinck, 31–33, 390, &c.

most opponents of the late minister. But they were, as yet, without spirit or organisation, disturbed in their faith,—and repining over the past, rather than hopeful of the future.[1]

<small>The Whigs in office under Lord J. Russell, 1846–1852.</small> Meanwhile the Whigs, under Lord John Russell, were ill at ease with their more advanced supporters, as they had been under Lord Melbourne. They had nearly worked out the political reforms comprised in the scheme of an aristocratic party; and Sir Robert Peel had left them small scope for further experiments in fiscal legislation. They resisted, for a time, all projects of change in the representation: but were at length driven, by the necessities of their position, to promise a further extension of the franchise.[2] With parties so disunited, a strong government was impossible: but Lord J. Russell's administration, living upon the distractions of the Conservatives, lasted for six years. In 1852, it fell at the first touch of Lord Palmerston, who had been recently separated from his colleagues.[3]

<small>Lord Derby's ministry, 1852.</small> Power was again within the reach of the Conservatives, and they grasped it. The Earl of Derby[4] was a leader worthy to inspire them with confidence: but he had the aid of few experienced statesmen. Free trade was flourishing; and the revival of a protective policy utterly out of the question. Yet protection was still the distinctive principle of the great body of his party. He could

---

[1] Disraeli's Lord G. Bentinck, 79, 173, &c.
[2] *Supra*, Vol. I. 450.   [3] *Supra*, Vol. I. 160.
[4] Lord Stanley had succeeded his father in the earldom, in 1851.

not abandon it, without unfaithfulness to his friends: he could not maintain it, without the certain destruction of his government. A party cannot live upon memories of the past: it needs a present policy and purpose: it must adapt itself to the existing views and needs of society. But the Conservatives clung to the theories of a past generation, which experience had already overthrown; and had adopted no new principles to satisfy the sentiment of their own time. In the interests of his party, Lord Derby would have done well to decline the hopeless enterprise which had fallen to his lot. The time was not yet ripe for the Conservatives. Divided, disorganised, and unprepared,—without a popular cry and without a policy,—their failure was inevitable. In vain did they advocate protection in counties, and free trade in towns. In vain did many 'Liberal Conservatives' outbid their Whig opponents in popular professions: in vain did others avoid perilous pledges, by declaring themselves followers of Lord Derby, wherever he might lead them. They were defeated at the elections: they were constrained to renounce the policy of protection:[1] they could do little to gratify their own friends; and they had again united all sections of their opponents.

And now the results of the schism of 1846 were apparent. The disciples of Sir Robert Peel's school had hitherto kept aloof from both parties. Having lost their eminent leader, they were free to form new connections.

*Junction of Whigs and Peelites under Lord Aberdeen.*

[1] Hans. Deb., 3rd Ser., cxxii. 637, 693; cxxiii. 54, 406.

Distinguished for their talents and political experience, their influence was considerable,—notwithstanding the smallness of their following. Their ambition had been unchecked and unsatisfied. Their isolation had continued for six years: an impassable gulf separated them from the Conservatives; and their past career and present sympathies naturally attracted them towards the Liberal party. Accordingly, a coalition ministry was formed, under Lord Aberdeen, comprising the Peelites,—as they were now called,—the Whigs, and Sir William Molesworth,—a representative of the philosophical school of Radicals. It united men who had laboured with Mr. Canning, Sir Robert Peel, Earl Grey, and Mr. Hume. The Liberal party had gained over nearly all the statesmanship of the Conservative ranks, without losing any of its own. Five and twenty years before, the foremost men among the Tories had joined Earl Grey; and now again, the first minds of another generation were won over, from the same party, to the popular side. A fusion of parties had become the law of our political system. The great principles of legislation, which had divided parties, had now been settled. Public opinion had accepted and ratified them; and the disruption of party ties which their adoption had occasioned, brought into close connection the persons as well as the principles of various schools of politicians.

No administration, in modern times, had been *Disunion and fall of this ministry.* stronger in talent, in statesmanship, and in parliamentary support, than that of Lord Aberdeen. But the union of parties, which gave the cabinet outward force, was not calculated to secure harmony and mutual confidence among its members. The Peelites engrossed a preponderance, in the number and weight of their offices, out of proportion to their following, which was not borne without jealousy by the Whigs. Unity of sentiment and purpose was wanting to the material strength of the coalition; and in little more than two years, discord, and the disastrous incidents of the Crimean war, dissolved it.

Lord Aberdeen, the Duke of Newcastle, and Lord J. Russell retired; and Lord Palmerston was entrusted with the reconstruction of the ministry. It was scarcely formed, when Sir James Graham, Mr. Gladstone, and Mr. Sidney Herbert, followed their Peelite colleagues into retirement. The union of these statesmen with the Liberal party,—so recently effected—was thus completely dissolved. The government was again reduced to the narrower basis of the Whig connection. Lord John Russell, who had rejoined it on the retirement of Mr. Sidney Herbert from the Colonial Office, resigned after the conferences at Vienna, and assumed an attitude of opposition.[1] The Radicals,—and especially the peace party,—pursued the ministry with determined hostility and resentment. The Peelites were estranged, critical, and unfriendly. *Separation of Peelites from Lord Palmerston.*

The ministerial party were again separated into their discordant elements, while the opposition were watching for an occasion to make common cause with any section of *Combination of parties against the minister.*

[1] Ann. Reg., 1855, p. 152, *et seq.*

the Liberals, against the government. But a successful military administration, and the conclusion of a peace with Russia, rendered Lord Palmerston's position too strong to be easily assailed. For two years he maintained his ground, from whatever quarter it was threatened. Early in 1857, however, on the breaking out of hostilities in China, he was defeated by a combination of parties.[1] He was opposed by Mr. Cobden and his friends, by Lord John Russell, by all the Peelites who had lately been his colleagues, and by the whole force of the Conservatives.[2] Coalition had recently formed a strong government; and combination now brought suddenly together a powerful opposition. It was not to be expected that Lord Palmerston would submit to a confederation of parties so casual and incongruous. He boldly appealed to the confidence of the country, and routed his opponents of every political section.[3]

In the new Parliament, Lord Palmerston was the minister of a national party. The people had given him their confidence; and men, differing widely from one another, concurred in trusting to his wisdom and moderation. He was the people's minister, as the first William

*Lord Palmerston's popularity and sudden fall.*

---

[1] Previous concert between the different parties was denied; and combination is, therefore, to be understood as a concurrence of opinion and of votes. Earl of Derby and Lord J. Russell; Hans. Deb., 3rd Ser., cxliv. 1910, 2322.

[2] The majority against government was 16; Hans. Deb., 3rd Ser., cxliv. 1846. Ann. Reg., 1857, ch. iii.

[3] Mr. Cobden, Mr. Bright, Mr. Milner Gibson, Mr. Layard, and Mr. Fox, among his Liberal supporters, and Mr. Cardwell and Mr. Roundell-Palmer among the Peelites, lost their seats.—*Ann. Reg.,* 1857, p. 84.

Pitt had been a hundred years before. But the parties whom he had discomfited at the elections,—smarting under defeat, and jealous of his ascendency,—were ready to thrust at any weak place in his armour. In 1858, our relations with France, after the Orsini conspiracy,—infelicitously involved with a measure of municipal legislation,—suddenly placed him at a disadvantage; when all the parties who had combined against him in the last Parliament, again united their forces and overpowered him.[1]

These parties had agreed in a single vote against the minister; but their union in the government of the country was inconceivable. The Conservatives, therefore, as the strongest party, were restored to power, under the Earl of Derby. The events of the last few years had exemplified the fusion of parties in the government, and their combination, on particular occasions, in opposition. The relations of all parties were disturbed and unsettled. It was now to be seen that their principles were no less undetermined. The broad distinctions between them had been almost effaced; and all alike deferred to public opinion, rather than to any distinctive policy of their own. The Conservatives were in a minority of not less than one hundred, as compared with all sections of the Liberal party;[2] and their only hopes were in the divided councils of the opposition, and in a policy which should satisfy public expectations. Accordingly,

*Lord Derby's second ministry, 1858.*

---

[1] The majority against him was 19—Ayes, 215; Noes, 234.—Ann. Reg., 1858, ch. ii.; Hans. Deb., 3rd Ser., cxlviii. 1844.
[2] Quarterly Rev., civ. 517.

though it had hitherto been their characteristic principle to resist constitutional changes, they accepted Parliamentary Reform as a political necessity; and otherwise endeavoured to conform to public opinion. For the first session, they were maintained solely by the disunion of their opponents. Their India Bill threatened them with ruin; but they were rescued by a dexterous manœuvre of Lord John Russell.[1] Their despatch disapproving Lord Canning's Oude proclamation imperilled their position: but they were saved by the resignation of Lord Ellenborough, and by a powerful diversion in their favour, concerted by Mr. Bright, Sir James Graham, and other members of the opposition.[2] It was clear that, however great their intrinsic weakness, they were safe until their opponents had composed their differences. Early in the following session, this reconciliation was accomplished; and all sections of the Liberal party concurred in a resolution fatal to the ministerial Reform Bill.[3]

Ministers appealed in vain to the country. Their own distinctive principles were so far lost, that they were unable to rely upon reactionary sentiments against constitutional change; and having committed themselves to popular measures, they were yet outbidden by their

*Lord Palmerston's second ministry, 1859.*

---

[1] Ann. Reg., 1858, ch. iii.; Hans. Deb., 3rd Ser., cxlix. 858.
[2] Ann. Reg. 1858, ch. iv.; Hans. Deb., 3rd Ser., cl. 944, 985.
[3] *Supra*, Vol. I., 455. It was moved by Lord J. Russell, and supported by Lord Palmerston, Mr. Bright, Mr. Cobden, Mr. Milner Gibson, Mr. Sidney Herbert, Sir James Graham, and Mr. Cardwell. —Hans. Deb., 3rd Ser., cliii. 405.

opponents. They fell;[1] and Lord Palmerston was restored to power, with a cabinet representing, once more, every section of the Liberal party.

The fusion of parties, and concurrence or compromise of principles, was continued. In 1859, the Conservatives gave in their adherence to the cause of Parliamentary reform; and in 1860, the Liberal administration which succeeded them, were constrained to abandon it.  {Fusion of parties.}  Thirty years of change in legislation, and in social progress, had brought the sentiments of all parties into closer approximation. Fundamental principles had been settled: grave defects in the laws and constitution had been corrected. The great battle-fields of party were now peaceful domains, held by all parties in common. To accommodate themselves to public opinion, Conservatives had become liberal: not to outstrip public opinion, ultra-Liberals were forced to maintain silence, or profess moderation.

Among the leaders of the Conservatives, and the leaders of the ministerial Liberals, there was little difference of policy and professions. But between their respective adherents, there were still essential diversities  {Essential difference between Conservatives and Liberals.}  of political sentiment. The greater number of Conservatives had viewed the progress of legislation,— which they could not resist,—as a hard necessity: they had accepted it grudgingly, and in an unfriendly spirit,—as defendants submitting to the adverse judgment of a court, whence there is no

[1] Hans. Deb., 3rd Ser., cliv. 416.

appeal. It had been repugnant to the principles and traditions of their party; and they had yielded to it without conviction. 'He that consents against his will, is of the same opinion still;' and the true Conservative, silenced but not convinced by the arguments of his opponents and the assent of his leaders, still believed that the world was going very wrong, and regretted the good old times, when it was less headstrong and perverse.

On the other hand, the Liberal party, which had espoused the cause of liberty and progress from the beginning, still maintained it with pride and satisfaction,—approving the past, and hopeful of the future,—leading public opinion, rather than following it, and representing the spirit and sentiment of the age. The sympathies of one party were still with power, and immutable prescription: the sympathies of the other were associated with popular self-government, and a progressive policy. The Conservatives were forced to concede as much liberty as would secure obedience and contentment: the Liberals, confiding in the people, favoured every liberty that was consistent with security and order.

At the same time, each party comprised within itself diversities of opinion, not less marked than those which distinguished it from the other. Various sections of each party. The old constitutional Whig was more nearly akin to the Liberal Conservative than to many of his democratic allies. Enlightened statesmen of the Conservative connection had more principles in common with the bold disciples of Sir

Robert Peel than with the halting rear-rank of their own Tory followers.

Such diversities of opinion, among men of the same parties, and such an approach to agreement between men of opposite parties, led attentive observers to speculate upon further combination and fusion hereafter. A free representation had brought together a Parliament reflecting the varied interests and sentiments of all classes of the people; and the ablest statesmen, who were prepared to give effect to the national will, would be accepted as members of the national party, by whom the people desired to be governed. Loving freedom and enlightened progress, but averse to democracy, the great body of the people had learned to regard the struggles of parties with comparative indifference. They desired to be well and worthily governed, by statesmen fit to accept their honourable service, rather than to assist at the triumph of one party over another.

Having traced the history of parties,—the principles by which they were distinguished,— their successes and defeats,—their coalitions and separations,—we must not overlook some material changes in their character and organisation. Of these the most important have arisen from an improved representative system, and the correction of the abuses of patronage. Changes in the character and organisation of parties.

When parliamentary majorities were secured by combinations of great families, acting in concert with the crown, and agreeing in the constitution of the government, the Former associations of great families.

organisation of parties was due rather to negotiations between high contracting powers, for the distribution of offices, honours, and pensions, than to considerations of policy, statesmanship, and popularity.[1] The crown and aristocracy governed the country; and their connections and nominees in the House of Commons were held to their party allegiance by a profuse dispensation of patronage. Men independent of constituents naturally looked up to the crown and the great nobles,—the source of all honour and profit. Long before the representation was reformed, the most flagrant abuses of parliamentary patronage had been corrected. Offices and pensions had been reduced, the expenditure of the civil list controlled, and political corruption in many forms abated.[2] But while a close representative system continued, parties were still compacted by family connections and interests, rather than by common principles and convictions. The Reform acts modified, but did not subvert, this organisation. The influence of great families, though less absolute, was still predominant. The constitution had been

[1] A spirited, but highly coloured, sketch of this condition of parties, appeared in Blackwood's Magazine, No. 350, p. 754. 'No game of whist in one of the lordly clubs of St. James's Square was more exclusively played. It was simply a question whether his grace of Bedford would be content with a quarter or a half of the cabinet; or whether the Marquess of Rockingham would be satisfied with two-fifths; or whether the Earl of Shelburne would have all, or share his power with the Duke of Portland. In those barterings and borrowings we never hear the name of the nation: no whisper announces that there is such a thing as the people; nor is there any allusion, in its embroidered conclave, to its interests, feelings, and necessities. All was done as in an assemblage of a higher race of beings, calmly carving out the world for themselves, a tribe of epicurean deities, with the cabinet for their Olympus.'

[2] See *supra*, Vol. I. 369 *et seq.*; also, Chap. IV.

invigorated by more popular elements: but society had not been shaken. Rank and ancestral property continued to hold at least their fair proportion of power, in a mixed government. But they were forced to wield that power upon popular principles, and in the interests of the public. They served the people in high places, instead of ruling them as irresponsible masters.

A reformed representation and more limited patronage have had an influence, not less marked, upon the organisation of parties, in another form. Politics then a profession. When great men ruled, in virtue of their parliamentary interest, they needed able men to labour for them in the field of politics. There were Parliaments to lead, rival statesmen to combat, foreign ministers to outwit, finances to economise, fleets and armies to equip, and the judgment of a free people to satisfy. But they who had the power and patronage of the crown in their hands, were often impotent in debate,—drivellers in council,—dunces in writing minutes and despatches. The country was too great and free to be governed wholly by such men; and some of their patronage was therefore spared from their own families and dependents, to encourage eloquence and statesmanship in others. They could bestow seats in Parliament without the costs of an election: they could endow their able but needy clients with offices, sinecures, and pensions; and could use their talents and ambition in all the arduous affairs of state. Politics became a dazzling profession,—a straight road to fame and fortune. It was the daydream of the first scholars of Oxford and Cambridge, Eton, Harrow, and Westminster. Men of genius and eloquence aspired to the most eminent positions in the government: men of administrative capacity, and useful talents for business, were gratified with lucrative but less conspicuous places in the various public departments. Such men were trained, from their youth upwards, to parliamentary and official aptitude; and were powerful agents in the consolidation of parties. Free from the intrusion of constituents, and the distractions and perils of contested elections, they devoted all their talents and energies to the service of their country, and the interests of their party. Lord Chatham, the brilliant ' cornet of horse,' owed the beginning of his great career to the mythical borough of Old Sarum. Mr. Burke was indebted to Lord Rockingham for a field worthy of his genius. William Pitt entered Parliament as the client of Sir James Lowther, and member for the insignificant borough of Appleby. His rival, Mr. Fox, found a path for his ambition, when little more than nineteen years of age,[1] through the facile suffrages of Midhurst. Mr. Canning owed his introduction to public life to Mr. Pitt, and the select constituency of Newport. These and other examples were adduced, again and again,—not only before but even since the Reform act,—in illustration of the virtues of rotten boroughs. Few men would now be found to contend that such boroughs ought to have been spared: but it must be admitted that the

---

[1] He was nineteen years and four months old, and spoke before he was of age.—*Lord J. Russell's Mem. of Fox*, i. 51.

attraction of so much talent to the public service, went far to redeem the vices of the old system of parliamentary government. Genius asserted its mastery; and the oligarchy of great families was constrained to share its power with the distinguished men whom its patronage had first brought forward. An aristocratic rule was graced and popularised by the talents of statesmen sprung from the people. Nay, such men were generally permitted to take the foremost places. The territorial nobles rarely aspired to the chief direction of affairs. The Marquess of Rockingham was by his character and principles, as well as by his eminent position, the acknowledged leader of the Whig party,[1] and twice accepted the office of premier: but the Dukes of Grafton and Portland, who filled the same office, were merely nominal ministers. The Earl of Shelburne was another head of a great house, who became first minister. With these exceptions, no chief of a great territorial family presided over the councils of the state, from the fall of the Duke of Newcastle in 1762, till the ministry of the Earl of Derby, in 1852.[2] Even in their own privileged chamber, eminent lawyers and other new men generally took the lead in debate, and constituted the intellectual strength of their order.

How different would have been the greatness and glory of English history if the nobles had failed to associate with themselves these *How far favourable to freedom.*

[1] Rockingham Mem., ii. 245; Lord J. Russell's Life of Fox, i. 319.
[2] Earl Grey was the acknowledged leader of the Whigs, irrespectively of his rank, which was scarcely that of a great territorial noble.

brilliant auxiliaries! Their union was a conspicuous homage to freedom. The public liberties were also advanced by the conflicts of great minds, and the liberal sympathies of genius.[1] But it must not be forgotten that the system which they embellished was itself opposed to freedom; and that the foremost men of the dominant party, during the reigns of the two last Georges, exercised all their talents in maintaining principles, which have since been condemned as incompatible with the rights and liberties of the people. Nor can it be doubted that without their aid, the aristocracy, whose cause they espoused, and whose ranks they recruited, would have been unable to hold out so long against the expanding intelligence, and advancing spirit of the times.

The prizes of public life were gradually diminished: pensions and sinecures were abolished: offices reduced in number and emolument; and at length, the greater part of the nomination boroughs were swept away. These privileged portals of the House of Commons were now closed against the younger son, the aspiring scholar, and the ambitious leader of a university

*Effects of suppression of rotten boroughs upon parties.*

---

[1] On the 29th March, 1859, Mr. Gladstone, in an eloquent speech upon Lord Derby's Reform Bill, asked, 'Is it not, under Providence, to be attributed to a succession of distinguished statesmen, introduced at an early age into this House, and, once made known in this House, securing to themselves the general favour of their countrymen, that we enjoy our present extension of popular liberty, and, above all, the durable form which that liberty has assumed?'— *Hans. Deb.*, 3rd Ser., cliii. 1059.

An able reviewer has lately said that 'historians will recognise the share which a privileged and endowed profession of politics had in the growth of English freedom and greatness, between the accession of the Hanoverian dynasty and the Reform Bill.'—*Edinb. Rev.*, April 1861, p. 368.

debating club. These candidates were now supplanted by men of riper age,—by men versed in other business, and disinclined to learn a new vocation,—by men who had already acquired fame or fortune elsewhere,—by men to whom Parliament was neither a school nor a profession, but a public trust.[1] Such men looked to their constituents, and to public opinion, rather than to leaders of parties, of whose favours they were generally independent. In parties composed of such materials as these, the same discipline and unity of purpose could not be maintained. Leaders sought to secure the adherence of their followers, by a policy which they and their constituents alike approved. They no longer led regular armies: but commanded bodies of volunteers. This change was felt less by the Conservatives than by the Liberal party. Their followers sat for few of the large towns. They mainly represented counties, and boroughs connected with the landed interest: they were homogeneous in character, and comprised less diversities of social position and pretensions. Their confederation, in short, resembled that of the old *régime*. These circumstances greatly aided their cause. They gained strength by repose and inaction: while their opponents were forced to bid high for the support of their disunited bands,

[1] It is by no means true that the general standard of instruction and accomplishment was superior under the system of nomination. Wraxall says: 'Mr. Pitt, who well knew how large a part of his audience, especially among the country gentlemen, were little conversant in the writings of the Augustan age, or familiar with Horace, always displayed great caution in borrowing from those classic sources.' . . . 'Barré usually condescended, whenever he quoted Latin, to translate for the benefit of the county members.'—*Hist. Mem.*, iii. 318.

by constant activity, and by frequent concessions to the demands of the extreme members of their party.

A moral cause also favoured the interests of the Conservatives. Conservatism is the normal state of most minds after fifty years of age,—resulting not so much from experience and philosophy, as from the natural temperament of age. The results of a life have then been attained. The rich and prosperous man thinks it a very good world that we live in, and fears lest any change should spoil it. The man who has struggled on with less success begins to weary of further efforts. Having done his best to very little purpose, he calmly leaves the world to take care of itself. And to men of this conservative age belongs the great bulk of the property of the country.

*Conservatism of age.*

Whatever the difficulties of directing parties so constituted, the new political conditions have, at least, contributed to improved government, and to a more vigilant regard to the public interests. It has been observed, however, that the leading statesmen who have administered affairs since the Reform act, had been trained under the old organisation; and that as yet the representatives of the new system have not given tokens of future eminence.[1] Yet there has been no lack of young men in the House of Commons. The Reform act left abundant opportunities to the territorial interest for promoting rising talent; and if they have not been turned to good account, the men,

*Statesmen under the old and new systems.*

---

[1] Mr. John Walsh's 'Practical Results of the Reform Act, 1832' (1860).

and not the constitution, have been at fault. Who is to blame, if young men have shown less of ambition and earnest purpose, than the youth of another generation: if those qualified by position and talents for public life, prefer ease and enjoyment, to the labours and sacrifices which a career of usefulness exacts? Let us hope that the resources of an enlightened society will yet call forth the dormant energies of rising orators and statesmen. Never has there been a fairer field for genius, ambition, and patriotism. Nor is Parliament the only school for statesmanship. Formerly, it reclaimed young men from the race-course, the prize-ring, and the cockpit. Beyond its walls there was little political knowledge and capacity. But a more general intellectual cultivation, greater freedom and amplitude of discussion, the expansion of society, and the wider organisation of a great community, have since trained thousands of minds in political knowledge and administrative ability; and already men, whose talents have been cultivated, and accomplishments acquired in other schools, have sprung at once to eminence in debate and administration. But should the public service be found to suffer from the want of ministers already trained in political life, leaders of parties and independent constituencies will learn to bring forward competent men to serve their country. Nor are such men wanting among classes independent in fortune, and needing neither the patronage of the great, nor any prize but that of a noble ambition.

It has been noticed elsewhere,[1] that while the

[1] Vol. I. 164.

number of places held by members of Parliament was being continually reduced, the general patronage of the government had been extended by augmented establishments and expenditure. But throughout these changes, patronage was the mainspring of the organisation of parties. It was used to promote the interests, and consolidate the strength of that party in which its distribution happened to be vested. The higher appointments offered attractions and rewards to the upper classes, for their political support. The lower appointments were not less influential with constituencies. The offer of places, as a corrupt inducement to vote at elections, had long been recognised by the legislature, as an insidious form of bribery.[1] But without committing any offence against the law, patronage continued to be systematically used as the means of rewarding past political service, and ensuring future support. The greater part of all local patronage was dispensed through the hands of members of Parliament, supporting the ministers of the day. They claimed and received it as their right; and distributed it, avowedly, to strengthen their political connection. Constituents learned too well to estimate the privileges of ministerial candidates, and the barren honours of the opposition; and the longer a party enjoyed power, the more extended became its influence with electors.

*Patronage an instrument of party.*

The same cause served to perpetuate party distinctions among constituent bodies, apart from varieties of

---

[1] 2 Geo. II. c. 24; 49 Geo. III. c. 118, &c.; Rogers on Elections, 316–347.

## The Evils and Merits of Parties. 235

interests and principles. The ministerial party were bound together by favours received and expected: the party in opposition,—smarting under neglect and hope deferred,—combined against their envied rivals, and followed, with all the ardour of self-interest, the parliamentary leaders, who were denied at once the objects of their own ambition and the power of befriending their clients. Hence, when the principles of contending parties have seemed to be approaching agreement, their interests have kept them nearly as far asunder as ever.

The principle of competition, lately applied to the distribution of offices, threatened to subvert the established influence of patronage. With open competition, candidates owe nothing to ministers. In this way, the civil and medical services of India, the scientific corps of the army, and some civil departments of the state, were wholly lost to ministers of the crown. This loss, however, was compensated for a time by the limited competition introduced into other departments. There, for every vacancy, a minister nominated three or more candidates. The best was chosen; and, with the same number of offices, the patronage of the minister was multiplied. Two of his nominees were disappointed: but the patron was not the less entitled to their gratitude. He lamented their failure, but could not avert it. Their lack of proficiency was no fault of his.[1]

*Effect of competition upon patronage.*

In the history of parties, there is much to deplore

[1] In 1870 open competition was extended to nearly all the other public departments.

and condemn : but more to approve and to commend. We observe the evil passions of our nature aroused,—'envy, hatred, malice, and all uncharitableness.' We see the foremost of our fellow-countrymen contending with the bitterness of foreign enemies, — reviling each other with cruel words,—misjudging the conduct of eminent statesmen, and pursuing them with vindictive animosity. We see the whole nation stirred with sentiments of anger and hostility. We find factious violence overcoming patriotism; and ambition and self-interest prevailing over the highest obligations to the state. We reflect that party rule excludes one half of our statesmen from the service of their country, and condemns them,—however wise and capable,—to comparative obscurity and neglect. We grieve that the first minds of every age should have been occupied in collision and angry conflict, instead of labouring together for the common weal.

*Review of the evils and merits of party.*

But, on the other side, we find that government without party is absolutism,—that rulers, without opposition, may be despots. We acknowledge, with gratitude, that we owe to party most of our rights and liberties. We recognise in the fierce contentions of our ancestors, the conflict of great principles, and the final triumph of freedom. We glory in the eloquence and noble sentiments which the rivalry of contending statesmen has inspired. We admire the courage with which power has been resisted; and the manly resolution and persistence by which popular rights have been established. We observe that, while the undue influence of the crown has been restrained, democracy has been also held in check. We exult in the final success of men who have suffered in a good cause. We admire the generous friendships, fidelity, and self-sacrifice,—akin to loyalty and patriotism,—which the honourable sentiments of party have called forth.[1] We perceive that an opposition may often serve the country far better than a ministry; and that where its principles are right, they will prevail. By argument and discussion truth is discovered, public opinion is expressed, and a free people are trained to self-government. We feel that party is essential to representative institutions. Every interest, principle, opinion, theory, and sentiment, finds expression. The majority governs: but the minority is never without sympathy, representation, and hope. Such being the two opposite aspects of party, who can doubt that good predominates over evil? Who can fail to recognise in party, the very life-blood of freedom?

[1] 'The best patriots in the greatest commonwealths have always commended and promoted such connections. *Idem sentire de republicâ* was with them a principal ground of friendship and attachment: nor do I know any other capable of forming firmer, dearer, more pleasing, more honourable, and more virtuous habitudes.'—*Burke's Present Discontents, Works*, ii. 332.

## CHAPTER IX.

FREEDOM OF OPINION THE GREATEST OF LIBERTIES, AND LAST ACQUIRED:—THE PRESS UNDER THE CENSORSHIP, AND AFTERWARDS:—ITS CONTESTS WITH GOVERNMENT EARLY IN THE REIGN OF GEORGE III.:—WILKES AND JUNIUS:—RIGHTS OF JURIES:—MR. FOX'S LIBEL ACT:—PUBLIC MEETINGS, ASSOCIATIONS, AND POLITICAL AGITATION:—PROGRESS OF FREE DISCUSSION, 1760–1792:—REACTION CAUSED BY FRENCH REVOLUTION AND ENGLISH DEMOCRACY:—REPRESSIVE POLICY, 1792–1799:—THE PRESS UNTIL THE REGENCY.

WE now approach the greatest of all our liberties,— liberty of opinion. We have to investigate the development of political discussion, —to follow its contests with power,—to observe it repressed and discouraged,—but gradually prevailing over laws and rulers, until the enlightened judgment of a free people has become the law by which the state is governed.

*Freedom of opinion, the greatest of liberties.*

Freedom in the governed to complain of wrongs, and readiness in rulers to redress them, constitute the ideal of a free state. Philosophers and statesmen of all ages have asserted the claims of liberty of opinion.[1] But the

*Free discussion the last liberty to be recognised.*

---

[1] Οὔτε ἐκ τοῦ κόσμου τὸν ἥλιον, οὔτε ἐκ τῆς παιδείας ἄρτεον τὴν παρρησίαν.—*Socrates*, Stobæi Florilegium. Ed. Gaisford, i. 328. Translated thus by Gilbert Wakefield: 'The sun might as easily be spared from the universe, as free speech from the liberal institutions of society.'

Οὐδὲν ἂν εἴη τοῖς ἐλευθέροις μεῖζον ἀτύχημα τοῦ στέρεσθαι τῆς παρρησίας.—*Demosthenes. Ibid.*, 323; translated by the same eminent scholar: 'No greater calamity could come upon a people than the privation of free speech.'

very causes which have filled enlightened thinkers with admiration for this liberty, have provoked the intolerance of rulers. It was nobly said by Erskine, that 'other liberties are held under governments, but the liberty of opinion keeps governments themselves in due subjection to their duties. This has produced the martyrdom of truth in every age; and the world has been only purged from ignorance with the innocent blood of those who have enlightened it.'[1] The church has persecuted freedom of thought in religion: the state has repressed it in politics. Everywhere authority has resented discussion, as hostile to its own sovereign rights. Hence, in states otherwise free, liberty of opinion has been the last political privilege which the people have acquired.

When the art of printing had developed thought, and multiplied the means of discussion, the press was subjected, throughout Europe, to a rigorous censorship. *Censorship of the press.* First, the church attempted to prescribe the bounds of human thought and knowledge; and next, the state assumed the same presumptuous office. No writings were suf-

> Τοὐλεύθερον δ' ἐκεῖνο εἴ τις θέλει πόλει
> χρηστόν τι βούλευμ' εἰς μέσον φέρειν, ἔχων.
> This is true liberty, when free-born men,
> Having to advise the public, may speak free.
> *Euripides.*

'For this is not the liberty which we can hope, that no grievance ever should arise in the commonwealth,—that let no man in the world expect: but when complaints are freely heard, deeply considered, and speedily reformed, then is the utmost bound of civil liberty attained that wise men look for.'—*Milton's Areopagitica, Works*, iv. 396: Ed. 1851.

'Give me the liberty to know, to utter, and to argue, freely according to conscience, above all liberties.'—*Ibid.*, 442.

[1] Erskine's speech for Paine.

fered to be published without the *imprimatur* of the licenser; and the printing of unlicensed works was visited with the severest punishments.

After the reformation in England the crown assumed the right which the church had previously exercised, of prohibiting the printing of all works 'but such as should be first seen and allowed.' The censorship of the press became part of the prerogative; and printing was further restrained by patents and monopolies. Queen Elizabeth interdicted printing save in London, Oxford, and Cambridge.[1]

Tracts, flying-sheets, and newspapers.

But the minds of men had been too deeply stirred to submit to ignorance and lethargy. They thirsted after knowledge; and it reached them through the subtle agency of the press. The theological controversies of the sixteenth century, and the political conflicts of the seventeenth, gave birth to new forms of literature. The heavy folio, written for the learned, was succeeded by the tract and flying sheet,—to be read by the multitude. At length, the printed sheet, continued periodically, assumed the shape of a news-letter or newspaper.

The press under the Stuarts.

The first example of a newspaper is to be found late in the reign of James I.,[2]—a period most inauspicious for the press. Political discussion was silenced by the licenser, the Star Chamber, the dungeon, the pillory, mutilation, and

[1] State Tr., i. 1263.
[2] The Weekly Newes, May 23rd, 1622, printed for Nicholas Bourne and Thomas Archer. The English Mercurie, 1588, in the British Museum, once believed to be the first English newspaper, has since been proved a fabrication.—*Letter to Mr. Panizzi by T. Watts, of the British Museum*, 1839; Disraeli's Curiosities of Literature, 14th Ed., i. 173; Hunt's Fourth Estate, i. 33.

branding. Nothing marked more deeply the tyrannical spirit of the two first Stuarts than their barbarous persecutions of authors, printers, and the importers of prohibited books: nothing illustrated more signally the love of freedom, than the heroic courage and constancy with which those persecutions were borne.

The fall of the Star Chamber[1] augured well for the liberty of the press; and the great struggle which ensued, let loose the fervid thoughts and passions of society in political discussion. *The commonwealth.* Tracts and newspapers entered hotly into the contest between the Court and the Parliament.[2] The Parliament, however, while it used the press as an instrument of party, did not affect a spirit of toleration. It passed severe orders and ordinances in restraint of printing;[3] and would have silenced all royalist and prelatical writers. In war none of the enemy's weapons were likely to be respected; yet John Milton, looking beyond the narrow bounds of party to the great interests of truth, ventured to brand its suppression by the licenser, as the slaying of 'an immortality rather than a life.'[4]

The Restoration brought renewed trials upon the

[1] February 1641.
[2] Upwards of 30,000 political pamphlets and newspapers were issued from the press between 1640 and the restoration. They were collected by Mr. Thomasson, and are now in the British Museum, bound up in 2,000 volumes.—*Knight's Old Printer and Modern Press*, 199: *Disraeli's Cur. of Literature*, i. 175.
[3] Orders June 14th, 1642; Aug. 26th, 1642; Husband's Ord., 591; Ordinance, June, 1643; Parl. Hist., iii. 131; Ordinance, Sept. 30th, 1647; Parl. Hist., iii. 780; Rushworth, ii. 957, &c.; Further Ordinances, 1649 and 1652; Scobell, i. 44, 134; ii. 88, 230.
[4] Areopagitica; a Speech for Liberty of Unlicensed Printing, Works, iv. 400; Ed. 1851.

press. The Licensing Act placed the entire control of printing in the government.[1] In the narrow spirit of Elizabeth, printing was confined to London, York, and the universities, and the number of master printers were limited to twenty. The severe provisions of this act were used with terrible vindictiveness. Authors and printers of obnoxious works were hung, quartered and mutilated, exposed in the pillory and flogged, or fined and imprisoned, according to the temper of their judges:[2] their productions were burned by the common hangman. Freedom of opinion was under interdict: even news could not be published without license. Nay, when the Licensing Act had been suffered to expire for a while, the twelve judges, under Chief Justice Scroggs, declared it to be criminal, at common law, to publish any public news, whether true or false, without the king's license.[3] Nor was this monstrous opinion judicially condemned, until the better times of that constitutional judge, Lord Camden.[4] A monopoly in news being created, the public were left to seek intelligence in the official summary of the 'London Gazette.' The press, debased and enslaved, took refuge in the licentious ribaldry of that age.[5] James II. and his infamous judges carried the Licensing Act into effect with

*The press after the restoration.*

[1] 13 & 14 Chas. II. c. 33.
[2] St. Tr., vi. 514. The sentence upon John Twyn, a poor printer, was one of revolting brutality; St. Tr., vi. 659; Keach's case, pillory, *Ib.*, 710; Cases of Harris, Smith, Curtis, Carr, and Cellier, *Ib.*, vii. 926-1043, 1111, 1183.
[3] Carr's Case, 1680; State Trials, vii. 929.
[4] Entinck *v.* Carrington, St. Tr., xix. 1071.
[5] See Macaulay's Hist., i. 365, for a good account of the newspapers of this period.

barbarous severity. But the Revolution brought indulgence even to the Jacobite press; and when the Commons, a few years later, refused to renew the Licensing Act,[1] a censorship of the press was for ever renounced by the law of England. Expiration of Licensing Act, 1695.

Henceforth the freedom of the press was theoretically established. Every writing could be freely published: but at the peril of a rigorous execution of the libel laws. The administration of justice was indeed improved. Scroggs and Jeffreys were no more: but the law of libel was undefined; and the traditions of the Star Chamber had been accepted as the rule of Westminster Hall. To speak ill of the government was a crime. Censure of ministers was a reflection upon the king himself.[2] Hence the first aim and use of free discussion was prohibited by law. But no sooner had the press escaped from the grasp of the licenser, than it began to give promise of its future energies. Newspapers were multiplied: news and gossip freely circulated among the people.[3] Theory of free press recognised.

With the reign of Anne opened a new era in the history of the press. Newspapers then assumed their present form, combining intelligence with political discussion;[4] and began to be published daily.[5] This reign was also marked by the higher intellectual character of its periodical The press in the reign of Anne.

---

[1] See Macaulay's Hist., iii. 656; iv. 540.
[2] See the law as laid down by Ch. J. Holt, St. Tr., xiv. 1103.
[3] Macaulay's Hist., iv. 604.
[4] Hallam's Const. Hist., ii. 331, 460.
[5] Disraeli's Cur. of Literature, i. 178; Nichols' Lit. Anecd., iv.80. The Daily Courant was the first daily paper, in 1709.—*Hunt's Fourth Estate*, i. 175.

literature, which engaged the first talents of that Augustan age,—Addison and Steele, Swift and Bolingbroke. The popular taste for news and political argument was becoming universal: all men were politicians, and every party had its chosen writers. The influence of the press was widely extended: but in becoming an instrument of party, it compromised its character, and long retarded the recognition of its freedom. Party rancour too often betrayed itself in outrageous license and calumny. And the war which rulers had hitherto waged against the press, was now taken up by parties. Writers in the service of rival factions had to brave the vengeance of their political foes, whom they stung with sarcasm and lampoon. They could expect no mercy from the courts, or from Parliament. Every one was a libeller who outraged the sentiments of the dominant party. The Commons, far from vindicating public liberty, rivalled the Star Chamber in their zeal against libels. Now they had 'a sermon to condemn and a parson to roast;'[1] now a member to expel:[2] now a journalist to punish, or a pamphlet to burn.[3] Society was no less intolerant. In the late reign, Dyer, having been reprimanded by the speaker, was cudgelled by Lord Mohun in a coffee-house;[4] and in this reign, Tutchin, who had

*The press an instrument of party.*

---

[1] Dr. Sacheverell, 1709; Bolingbroke Works, iii. 9; Preface to Bishop of St. Asaph's Four Sermons, burned 1712; Parl. Hist., vi. 1151.

[2] Steele, in 1713. See Sir R. Walpole's admirable speech; Parl. Hist., vi. 1268; Coxe's Walpole, i. 72.

[3] Dr. Drake and others, 1702; Parl. Hist., vi. 19; Dr. Coward, 1704; *Ibid.*, 331; David Edwards, 1706; *Ibid.*, 512; Swift's Public Spirit of the Whigs, 1713 (Lords); Parl. Hist., vi. 1261.

[4] 1694; Kennet's Hist., iii. 666; Hunt's Fourth Estate, i. 164.

braved the Commons and the attorney-general, was waylaid in the streets, and actually beaten to death.¹ So strong was the feeling against the press, that proposals were even made for reviving the Licensing Act. It was too late to resort to such a policy: but a new restraint was devised in the form of a stamp duty on newspapers and advertisements,² —avowedly for the purpose of repressing libels. This policy, being found effectual in limiting the circulation of cheap papers,³ was improved upon in the two following reigns,⁴ and continued in high esteem until our own time.⁵

First stamp duty, 1712.

The press of the two first Georges made no marked advances in influence or character. An age adorned by Pope, Johnson, and Goldsmith,— by Hume and Robertson,— by Sterne, Gray, Fielding, and Smollett, claims no mean place in the history of letters. But its political literature had no such pretensions. Falling far below the intellectual standard of the previous reign, it continued to express the passions and malignity of parties. Writers were hired by statesmen to decry the measures and blacken the charac-

The press in the reigns of Geo. I. and II.

---

¹ St. Tr., xiv. 1199; Hunt, i. 173.
² 10 Anne, c. 19, § 101, 118; Resolutions, June 2nd, 1712; Parl. Hist., vi. 1141; Queen's Speech, April 1713: *Ib.*, 1173.
³ 'Do you know that Grub Street is dead and buried during the last week.'—*Swift's Journ. to Stella*, Aug. 7th, 1712.

> 'His works were hawked in every street,
> But seldom rose above a sheet:
> Of late, indeed, the paper stamp
> Did very much his genius cramp;
> And since he could not spend his fire
> He now intended to retire.'
> —*Swift's Poems*, iii. 44, Pickering's Edition.

⁴ 11 G. I. c. 8; 30 G. II. c. 19.   ⁵ See *infra*, p. 382.

ters of their rivals; and, instead of seeking to instruct the people, devoted their talents to the personal service of their employers, and the narrowest interests of faction. Exercising unworthily a mean craft, they brought literature itself into disrepute.[1]

The press, being ever the tool of party, continued to be exposed to its vengeance:[2] but, except when Jacobite papers, more than usually disloyal, openly prayed for the restoration of the Stuarts,[3] the press generally enjoyed a fairer toleration. Sir Robert Walpole, good-humoured, insensitive, liberal,—and no great reader,—was indifferent to the attacks of the press, and avowed his contempt for political writers of all parties.[4] And other ministers, more easily provoked, found a readier vengeance in the gall of their own bitter scribes, than in the tedious processes of the law.

Such was the condition of the press on the accession of George III. However debased by the servile uses of party, and the low es-

*Press on accession of Geo. III.*

[1] Speaking in 1740, Mr. Pulteney termed the ministerial writers 'a herd of wretches, whom neither information can enlighten, nor affluence elevate.' 'If their patrons would read their writings, their salaries would quickly be withdrawn: for a few pages would convince them that they can neither attack nor defend, neither raise any man's reputation by their panegyric, nor destroy it by their defamation.'—*Parl. Hist.*, xi. 882.—See also some excellent passages in Forster's Life of Goldsmith, 71; Ed. 1848.

[2] Parl. Hist., viii. 1166; ix. 867.

[3] Mist's Journ., May 27th, 1721; Parl. Hist., vii. 804; Trial of Mathews, 1719; St. Tr., xv. 1323.

[4] On the 2nd Dec., 1740, he said: 'Nor do I often read the papers of either party, except when I am informed by some who have more inclination to such studies than myself, that they have risen by some accident above their common level.' Again: 'I have never discovered any reason to exalt the authors who write against the administration, to a higher degree of reputation than their opponents.'—*Parl. Hist.*, xi. 882.

teem of its writers,[1] its political influence was not the less acknowledged. With an increasing body of readers, interested in public affairs, and swayed by party feelings and popular impulses, it could not fail to become a powerful friend, or formidable foe, to ministers. 'A late nobleman, who had been a member of several administrations,' said Smollett, 'observed to me, that one good writer was of more importance to the government, than twenty placemen in the House of Commons.'[2] Its influence, as an auxiliary in party warfare, had been proved. It was now to rise above party, and to become a great popular power,—the representative of public opinion. The new reign suddenly developed a freedom of discussion hitherto unknown; and within a few years, the people learned to exercise a powerful control over their rulers, by an active and undaunted press, by public meetings, and, lastly, by political concert and association.

The government was soon at issue with the press. Lord Bute was the first to illustrate its power. Overwhelmed by a storm of obloquy and ridicule, he bowed down before it and fled. He did not attempt to stem it by the terrors of the law. Vainly did his own hired writers endeavour to shelter him:[3] vainly did the king uphold his favourite. The unpopular minister was

<small>Wilkes and the 'North Briton.'</small>

---

[1] Walpole's Mem., iii. 115, 164; Forster's Life of Goldsmith, 387.
[2] Forster's Life of Goldsmith, 665. In 1738, Mr. Danvers said: 'The sentiments of one of these scribblers have more weight with the multitude than the opinion of the best politician in the kingdom.' —*Parl. Hist.*, x. 448.
[3] Dodington's Diary, 245, 419, &c.; History of a Late Minority, 77.

swept away: but the storm continued. Foremost among his assailants had been the 'North Briton,' conducted by Wilkes, who was not disposed to spare the new minister, Mr. Grenville, or the court. It had hitherto been the custom for journalists to cast a thin veil over sarcasms and abuse directed against public men;[1] but the 'North Briton' assailed them openly and by name.[2] The affected concealment of names, indeed, was compatible neither with the freedom nor the fairness of the press. In shrinking from the penalties of the law, a writer also evaded the responsibilities of truth. Truth is ever associated with openness. The free use of names was therefore essential to the development of a sound political literature. But as yet the old vices of journalism prevailed; and to coarse invective and slander, was added the unaccustomed insult of a name openly branded by the libeller.

'North Briton,' No. 45.
On the 23rd of April, 1763, appeared the memorable number 45 of the 'North Briton,' commenting upon the king's speech at the prorogation, and upon the unpopular peace recently concluded.[3] It was at once stigmatised by the court as an audacious libel, and a studied insult to

---

[1] Even the Annual Register, during the first few years of this reign, in narrating domestic events, generally avoided the use of names, or gave merely the initials of ministers and others: e.g. 'Mr. P.,' 'D. of N.,' 'E. of B.,' 1762, p. 46; 'Mr. F.,' 'Mr. Gr.,' p. 62; 'Lord H.' and 'Lord E-r-t,' 1763, p. 40; 'M. of R.,' 1765, p. 44; 'Marquis of R——,' and 'Mr. G——,' 1769, p. 50; 'The K——,' 1770, p. 59, &c. &c.

[2] 'The highest names, whether of statesmen or magistrates, were printed at length, and the insinuations went still higher.'—*Walpole's Mem.*, i. 179.

[3] Parl. Hist., xv. 1331, *n*.

the king himself; and it has since been represented in the same light, by historians not heated by the controversies of that time.[1] But however bitter and offensive, it unquestionably assailed the minister rather than the king. Recognising, again and again, the constitutional maxim of ministerial responsibility, it treated the royal speech as the composition of the minister.[2]

The court were in no mood to brook the license of the press. Why had great lords been humbled, parties broken up, and the Commons managed by the paymaster, if the king was to be defied by a libeller?[3] It was resolved that he should be punished,—not like common libellers, by the attorney-general, but by all the powers of the state. Prerogative was strained by the issue of a general warrant for the discovery of the authors and printers:[4] privilege was perverted for the sake of vengeance and persecution;[5] and an information for libel was filed against Wilkes in the Court of King's Bench. Had the court contented themselves with the last proceeding, they would have had the libeller at their feet. A verdict was obtained against Wilkes for printing and publishing a seditious and scandalous libel. At the same time the jury found his 'Essay on Woman' to be an 'obscene and impious libel.'[6] But the other measures taken to crush Wilkes were so repugnant to justice and decency,

*Proceedings against Wilkes.*

---

[1] Adolphus' Hist., i. 116; Hughes' Hist., i. 312.
[2] Lord Mahon's Hist., v. 45; Massey's Hist., i. 157.
[3] Dodington's Diary, 245, 419, &c.; Hist. of a late Minority, 77.
[4] *Infra*, Vol. III. p. 2.   [5] See *supra*, Vol. II. 2.
[6] Burrow's Reports, iv. 2527; St. Tr., xix. 1075

that these verdicts were resented by the people as part of his persecutions. The Court of King's Bench shared the odium attached to the government, which Wilkes spared no pains to aggravate. He complained that Lord Mansfield had permitted the informations against him to be irregularly amended on the eve of his trial: he inveighed against the means by which a copy of his 'Essay on Woman' had been obtained by the bribery of his servant; and by questions arising out of his outlawry, he contrived to harass the court, and keep his case before the public for the next six years.[1] The people were taught to be suspicious of the administration of justice, in cases of libel; and, assuredly, the proceedings of the government and the doctrines of the courts, alike justified their suspicions.

The printers of the 'North Briton' suffered as well as the author; and the government, having secured these convictions, proceeded with unrelenting rigour against other printers.[2] No grand jury stood between the attorney-general and the defendants; and the courts, in the administration of the law, were ready instruments of the government. Whether this severity tended to check the publication of libels or not, it aroused the sympathies of the people on the side of

*Printers of the 'North Briton,' 1764.*

---

[1] State Tr., xix. 1136.

[2] Horace Walpole affirms that 200 informations were filed, a larger number than had been prosecuted in the whole thirty-three years of the last reign.—*Walp. Mem.*, ii. 15, 67. But many of these must have been abandoned, for in 1791 the attorney-general stated that in the last thirty-one years there had been seventy prosecutions for libel, and about fifty convictions: twelve had received severe sentences; and in five cases the pillory had formed part of the punishment.—*Parl. Hist.*, xxix. 551.

the sufferers. Williams, who had reprinted the 'North Briton,' being sentenced to the pillory, drove there in a coach marked '45.' Near the pillory the mob erected a gallows, on which they hung the obnoxious symbols of a boot and a Scotch bonnet; and a collection was made for the culprit, which amounted to 200*l*.[1]

Meanwhile *ex-officio* informations had become so numerous as to attract observation in Parliament; where Mr. Nicholson Calvert moved for a bill to discontinue them. He referred the origin of the practice to the Star Chamber,—complained of persons being put upon their trial without the previous finding of a grand jury,—and argued that the practice was opposed to the entire policy of our laws. His motion, however, was brought forward in opposition to the advice of his friends,[2] and being coldly seconded by Mr. Serjeant Hewitt, was lost on a division, by a large majority.[3]

*Ex-officio informations. Mr. Calvert's motion, March 4th, 1765.*

The excitement which Wilkes and his injudicious oppressors had aroused had not yet subsided, when a more powerful writer arrested public attention.[4] Junius was by far the most remarkable public writer of his time.[5] He was clear, terse, and logical in statement,—learned, in-

*Junius.*

*Character of Junius.*

---

[1] Walp. Mem., ii. 80; Walp. Letters, iv. 49.
[2] Walp. Mem., ii. 84.
[3] Ayes, 204; Noes, 78; Parl. Hist., xvi. 40.
[4] Walp. Mem., iii. 164; Lord Brougham's Works, iii. 425, *et seq.*
[5] Burke, speaking of his letter to the king, said:—'It was the rancour and venom with which I was struck. In these respects the "North Briton" is as much inferior to him, as in strength, wit, and judgment.'—*Parl. Hist.*, xvi. 1154.

genious, and subtle in disputation,—eloquent in appeals to popular passion,—polished, and trenchant as steel, in sarcasm,—terrible in invective. Ever striving to wound the feelings, and sully the reputation of others, he was even more conspicuous for rancour and envenomed bitterness than for wit. With the malignant spirit of a libeller,—without scruple or regard for truth,—he assailed the private character, no less than the actions of public men. In the 'Morning Advertiser' of the 19th of December 1769, appeared Junius's celebrated letter to the king.[1] Inflammatory and seditious, it could not be overlooked; and as the author was unknown, informations were immediately filed against the printers and publishers of the letter. But before they were brought to trial, Almon, the bookseller, was tried for selling the 'London Museum,' in which the libel was reprinted.[2] His connection with the publication proved to be so slight that he escaped with a nominal punishment. Two doctrines, however, were maintained in this case, which excepted libels from the general principles of the criminal law. By the first, a publisher was held criminally answerable for the acts of his servants, unless proved to be neither privy nor assenting to the publication of a libel. So long as exculpatory evidence was admitted, this doctrine was defensible: but judges afterwards refused to admit such evidence, holding that the

*Junius's letter to the king.*

*Publisher criminally liable for acts of his servants.*

---

[1] Letter, No. xxxv.; Woodfall's Ed., ii. 62.
[2] Walp. Mem., iv. 160; Notes to the St. Tr., xx. 821; Parl. Hist., xvi. 1153, 1156.

publication of a libel by a publisher's servant was proof of his criminality. And this monstrous rule of law prevailed until 1843, when it was condemned by Lord Campbell's Libel Act.¹

The second doctrine was wholly subversive of the rights of juries, in cases of libel. Already, on the trial of the printers of the 'North Briton,' Lord Mansfield had laid it down that it was the province of the court alone to judge of the criminality of a libel. This doctrine, however questionable, was not without authority;² and was now enforced with startling clearness by his lordship. The only material issue for the jury to try, was whether the paper was libellous or not; and this was emphatically declared to be entirely beyond their jurisdiction.³ Trial by jury was the sole security for freedom of the press; and it was found to have no place in the law of England. *Right of Jury to judge of the offences of libel, denied.*

Again, on the trial of Woodfall, his lordship told the jury that, 'as for the intention, the malice, the sedition, or any other harder words which might be given in informations for libels, public or private, they were merely formal words, mere words of course, mere inferences of law, —with which the jury were not to concern themselves.' The jury, however, learning that the offence which they were trying was to be withdrawn from *Woodfall's trial, June 13th, 1770.*

---

¹ 6 & 7 Vict., c. 96, § 7; Hans. Deb., 3rd Ser., lvi. 395, &c.
² Lord Raymond in Franklin's Case, 1731; Ch. Justice Lee in Owen's case, 1752.—St. Tr., xvii. 1243; xviii. 1203; Parl. Hist., xvi. 1275.
³ Burr., 2686; State Tr., xx. 803.

their cognisance, adroitly hit the palpable blot of such a doctrine, by finding Woodfall 'guilty of printing and publishing only.' In vain was it contended, on the part of the crown, that this verdict should be amended, and entered as a general verdict of guilty. The court held the verdict to be uncertain, and that there must be a new trial.[1] Miller, the printer and publisher of the 'Evening Post,' was next tried, at Guildhall. To avert such a verdict as that in Woodfall's case, Lord Mansfield, in language still stronger and more distinct, laid it down that the jury must not concern themselves with the character of the paper charged as criminal, but merely with the fact of its publication, and the meaning of some few words not in the least doubtful. In other words, the prisoner was tried for his offence by the judge, and not by the jury. In this case, however, the jury boldly took the matter into their own hands, and returned a verdict of not guilty.[2]

*Nov. 20th, 1770.*

*Miller's trial, July 18th, 1770.*

Other printers were also tried for the publication of this same letter of Junius, and acquitted. Lord Mansfield had, in fact, overshot the mark; and his dangerous doctrines recoiled upon himself.[3] Such startling restrictions upon the natural rights of a jury excited general alarm and disapprobation.[4] They were impugned in several able letters and pamphlets; and above all, in the terrible letter of Junius to Lord

*Disapproval of Lord Mansfield's doctrines.*

---

[1] State Tr., xx. 895.  
[2] Ibid., xx. 870.  
[3] Walp. Mem., iv. 160, 168.  
[4] See Lord Chatham's Corr., iv. 50.

Mansfield himself.[1] It was clear that they were fatal to the liberty of the press. Writers, prosecuted by an officer of the crown, without the investigation of a grand jury, and denied even a trial by their peers, were placed beyond the pale of the law.

These trials also became the subject of animadversion in Parliament. On a motion of Captain Constantine Phipps, for a bill to restrain *ex-officio* informations, grave opinions were expressed upon the invasion of the rights of juries, and the criminal responsibility of a publisher for the acts of his servants. Lord Mansfield's doctrines were questioned by Mr. Cornwall, Mr. Serjeant Glynn, Mr. Burke, Mr. Dunning, and Sir W. Meredith;[2] and defended by Mr. Attorney-General De Grey, and Mr. Solicitor-General Thurlow.[3] *Debates in Parliament. Captain Phipps' motion, Nov. 27th, 1770.*

Lord Chatham, in the House of Lords, assailed Lord Mansfield for his directions to juries in the recent libel cases. Lord Mansfield justified them, and Lord Camden desired that they should be fully stated, in order that the House might judge of their legality.[4] *Lord Chatham, Dec. 5th, 1770.*

This debate was followed, in the Commons, by a motion of Mr. Serjeant Glynn for a committee, to inquire into the administration of criminal justice, particularly in cases relating to the liberty of the press, and the constitutional power and duty of juries. The same contro- *Mr. Serjeant Glynn's motion, Dec. 6th, 1770.*

---

[1] Nov. 14th, 1770; Letter No. 41, Woodfall's Ed., ii. 159.
[2] Mr. Wedderburn also spoke against *ex-officio* informations.
[3] Parl. Hist., xvi. 1127, 1175 (two reports).
[4] Parl. Hist., xvi. 1302.

verted questions were again discussed; and such was the feeling of the House, that the motion was lost by a majority of eight only.[1] In this debate, Mr. Charles Fox gave little promise of his future exertions to improve the law of libel. He asked, where was the proof, 'that juries are deprived of their constitutional rights?' 'The abettors of the motion,' he said, 'refer us to their own libellous remonstrances, and to those infamous lampoons and satires which they have taken care to write and circulate.'

The day after this debate, Lord Mansfield desired that the Lords might be summoned on the 10th of December, as he had a communication to make to their Lordships. On that day, however, instead of submitting a motion, or making a statement to the House, he merely informed their Lordships that he had left with the clerk of the House a copy of the judgment of the Court of King's Bench, in Woodfall's case, which their Lordships might read, and take copies of, if they pleased. This, however, was enough to invite discussion; and on the following day, Lord Camden accepted this paper as a challenge directed personally to himself. 'He has thrown down the glove,' he said, 'and I take it up. In direct contradiction to him, I maintain that his doctrine is not the law of England.' He then proposed six questions to Lord Mansfield upon the subject. His lordship, in great distress and confusion, said, 'he

*Lord Mansfield produces the judgment in Woodfall's case.*

[1] Ayes, 176; Noes, 184; Parl. Hist., xvi. 1211; Cavendish Deb., ii. 89; Walp. Mem., iv. 211.

would not answer interrogatories,' but that the matter should be discussed.¹ No time, however, was fixed for this discussion; and notwithstanding the warmth of the combatants, it was not resumed.

So grave a constitutional wrong, however, could not be suffered without further remonstrances. Mr. Dowdeswell moved for a bill to settle doubts concerning the rights of jurors in prosecutions for libels, which formed the basis of that brought in, twenty years later, by Mr. Fox.² The motion was seconded by Sir G. Savile, and supported by Mr. Burke, in a masterly speech, in which be showed, that if the criminality of a libel were properly excluded from the cognisance of a jury,—then should the malice in charges of murder, and the felonious intent in charges of stealing, be equally removed from their jurisdiction, and confided to the judge. If such a doctrine were permitted to encroach upon our laws, juries would 'become a dead letter in our constitution.' The motion was defeated on a question of adjournment.³ All the Whig leaders were sensible of the danger of leaving public writers at the mercy of the courts; and Lord Rockingham, writing to Mr. Dowdeswell, said, 'he who would really assist in re-establishing and confirming the right in juries to judge of both law and fact, would be the best friend to posterity.'⁴ This work, however, was not

*Mr. Dowdeswell's motion, March 7th, 1771.*

¹ Parl. Hist., xvi. 1321; Preface to Woodfall's Junius, i. 49; Letter No. 82, Junius; Woodfall's Ed., iii. 295; Walpole's Mem., iv. 220; Lord Campbell's Lives of the Chancellors, v. 295.
² Rockingham Mem., ii. 198.
³ 218 to 72; Parl. Hist., xvii. 43; Burke's Works, x. 109; Ed. 1812.
⁴ Rockingham Mem., ii. 200.

yet to be accomplished for many years; and the law of libel continued to be administered by the courts, according to the doctrine which Parliament had hitherto shrunk from condemning.

But the rights of juries continued to be inflexibly maintained in the courts, by the eloquence and noble courage of Mr. Erskine. The exertions of that consummate advocate in defence of the Dean of St. Asaph, are memorable in forensic history.[1] At various stages of the proceedings, in this case, he vindicated the right of the jury to judge of the criminality of the libel; and in arguing for a new trial, delivered a speech, which Mr. Fox repeatedly declared to be 'the finest argument in the English language.'[2] He maintained 'that the defendant had had, in fact, no trial; having been found guilty without any investigation of his guilt, and without any power left to the jury to take cognisance of his innocence.' And by the most closely connected chain of reasoning,—by authorities, —and by cases, he proved that the anomalous doctrine against which he was contending was at variance with the laws of England. The new trial was refused; and so little did Lord Mansfield anticipate the approaching condemnation of his doctrine, that he sneered at the 'jealousy of leaving the law to the court,' as 'puerile rant and declamation.' Such, however, was not the opinion of the first statesmen of his own time, nor of posterity.

*Mr. Erskine supports the rights of Juries.*

*Case of Dean of St. Asaph.*

*Nov. 15th, 1779.*

[1] In 1778. He had only been called to the bar on the last day of the preceding term.—St. Tr., xxi. 1; Erskine's Speeches, i. 4; Edinburgh Review, vol. xvi. 103.
[2] Note to St. Tr., xxi. 971.

Mr. Erskine then moved in arrest of judgment. He had known throughout that no part of the publication, as charged in the indictment, was criminal: but had insisted upon maintaining the great public rights which he had so gloriously defended. He now pointed out the innocence of the publication in point of law: the court were unanimously of opinion that the indictment was defective; and the dean was at length discharged from his prosecution.[1]

The trial of Stockdale, in 1789, afforded Mr. Erskine another opportunity of asserting the liberty of the press, in the most eloquent speech ever delivered in a British Court of Justice. Stockdale was prosecuted by the attorney-general, at the instance of the House of Commons,[2] for publishing a defence of Warren Hastings, written by the Rev. Mr. Logan. This pamphlet was charged in the information as a scandalous and seditious libel, intended to vilify the House of Commons as corrupt and unjust, in its impeachment of Warren Hastings. After urging special grounds of defence, Mr. Erskine contended, with consummate skill and force of argument, that the defendant was not to be judged by isolated passages, selected and put together in the information, but by the entire context of the publication, and its general character and objects. If these were fair and proper, the defendant must be acquitted. That question he put to the jury as one which 'cannot, in common sense, be anything resembling a question of law, but is a pure

*Stockdale's trial, 1789.*

---
[1] St. Tr., xxi. 847–1046; Erskine's Speeches, i. 386; Lord Campbell's Chief Justices, ii. 540.
[2] Parl. Hist., xxvii. 1, 7.

question of fact.' Lord Kenyon, who tried the cause, did not controvert this doctrine, and the jury fairly comparing the whole pamphlet with the information, returned a verdict of not guilty.[1] Thus Mr. Erskine succeeded in establishing the important doctrine that full and free discussion was lawful,—that a man was not to be punished for a few unguarded expressions, but was entitled to a fair construction of his general purpose and *animus* in writing,—of which the jury were to judge. This was the last trial for libel which occurred, before Mr. Fox's libel bill. Mr. Erskine had done all that eloquence, courage, and forensic skill could do for the liberty of the press and the rights of juries.

It now only remained for the legislature to accomplish what had been too long postponed. In May, 1791, Mr. Fox made noble amends for his flippant speech upon the libel laws, twenty years before. Admitting that his views had then been mistaken, he now exposed the dangerous anomaly of the law, in a speech of great argumentative power and learning. Mr. Erskine's defence of the Dean of St. Asaph he pronounced to be 'so eloquent, so luminous, and so convincing, that it wanted but in opposition to it, not a man, but a giant.' If the doctrine of the courts was right in cases of libel, it would be right in cases of treason. He might himself be tried for writing a paper charged to be an overt act of treason. In the fact of publication the jury would find a verdict of guilty; and if no motion were made in arrest of judgment, the court would say 'let him be hanged

Mr. Fox's Libel Bill, May 20th, 1791.

[1] St. Tr., xxii. 237; Erskine's Speeches, ii. 205.

and quartered.' A man would thus lose his life without the judgment of his peers. He was worthily seconded[1] by Mr. Erskine, whose name will ever be associated with that important measure. His arguments need not be recapitulated. But one statement, illustrative of the law, must not be omitted. After showing that the judges had usurped the unquestionable privilege of the jury to decide upon the guilt or innocence of the accused, he stated, 'that if, upon a motion in arrest of judgment, the innocence of the defendant's intention was argued before the court, the answer would be and was given uniformly, that the verdict of guilty had concluded the criminality of the intention, though the consideration of that question had been, by the judge's authority, wholly withdrawn from the jury at the trial.'

The opinion of the Commons had now undergone so complete a change upon this question, that Mr. Fox's views found scarcely any opponents. The attorney-general supported him, and suggested that a bill should be at once brought in for declaring the law, to which Mr. Fox readily assented. Mr. Pitt thought it necessary ' to regulate the practice of the courts in the trial of libels, and render it conformable to the spirit of the constitution.' The bill was brought in without a dissentient voice, and passed rapidly through the House of Commons.[2]

In the Lords, however, its further progress was opposed by Lord Thurlow, on account of its importance, and the late period of the session. Lord

---

[1] The motion was one of form, 'that the Grand Committee for Courts of Justice do sit on Tuesday next.'
[2] Parl. Hist., xxix. 551–602.

Camden supported it, as a declaration of what he had ever maintained to be the true principles of the law of England. The bill was put off for a month, without a division: but two protests were entered against its postponement.[1]

In the following session Mr. Fox's bill was again unanimously passed by the Commons. In the Lords it met with renewed opposition from Lord Thurlow, at whose instance the second reading was postponed, until the opinions of the judges could be obtained upon certain questions.[2]

*Libel Bill, 1792. March 20th, 1792.*

*Opinion of the judges, April 27th. May 11th.*

Seven questions were submitted to the judges,[3] and on the 11th of May their answers were returned. Had anything been wanting to prove the danger of those principles of law which it was now sought to condemn, it would have been supplied from the unanimous answers of the judges. These principles, it seemed, were not confined to libel: but the criminality or innocence of any act was 'the result of the judgment which the law pronounces upon that act, and must, therefore, be, in all cases and under all circumstances, matter of law, and not matter of fact.' They even maintained,—as Mr. Fox had argued,—that the criminality or innocence of letters or papers set forth as overt acts of treason was matter of law, and not of fact; yet shrinking from so alarming a conclusion, they added that they had offered no opinion ' which will have the effect of taking matter of law out of the general issue, or out of a general verdict.'[4]

[1] Parl. Hist., xxix. 726-742.
[2] Ibid., 1036.
[3] Ibid., 1293.
[4] Ibid., 1361.

Lord Camden combated the doctrines of the judges, and repeated his own matured and reiterated opinion of the law. The bill was now speedily passed; with a protest, signed by Lord Thurlow and five other lords, predicting 'the confusion and destruction of the law of England.'[1]

And thus, to the immortal honour of Mr. Fox, Mr. Erskine, Lord Camden, and the legislature, was passed the famous Libel Bill of 1792,[2] in opposition to all the judges and chief legal authorities of the time. Being in the form of a declaratory law, it was in effect a reversal of the decisions of the judges by the High Court of Parliament. Its success was undoubted, for all the purposes for which it was designed. While it maintained the rights of juries, and secured to the subject a fair trial by his peers, it introduced no uncertainty in the law, nor dangerous indulgence to criminals. On the contrary, it was acknowledged that government was better protected from unjust attacks, when juries were no longer sensitive to privileges withheld, and jealous of the bench which was usurping them.[3]

*Results of the Libel Act.*

Since the beginning of this reign, the press had

---

[1] Parl. Hist., xix. 1404, 1534–1538; Ann. Reg., 1792, p. 353; Chron. 69; Lord Campbell's Lives of the Chancellors, v. 346. It was followed by a similar law passed by the Parliament of Ireland.

[2] 32 Geo. III. c. 60. Lord Macaulay says:—'Fox and Pitt are fairly entitled to divide the high honour of having added to our statute book the inestimable law which places the liberty of the press under the protection of juries.' This is cited and accepted by Lord Stanhope in his Life of Pitt, ii. 148: but why such prominence to Pitt, and exclusion of Erskine?

[3] Lord Erskine's Speeches, i. 382, *n.*; Lord Campbell's Lives of the Chancellors, v. 350.

made great advances in freedom, influence, and consideration. The right to criticise public
affairs, to question the acts of the government, and the proceedings of the legislature,
had been established. Ministers had been taught,
by the constant failure of prosecutions,[1] to trust to
public opinion for the vindication of their measures,
rather than to the errors of the law for the silencing
of libellers. Wilkes and Junius had at once stimulated the activity of the press, and the popular interest in public affairs. Reporters and printers having
overcome the resistance of Parliament to the publication of debates,[2] the press was brought into closer
relations with the state. Its functions were elevated,
and its responsibilities increased. Statesmen now
had audience of the people. They could justify
their own acts to the world. The falsehoods and
misrepresentations of the press were exposed. Rulers
and their critics were brought face to face, before
the tribunal of public opinion. The sphere of the
press was widely extended. Not writers only, but
the first minds of the age,—men ablest in council
and debate,—were daily contributing to the instruction of their countrymen. Newspapers promptly
met the new requirements of their position. Several
were established during this period, whose high reputation and influence have survived to our own
time;[3] and by fullness and rapidity of intelligence,

*General progress of free discussion in the press.*

---

[1] On the 27th Nov., 1770, the Attorney-General De Grey 'declared solemnly that he had hardly been able to bring a single offender to justice.'—*Parl. Hist.*, xvi. 1138.

[2] *Supra*, p. 33, *et seq.*

[3] Viz., The Morning Chronicle, 1769 (extinct in 1862); The Morning Post, 1772; The Morning Herald, 1780 (extinct in 1869);

frequency of publication, and literary ability, proved themselves worthy of their honourable mission to instruct the people.

Nor is it unworthy of remark that art had come to the aid of letters, in political contro- Caricatures. versy. Since the days of Walpole, caricatures had occasionally pourtrayed ministers in grotesque forms, and with comic incidents : but during this period, caricaturists had begun to exercise no little influence upon popular feeling. The broad humour and bold pencil of Gillray had contributed to foment the excitement against Mr. Fox and Lord North ; and this skilful limner elevated caricature to the rank of a new art. The people were familiarised with the persons and characters of public men : crowds gathered round the printsellers' windows; and as they passed on, laughing goodhumouredly, felt little awe or reverence for rulers whom the caricaturist had made ridiculous. The press had found a powerful ally, which, first used in the interests of party, became a further element of popular force.[1]

Meanwhile, other means had been devised,—more powerful than the press,—for directing public meetings public opinion, and exercising influence and associations. over the government and the legislature. Public meetings had been assembled, political associations organised, and 'agitation'—as it has since

The Times, founded in 1788, holds an undisputed position as the first newspaper in the world.—*Hunt's Fourth Estate*, ii. 99–189.

[1] Wright's England under the House of Hanover, i. 136, 403 ; ii. 74–83, &c. ; Twiss's Life of Eldon, i. 162 ; Lord Stanhope's Life of Pitt, i. 239.

been termed,—reduced to a system. In all ages and countries, and under every form of government, the people have been accustomed, in periods of excitement, to exercise a direct influence over their rulers. Sometimes by tumults and rebellions, sometimes by clamours and discontent, they have made known their grievances, and struggled for redress.[1] In England, popular feelings had too often exploded in civil wars and revolutions; and, in more settled times, the people had successfully overborne the government and the legislature. No minister, however powerful, could be wholly deaf to their clamours. In 1733, Sir Robert Walpole had been forced to withdraw his excise scheme.[2] In 1754, Parliament had been compelled to repeal a recent act of just toleration, in deference to popular prejudices.[3]

In the beginning of this reign, the populace had combined with the press in hooting Lord Bute out of the king's service; and for many years afterwards popular excitement was kept alive by the ill-advised measures of the Court and Parliament. It was a period of discontent and turbulence.

In 1765, the Spitalfields' silk-weavers, exasperated by the rejection of a bill for the protection of their trade by the House of Lords, paraded in front of St. James' Palace with black flags, surrounded the Houses of Parliament at Westminster, and questioned the peers as they

*The Silk-weavers' riots, 1765.*

*May 15th.*

---

[1] 'Pour la populace, ce n'est jamais par envie d'attaquer qu'elle se soulève, mais par impatience de souffrir.'—*Mem. de Sully*, i. 133.
[2] Parl. Hist., viii. 1306; ix. 7; Coxe's Walpole, i. 372; Lord Hervey's Mem., i. 185, *et seq.*
[3] Naturalisation of Jews, 1754.

came out, concerning their votes. They assailed the Duke of Bedford, at whose instance the bill had been thrown out; and having been dispersed by cavalry in Palace Yard, they proceeded to attack May 17th. Bedford House, whence they were repulsed by the guards.¹ It was an irregular and riotous attempt to overawe the deliberations of Parliament. It was tumult of the old type, opposed alike to law and rational liberty : but it was not the less successful. Encouraged by the master manufacturers, and exerted in a cause then in high favour with statesmen, it was allowed to prevail. Lord Halifax promised to satisfy the weavers;² and in the next year, to their great joy, a bill was passed restraining the importation of foreign silks.³

But the general discontents of the time shortly developed other popular demonstrations far more formidable, which were destined to form a new era in constitutional government. *Popular excitement, 1768.* In 1768, the excitement of the populace in the cause of Wilkes, led to riots and a conflict with the military. But the tumultuous violence of mobs was succeeded by a deeper and more constitutional agitation. The violation of the rights of the electors of Middlesex by the Commons,⁴ united, in support of Wilkes, the first statesmen of the time, the parliamentary opposition, the wronged electors, the

¹ Ann. Reg., 1765, p. 41 ; Grenville Papers, iii. 168-172 ; Walp. Mem., ii. 155, *et seq.* ; Rockingham Mem., i. 200, 207 ; Adolphus' Hist., i. 177 ; Lord Mahon's Hist., v. 152.
² He wrote to Lord Hillsborough to assure the master-weavers that the bill should pass both Houses.—*Rockingham Mem.*, i. 200-207.
³ 6 Geo. III. c. 28. ⁴ *Supra*, p. 13.

magistrates and citizens of London, a large body of the middle classes, the press, and the populace.

*Public meetings and associations, 1768-70.* Enthusiastic meetings of freeholders were assembled to support their champion, with whom the freeholders of other counties made common cause. The throne was approached by addresses and remonstrances. Junius thundered forth his fearful invectives. Political agitation was rife in various forms: but its most memorable feature was that of public meetings, which at this period began to take their place among the institutions of the country.[1] No less than seventeen counties held meetings to support the electors of Middlesex.[2] Never had so general a demonstration of public sentiment been made, in such a form. It was a new phase in the development of public opinion. This movement was succeeded by the formation of a 'society for supporting the bill of rights.'

Ten years later, public meetings assumed more *Public meetings, 1779-80.* importance and a wider organisation. The freeholders of Yorkshire and twenty-three other counties, and the inhabitants of many cities, were assembled, by their sheriffs and chief magistrates, to discuss economical and parliamentary reform. These meetings were attended by the leading men of each neighbourhood; and speeches were

---

[1] Ann. Reg., 1770, p. 58, 60. On the 31st October, 1770, a large meeting of the electors of Westminster was held in Westminster Hall, when Mr. Wilkes counselled them to instruct their members to impeach Lord North.—Adolphus' Hist., i. 451; Ann. Reg., 1770, p. 159; Chron., 206; Lord Rockingham's Mem., ii. 93; Cooke's Hist. of Party, iii. 187.

[2] Ann. Reg., 1770, p. 58.

made, and resolutions and petitions agreed to, with a view to influence Parliament, and attract public support to the cause. A great meeting was held in Westminster Hall, with Mr. Fox in the chair, which was attended by the Duke of Portland, and many of the most eminent members of the opposition. Nor were these meetings spontaneous in each locality. They were encouraged by active correspondence, association, and concerted movements throughout the country.[1] Committees of correspondence and association were appointed by the several counties, who kept alive the agitation; and delegates were sent to London to give it concentration. This practice of delegation was severely criticised in Parliament. Its representative principle was condemned as a derogation from the rights of the legislature: no county delegates could be recognised, but knights of the shire returned by the sheriff. Mainly on this ground, the Commons refused to consider a petition of thirty-two delegates who signed themselves as freeholders only.[2] The future influence of such an organisation over the deliberations of Parliament was foreseen: but it could not be prevented. Delegates were a natural incident to association. Far from arrogating to themselves the power of the Commons, they approached that body as humble petitioners for redress.

*Political associations.*

---

[1] *Supra*, p. 63; Ann. Reg., 1780, p. 85; Parl. Hist., xx. 1378; Wyvill's Political Papers, i. 1, *et seq.*; Wraxall's Mem., iii. 292, &c.; Rockingham Mem., ii. 391–403; Lord J. Russell's Life of Fox, i. 222; Walpole's Journ., ii. 389–441.
[2] 13th Nov., 1780; 2nd April and 8th May, 1781; Parl. Hist., xxi. 844; xxii. 95, 138.

They represented a cause,—not the people. So long as it was lawful for men to associate, to meet, to discuss, to correspond, and to act in concert for political objects, they could select delegates to represent their opinions. If their aims were lawful and their conduct orderly, no means which they deemed necessary for giving effect to free discussion were unconstitutional; and this system,—subject, however, to certain restraints,[1]—has generally found a place in later political organisations. Other political societies and clubs were now established;[2] and the principle of association was brought into active operation, with all its agencies. At this time Mr. Pitt, the future enemy of political combinations, encouraged associations to forward the cause of parliamentary reform, took counsel with their delegates, and enrolled himself a member of the society for constitutional information.[3]

Here were further agencies for working upon the public mind, and bringing the popular will to bear upon affairs of state. Association for political purposes, and large assemblages of men, henceforth became the most powerful and impressive form of agitation. Marked by reality and vital power, they were demonstrations at once of moral conviction and numerical force. They combined discussion with action. However forcibly the press might persuade and convince, it moved men

*Political associations considered.*

---

[1] *Infra*, p. 187.  [2] Adolphus' Hist., iii. 233.
[3] See resolutions agreed to at a meeting of members and delegates at the Thatched House Tavern, May 18th, 1782, in Mr. Pitt's own writing. St. Tr., xxii. 492; also Mr. Pitt's evidence on the Trial of Horne Tooke.—*Ibid.*, xxv. 381.

singly in their homes and business: but here were men assembled to bear witness to their earnestness: the scattered forces of public opinion were collected and made known: a cause was popularised by the sympathies and acclamations of the multitude. The people confronted their rulers bodily, as at the hustings.[1]

Again, association invested a cause with permanent interest. Political excitement may subside in a day: but a cause adopted by a body of earnest and active men is not suffered to languish. It is kept alive by meetings, deputations, correspondence, resolutions, petitions, tracts, advertisements. It is never suffered to be forgotten: until it has triumphed, the world has no peace.

Public meetings and associations were now destined to exercise a momentous influence on the state. Their force was great and perilous. In a good cause, directed by wise and honourable men, they were designed to confer signal benefits upon their country and mankind. In a bad cause, and under the guidance of rash and mischievous leaders, they were ready instruments of tumult and sedition. The union of moral and physical force may convince, but it may also practise intimidation: arguments may give place to threats, and fiery words to deeds of lawless violence.[2] Our history abounds with

---

[1] 'L'association possède plus de puissance que la presse.' . . . . 'Les moyens d'exécution se combinent, les opinions se déploient avec cette force, et cette chaleur, que ne peut jamais attendre la pensée écrite.'—*De Tocqueville, Démocr. en Amérique*, i. 277.

[2] 'On ne peut se dissimuler que la liberté illimitée d'association, en matière politique, ne soit, de toutes les libertés, la dernière qu'un peuple puisse supporter. Si elle ne la fait pas tomber dans l'anar-

examples of the uses and perils of political agitation.

The dangers of such agitation were exemplified at this very time, in their worst form, by the Protestant associations. In 1778, the legislature having conceded to the Catholics of England a small measure of indulgence, a body of Protestant zealots in Scotland associated to resist its extension to that country. So rapidly had the principle of association developed itself, that no less than eighty-five societies, or corresponding committees, were established in communication with Edinburgh. The fanaticism of the people was appealed to by speeches, pamphlets, handbills, and sermons, until the pious fury of the populace exploded in disgraceful riots. Yet was this wretched agitation too successful. The Catholics of Scotland waived their just rights, for the sake of peace; and Parliament submitted its own judgment to the arbitrament of Scottish mobs.[1]

This agitation next extended to England. A Protestant association was formed in London, with which numerous local societies, committees, and clubs in various parts of the kingdom, were affiliated. Of this extensive confederation, in both countries, Lord George Gordon was elected president. The Protestants of Scotland had overawed the legislature: might not the Protestants of England advance their cause by intimidation? The experiment was now to be tried. On the 29th of

chie, elle la lui fait, pour ainsi dire, toucher à chaque instant.'—*De Tocqueville, Democr.*, i. 231.

[1] *Infra*, Chap. XII.

May, 1780, Lord George Gordon called a meeting of the Protestant Association, at Coachmakers' Hall, where a petition to the Commons was agreed to, praying for the repeal of the late Catholic relief act. Lord George, in haranguing this meeting, said that, 'if they meant to spend their time in mock debate and idle opposition, they might get another leader;' and declared that he would not present their petition, unless attended by 20,000 of his fellow-citizens. For that purpose, on the 2nd of June, a large body of petitioners and others, distinguished by blue cockades, assembled in St. George's Fields, whence they proceeded by different routes to Westminster, and took possession of Palace Yard, before the two Houses had yet met. As the peers drove down to the meeting of their House, several were assailed and pelted. Lord Boston was dragged from his coach, and escaped with difficulty from the mob. At the House of Commons, the mob forced their way into the lobby and passages, up to the very door of the House itself. They assaulted and molested many members, obliged them to wear 'blue cockades, and shout 'no popery!' *Meeting at Coach-makers' Hall, May 29th, 1780.*

*Disorders at Westminster, June 2nd.*

Though full notice had been given of such an irregular assemblage, no preparations had been made for maintaining the public peace, and securing Parliament from intimidation. The Lords were in danger of their lives; yet six constables only could be found to protect them. The Commons were invested: but their doorkeepers *Houses of Parliament invested.*

VOL. II.    T

alone resisted the intrusion of the mob. While this tumult was raging, Lord George Gordon proceeded to present the Protestant petition, and moved that it should be immediately considered in committee. Such a proposal could not be submitted to in presence of a hooting mob; and an amendment was moved to postpone the consideration of the petition till another day. A debate ensued, during which disorders were continued in the lobby, and in Palace Yard. Sometimes the House was interrupted by violent knocks at the door, and the rioters seemed on the point of bursting in. Members were preparing for defence, or to cut their way out with their swords. Meanwhile, the author of these disorders went several times into the lobby, and to the top of the gallery stairs, where he harangued the people, telling them that their petition was likely to meet with small favour, and naming the members who opposed it. Nor did he desist from this outrageous conduct, until Colonel Murray, a relative of his own, threatened him with his sword, on the entrance of the first rioter. When a division was called, the serjeant reported that he could not clear the lobby; and the proceedings of the House were suspended for a considerable time. At length, a detachment of military having arrived, the mob dispersed, the division was taken, and the House adjourned.[1]

*Riots in London.* The scene at Westminster had been sufficiently disgraceful: but it was merely the prelude to riots and incendiarism, by which London

[1] Ann. Reg., 1780, 190, *et seq.*; Parl. Hist., xxi. 654-666; State Tr., xxi. 486.

was desolated for a week. On the 6th of June, the Protestant petition was to be considered. Measures had been taken to protect the legislature from further outrage: but Lord Stormont's carriage was attacked, and broken to pieces; Mr. Burke was for some time in the hands of the mob; and an attempt was made upon Lord North's official residence, in Downing Street. The Commons agreed to resolutions in vindication of their privileges, and pledging themselves to consider the petition when the tumults should subside.[1]

Meanwhile, the outrages of the mob were encouraged by the supineness and timidity of the government and magistracy, until the whole metropolis was threatened with conflagration. The chapels of Catholic ambassadors were burned, prisons broken open, the houses of magistrates and statesmen destroyed; the residence of the venerable Mansfield, with his books and priceless manuscripts, was reduced to ashes. Even the bank of England was threatened. The streets swarmed with drunken incendiaries. At length the devastation was stayed by the bold decision of the king. 'There shall, at least, be one magistrate in the kingdom,' said he, 'who will do his duty;' and by his command a proclamation was immediately issued, announcing that the king's officers were instructed to repress the riots; and the military received orders to act without waiting for directions from the civil magistrate. The military were prompt in action; and

---

[1] Parl. Hist., xxi. 661.

the rioters were dispersed with bloodshed and slaughter.¹

<small>Military action in the absence of a magistrate.</small> The legality of military interference, in the absence of a magistrate, became afterwards the subject of discussion. It was laid down by Lord Mansfield, that the insurgents, having been engaged in overt acts of treason, felony and riot, it was the duty of every subject of His Majesty,—and not less of soldiers than of citizens,—to resist them. On this ground was the proclamation justified, and the action of the military pronounced to be warranted by law. His authority was accepted as conclusive. It was acknowledged that the executive, in times of tumult, must be armed with necessary power: but with how little discretion had it been used? Its timely exercise might have averted the anarchy and outrages of many days,—perhaps without bloodshed. Its tardy and violent action, at the last, had added to the evils of insurrection a sanguinary conflict with the people.²

Such was the sad issue of a distempered agitation in an unworthy cause, and conducted with intimidation and violence. The foolish and guilty leader of the movement escaped a conviction for high treason, to die, some years afterwards, in Newgate, a victim to the cruel administration of the law of libel;³

---

¹ Ann. Reg., 1780, 265, *et seq.* Nearly three hundred lives were known to have been lost; and one hundred and seventy-three wounded persons were received into the hospitals.

² Debates of Lords and Commons, June 19th, 1780; Parl. Hist., xxi. 690–701; Debate on Mr. Sheridan's motion (Westminster Police), March 5th, 1781; *Ibid.*, 1305.

³ State Tr., xxii., 175–236; Ann. Reg., 1793, Chron. 3.

and many of the rioters expiated their crimes on the scaffold.

A few years later another association was formed, to forward a cause of noble philanthropy, —the abolition of the slave trade. It was almost beyond the range of politics. It had no constitutional change to seek: no interest to promote: no prejudice to gratify: not even the national welfare to advance. Its clients were a despised race, in a distant clime,—an inferior type of the human family,—for whom natures of a higher mould felt repugnance rather than sympathy. Benevolence and Christian charity were its only incentives. On the other hand, the slave trade was supported by some of the most powerful classes in the country,— merchants, shipowners, planters. Before it could be proscribed, vested interests must be overborne,— ignorance enlightened,—prejudices and indifference overcome,—public opinion converted. And to this great work did Granville Sharpe, Wilberforce, Clarkson, and other noble spirits devote their lives. Never was cause supported by greater earnestness and activity. The organisation of the society comprehended all classes and religious denominations. Evidence was collected from every source, to lay bare the cruelties and iniquity of the traffic. Illustration and argument were inexhaustible. Men of feeling and sensibility appealed, with deep emotion, to the religious feelings and benevolence of the people. If extravagance and bad taste sometimes courted ridicule, the high purpose, just sentiments, and eloquence of the leaders of this movement won

*Slave-Trade Association, 1787.*

respect and admiration. Tracts found their way into every house : pulpits and platforms resounded with the wrongs of the negro : petitions were multiplied : ministers and Parliament moved to inquiry and action. Such a mission was not to be soon accomplished. The cause could not be won by sudden enthusiasm,—still less by intimidation : but conviction was to be wrought in the mind and conscience of the nation. And this was done. Parliament was soon prevailed upon to attempt the mitigation of the worst evils which had been brought to light; and in little more than twenty years, the slave trade was utterly condemned and prohibited.[1] A good cause prevailed,—not by violence and passion,—not by demonstrations of popular force,—but by reason, earnestness, and the best feelings of mankind.

At no former period had liberty of opinion made advances so signal, as during the first thirty years of this reign. Never had the voice of the people been heard so often, and so loudly, in the inner councils of the state. Public opinion was beginning to supply the defects of a narrow representation. But evil days were now approaching, when liberties so lately won were about to be suspended. Wild and fanatical democracy, on the one hand, transgressing the bounds of rational liberty ; and a too sensitive apprehension of its dangers, on the other, were introducing a period of reaction, unfavourable to popular rights.

*Progress of public opinion, 1760-1792.*

---

[1] Clarkson's Hist. of the Slave Trade, i. 288, &c.; Wilberforce's Life, i. 139-173, &c.

In 1792, the deepening shadows of the French revolution had inspired the great body of the people with sentiments of fear and repugnance; while a small, but noisy and turbulent, party, in advocating universal suffrage and annual parliaments, were proclaiming their admiration of French principles, and sympathy with the Jacobins of Paris. Currency was given to their opinions in democratic tracts, handbills, and newspapers, conceived in the spirit of sedition. Some of these papers were the work of authors expressing, as at other times, their own individual sentiments: but many were disseminated, at a low price, by democratic associations, in correspondence with France.[1] One of the most popular and dangerous of these publications was Paine's second part of the 'Rights of Man.'

*Democratic publications, 1792.*

Instead of singling out any obnoxious work for a separate prosecution, the government issued, on the 21st of May, 1792, a proclamation warning the people against wicked and seditious writings, industriously dispersed amongst them,—commanding magistrates to discover the authors, printers, and promulgators of such writings,—and sheriffs and others to take care to prevent tumults and disorders. This proclamation, having been laid before Parliament, was strongly denounced by Mr. Grey, Mr. Fox, and other members of the opposition, who alleged that it was calculated to excite

*Proclamation, May 21st, 1792.*

---

[1] Ann. Reg., 1792, p. 365; Hist. of the Two Acts, Introd., xxxvii; Adolphus' Hist. v. 67; Tomline's Life of Pitt, iii. 272.

groundless jealousies and alarms,[1]—the government already having sufficient powers, under the law, to repress license or disaffection.

Both Houses, however, concurred in an address to the king, approving of the objects of the proclamation, and expressing indignation at any attempts to weaken the sentiments of the people in favour of the established form of government.[2]

Thomas Paine was soon afterwards brought to trial. He was defended by Mr. Erskine, whom neither the displeasure of the king and the Prince of Wales, nor the solicitations of his friends, nor public clamours, had deterred from performing his duty as an advocate.[3] To vindicate such a book, on its own merits, was not to be attempted: but Mr. Erskine contended that, according to the laws of England, a writer is at liberty to address the reason of the nation upon the constitution and government, and is criminal only if he seeks to excite them to disobey the law, or calumniates living magistrates. He maintained 'that opinion is free, and that conduct alone is amenable to the law.' He himself condemned Mr. Paine's opinions: but his client was not to be punished because the jury disapproved of them as opinions, unless their character and intention were criminal. And he showed from the writings of

*Trial of Thomas Paine, Dec. 18th, 1792.*

---

[1] See also *supra*, p. 165.
[2] Parl. Hist., xxix. 1476-1534; Tomline's Life of Pitt, iii. 347; Lord Malmesbury's Corr., ii. 441. There had been similar proclamations in the reigns of Queen Anne and George I.
[3] St. Tr., xxvi. 715; Lord Campbell's Lives of the Chancellors, vi. 455.

Locke, Milton, Burke, Paley, and other speculative writers, to what an extent abstract opinions upon our constitution had been expressed, without being objected to as libellous. The obnoxious writer was found guilty:[1] but the general principles expounded by his advocate, to which his contemporaries turned a deaf ear, have long been accepted as the basis on which liberty of opinion is established.

Meanwhile, the fears of democracy, of the press, and of speculative opinions, were further aggravated by the progress of events in France, and the extravagance of English democrats. *Alarm of the government and magistracy.*

Several societies, which had been formed for other objects, now avowed their sympathy and fellowship with the revolutionary party in France, — addressed the National Convention, — corresponded with political clubs and public men in Paris; and imitated the sentiments, the language, and the cant then in vogue across the channel.[2] Of these the most conspicuous were the 'Revolution Society,' the 'Society for Constitutional Information,' and the 'London Corresponding Society.' The Revolution Society had been formed long since, to commemorate the English revolution of 1688, and not that of France, a century later. It met annually on the 4th of November, when its principal toasts were the memory of King William, trial by jury, and the liberty of the press. On the 4th of Nov., 1788, the centenary of the *Democratic associations.* *The Revolution Society.*

---

[1] St. Tr., xxii. 357.
[2] Ann. Reg., 1792, part ii. 128-170, 344.

Revolution had been commemorated throughout the country, by men of all parties; and the Revolution Society had been attended by a secretary of state, and other distinguished persons.[1] But the excitement of the times quickened it with a new life; and historical sentiment was lost in political agitation. The example of France almost effaced the memory of William.[2] The Society for Constitutional Information had been formed in 1780, to instruct the people in their political rights, and to forward the cause of parliamentary reform. Among its early members were the Duke of Richmond, Mr. Fox, Mr. Pitt himself, and Mr. Sheridan. These soon left the society: but Mr. Wyvill, Major Cartwright, Mr. Horne Tooke, and a few more zealous politicians, continued to support it, advocating universal suffrage, and distributing obscure tracts. It was scarcely known to the public: its funds were low; and it was only saved from a natural death by the French revolution.[3]

*Society for Constitutional Information.*

The London Corresponding Society,—composed chiefly of working men,—was founded in the midst of the excitement caused by events in France. It sought to remedy all the grievances

*London Corresponding Society.*

---

[1] History of the Two Acts, Introd., xxxv.
[2] Abstract of the History and Proceedings of the Revolution Society, 1789; Sermon by Dr. Price, with Appendix, 1789; 'The Correspondence of the Revolution Society in London,' &c., 1792; Ann. Reg., 1792, part i. 165, 311, 366; part ii. 135; App. to Chron., 128, et seq.; Adolphus' Hist., iv. 543, v. 211.
[3] Stephens' Life of Horne Tooke, i. 435; ii. 144; Hist. of the Two Acts, Introd., xxxvii. Wyvill's Pol. Papers, ii. 537; Adolphus' Hist., v. 212; Lord Stanhope's Life of Pitt, ii. 65.

of society, real or imaginary,—to correct all political abuses,—and particularly to obtain universal suffrage and annual parliaments. These objects were to be secured by the joint action of affiliated societies throughout the country. The scheme embraced a wide correspondence, not only with other political associations in England, but with the National Convention of France, and the Jacobins of Paris. The leaders were obscure and, for the most part, illiterate men; and the proceedings of the society were more conspicuous for extravagance and folly than for violence. Arguments for universal suffrage were combined with abstract speculations, and conventional phrases, borrowed from France,—wholly foreign to the sentiments of Englishmen and the genius of English liberty. Their members were 'citizens,' the king was 'chief magistrate.'[1]

These societies, animated by a common sentiment, engaged in active correspondence; and published numerous resolutions and addresses of a democratic, and sometimes of a seditious character. Their wild and visionary schemes,—however captivating to a lower class of politicians,—served only to discredit and endanger liberty. They were repudiated by the 'Society of the Friends of the People,'[2] and by all the earnest but temperate reformers of that time: they shocked the sober, alarmed the timid, and provoked,

---

[1] Ann. Reg., 1792, p. 366; 1793, p. 165; App. to Chron., 75; 1794, p. 129; Adolphus' Hist., v. 212; Tomline's Life of Pitt, iii. 272, 321; Lord J. Russell's Life of Fox, ii. 284; Belsham's Hist., viii. 495, 499.
[2] See *supra*, Vol. I. 402; Lord J. Russell's Life of Fox, ii. 293.

—if they did not justify,—the severities of the government.

In ordinary times, the insignificance of these societies would have excited contempt rather than alarm: but as clubs and demagogues, originally not more formidable, had obtained a terrible ascendency in France, they aroused apprehensions out of proportion to their real danger. In presence of a political earthquake, without a parallel in the history of the world, every symptom of revolution was too readily magnified.

There is no longer room for doubt that the alarm of this period was exaggerated and excessive. Evidence was not forthcoming to prove it just and well-founded. The societies, however mischievous, had a small following: they were not encouraged by any men of influence : the middle classes repudiated them: society at large condemned them. None of the causes which had precipitated the revolution in France were in existence here. None of the evils of an absolute government provoked popular resentment. We had no *lettres de cachet*, or Bastille: no privileged aristocracy: no impassable gulf between nobles and the commonalty: no ostracism of opinion. We had a free constitution, of which Englishmen were proud,—a settled society,—with just gradations of rank, bound together by all the ties of a well-ordered commonwealth; and our liberties, long since secured, were still growing with the greatness and enlightenment of the people. In France there was no bond between the government and its subjects but author-

*[marginal note: Exaggerated alarms.]*

ity: in England, power rested on the broad basis of liberty. So stanch was the loyalty of the country, that where one person was tainted with sedition, thousands were prepared to defend the law and constitution with their lives. The people, as zealous in the cause of good order as their rulers, were proof against the seductions of a few pitiful democrats. Instead of sympathising with the French revolution, they were shocked at its bloody excesses, and recoiled with horror from its social and religious extravagances. The core of English society was sound. Who that had lately witnessed the affectionate loyalty of the whole people, on the recovery of the king from his affliction, could suspect them of republicanism?

Yet their very loyalty was now adverse to the public liberties. It showed itself in dread and hatred of democracy. Repression and severity were popular, and sure of cordial support. The influential classes, more alarmed than the government, eagerly fomented the prevailing spirit of reaction. They had long been jealous of the growing influence of the press and popular opinion. Their own power had been disturbed by the political agitation of the last thirty years, and was further threatened by parliamentary reform. But the time had now come for recovering their ascendency. The democratic spirit of the people was betraying itself; and must be crushed out, in the cause of order. The dangers of parliamentary reform were illustrated by clamours for universal suffrage, annual parliaments, and the rights of man; and

*Repressive policy, 1792.*

reformers of all degrees were to be scouted as revolutionary.

The calm and lofty spirit of Mr. Pitt was little prone to apprehension. He had discountenanced Mr. Burke's early reprobation of the French revolution: he had recently declared his confidence in the peace and prosperity of his country; and had been slow to foresee the political dangers of events in France. But he now yielded to the pressure of Mr. Burke and an increasing party in Parliament; and while he quieted their apprehensions, he secured for himself a vast addition of moral and material support. Enlarging his own party, and breaking up the opposition, he at the same time won public confidence.

It was a crisis of unexampled difficulty,—needing the utmost vigilance and firmness. Ministers, charged with the maintenance of order, could not neglect any security which the peril of the time demanded. They were secure of support in punishing sedition and treason: the guilty few would meet with no sympathy among a loyal people. But, counselled by their new chancellor and convert, Lord Loughborough, and the law officers of the crown, the government gave too ready a credence to the reports of their agents; and invested the doings of a small knot of democrats,—chiefly working men, —with the dignity of a wide-spread conspiracy to overturn the constitution. Ruling over a free state, they learned to dread the people, in the spirit of tyrants. Instead of relying upon the sober judgment of the country, they appealed to its fears;

and in repressing seditious practices, they were prepared to sacrifice liberty of opinion. Their policy, dictated by the circumstances of a time of strange and untried danger, was approved by the prevailing sentiment of their contemporaries: but has not been justified,—in an age of greater freedom,—by the maturer judgment of posterity.

The next step taken by the government was calculated to excite a panic. On the 1st of December, 1792, a proclamation was issued, stating that so dangerous a spirit of tumult and disorder had been excited by evil-disposed persons, acting in concert with persons in foreign parts, that it was necessary to call out and embody the militia. And Parliament, which then stood prorogued until the 3rd of January, was directed to meet on the 13th of December. *Proclamation, Dec. 1st, 1792.*

The king's speech, on the opening of Parliament, repeated the statements of the proclamation; and adverted to designs, in concert with persons in foreign countries, to attempt 'the destruction of our happy constitution, and the subversion of all order and government.'[1] These statements were warmly combated by Mr. Fox, who termed them 'an intolerable calumny upon the people of Great Britain,' and argued that the executive government were about to assume control, not only over the acts of the people, but over their very thoughts. Instead of silencing discussion, he counselled a forwardness to redress every grievance. *King's speech, Dec. 13th, 1792.*

[1] Comm. Journ., xlviii. 4; Parl. Hist., xxx. 6; Fox's Speeches, iv. 445.

Other speakers also protested against the exaggerated views of the state of the country which the administration had encouraged. They exhorted ministers to have confidence in the loyalty and sound judgment of the people; and, instead of fomenting apprehensions, to set an example of calmness and sobriety. But in both Houses addresses were voted,[1] giving the sanction of Parliament to the sentiments expressed from the throne.[2] The majority did not hesitate to permit popular privileges to be sacrificed to the prevailing panic.

But as yet no evidence of the alleged dangers had been produced; and on the 28th of February, Mr. Sheridan proposed an inquiry, in a committee of the whole House.

*Mr. Sheridan's motion Feb. 28th, 1793.*

He denied the existence of seditious practices; and imputed to the government a desire to create a panic, in order to inflame the public mind against France, with which war was now declared; and to divert attention from parliamentary reform. The debate elicited no further evidence of sedition: but the motion was negatived without a division.[3]

Meanwhile, prosecutions of the press abounded, especially against publishers of Paine's works.[4] Seditious speaking was also vigilantly repressed. A few examples will illustrate the rigorous adminis-

---

[1] In the Commons by a majority of 290 to 50.
[2] Parl. Hist., xxx. 1–80. Ann. Reg., 1793, p. 244–249.
[3] Parl. Hist., xxx. 523.
[4] E. g., Daniel Isaac Eaton, Daniel Holt, and others; State Tr., xxii. 574–822; *Ibid.*, xxiii. 214, &c., The Attorney-General stated, on the 13th December, 1792, that he had on his file 200 informations for seditious libels.—Adolphus' Hist., v. 524. See also Currie's Life, i. 185; Roscoe's Life, i. 124; Holcroft's Mem., ii. 151.

tration of the laws. John Frost, a respectable attorney, who had been associated with the Duke of Richmond and Mr. Pitt, a few years before, in promoting parliamentary reform, was prosecuted for seditious words spoken in conversation, after dinner, at a coffee-house. His words, reprehensible in themselves, were not aggravated by evidence of malice or seditious intent. They could scarcely be termed advised speaking; yet was he found guilty, and sentenced to six months' imprisonment, to stand in the pillory at Charing Cross, and to be struck off the roll of attorneys.[1] Mr. Winterbotham, a Baptist Minister, was tried for uttering seditious words in two sermons. The evidence brought against him was distinctly contradicted by several witnesses; and in the second case, so weak was the evidence for the crown, and so conclusive his defence, that the judge directed an acquittal; yet in both cases the jury returned verdicts of guilty. The luckless minister was sentenced to four years' imprisonment, to pay two fines of 100*l*., and to give security for his good behaviour.[2] Thomas Briellat was tried for the use of seditious words in conversations at a public-house, and in a butcher's shop. Here again the evidence for the prosecution was contradicted by witnesses for the defence: but no credit being given to the latter, the jury returned a verdict of guilty; and Briellat was sentenced to twelve months' imprisonment, and to pay a fine of 100*l*.[3]

Trial of Frost, March 1793.

Mr. Winterbotham, 1793.

Case of Thomas Briellat, 1793.

[1] St. Tr., xxii. 522.   [2] *Ibid.*, 823, 875.   [3] *Ibid.*, 910.

The trial of Dr. Hudson, for seditious words spoken at the London Coffee-House, affords another illustration of the alarmed and watchful spirit of the people. Dr. Hudson had addressed toasts and sentiments to his friend Mr. Pigott, who was dining with him in the same box. Other guests in the coffee-house overheard them, and interfered with threats and violence. Both the friends were given in charge to a constable: but Dr. Hudson was alone brought to trial.[1] He was found guilty, and sentenced to two years' imprisonment, and to pay a fine of 200*l*.[2]

*Dr. Hudson, Dec. 9th, 1793.*

Nor were such prosecutions confined to the higher tribunals. The magistrates, invited to vigilance by the king's proclamation, and fully sharing the general alarm, were satisfied with scant evidence of sedition; and if they erred in their zeal, were sure of being upheld by higher authorities.[3] And thus every incautious disputant was at the mercy of panic-stricken witnesses, officious constables, and country justices.

*Trials at Quarter Sessions.*

Another agency was evoked by the spirit of the times,—dangerous to the liberty of the press, and to the security of domestic life. Voluntary societies were established in

*Voluntary societies for repressing sedition.*

---

[1] The bill of indictment against Pigott was rejected by the grand jury.

[2] St. Tr., xxii. 1019.

[3] A yeoman in his cups being exhorted by a constable, as drunk as himself, to keep the peace in the king's name, muttered, 'D—— you and the king too:' for which the loyal quarter sessions of Kent sentenced him to a year's imprisonment. A complaint being made of this sentence to Lord Chancellor Loughborough, he said, 'that to save the country from revolution, the authority of all tribunals, high and low, must be upheld.'—*Lord Campbell's Lives of the Chancellors*, vi. 265.

London and throughout the country, for the purpose of aiding the executive government in the discovery and punishment of seditious writings or language. Of these the parent was the 'Society for the protection of liberty and property against republicans and levellers.' These societies, supported by large subscriptions, were busy in collecting evidence of seditious designs,—often consisting of anonymous letters,—often of the reports of informers, liberally rewarded for their activity. They became, as it were, public prosecutors, supplying the government with proofs of supposed offences, and quickening its zeal in the prosecution of offenders. Every unguarded word at the club, the market-place, or the tavern, was reported to these credulous alarmists, and noted as evidence of disaffection.

Such associations were repugnant to the policy of our laws, by which the crown is charged with the office of bringing offenders to justice, while the people, represented by juries, are to judge, without favour or prejudice, of their guilt or innocence. But here the people were invited to make common cause with the crown against offenders, to collect the evidence, and prejudge the guilt. How then could members of these societies assist in the pure administration of justice, as jurymen and justices of the peace? In the country especially was justice liable to be warped. Local cases of sedition were tried at the Quarter Sessions, by magistrates who were leaders of these societies, and by jurors who, if not also members, were the tenants or neighbours of the gentlemen on the bench. Prosecutor, judge, and jury being all leagued against the accused, in a time of panic, how could any man demand with confidence to be tried by his peers?[1]

Meanwhile, the authorities in Scotland were more alarmed by the French revolution than the English government; and their apprehensions were increased by the proceedings of several societies for democratic reform, and by the assembling in Edinburgh of a 'convention of delegates of the associated friends of the people,' from various parts of England and Scotland. The mission of these delegates was to discuss annual parliaments and universal suffrage: but the excitement of the times led them to an extravagance of language, and proceedings which had characterised other associations.[2] The government resolved to confront democracy and overawe sedition: but in this period of panic, even justice was at fault; and the law was administered with a severity discreditable to the courts, and to the public sentiments of that country. Some of the persons implicated in obnoxious publications withdrew from the jurisdiction of the courts;[3] while those who remained found little justice or mercy.[4]

*Apprehensions of democracy in Scotland.*

Thomas Muir, a young advocate of high talents and attainments, having exposed himself to suspicion by his activity in promoting

*Trial of Muir, Aug. 30th, 1793.*

[1] Proceedings of the Friends of the liberty of the Press, Jan. 1793; Erskine's Speeches, iv. 411.
[2] Ann. Reg., 1794, p. 129; State Tr., xxiii. 385, *et seq.*, 398.
[3] James Tytler, St. Tr., xxiii. 2; John Elder and William Stewart, *Ibid.*, 25; James Smith and John Mennons, *Ibid.*, 34; James T. Callender, *Ibid.*, 84.
[4] See Trial of Walter Berry and James Robertson, St. Tr., xxiii. 79.

the proscribed cause of parliamentary reform, and as a member of the convention of delegates, was brought to trial before the High Court of Justiciary at Edinburgh, for sedition. Every incident of this trial marked the unfairness and cruel spirit of his judges.

In deciding upon the relevancy of the indictment, they dilated upon the enormity of the offences charged, which, in their judgment, amounted almost to high treason,—upon the excellence of our constitution,[1] and the terrors of the French revolution. It was plain that any attempt to amend our institutions was, in their eyes, a crime. All the jurymen, selected by the sheriff and picked by the presiding judge,[2] were members of an association at Goldsmith's Hall, who had erased Muir's name from their books as an enemy to the constitution. He objected that such men had already prejudged his cause, but was told he might as well object to his judges, who had sworn to maintain the constitution! The witnesses for the crown failed to prove any seditious speeches, —while they all bore testimony to the earnestness with which he had counselled order and obedience to the law. Throughout the trial, he was browbeaten and threatened by the judges. A contemptible witness against him was 'caressed by the prosecutor, and complimented by the court,'—while a witness of his own was hurriedly committed for concealing the truth, without hearing Muir on his behalf, who was

---

[1] The Lord Justice Clerk (Lord Braxfield) termed it 'the happiest, the best, and the most noble constitution in the world, and I do not believe it possible to make a better.'—*St. Tr.*, xxiii. 132.

[2] State Tr., xix. 11 *n.*; Cockburn's Mem., 87.

told that 'he had no right or title to interfere in the business.' In the spirit of a bygone age of judicature, the Lord Advocate denounced Muir as a demon of sedition and mischief. He even urged it as a proof of guilt that a letter had been found among his papers, addressed to Mr. Fyshe Palmer, who was about to be tried for sedition!

Muir defended himself in a speech worthy of the talents and courage which were to be crushed by this prosecution. Little did they avail him. He knew that he was addressing men by whom his cause had been prejudged: but he appealed worthily to the public and to posterity; and affirmed that he was tried, in truth, for promoting parliamentary reform. The Lord Justice Clerk, Braxfield,[1] confirmed this assertion, by charging the jury that to preach the necessity of reform, at a time of excitement, was seditious. This learned judge also harangued the jury upon parliamentary reform. 'The landed interest alone had a right to be represented,' he said; 'as for the rabble, who have nothing but personal property, what hold has the nation of them?' Need it be told that the jury returned a verdict of guilty? And now the judges renewed their reflections upon the enormity of the prisoner's crimes. Lord Henderland noticed the applause with which Muir's noble defence had been received by the audience,—which could not but admire his spirit and eloquence,—as a proof of the seditious feelings of the people; and

---

[1] Robert McQueen of Braxfield—Lord Braxfield, 'was the Jeffreys of Scotland.' 'Let them bring me more prisoners, and I will find them law,' was said to have been his language to the government.— *Lord Cockburn's Mem.*, 116.

though his lordship allowed that this incident should not aggravate Muir's punishment, he proceeded to pass a sentence of transportation for fourteen years. Lord Swinton could scarcely distinguish Muir's crime from high treason, and said, with a ferocity unworthy of a Christian judge, 'if punishment adequate to the crime of sedition were to be sought for, it could not be found in our law, now that torture is happily abolished.' He concurred in the sentence of transportation,— referring to the Roman law where seditious criminals '*aut in furcam tolluntur, aut bestiis objiciuntur, aut in insulam deportantur.*' 'We have chosen the mildest of these punishments,' said his lordship! Lord Abercromby and the Lord Justice Clerk thought the defendant fortunate in having escaped with his life,—the penalty of treason; and the latter, referring to the applause with which Muir had been greeted, admitted that the circumstance had no little weight with him in considering the punishment.[1]

What was this but an avowal that public opinion was to be repressed and punished in the person of Muir, who was now within the grasp of the law? And thus, without even the outward show of a fair trial, Muir stood sentenced to a punishment of unwarrantable, if not illegal, severity.[2]

[1] St. Tr., xxiii. 118-238; Lord Campbell's Lives of the Chancellors, vi. 261. In reference to this trial, Lord Cockburn says, 'if, instead of being a Supreme Court of Justice, sitting for the trial of guilt or innocence, it had been an ancient commission appointed by the crown to procure convictions, little of its judicial manner would have required to be changed.'—*Memorials*, p. 100.

[2] There is little doubt that the law of Scotland did not authorise

A few days after this trial, the Rev. T. Fyshe Palmer[1] was tried for sedition before the Circuit Court of Justiciary at Perth. He was charged with circulating an address from 'A society of the friends of liberty to their fellow-citizens.' However strong the language of this paper,[2] its sole object was to secure a reform of the House of Commons, to whose corruption and dependence were attributed all the evils which it denounced. His trial was conducted with less intemperance than that of Muir, but scarcely with more fairness. In deciding upon the relevancy of the indictment, the judges entertained no doubt that the paper was seditious, which they proved mainly by combating the truth of the propositions contained in it. The witnesses for the crown, who gave their evidence with much reluctance, proved that Palmer was not the author of the address: but had corrected it, and softened many of its expres-

*The Rev. T. Fyshe Palmer, Sept. 12th, 1793.*

---

the sentence of transportation for sedition, but of banishment only. This was affirmed over and over again. In 1797 Mr. Fox said he was satisfied, "not merely on the authority of the most learned men of that country, but on the information he had himself been able to acquire, that no such law did exist in Scotland, and that those who acted upon it, will one day be brought to a severe retribution for their conduct.'—*Parl. Hist.*, xxxiii. 616.

It seems also that the Act 25 Geo. III. c. 46, for removing offenders, in Scotland, to places of temporary confinement, had expired in 1788; and that 'Muir and Palmer were nevertheless removed from Scotland and transported to Botany Bay, though there was no statute then in force to warrant it.'—*Lord Colchester's Diary*, i. 50.

[1] Mr. Palmer had taken orders in the Church of England, but afterwards became an Unitarian Minister.

[2] 'That portion of liberty you once enjoyed is fast setting, we fear, in the darkness of despotism and tyranny,' was the strongest sentence.

sions. That he was concerned in its printing and circulation, was clearly proved.

The judicial views of sedition may be estimated from part of Lord Abercromby's summing up. 'Gentlemen,' said he, 'the right of universal suffrage, the subjects of this country never enjoyed; and were they to enjoy it, they would not long enjoy either liberty or a free constitution. You will, therefore, consider whether telling the people that they have a just right to what would unquestionably be tantamount to a total subversion of this constitution, is such a writing as any person is entitled to compose, to print, and to publish.' When such opinions were declared from the bench, who can wonder if complaints were heard that the law punished as sedition, the advocacy of parliamentary reform? Palmer was found guilty and sentenced to seven years' transportation,—not without intimations from Lord Abercromby and Lord Eskgrove that his crime so nearly amounted to treason, that he had narrowly escaped its punishment.[1]

After these trials, the government resolved to put down the Convention of the Friends of the People in Edinburgh, whose proceedings had become marked by greater extravagance.[2] Its leaders were arrested, and its papers seized. In January 1794, William Skirving,

*Trial of William Skirving, Jan. 6th and 7th, 1794.*

---

[1] St. Tr., xxiii. 237.
[2] It was now called the British Convention of Delegates, &c. Its members were citizens: its place of meeting was called Liberty Hall: it appointed secret committees, and spoke mysteriously of a convention of emergency.

the secretary, was tried for sedition, as being concerned in the publication of the address to the people, for which Palmer had already been convicted, and in other proceedings of the convention. He was found guilty and sentenced to fourteen years' transportation. On hearing his sentence, Skirving said:—'My Lords, I know that what has been done these two days will be rejudged; that is my comfort, and all my hope.'[1] That his guilt was assumed and prejudged, neither prosecutor nor judge attempted to disguise. The solicitor-general, in his opening speech, said:—'The very name of British convention carries sedition along with it.' —'And the British convention associated for what? For the purpose of obtaining universal suffrage: in other words, for the purpose of subverting the government of Great Britain.' And when Skirving, like Muir, objected to the jurors, as members of the Goldsmiths' Hall Association, Lord Eskgrove said, 'by making this objection, the panel is avowing that it was their purpose to overturn the government.'

Maurice Margarot[2] and Joseph Gerrald,[3] who had been sent by the London Corresponding Society to the Convention of the Friends of the People at Edinburgh, were tried for

*Margarot and Gerrald, Jan. and March, 1794.*

---

[1] State Trials, xxiii. 391–602. Hume's Criminal Commentaries were compiled 'in a great measure for the purpose of vindicating the proceedings of the Criminal Court in these cases of sedition;' but 'there is scarcely one of his favourite points that the legislature, with the cordial assent of the public and of lawyers, has not put down.'—*Lord Cockburn's Mem.*, 164; and see his art. in Edinb. Rev. No. 167, art. 7.

[2] St. Tr., xxiii. 603.     [3] *Ibid.*, 805.

seditious speeches and other proceedings, in connection with that convention; and on being found guilty, were sentenced to fourteen years' transportation.[1]

The circumstances attending these trials, and the extreme severity of the sentences, could not fail to raise animadversions in Parliament. The case of Mr. Muir was brought before the Lords by Earl Stanhope;[2] and that of Mr. Fyshe Palmer before the Commons, on a petition from himself, presented by Mr. Sheridan.[3]

*These trials noticed in Parliament. Jan. 31st, 1794. Feb. 24th, Mar. 10th.*

The cases of Muir and Palmer were afterwards more fully laid before the House of Commons, by Mr. Adam. He contended, in an able speech, that the offences with which they had been charged were no more than leasing-making, according to the law of Scotland,[4] for which no such punishment as transportation could be inflicted. He also called attention to many of the circumstances connected with these trials, in order to show their unfairness; and moved for a copy of the record of Muir's trial. The trials and sentences were defended by the Lord Advocate, Mr. Windham, and Mr. Pitt; and strongly censured by Mr. Sheridan, Mr. Whitbread, Mr. Grey, and Mr. Fox. The latter denounced, with eloquent indig-

---

[1] Mr. Fox said of Gerrald, in 1797, 'his elegant and useful attainments made him dear to the circles of literature and taste. Bred to enjoyments, in which his accomplishments fitted him to participate, and endowed with talents that rendered him valuable to his country, . . . the punishment to such a man was certain death, and accordingly he sank under the sentence, the victim of virtuous, wounded sensibility.'—*Parl. Hist.*, xxxiii. 617

[2] Parl. Hist., xxx. 1298.   [3] *Ibid.*, xxx. 1449.

[4] Scots Act of Q. Anne, 1703, c. 4.

nation, some of the extravagant expressions which had proceeded from the bench, and exclaimed, 'God help the people who have such judges!' The motion was refused by a large majority.[1]

Mar 25th. These cases were again incidentally brought into discussion, upon a motion of Mr. Adam respecting the criminal law of Scotland.[2] They were also discussed in the House of Lords, upon a motion April.15th. of Lord Lauderdale, but without any results.[3]

Sympathy for the prisoners. The prisoners were without redress, but their sufferings excited a strong popular sympathy, especially in Scotland. 'These trials,' says Lord Cockburn, 'sank deep, not merely into the popular mind, but into the minds of all men who thought. It was by these proceedings, more than by any other wrong, that the spirit of discontent justified itself throughout the rest of that age.'[4] This strong sense of injustice rankled in the minds of a whole generation of Scotchmen, and after fifty years, found expression in the Martyrs' Memorial on Calton Hill.[5]

Other cases of sedition in England. Meanwhile, some of the cases of sedition tried by the courts, in England, brought ridicule upon the administration of justice. Daniel

---

[1] Ayes, 32; Noes, 171; Parl. Hist., xxx. 1486.
[2] *Ibid.*, xxxi. 54.
[3] *Ibid.*, 263. For an account of the sufferings of Muir and Palmer on board of the hulks, see St. Tr., xxiii. 377, *note*. Palmer, Gerrald, and Skirving died abroad; Muir escaped to Europe, and died in Paris, in 1799.—Ann. Reg., 1797, Chron., p. 14, and 1799, Chron., p. 9.
[4] Lord Cockburn's Mem., 102: Belsham's Hist., ix. 77-80.
[5] Erected 1844.

Isaac Eaton was tried for publishing a contemptible pamphlet entitled 'Politics for the people, or Hog's Wash,' in which the king was supposed to be typified under the character of a game cock. It was a ridiculous prosecution, characteristic of the times: the culprit escaped, and the lawyers were laughed at.[1] Daniel Isaac Eaton, Feb. 24th, 1794.

Another prosecution, of more formidable pretensions, was brought to an issue, in April 1794. Thomas Walker, an eminent merchant of Manchester, and six other persons, were charged with a conspiracy to overthrow the constitution and government, and to aid the French in the invasion of these shores. This charge expressed all the fears with which the government were harassed, and its issue exposed their extravagance. The entire charge was founded upon the evidence of a disreputable witness, Thomas Dunn, whose falsehoods were so transparent that a verdict of acquittal was immediately taken, and the witness was committed for his perjury. The arms that were to have overturned the government and constitution of the country, proved to be mere children's toys, and some firearms which Mr. Walker had obtained to defend his own house against a church and king mob, by whom it had been assailed.[2] Thomas Walker, of Manchester, and others, April 1794. That such a case could have appeared to the officers of the crown worthy of a public trial, is evidence of the heated imagination of the time, which discovered conspiracies and treason in all the actions of men.

[1] St. Tr., xxiii. 1014.     [2] *Ibid.*, 1055.

It was not until late in the session of 1794, that the ministers laid before Parliament any evidence of seditious practices. But in May 1794, some of the leading members of the democratic societies having been arrested, and their papers seized, a message from the king was delivered to both Houses, stating that he had directed the books of certain corresponding societies to be laid before them.[1] In the Commons, these papers were referred to a secret committee, which first reported upon the proceedings of the Society for Constitutional Information, and the London Corresponding Society; and pronounced its opinion that measures were being taken for assembling a general convention 'to supersede the House of Commons in its representative capacity, and to assume to itself all the functions and powers of a national legislature.'[2] It was also stated that measures had recently been taken for providing arms, to be distributed amongst the members of the societies. No sooner had the report been read, than Mr. Pitt, after recapitulating the evidence upon which it was founded, moved for a bill to suspend the habeas corpus act, which was rapidly passed through both Houses.[3]

A secret committee of the Lords reported that 'a traitorous conspiracy had been formed for the subversion of the established laws and constitution, and the introduction of that system of anarchy and confusion which has fatally

---

[1] Parl. Hist., xxxi. 471.  [2] *Ibid.*, 495.
[3] See Chap. XI.

prevailed in France.'[1] And the committee of the Commons, in a second report, revealed evidence of the secret manufacture of arms, in connection with the societies,—of other designs dangerous to the public peace,— and of proceedings ominously formed upon the French model.[2] A second report was also issued, on the following day, from the committee of the Lords.[3] They were followed by loyal addresses from both Houses, expressing their indignation at these seditious practices, and the determination to support the constitution and peace of the country.[4] The warmest friends of free discussion had no sympathy with sedition, or the dark plots of political fanatics: but, relying upon the loyalty and good conduct of the people, and the soundness of the constitution, they steadily contended that these dangers were exaggerated, and might be safely left to the ordinary administration of the law.

*Second Report of Secret Committee (Commons), June 6th.*

Notwithstanding the dangers disclosed in these reports, prosecutions for seditious libel, both in England and Ireland, were singularly infelicitous. The convictions secured were few compared with the acquittals; and the evidence was so often drawn from spies and informers, that a storm of unpopularity was raised against the government. Classes, heartily on the side of order, began to be alarmed for the public liberties. They were willing that libellers should be punished: but protested against the privacy of domestic life being

*Trials for seditious libels, 1794.*

---

[1] Parl. Hist., xxxi. 574.     [2] *Ibid.*, 688.
[3] *Ibid.*    [4] *Ibid.*, 909–931.

invaded by spies, who trafficked upon the excitement of the times.¹

Crimes more serious than seditious writings were now to be repressed. Traitorous societies, conspiring to subvert the laws and constitution, were to be assailed, and their leaders brought to justice. If they had been guilty of treason, all good subjects prayed that they might be convicted: but thoughtful men, accustomed to free discussion and association for political purposes, dreaded lest the rights and liberties of the people should be sacrificed to the public apprehensions.

<small>State trials, 1794.</small>

In 1794, Robert Watt and David Downie were tried, in Scotland, for high treason. They were accused of a conspiracy to call a convention, with a view to usurp legislative power, to procure arms, and resist the royal authority. That their designs were dangerous and criminal was sufficiently proved, and was afterwards confessed by Watt. A general convention was to be assembled, comprising representatives from England, Scotland, and Ireland, and supported by an armed insurrection. The troops were to be seduced or overpowered, the public offices and banks secured, and the king compelled to dismiss his ministers and dissolve parliament. These alarming projects were discussed by seven obscure individuals in Edinburgh, of whom Watt, a spy, was the leader, and David Downie, a mechanic, the treasurer. Two of the seven soon withdrew from the conferences of

<small>Trials of Robert Watt and David Downie for high treason, Aug. and Sept. 1794.</small>

---

¹ Adolphus' Hist., vi. 45, 46.

the conspirators ; and four became witnesses for the crown. Forty-seven pikes had been made, but none had been distributed. Seditious writing and speaking, and a criminal conspiracy, were too evidently established: but it was only by straining the dangerous doctrines of constructive treason, that the prisoners could be convicted of that graver crime. They were tried separately, and both being found guilty, received sentence of death.[1] Watt was executed: but Downie, having been recommended to mercy by the jury, received a pardon.[2] It was the first conviction yet obtained for any of those traitorous designs, for the reality of which Parliament had been induced to vouch.

While awaiting more serious events, the public were excited by the discovery of a regicide plot. The conspirators were members of the much-dreaded Corresponding Society, and had concerted a plan for assassinating the king. Their murderous instrument was a tube, or air-gun, through which a poisoned arrow was to be shot! No wonder that this foul conspiracy at once received the name of the 'Pop-Gun Plot!' A sense of the ridiculous prevailed over the fears and loyalty of the people.[3]

*The pop-gun plot, Sept. 1794.*

---

[1] St. Tr., xxiii. 1167; *Ibid.*, xxiv. 11. Not long before the commission of those acts which cost him his life, Watt had been giving information to Mr. Secretary Dundas of dangerous plots which never existed; and suspicions were entertained that if his criminal suggestions had been adopted by others, and a real plot put in movement, he would have been the first to expose it and to claim a reward for his disclosures. If such was his design the 'biter was bit,' as he fell a sacrifice to the evidence of his confederates.—St. Tr., xxiii. 1325; Belsham's Hist., ix. 227.

[2] Speech of Mr. Curwen in defence of Downie, St. Tr., xxiv. 150; Speech of Mr. Erskine in defence of Hardy, *Ibid.*, 964, &c.

[3] Crossfield, the chief conspirator, being abroad, the other traitors

But before the ridicule excited by the discovery of such a plot had subsided, trials of a far graver character were approaching, in which not only the lives of the accused, but the credit of the executive, the wisdom of Parliament, and the liberties of the people were at stake.

Parliament had declared in May[1] 'that a traitorous and detestable conspiracy had been formed for subverting the existing laws and constitution, and for introducing the system of anarchy and confusion which has so lately prevailed in France.' In October, a special commission was issued for the trial of the leaders of this conspiracy. The grand jury returned a true bill against Thomas Hardy, John Horne Tooke, John Thelwall, and nine other prisoners, for high treason. These persons were members of the London Corresponding Society, and of the Society for Constitutional Information, which had formed the subject of the reports of secret committees, and had inspired the government with so much apprehension. It had been the avowed object of both these societies to obtain parliamentary reform : but the prisoners were charged with conspiring to break the public peace, —to excite rebellion,—to depose the king and put him to death, and alter the legislature and government of the country,—to summon a convention of the people for effecting these traitorous designs,— to write and issue letters and addresses, in order to

*State trials, 1794.*

*Oct. 6th, 1794.*

---

were not brought to trial for nearly two years, when Crossfield and his confederates were all acquitted.—St. Tr., xxvi. 1.

[1] Preamble to Habeas Corpus Suspension Act, 34 Geo. III. c. 54.

assemble such a convention; and to provide arms for the purpose of resisting the king's authority.

Never, since the revolution, had prisoners been placed at so great a disadvantage, in defending themselves from charges of treason. They were accused of the very crimes which Parliament had declared to be rife throughout the country; and in addressing the grand jury, Chief Justice Eyre had referred to the recent act, as evidence of a wide-spread conspiracy to subvert the government.

The first prisoner brought to trial was a simple mechanic, Thomas Hardy,—a shoemaker by trade, and secretary of the London Corresponding Society. Day after day, evidence was produced by the crown, first to establish the existence and character of this conspiracy; and secondly to prove that the prisoner was concerned in it. This evidence having already convinced Parliament of a dangerous conspiracy, the jury were naturally predisposed to accept it as conclusive; and a conspiracy being established, the prisoner, as a member of the societies concerned in it, could scarcely escape from the meshes of the general evidence. Instead of being tried for his own acts or language only, he was to be held responsible for all the proceedings of these societies. If they had plotted a revolution, he must be adjudged a traitor; and if he should be found guilty, what members of these societies would be safe.

*Trial of Hardy, Oct. 28th, 1794.*

The evidence produced in this trial proved, indeed, that there had been strong excitement, intemperate language, impracticable projects of reform, an extensive correspondence and popular organisation. Many things had been said and done, by persons connected with these societies, which probably amounted to sedition: but nothing approaching either the dignity or the wickedness of treason. Their chief offence consisted in their efforts to assemble a general convention of the people, ostensibly for obtaining parliamentary reform,—but in reality, it was said, for subverting the government. If their avowed object was the true one, clearly no offence had been committed. Such combinations had already been formed, and were acknowledged to be lawful. Mr. Pitt himself, the Duke of Richmond, and some of the first men in the state had been concerned in them. If the prisoner had other designs,—concealed and unlawful,—it was for the prosecution to prove their existence, by overt acts of treason. Many of the crown witnesses, themselves members of the societies, declared their innocence of all traitorous designs; while other witnesses gained little credit when exposed as spies and informers.

It was only by pushing the doctrines of constructive treason to the most dangerous extremes, that such a crime could even be inferred. Against these perilous doctrines Mr. Erskine had already successfully protested in the case of Lord George Gordon; and now again he exposed and refuted them, in a speech which, as Mr. Horne Tooke justly said, 'will live for ever.'[1] The shortcomings of the

[1] The conclusion of his speech was received with acclamations by the spectators who thronged the court, and by the multitudes sur-

evidence, and the consummate skill and eloquence of the counsel for the defence, secured the acquittal of the prisoner.[1]

Notwithstanding their discomfiture, the advisers of the crown resolved to proceed with the trial of Mr. John Horne Tooke, an accomplished scholar and wit, and no mean disputant. His defence was easier than that of Hardy. It had previously been doubtful how far the fairness and independence of a jury could be relied upon. Why should they be above the influences and prejudices which seemed to prevail everywhere? In his defence of Horne Tooke, Mr. Erskine could not resist adverting to his anxieties in the previous trial, when even the 'protecting Commons had been the accusers of his client, and had acted as a solicitor to prepare the very briefs for the prosecution.' But now that juries could be trusted, as in ordinary times, the case was clear; and Horne Tooke was acquitted.[2]

The groundless alarm of the government, founded upon the unfaithful reports of spies, was well exemplified in the case of Horne Tooke. He had received a letter from Mr. Joyce, containing the ominous words 'Can you be ready by Thursday?' The question was believed to refer to some rising,

---

rounding it. Fearful that their numbers and zeal should have the appearance of overawing the judges and jury, and interfering with the administration of justice, Mr. Erskine went out and addressed the crowd, beseeching them to disperse. 'In a few minutes there was scarcely a person to be seen near the Court.'—*Notes to Erskine's Speeches*, iii. 502.

[1] State Tr., xxiv. 19; Erskine's Speeches, iii. 53; Lord Campbell's Lives of the Chancellors, vi. 471.
[2] St. Tr., xxv. 745.

or other alarming act of treason: but it turned out that it related only to 'a list of the titles, offices, and pensions bestowed by Mr. Pitt upon Mr. Pitt, his relations, friends, and dependents.'[1] And again, Mr. Tooke, seeing Mr. Gay, an enterprising traveller, present at a meeting of the Constitutional Society, had humorously observed that he 'was disposed to go to greater lengths than any of us would choose to follow him;' an observation which was faithfully reported by a spy, as evidence of dangerous designs.[2]

Messrs. Bonney, Joyce, Kyd, and Holcroft were next arraigned, but the attorney-general, having twice failed in obtaining a conviction upon the evidence at his command, consented to their acquittal and discharge.[3] But Thelwall, against whom the prosecution had some additional evidence personal to himself, was tried, and acquitted. After this last failure, no further trials were adventured upon. The other prisoners, for whose trial the special commission had been issued, were discharged, as well as several prisoners in the country, who had been implicated in the proceedings of the obnoxious societies.

*Other prisoners discharged, Dec. 1st, 1794. Trial of Thelwall.*

Most fortunate was the result of these trials. Had the prisoners been found guilty, and suffered death, a sense of injustice would have aroused the people to dangerous exasperation. The right of free discussion and asso-

*Fortunate results of these trials.*

[1] Mr. Erskine's Speech, St. Tr., xxv. 309.
[2] St. Tr., xxv. 310. [3] *Ibid.*, 746.

ciation would have been branded as treason : public liberty would have been crushed ; and no man would have been safe from the vengeance of the government. But now it was acknowledged, that if the executive had been too easily alarmed, and Parliament too readily persuaded of the existence of danger, the administration of justice had not been tampered with ; and that, even in the midst of panic, an English jury would see right done between the crown and the meanest of its subjects.[1] And while the people were made sensible of their freedom, ministers were checked for a time in their perilous career. Nor were these trials, however impolitic, without their uses. On the one hand, the alarmists were less credulous of dangers to the state: on the other, the folly, the rashness, the ignorance, and criminality of many of the persons connected with political associations were exposed.

On the meeting of Parliament, in December, the failure of these prosecutions at once became the subject of discussion. Even on the formal reading of the Clandestine Outlawries Bill, Mr. Sheridan urged the immediate repeal of the act for the suspension of the Habeas Corpus. While he and other members of the opposition contended that the trials had discredited the evidence of dangerous plots, ministers declined

*Debates in Parliament on the trials, Dec. 30th, 1794.*

---

[1] Mr. Speaker Addington, writing after these events, said, 'It is of more consequence to maintain the credit of a mild and unprejudiced administration of justice than even to convict a Jacobin.'— *Pellew's Life of Lord Sidmouth*, i. 132. See also Belsham's Hist., ix. 244; Cartwright's Life, i. 210; Holcroft's Mem., ii. 180.

to accept any such conclusion. The solicitor-general maintained that the only effect of the late verdicts was, that the persons acquitted could not be again tried for the same offence;' and added, that if the juries had been as well informed as himself, they would have arrived at a different conclusion! These expressions, for which he was rebuked and ridiculed by Mr. Fox, were soon improved upon by Mr. Windham. The latter wished the opposition 'joy of the innocence of an acquitted felon,'—words which, on being called to order, he was obliged to explain away.[1]

A few days afterwards, Mr. Sheridan moved for the repeal of the Habeas Corpus Suspension Act, in a speech abounding in wit, sarcasm, and personalities. The debate elicited a speech from Mr. Erskine, in which he proved, in the clearest manner, that the acquittal of the prisoners had been founded upon the entire disbelief of the jury in any traitorous conspiracy,—such as had been alleged to exist. His arguments were combated by Mr. Serjeant Adair, who, in endeavouring to prove that the House had been right, and the juries in error, was naturally rewarded with the applause of his audience. His speech called forth this happy retort of Mr. Fox. The learned gentleman, he said, 'appealed from the jury to the House. And here let me adore the trial by jury. When this speech was made to another jury,—a speech which has been to-night received with such plaudits that we seemed

<small>Jan. 5th, 1795.</small>

---

[1] Parl. Hist., xxxi. 994-1061.

ready *ire pedibus in sententiam*,— it was received with a cold "not guilty."' The minister maintained a haughty silence: but being appealed to, said that it would probably be necessary to continue the act. Mr. Sheridan's motion was supported by no more than forty-one votes.[1]

The debate was soon followed by the introduction of the Continuance Bill. The government, not having any further evidence of public danger, relied upon the facts already disclosed in Parliament and in the courts. Upon these they insisted, with as much confidence as if there had been no trials; while, on the other side, the late verdicts were taken as a conclusive refutation of all proofs hitherto offered by the executive. These arguments were pressed too far, on either side. Proofs of treason had failed: proofs of seditious activity abounded. To condemn men to death on such evidence was one thing: to provide securities for the public peace was another: but it was clear that the public danger had been magnified, and its character misapprehended. The bill was speedily passed by both Houses.[2]

<small>Suspension of Habeas Corpus Act, continued, 1795.</small>

While many prisoners charged with sedition had been released, after the state trials, Henry Redhead Yorke was excepted from this indulgence. He was a young man of considerable talent, just twenty-two years old; and had entered into politics when a mere boy, with more zeal than discretion. In April 1794, he had

<small>Trial of Henry Redhead Yorke for conspiracy, July 23rd, 1795.</small>

---

[1] Ayes 41, noes 185; Parl. Hist., xxxi. 1062.
[2] Parl. Hist., xxxi. 1144–1194; 1280–1293.

assembled a meeting at Castle Hill, Sheffield, whom he addressed, in strong and inflammatory language, upon the corruptions of the House of Commons, and the necessity for parliamentary reform. The proceedings at this meeting were subsequently printed and published: but it was not proved that Mr. Yorke was concerned in the publication, nor that it contained an accurate report of his speech. Not long afterwards, he was arrested on a charge of high treason. After a long imprisonment, this charge was abandoned: but in July 1795, he was at length brought to trial at the York Assizes, on a charge of conspiracy to defame the House of Commons, and excite a spirit of disaffection and sedition amongst the people. He spoke ably in his own defence; and Mr. Justice Rooke, before whom he was tried, admitted in his charge to the jury that the language of the prisoner,—presuming it to be correctly reported,— would have been innocent at another time and under other circumstances: but that addressed to a large meeting, at a period of excitement, it was dangerous to the public peace. The jury being of the same opinion, found a verdict of guilty; and the defendant was sentenced to a fine of 200*l.*, and two years' imprisonment in Dorchester gaol.[1]

*Distress and riots, 1795.* The year 1795 was one of suffering, excitement, uneasiness, and disturbance: 'the time was out of joint.' The pressure of the war upon industry, aggravated by two bad harvests, was already beginning to be felt. Want of employment

---

[1] St. Tr., xxv. 1003.

and scarcity of food, as usual, provoked political discontent; and the events of the last three years had made a wide breach between the government and the people.[1] Until then, the growth of freedom had been rapid: many constitutional abuses had already been corrected; and the people, trained to free thought and discussion, had been encouraged by the first men of the age,—by Chatham, Fox, Grey, and the younger Pitt himself,—to hope for a wider representation as the consummation of their liberties. But how had the government lately responded to these popular influences? By prosecutions of the press,—by the punishment of political discussion as a crime,—by the proscription of parliamentary reformers, as men guilty of sedition and treason,—and by startling restraints upon public liberty. Deeply disturbed and discontented was the public mind. Bread riots, and excited meetings in favour of parliamentary reform, disclosed the mixed feelings of the populace. These discontents were inflamed by the mischievous activity of the London Corresponding Society,[2] emboldened by its triumphs over the government, and by demagogues begotten by the agitation of the times. On the 26th of October a vast meeting was assembled by the London Corresponding Society at Copenhagen House, at which 150,000 persons were said to have been present. An address to the nation was agreed to, in which, among other stirring appeals, it was

[1] Ann. Reg., 1796, p. 7; History of the Two Acts, Introduction.
[2] See their addresses to the nation and the king, June 29th, 1795, in support of universal suffrage and annual parliaments.—*Hist. of the Two Acts*, 90-97.

said 'We have lives, and are ready to devote them, either separately or collectively, for the salvation of the country.' This was followed by a remonstrance to the king, urging parliamentary reform, the removal of ministers, and a speedy peace. Several resolutions were also passed describing the sufferings of the people, the load of taxation, and the necessity of universal suffrage and annual parliaments. The latter topic had been the constant theme of all their proceedings; and however strong their language, no other object had ever been avowed. The meeting dispersed without the least disorder.

Popular excitement was at its height, when the king was about to open Parliament in person. On the 29th of October, the Park and streets were thronged with an excited multitude, through which the royal procession was to pass, on its way to Westminster. Instead of the cordial acclamations with which the king had generally been received, he was now assailed with groans and hisses, and cries of 'Give us bread,'—'No Pitt,'—'No war,'—'No famine.' His state carriage was pelted, and one missile, apparently from an air-gun, passed through the window. In all his dominions, there was no man of higher courage than the king himself. He bore these attacks upon his person with unflinching firmness; and proceeded to deliver his speech from the throne, without a trace of agitation. On his return to St. James's, these outrages were renewed, the glass panels and windows

*Attack upon the king, Oct. 29th, 1795.*

[1] Hist. of the Two Acts, 98-108.

of the carriage were broken to pieces;[1] and after the king had alighted, the carriage itself was nearly demolished by the mob. His Majesty, in passing from St. James's to Buckingham House in his private carriage, was again beset by the tumultuous crowd; and was only rescued from further molestation by the timely arrival of some horse-guards, who had been dismissed from duty.[2]

These disgraceful outrages, reprobated by good men of all classes, were made the occasion of further encroachments upon the political privileges of the people. Both Houses immediately concurred in an address to his Majesty, expressing their abhorrence of the late events. This was succeeded by two proclamations,—one offering rewards for the apprehension of the authors and abettors of these outrages; and the other adverting to recent meetings near the metropolis, followed by the attack upon the king; and calling upon the magistrates and all good subjects to aid in preventing such meetings, and in apprehending persons who should deliver inflammatory speeches or distribute seditious papers. Both these proclamations were laid before Parliament, and Lord Grenville introduced into the House of Lords a bill founded upon them, for the 'preservation of his Majesty's person and government against treasonable practices and attempts.' *Proclamations and addresses.* *Oct. 31st, 1795.* *Nov. 4.* *Treasonable Practices Bill, Nov. 4th.* *Nov. 6th.*

[1] 'When a stone was thrown at one of his glasses in returning home, the king said, "That is a stone,—you see the difference from a bullet."'—*Lord Colchester's Diary*, i. 3.
[2] Ann. Reg., 1796, p. 9; History of the Two Acts, 1796, 4–21; Lord Colchester's Diary, i. 2.

This bill introduced a new law of treason, at variance with the principles of the existing law, the operation of which had gravely dissatisfied the government, in the recent state trials. The proof of overt acts of treason was now to be dispensed with; and any person compassing and devising the death, bodily harm, or restraint of the king, or his deposition, or the levying of war upon him, in order to compel him to change his measures or counsels, or who should express such designs by any printing, writing, preaching, or malicious and advised speaking, should suffer the penalties of high treason.[1] Any person who by writing, printing, preaching, or speaking should incite the people to hatred or contempt of his Majesty, or the established government and constitution of the realm, would be liable to the penalties of a high misdemeanour; and on a second conviction, to banishment or transportation. The act was to remain in force during the life of the king, and till the end of the next session after his decease.

It was at once perceived that the measure was an alarming encroachment upon freedom of opinion. Its opponents saw in it a statutory prohibition to discuss parliamentary reform. The most flagrant abuses of the government and constitution were henceforth to be sacred from exposure. To speak of them at all would excite hatred and contempt: and silence was therefore to be imposed by law. Nor were the arguments by which this measure was

---

[1] The provision concerning preaching and advised speaking was afterwards omitted.

supported such as to qualify its obnoxious provisions. So grave a statesman as Lord Grenville claimed credit for it as being copied from acts passed in the reigns of Queen Elizabeth and Charles II.,—'approved times,' as his Lordship ventured to affirm.[1] Dr. Horsley, Bishop of Rochester, 'did not know what the mass of the people in any country had to do with the laws, but to obey them.' This constitutional maxim he repeated on another day, and was so impressed with its excellence that he exclaimed, ' My Lords, it is a maxim which I ever will maintain,—I will maintain it to the death,—I will maintain it under the axe of the guillotine.'[2] And notwithstanding the obloquy which this sentiment occasioned, it was, in truth, the principle and essence of the bill which he was supporting.

Within a week the bill was passed through all its stages,—there being only seven dissentient peers,—and sent to the House of Commons.[3]  *Nov. 13th, 1795.*

But before it reached that house, the Commons had been occupied by the discussion of another measure equally alarming. On the 10th November, the king's proclamations were considered, when Mr. Pitt founded upon them a bill to prevent seditious meetings. Following the  *Seditious meetings Bill, Nov. 10th.*

---

[1] Parl. Hist., xxxii. 245; Lord Colchester's Diary, i. 5.
[2] Parl. Hist., xxxii. 268. His explanations in no degree modified the extreme danger of this outrageous doctrine. He admitted that where there were laws bearing upon the particular interests of certain persons or bodies of men, such persons might meet and discuss them. In no other cases had the people anything to do with the laws, i. e., they had no right to an opinion upon any question of public policy! See *supra*, Vol. II. 61.
[3] *Ibid.*, xxxii. 244-272; Lord Colchester's Diary, i. 5, 6.

same reasoning as these proclamations, he attributed the outrages upon his Majesty, on the opening of Parliament, to seditious meetings, by which the disaffection of the people had been inflamed. He proposed that no meeting of more than fifty persons (except county and borough meetings duly called) should be held, for considering petitions or addresses for alteration of matters in church or state, or for discussing any grievance, without previous notice to a magistrate, who should attend to prevent any proposition or discourse tending to bring into hatred or contempt the sovereign, or the government and constitution. The magistrate would be empowered to apprehend any person making snch proposition or discourse. To resist him would be felony, punishable with death. If he deemed the proceedings tumultuous, he might disperse the meeting; and was indemnified if any one was killed in its dispersion. To restrain debating societies and political lectures, he proposed to introduce provisions for the licensing and supervision of lecture-rooms by magistrates.

When this measure had been propounded, Mr. Fox's indignation burst forth. That the outrage upon the king had been caused by public meetings, he denounced as a flimsy pretext; and denied that there was any ground for such a measure. 'Say at once,' he exclaimed, 'that a free constitution is no longer suited to us; say at once, in a manly manner, that on a review of the state of the world, a free constitution is not fit for you; conduct yourselves at once as the senators of Denmark did,—lay down your freedom, and acknowledge and accept of despotism. But do not mock the understandings and feelings of mankind, by telling the world that you are free.'

He showed that the bill revived the very principles of the Licensing Acts. They had sought to restrain the printing of opinions of which the government disapproved: this proposed to check the free utterance of opinions upon public affairs. Instead of leaving discussion free, and reserving the powers of the law for the punishment of offences, it was again proposed, after an interval of a hundred years, to license the thoughts of men, and to let none go forth without the official *dicatur*. With the views of a statesman in advance of his age, he argued, 'We have seen and heard of revolutions in other states. Were they owing to the freedom of popular opinions? Were they owing to the facility of popular meetings? No, sir, they were owing to the reverse of these; and therefore, I say, if we wish to avoid the danger of such revolutions, we should put ourselves in a state as different from them as possible.' Forty-two members only could be found to resist the introduction of this bill.[1]

Each succeeding stage of the bill occasioned renewed discussions upon its principles.[2] But when its details were about to be considered in committee, Mr. Fox, Mr. Erskine, Mr. Grey, Mr. Lambton, Mr. Whitbread, and the other

Nov. 27th, 1795.

---

[1] Ayes, 244; Noes, 42, Parl. Hist., xxxii. 272-300. Lord Colchester's Diary, i. 6.

[2] Parl. Hist., xxxii. 300-364, 387-422.

opponents of the measure, rose from their seats and withdrew from the House.¹ Mr. Sheridan alone remained, not, as he said, to propose any amendments to the bill,—for none but the omission of every clause would make it acceptable,—but merely to watch its progress through the committee.² The seceders returned on the third reading, and renewed their opposition to the bill; but it was passed by a vast majority.³

<small>Dec. 3rd.</small>

Meanwhile, the Treasonable Practices Bill having been brought from the Lords, had also encountered a resolute opposition. The irritation of debate provoked expressions on both sides tending to increase the public excitement. Mr. Fox said that if 'ministers were determined, by means of the corrupt influence they possessed in the two Houses of Parliament, to pass the bills, in direct opposition to the declared sense of a great majority of the nation; and should they be put in force with all their rigorous provisions, if his opinion were asked by the people, as to their obedience, he should tell them that it was no longer a question of moral obligation and duty, but of prudence.' He expressed this strong opinion advisedly, and repeated and justified it again and again, with the encouragement of Mr. Sheridan, Mr. Grey, Mr. Whitbread, and other earnest opponents of the bills.⁴ On the other side, this menace was

<small>Treasonable practices bill in the Commons, Nov. 16th.</small>

---

¹ Parl. Hist., xxxii. 300-364, 387-422; Lord Colchester's Diary, i. 11.
² Parl. Hist. xxxii., 422.
³ Ayes, 266; Noes, 51. *Ibid.*, 422-470.
⁴ Parl. Hist., xxxii. 383, 385, 386, 392, 451-460; Lord Col-

met by a statement of Mr. Windham, 'that ministers were determined to exert a rigour beyond the law, as exercised in ordinary times and under ordinary circumstances.'[1]

After repeated discussions in both Houses, the bills were eventually passed.[2] During their progress, however, large classes of the people, whose liberties were threatened, had loudly remonstrated against them. The higher classes generally supported the government, in these and all other repressive measures. In their terror of democracy, they had unconsciously ceased to respect the time-honoured doctrines of constitutional liberty. They saw only the dangers of popular license; and scarcely heeded the privileges which their ancestors had prized. But on the other side were ranged many eminent men, who still fearlessly asserted the rights of the people, and were supported by numerous popular demonstrations. *The bills passed. Opposition out of doors.*

On the 10th November, the Whig Club held an extraordinary meeting, which was attended by the first noblemen and gentlemen of that party. It was there agreed, that before the right of discussion and meeting had been abrogated, the utmost exertions should be used to oppose these dangerous measures. Resolutions were accordingly passed, expressing abhorrence of the attack upon the king, and deploring that it should have been made *The Whig Club.*

---

chester's Diary, i. 9. Nov. 24th: 'Grey to-night explained his position of resistance to the theoretical, which in the preceding night he had stated to be practically applicable to the present occasion.'—*Ibid.*, i. 10. And see Lord Malmesbury's Diary, iii. 247.

[1] Parl. Hist., xxxii. 386.     [2] 36 Geo. III. c. 7, 8.

the pretext for bills striking at the liberty of the press, the freedom of public discussion, and the right to petition Parliament for redress of grievances; and advising that meetings should be immediately held and petitions presented against measures which infringed the rights of the people.[1] The London Corresponding Society published an address to the nation, indignantly denying that the excesses of an aggrieved and uninformed populace could be charged upon them, or the late meeting at Copenhagen House,—professing the strictest legality in pursuit of parliamentary reform,—and denouncing the minister as seeking pretences 'to make fresh invasion upon our liberties, and establish despotism on the ruins of popular association.'[2]

The same society assembled a prodigious meeting at Copenhagen House, which agreed to an address, petition, and remonstrance to the king, and petitions to both Houses of Parliament, denouncing these 'tremendous bills, which threatened to overthrow the constitutional throne of the house of Brunswick, and to establish the despotism of the exiled Stuarts.'[3] A few days afterwards, a great meeting was held in Palace Yard, with Mr. Fox in the chair, which voted an address to the king and a petition to the House of Commons against the bills.[4] Mr. Fox there denounced the bills 'as a daring attempt upon your

*Meeting at Copenhagen House, Nov. 12th.*

*Meeting in Palace Yard.*

[1] Hist of the Two Acts, 120.
[2] Ibid., 39.   [3] Ibid., 125–134.
[4] Ibid., 232–236, 239; Adolphus'. Hist., vi. 370; Lord Colchester's Diary, i. 7. This meeting had been convened to assemble in Westminster Hall; but as the Courts were sitting, it adjourned to Palace Yard.

liberties,—an attempt to subvert the constitution of England. The Bill of Rights is proposed to be finally repealed, that you shall be deprived of the right of petitioning.' And the people were urged by the Duke of Bedford to petition while that right remained to them.

Numerous meetings were also held in London, Edinburgh, Glasgow, York, and in various parts of the country, to petition against the bills. At the same time, other meetings were held at the Crown and Anchor, and elsewhere in support of ministers, which declared their belief that the seditious excesses of the people demanded these stringent measures, as a protection to society.[1] *Other meetings.*

The debates upon the Treason and Sedition bills had been enlivened by an episode, in which the opposition found the means of retaliating upon the government and its supporters. A pamphlet, of ultra-monarchical principles, was published, entitled 'Thoughts on the English Government.' One passage represented the king as the ancient stock of the constitution,—and the Lords and Commons as merely branches, which might be 'lopped off' without any fatal injury to the constitution itself. It was a speculative essay which, at any other time, would merely have excited a smile: but it was discovered to be the work of Mr. Reeves, chairman of the 'Society for protecting liberty and property from Republicans and Levellers,'—better known as the 'Crown and Anchor *Mr. Reeves's pamphlet.*

[1] Hist. of the Two Acts, 135, 165, 244, 306–361, 389–392, 466, et seq.; Belsham's Hist., x. 10–23.

Association.'[1] The work was published in a cheap form, and extensively circulated amongst the numerous societies of which Mr. Reeves was the moving spirit; and its sentiments were in accordance with those which had been urged by the more indiscreet supporters of repressive measures. Hence the opposition were provoked to take notice of it. Having often condemned the government for repressing speculative opinions, it would have been more consistent with their principles to answer than to punish the pamphleteer: but the opportunity was too tempting to be lost. The author was obnoxious, and had committed himself: ministers could scarcely venture to defend his doctrines; and thus a diversion favourable to the minority was at last feasible. Mr. Sheridan, desirous, he said, of setting a good example, did not wish the author to be prosecuted: but proposed that he should be reprimanded at the bar, and his book burned in New Palace Yard by the common hangman. Ministers, however, preferred a prosecution to another case of privilege. The attorney-general was therefore directed to prosecute Mr. Reeves; and, on his trial, the jury, while they condemned his doctrines, acquitted the author.[2]

In 1797, Mr. Fox moved for the repeal of the Treason and Sedition Acts, in a speech abounding

---

[1] Mr. Reeves was the author of the learned 'History of the Law of England,' well known to posterity, by whom his pamphlet would have been forgotten but for these proceedings.

[2] Parl. Hist., xxxii. 608, 627, 651, 662. In the Lords, notice was also taken of the pamphlet, but no proceedings taken against it. *Ibid.*, 681; St. Tr., xxvi. 529; Lord Colchester's Diary, i. 8.

in political wisdom. The truth of many of his sentiments has since received remarkable confirmation. 'In proportion as opinions are open,' he said, 'they are innocent and harmless. Opinions become dangerous to a state only when persecution makes it necessary for the people to communicate their ideas under the bond of secrecy.' And, again, with reference to the restraints imposed upon public meetings: 'What a mockery,' he exclaimed, 'to tell the people that they shall have a right to applaud, a right to rejoice, a right to meet when they are happy: but not a right to condemn, not a right to deplore their misfortunes, not a right to suggest a remedy!' And it was finely said by him, 'Liberty is order; Liberty is strength,'—words which would serve as a motto for the British constitution. His motion, however, found no more than fifty-two supporters.[1] *Mr. Fox's motion to repeal Treason and Sedition Acts, May 14th, 1797.*

During this period of excitement, the regulation of newspapers often occupied the attention of the legislature. The stamp and advertisement duties were increased: more stringent provisions made against unstamped publications; and securities taken for ensuring the responsibility of printers.[2] By all these laws it was sought to restrain the multiplication of cheap political papers among the poorer classes; and to subject the press, generally, to a more effectual control. But more serious matters were still engaging the attention of government. *Regulation of newspapers, 1789–1798.*

[1] Parl. Hist., xxxiii. 613.
[2] 29 Geo. III. c. 50; 34 Geo. III. c. 72; 37 Geo. III. c. 90; 38 Geo. III. c. 78; Parl. Hist., xxx. iii. 1415, 1482.

The London Corresponding Society and other similar societies continued their baneful activity. Their rancour against the government knew no bounds. Mr. Pitt and his colleagues were denounced as tyrants and enemies of the human race. Hitherto their proceedings had been generally open: they had courted publicity, paraded their numbers, and prided themselves upon their appeals to the people. But the acts of 1795 having restrained their popular meetings, and put a check upon their speeches and printed addresses, they resorted to a new organisation, in evasion of the law. Secrecy was now the scheme of their association. Secret societies, committees, and officers were multiplied throughout the country, by whom an active correspondence was maintained: the members were bound together by oaths: inflammatory papers were clandestinely printed and circulated: seditious handbills secretly posted on the walls. Association degenerated into conspiracy. Their designs were congenial to the darkness in which they were planned. A general convention was projected; and societies of United Englishmen, and United Scotsmen, established an intercourse with the United Irishmen. Correspondence with France continued: but it no longer related to the rights of men, and national fraternity. It was undertaken in concert with the United Irishmen, who were encouraging a French invasion.[1] In this basest of all treasons some of the English

[1] See Chap. XVI.

societies were concerned. They were further compromised by seditious attempts to foment discontent in the army and navy, and by the recent mutiny in the fleet.¹ But whatever their plots, or crimes, their secrecy alone made them dangerous. They were tracked to their hiding places by the agents of the government; and in 1799, when the rebellion had broken out in Ireland, papers disclosing these proceedings were laid before the House of Commons. A secret committee related, in great detail, the history of these societies; and Mr. Pitt brought in a bill to repress them.

It was not sought to punish the authors of past excesses: but to prevent future mischiefs. The societies of United Englishmen, Scotsmen, and Irishmen, and the London Corresponding Society, were suppressed by name; and all other societies were declared unlawful of which the members were required to take any oath not required by law, or which had any members or committees not known to the society at large, and not entered in their books, or which were composed of distinct divisions or branches. The measure did not stop here. Debating clubs and reading-rooms, not licensed, were to be treated as disorderly houses. All printing presses and type foundries were to be registered. Printers were to print their names on every book or paper, and register the names of their employers. Restraints were even imposed upon the lending of books and newspapers for hire. This

*Corresponding Societies Bill, April 19th, 1799.*

---

¹ An Act had been passed in 1797 to punish this particular crime, 37 Geo. III. c. 70.

rigorous measure encountered little resistance. Repression had been fully accepted as the policy of the state; and the opposition had retired from a hopeless contest with power. Nor for societies conducted on such principles, and with such objects, could there be any defence. The provisions concerning the press introduced new rigours in the execution of the law, which at another time would have been resisted: but a portion of the press had, by outrages on decency and order, disconcerted the stanchest friends of free discussion.[1]

*Repressive measures completed, 1799.* The series of repressive measures was now complete. We cannot review them without sadness. Liberty had suffered from the license and excesses of one party, and the fears and arbitrary temper of the other. The government and large classes of the people had been brought into painful conflict. The severities of rulers, and the sullen exasperation of the people, had shaken that mutual confidence which is the first attribute of a free state. The popular constitution of England was suspended. Yet was it a period of trial and transition, in which public liberty, repressed for a time, suffered no permanent injury. Subdued in one age, it was to arise with new vigour in another.

*Administration of the libel laws, 1799-1811.* Political agitation, in its accustomed forms of public meetings and association, was now checked for several years,[2]—and freedom of discussion in the press continued to be re-

[1] Reports of Committees on Sealed Papers, 1799; Parl. Hist., xxxiv. 579, 1000; Debates, *Ibid.*, 984, &c.; 39 Geo. III. c. 79.

[2] In Scotland, 'as a body to be deferred to, no public existed.'— *Cockburn's Mem.*, 88. See also *Ibid.*, 282, 302, 376.

strained by merciless persecution. But the activity of the press was not abated. It was often at issue with the government; and the records of our courts present too many examples of the license of the one, and the rigours of the other. Who can read without pain the trials of Mr. Gilbert Wakefield and his publishers, in 1799? On one side we see an eminent scholar dissuading the people, in an inflammatory pamphlet, from repelling an invasion of our shores: on the other, we find publishers held criminally responsible for the publication of a libel, though ignorant of its contents; and the misguided author punished with two years' imprisonment in Dorchester gaol,[1]—a punishment which proved little short of a sentence of death.[2] Who can peruse without indignation the trial of the conductors of the 'Courier,' in the same year, for a libel upon the Emperor of Russia,[3] in which the pusillanimous doctrine was laid down from the Bench, that public writers were to be punished, not for their

*marginal note: The Rev. Gilbert Wakefield.*

---

[1] St. Tr., xxvii. 679; Erskine's Speeches, v. 213; Lord Campbell's Chancellors, vi. 517.

[2] £5,000 was subscribed for him, but he died a fortnight after his release. Mr. Fox, writing March 1st, 1799, to Mr. Gilbert Wakefield, says :—' The liberty of the press I consider as virtually destroyed by the proceedings against Johnson and Jordan; and what has happened to you I cannot but lament, therefore, the more, as the sufferings of a man whom I esteem, in a cause that is no more.' —*Fox Mem.*, iv. 337.—And again on June 9th :—' Nothing could exceed the concern I felt at the extreme severity (for such it appears to me) of the sentence pronounced against you.'—*Ibid.*, 339.

[3] This libel was as follows :—

' The Emperor of Russia is rendering himself obnoxious to his subjects by various acts of tyranny, and ridiculous in the eyes of Europe by his inconsistency. He has now passed an edict prohibiting the exportation of timber, deals, &c. In consequence of this ill-timed law, upwards of one hundred sail of vessels are likely to return to this kingdom without freights.'

guilt, but from fear of the displeasure of foreign powers.[1]

*The First Consul and the English press, 1802.* From such a case, it is refreshing to turn to worthier principles of freedom, and independence of foreign dictation. However often liberty may have been invaded, it has ever formed the basis of our laws. When the First Consul, during the peace of Amiens, demanded that liberty of the press in England should be placed under restraints not recognised by the constitution, he was thus answered by the British government:— 'His Majesty neither can nor will, in consequence of any representation or menace from a foreign power, make any concession which may be in the smallest degree dangerous to the liberty of the press, as secured by the constitution of this country. This liberty is justly dear to every British subject: the constitution admits of no previous restraints upon publications of any description: but there exist judicatures wholly independent of the executive, capable of taking cognisance of such publications as the law deems to be criminal; and which are bound to inflict the punishment the delinquents may deserve. These judicatures may investigate and punish not only libels against the government and magistracy of this kingdom, but, as has been repeatedly experienced, of publications defamatory of those in

---

[1] Lord Kenyon said:—'When these papers went to Russia and held up this great sovereign as being a tyrant and ridiculous over Europe, it might tend to his calling for satisfaction as a national affront, if it passed unreprobated by our government and our courts of justice.' Trial of Vint, Ross, and Perry: St. Tr., xxvii. 627; Starkie's Law of Libel, ii. 217.

whose hands the administration of foreign governments is placed. Our government neither has, nor wants, any other protection than what the laws of the country afford; and though they are willing and ready to give to every foreign government all the protection against offences of this nature, which the principle of their laws and constitution will admit, they never can consent to new-model their laws, or to change their constitution, to gratify the wishes of any foreign power.'[1]

But without any departure from the law of England, the libeller of a foreign power could be arraigned;[2] and this correspondence was followed by the memorable trial of Jean Peltier.[3] Mr. Mackintosh, in his eloquent and masterly defence of the defendant,[4] dreaded this prosecution 'as the first of a long series of conflicts between the greatest power in the world, and the only free press remaining in Europe;' and maintained, by admirable arguments and illustrations, the impolicy of restraining the free discussion of questions of foreign policy, and the character and conduct of foreign princes, as affecting the interest of this country. The genius of his advocate did not

*Trial of Jean Peltier, Feb. 21st, 1803.*

---

[1] Lord Hawkesbury to Mr. Merry, Aug. 28th, 1802; Parl. Hist., xxxvi. 1273.

[2] R. v. D'Eon, 1764; Starkie's Law of Libel, ii. 216; R. v. Lord George Gordon, 1787; State Tr., xxii. 175; Vint, Ross, and Perry, 1799, *supra*, p. 331.

[3] Letter from M. Otto to Lord Hawkesbury, July 25th, 1862; Parl. Hist., xxxvi. 1267.

[4] The Attorney-General (Spencer Perceval) spoke of it as 'one of the most splendid displays of eloquence he ever had occasion to hear;' and Lord Ellenborough termed it 'eloquence almost unparalleled.'

save Peltier from a verdict of guilty: but as hostilities with France were soon renewed, he was not called up for judgment.[1] Meanwhile the First Consul had continued to express his irritation at the English newspapers, between which and the newspapers of France a warm controversy was raging; and finding that they could not be repressed by law, he desired that the government should at least restrain those newspapers which were supposed to be under its influence. But here again he was met by explanations concerning the independence of English editors, which he found it difficult to comprehend;[2] and no sooner was war declared, than all the newspapers joined in a chorus of vituperation against Napoleon Bonaparte, without any fears of the attorney-general.

In following the history of the press, we now approach names familiar in our own time. William Cobbett having outraged the republican feelings of America by his loyalty, now provoked the loyal sentiments of England by his radicalism. His strong good sense, his vigorous English style, and the bold independence of his opinions, soon obtained for his 'Political Register' a wide popularity. But the unmeasured terms in which he assailed the conduct and measures of the government exposed him to frequent prosecutions. In 1804, he suffered for the publication of two letters from an Irish judge, ridiculing Lord Hardwicke, Lord

*William Cobbett's trials, 1804.*

---

[1] St. Tr., xxviii. 529.
[2] Lord Whitworth to Lord Hawkesbury, Jan. 27th, and Feb. 21st, 1803.

Redesdale, and the Irish executive.¹ Ridicule being held to be no less an offence than graver obloquy, Cobbett was fined; and Mr. Justice Johnson, the author of the libels, retired from the bench with a pension.²

In 1809, another libel brought upon Cobbett a severer punishment. Some soldiers in a regiment of militia having been flogged, under a guard of the German legion, Cobbett seized the occasion for inveighing at once against foreign mercenaries and military flogging. He was indicted for a libel upon the German legion; and being found guilty, was sentenced to two years' imprisonment, a fine of 1,000*l*., and to give security for 3,000*l*., to keep the peace for seven years. The printer of the Register, and two persons who had sold it, were also punished for the publication of this libel. The extreme severity of Cobbett's sentence excited a general sympathy in his favour, and indignation at the administration of the libel laws.³ [margin: His libel on the German legion, 1809.]

Another similar case illustrates the grave perils of the law of libel. In 1811, Messrs. John and Leigh Hunt were prosecuted for the re-publication of a spirited article against [margin: Messrs. John and Leigh Hunt, Feb. 24th, 1811.]

---

¹ There was far more of ridicule than invective. Lord Hardwicke was termed 'a very eminent sheep-feeder from Cambridgeshire' with 'a wooden head;' and Lord Redesdale 'a very able and strong-built chancery pleader from Lincoln's Inn.'
² St. Tr., xxix. 1, 54, 422, 437; Hans. Deb., 1st ser., v. 119.
³ Sydney Smith, in a letter to Lady Holland, Feb. 11th, 1810, said: 'Who would have mutinied for Cobbett's libel? or who would have risen up against the German soldiers? and how easily might he have been answered? He deserved some punishment; but to shut a man up in gaol for two years for such an offence is most atrocious.'— *Sydney Smith's Mem.*, ii. 86.

military flogging from the 'Stamford News.' They were defended by the vigour and eloquence of Mr. Brougham, and were acquitted.¹

Yet a few days afterwards, John Drakard, the printer of the 'Stamford News,' though defended by the same able advocate, was convicted at Lincoln for the publication of this very article.² Lord Ellenborough had laid it down that 'it is competent for all the subjects of his Majesty, freely but temperately to discuss, through the medium of the press, every question connected with public policy.' But on the trial of Drakard, Baron Wood expressed opinions fatal to the liberty of the press. 'It is said that we have a right to discuss the acts of our legislature. This would be a large permission indeed. Is there, gentlemen, to be a power in the people to counteract the acts of the Parliament; and is the libeller to come and make the people dissatisfied with the government under which he lives? This is not to be permitted to any man,—it is unconstitutional and seditious.'³ Such doctrines were already repugnant to the law: but a conviction obtained by their assertion from the bench, proves by how frail a thread the liberty of the press was then upheld.

*The 'Stamford News,' March 13th, 1811.*

The last three years before the regency were marked by unusual activity, as well as rigour, in the administration of the libel laws. Informations were multiplied; and the attorney-general was armed with a new power of holding the accused to bail.⁴

*Last three years before the regency.*

---

¹ St. Tr., xxxi. 367.   ² *Ibid.*, xxxi. 495.   ³ *Ibid.*, xxxi. 535.
⁴ From 1808 to 1811, forty-two informations were filed, of which

## The Press before the Regency.

It is now time again to review the progress of the press, during this long period of trial and repression. Every excess and indiscretion had been severely visited: controversial license had often been confounded with malignant libel: but the severities of the law had not subdued the influence of the press. Its freedom was often invaded: but its conductors were ever ready to vindicate their rights with a noble courage and persistence. Its character was constantly improving. The rapidity with which intelligence of all the incidents of the war was collected,—in anticipation of official sources,—increased the public appetite for news: its powerful criticisms upon military operations, and foreign and domestic policy, raised its reputation for judgment and capacity. Higher intellects, attracted to its service, were able to guide and instruct public opinion. Sunday newspapers were beginning to occupy a place in the periodical press,—destined to future eminence,—and attempts to repress them, on the grounds of religion and morality, had failed.[1] But in the press, as in society, there were many grades; and a considerable class of newspapers were still wanting in the sobriety, and honesty of purpose necessary to maintain the permanent influence of

*Progress of the press.*

twenty-six were brought to trial. Lords' Deb. on Lord Holland's motion, March 4th, 1811; Hans. Deb., 1st Ser., xix. 140; Commons' Deb. on Lord Folkestone's motion, March 28th, 1811; *Ibid.*, 548; Ann. Reg., 1811, p. 142; Romilly's Life, ii. 380; Horner's Life, ii. 139.

[1] In 1799 Lord Belgrave, in concert with Mr. Wilberforce, brought in a bill for that purpose, which was lost on the second reading. Its loss was attributed by its promoters to the fact that three out of the four Sunday newspapers supported the government. Parl. Hist., xxxiv. 1006; Life of Wilberforce, ii. 424.

political literature. They were intemperate, and too often slanderous.¹ A lower class of papers, clandestinely circulated in evasion of the stamp laws, went far to justify reproaches upon the religion and decency of the press. The ruling classes had long been at war with the press; and its vices kept alive their jealousies and prejudice. They looked upon it as a noxious weed, to be rooted out, rather than a plant of rare excellence, to be trained to a higher cultivation. Holding public writers in low esteem, —as instruments of party rancour,—they failed to recognise their transcendent services to truth and knowledge.²

But all parties, whether regarding the press with jealousy or favour, were ready to acknowledge its extraordinary influence in affairs of state. 'Give me,'

---

¹ In his defence of John and Leigh Hunt, in 1811, Mr. Brougham gave a highly-coloured sketch of the licentiousness of the press: 'There is not only no personage so important or exalted,—for of that I do not complain,—but no person so humble, harmless, and retired, as to escape the defamation which is daily and hourly poured forth by the venal crew, to gratify the idle curiosity, or still less excusable malignity; to mark out, for the indulgence of that propensity, individuals retiring into the privacy of domestic life; to hunt them down and drag them forth as a laughing-stock to the vulgar, has become, in our days, with some men, the road even to popularity; but with multitudes the means of earning a base subsistence.'—*St. Tr.*, xxxi. 380.

² In 1808, the benchers of Lincoln's Inn passed a bye-law, excluding all persons who had written for hire, in the daily papers, from being called to the bar. The other Inns of Court refused to accede to such a proposition. On the 23rd March 1809, Mr. Sheridan presented a petition complaining of this bye-law, which was generally condemned in debate, and it was soon afterwards rescinded by the benchers.—*Lord Colchester's Diary*, ii. 240. In 1810, Mr. Windham spoke of the reporters as having amongst them 'bankrupts, lottery-office keepers, footmen, and decayed tradesmen.' And he understood the conductors of the press to be 'a set of men who would give in to the corrupt misrepresentation of opposite sides.'—*Hans. Deb.*, 1st Ser., xv. 330.

said Mr. Sheridan, 'but the liberty of the press, and I will give the minister a venal House of Peers,—I will give him a corrupt and servile House of Commons,—I will give him the full swing of the patronage of office,—I will give him the whole host of ministerial influence,—I will give him all the power that place can confer upon him to purchase submission, and overawe resistance; and yet, armed with the liberty of the press, I will go forth to meet him undismayed: I will attack the mighty fabric he has reared, with that mightier engine: I will shake down from its height corruption, and lay it beneath the ruins of the abuses it was meant to shelter.'[1]

[1] Feb. 6th, 1810.—Hans. Deb., 1st Ser., xv. 341.

# CHAPTER X.

REPRESSIVE POLICY OF THE REGENCY :—MEASURES OF 1817 :—THE MANCHESTER MEETING, 1819 :—THE SIX ACTS :—ADVANCING POWER OF PUBLIC OPINION :—THE CATHOLIC ASSOCIATION :—FREEDOM OF THE PRESS ASSURED :—POLITICAL UNIONS, AND THE REFORM AGITATION :—REPEAL AGITATION :—ORANGE LODGES ,—TRADES' UNIONS :—THE CHARTISTS :—THE ANTI-CORN-LAW LEAGUE :—GENERAL REVIEW OF POLITICAL AGITATION.

THE regency was a period memorable for the discontents and turbulence of the people, and for the severity with which they were repressed. The working classes were suffering from the grievous burthens of the protracted war, from the high prices of food, from restraints upon trade, and diminished employment. Want engendered discontent; and ignorant and suffering men were misled into disorder, tumult, and violence. In June 1812, Lord Sidmouth was appointed secretary of state. Never was statesman more amiable and humane: but falling upon evil times, and committed to the policy of his generation, his rule was stern and absolute.

<small>Lord Sidmouth secretary of state, 1812.</small>

The mischievous and criminal outrages of the 'Luddites,' and the measures of repression adopted by the government, must be viewed wholly apart from the history of freedom of opinion. Bands of famished operatives in the manufacturing districts, believing their distresses to be due to the

<small>The Luddites, 1811-1814.</small>

encroachment of machinery upon their labour, associated for its destruction. Bound together by secret oaths, their designs were carried out with intimidation, outrage, incendiarism, and murder.[1] Life and property were alike insecure; and it was the plain duty of the government to protect them, and punish the wrong-doers. Attempts, indeed, were made to confound the ignorance and turbulence of a particular class, suffering under a specific grievance, with a general spirit of sedition. It was not enough that the frame-breakers were without work, and starving; that they were blind to the causes of their distress; and that the objects of their fury were near at hand: but they were also accused of disaffection to the state.[2] In truth, however, their combinations were devoid of any political aims; and the measures taken to repress them were free from just imputations of interference with the constitutional rights of the subject. They were limited to the particular evil, and provided merely for the discovery of concealed arms in the disturbed districts, the dispersion of tumultuous assemblies, and the enlargement of the jurisdiction of magistrates, so as to prevent the escape of offenders.[3]

In 1815, the unpopular Corn bill,—expressly designed to raise the price of food,—was not passed without riots in the metro- *Riots, 1815, 1816.*

---

[1] A full account of these lawless excesses will be found in the State Trials, xxxi. 959; Ann. Reg., 1812, 54–66, &c. The Reports of the Secret Committees, 14th July, 1812, are extremely meagre; Hans. Deb., 1st Ser., xxiii. 951, 1029.

[2] Hans. Deb., 1st Ser., xxiii. 962, 996, &c.; Pellew's Life of Lord Sidmouth, iii. 79–96.

[3] 52 Geo. III. c. 162.

polis.[1] In the following year there were bread riots and tumultuous assemblages of workmen at Nottingham, Manchester, Birmingham, and Merthyr Tydvil. London itself was the scene of serious disturbances.[2] All these were repressed by the executive government, with the ordinary means placed at its disposal.

But in 1817, the excesses of mischievous and misguided men led, as on former occasions, to restraints upon the public liberties. On the opening of Parliament some bullets, stones, or other missiles, struck the state-carriage of the prince regent, on his return from the House of Lords.[3] This outrage was followed by a message from the prince regent, communicating to both Houses papers containing evidence of seditious practices. These were referred to secret committees, which reported that dangerous associations had been formed in different parts of the country, and other seditious practices carried on which the existing laws were inadequate to prevent. Attempts had been made to seduce soldiers; arms and banners had been provided, secret oaths taken, insurrection plotted, seditious and blasphemous publications circulated. The gaols were to be broken open, and the prisoners set free: the Bank of England and the Tower were to be stormed: the government subverted: property plundered and divided. Hampden clubs were plot-

*Outrage on prince regent, Jan. 28th, 1817.*

---

[1] Ann. Reg. 1815, p. 140; Pellew's Life of Lord Sidmouth, iii. 125.
[2] *Ibid.*, 143–162; Bamford's Passages in the Life of a Radical, i. 7, &c.; Ann. Reg., 1816, p. 95.
[3] Evidence of Lord James Murray; Hans. Deb., 1st Ser., xxxv. 34; Ann. Reg. 1817, p. 3.

ting revolution: Spenceans were preparing to hunt down the owners of the soil, and the 'rapacious fundholders.'[1]

The natural consequence of these alarming disclosures was a revival of the repressive policy of the latter years of the last century, to which this period affords a singular parallel. The act of 1795, for the protection of the king from treasonable attempts, was now extended to the prince regent; and another act renewed, to restrain the seduction of soldiers and sailors from their allegiance. To such measures none could object: but there were others, directed by the same policy and considerations as those which on former occasions, had imposed restraints upon public liberty. Again, the criminal excesses of a small class were accepted as evidence of wide-spread disaffection. In suffering and social discontent were detected the seeds of revolution; and to remedies for partial evils were added jealous restrictions upon popular rights. It was proposed to extend the acts of 1795 and 1799, against corresponding societies, to other political clubs and associations whether affiliated or not: to suppress the Spencean clubs, to regulate meetings of more than fifty persons, to license debating societies; and lastly, to suspend the Habeas Corpus Act.[2] These measures, especially the latter, were not passed without remonstrance and opposi-

*Repressive measures proposed.*

---

[1] Reports of Secret Committees, Lords and Commons; Hans. Deb., 1st Ser., xxxv. 411, 438.

[2] Speeches of Lord Sidmouth in the House of Lords, and Lord Castlereagh in the House of Commons; Hans. Deb., 1st Ser., xxxv. 551, 590; Pellew's Life of Lord Sidmouth, iii. 172; Acts 57 Geo. III. c. 3, 6, 7, 19.

tion. It was maintained that the dangers were exaggerated,—that the existing laws were sufficient to repress sedition,—and that no encroachment should be suffered on the general liberties of the people, for the sake of reaching a few miscreants whom all good citizens abhorred. While the inadequacy of the means of the conspirators to carry out their fearful designs was ridiculed, it was urged that the executive were already able to cope with sedition,— to put down secret and other unlawful societies,— and to restrain the circulation of blasphemous and seditious libels. But so great was the power of the government, and so general the repugnance of society to the mischievous agitation which it was proposed to repress, that these measures were rapidly passed through both Houses, without any formidable opposition.[1]

The restraints upon public liberty expired in the following year: but other provisions, designed to ensure Parliament against intimidation and insult, were allowed a permanent place in our constitutional law. Public meetings were prohibited within a mile of Westminster Hall, during the sitting of Parliament or the courts; and to arrest the evil of conventions assuming to dictate to the legislature, restraints were imposed on the appointment and co-operation of delegates from different societies.[2]

The state prosecutions for treason were as infelici-

---

[1] For the third reading of the Habeas Corpus Suspension Bill there were 265 votes against 103—the minority including nearly all the opposition.—*Hans. Deb.*, 1st Ser. xxxv. 822; Edinburgh Review, Aug. 1817, p. 524–543.

[2] 57 Geo. III. c. 19, § 23, 25; amended by 9 and 10 Vict. c. 33.

tous as those of 1794, which had been undertaken under similar circumstances. James Wat- son, Arthur Thistlewood, James Watson the younger, Thomas Preston, and John Hooper, were indicted for high treason, arising out of a riotous meeting in Spa Fields, which they had called together, and other riotous and seditious proceedings for which none will deny that they deserved condign punishment. They were entitled to no sympathy as patriots or reformers; and the wickedness of their acts was only to be equalled by their folly. But the government,—not warned by the experience of 1794, —indicted them, not for sedition and riot, of which they were unquestionably guilty, but for treason; and so allowed them to escape with impunity.[1] *Trials of Watson and others, 1817.*

In the month of June disturbances, approaching the character of insurrection, broke out in Derbyshire; and the ringleaders were tried and convicted. Brandreth, commonly known as the Nottingham Captain, Turner and Ludlam, were executed: Weightman and twenty-one others received His Majesty's pardon, on condition of transportation or imprisonment; and against twelve others no evidence was offered by the attorney-general.[2] *Derbyshire insurrection, 1817.*

When the repressive measures of this session had been passed, the government commenced a more rigorous execution of the laws against the press. Lord Sidmouth addressed a circular letter to the lords lieutenants of counties, *Lord Sidmouth's circular, March 27th, 1817.*

[1] St. Tr., xxxii. 1, 674; Pellew's Life of Lord Sidmouth, iii. 158.
[2] St. Tr., xxxii. 755-1394; Pellew's Life of Lord Sidmouth, iii. 179-183; Reports on the state of the country; Hans. Deb., 1st Ser., xxxvij. 568, 679.

acquainting them that the law officers of the crown were of opinion, that a justice of the peace may issue a warrant to apprehend any person charged on oath with the publication of a blasphemous or seditious libel, and compel him to give bail to answer the charge; and desiring them to communicate this opinion to the magistrates at the ensuing quarter sessions, and to recommend them to act upon it. He further informed them that the vendors of pamphlets or tracts should be considered as within the provisions of the Hawkers' and Pedlars' Act, and should be dealt with accordingly, if selling such wares without a licence. Doubts were immediately raised concerning the lawfulness and policy of this circular; and the question was brought by Earl Grey before the Lords,[1] and by Sir Samuel Romilly before the Commons.[2] Their arguments were briefly these. The law itself, as declared in this circular, was ably contested, by reference to authorities and principles. It could not be shown that justices had this power by common law: it had not been conferred by statute; nor had it been recognised by any express decision of the courts. But at all events, it was confessedly doubtful, or the opinion of the law officers would not have been required. In 1808, it had been doubted if judges of the Court of King's Bench could commit or hold to bail persons charged with the publication of libels, before indictment or informa-

*Its lawfulness questioned, May 12th and June 25th, 1817.*

---

[1] May 12th, 1817 (Lords); Hans. Deb., 1st Ser., xxxvi. 445. See also Lord Sidmouth's Life, iii. 176.
[2] *Ibid.*, June 25th (Commons), 1158.

tion; and this power was then conferred by statute.[1] But now the right of magistrates to commit, like the judges, was determined, neither by Parliament, nor by any judicial authority, but by the crown, through its own executive officers. The secretary of state had interfered with the discretion of justices of the peace. What if he had ventured to deal, in such a manner, with the judges? The justices had been instructed, not upon a matter of administration, or police, but upon their judicial duties. The constitution had maintained a separation of the executive and judicial authorities: but here they had been confounded. The crown, in declaring the law, had usurped the province of the legislature; and in instructing the magistrates, had encroached upon an independent judicature. And, apart from these constitutional considerations, it was urged that the exercise of such powers by justices of the peace was exposed to grave abuses. Men might be accused before a magistrate, not only of publishing libels, but of uttering seditious words: they might be accused by spies and informers of incautious language, spoken in the confidence of private society; and yet, upon such testimony, they might be committed to prison by a single magistrate,—possibly a man of violent prejudices and strong political prepossessions.

On the part of ministers it was replied that magistrates, embarrassed in the discharge of their duties, having applied to the secretary of state for information, he had consulted the law officers, and

[1] 48 Geo. III. c. 58.

communicated their opinion. He had no desire to interfere with their discretion, but had merely promulgated a law. The law had been correctly expounded, and if disputed, it could be tried before a court of law on a writ of *habeas corpus*. But, in the meantime, unless the hawkers of seditious tracts could be arrested, while engaged in their pernicious traffic, they were able to set the police at defiance. Whatever the results of these discussions, they at least served as a warning to the executive, ever to keep in view the broad principle of English freedom, which distinguishes independent magistrates from prefects of police.

Threatening, indeed, were now the terrors of the law. While every justice of the peace could issue his warrant against a supposed libeller, and hold him to bail; the secretary of state, armed with the extraordinary powers of the Habeas Corpus suspension act, could imprison him, upon bare suspicion, and detain him in safe custody, without bringing him to trial. The attorney-general continued to wield his terrible *ex-officio* informations,—holding the accused to bail, or keeping them in prison in default of it, until their trial.[1] Defendants were punished, if convicted, with fine and imprisonment, and even if acquitted, with ruinous costs. Nor did the judges spare any exertion to obtain convictions. Ever jealous and distrustful of the press, they had left as little discretion to juries as they were able; and using freely the power reserved to them by the Libel Act of 1792, of stating their

*Powers exercised against the press, 1817.*

[1] 48 Geo. III. c. 58.

own opinion, they were eloquent in summing up the sins of libellers.¹

William Cobbett, who had already suffered from the severities of the attorney-general, was not disposed to brave the secretary of state, but suspended his 'Political Register,' and sailed to America. 'I do not retire,' said he, 'from a combat with the attorney-general: but from a combat with a dungeon, deprived of pen, ink, and paper. A combat with the attorney-general is quite unequal enough. That, however, I would have encountered. I know too well what a trial by special jury is: yet that, or any sort of trial, I would have stayed to face. But against the absolute power of imprisonment, without even a hearing, for time unlimited, in any gaol in the kingdom, without the use of pen, ink, and paper, and without communication with any soul but the keepers,—against such a power it would have been worse than madness to attempt to strive.'² *Cobbett's withdrawal from England.*

·Ministers had silenced and put to flight their most formidable foe: but against this success must be set their utter discomfiture by an obscure bookseller, who would never have been known to fame, had he not been drawn out from his dingy shop, into a court of justice. William Hone had published some political squibs, in the form of parodies upon the liturgy of the church; and for this pitiful trash was thrice put upon his trial, for blasphemous and seditious libels. Too poor *Trials of Hone, 1817.*

---

¹ Lord Campbell's Lives of the Chancellors, vi. 517.
² Political Register, 28th March, 1817.

to seek professional aid, he defended himself in person. But he was a man of genius in his way; and with singular ingenuity and persistence, and much quaint learning, he proved himself more than a match for the attorney-general and the bench.

In vain did Lord Ellenborough, uniting the authority of the judge with the arts of a counsel, strive for a conviction. Addressing the jury,— 'under the authority of the Libel Act, and still more in obedience to his conscience and his God, he pronounced this to be a most impious and profane libel.' But the jury were proof alike against his authority and his persuasion. The humble bookseller fairly overcame the awful chief justice; and after intellectual triumphs which would have made the reputation of a more eminent man, was thrice acquitted.[1]

These proceedings savoured so strongly of persecution, that they excited a wide sympathy for Hone, amongst men who would have turned with disgust from his writings; and his trial, in connection with other failures, ensured at least a temporary mitigation of severity in the administration of the libel laws.[2]

*Trials in Scotland.* At this time some trials in Scotland, if they remind us of 1793, afford a gratifying contrast to the administration of justice at that

---

[1] Mr. Justice Abbott presided at the first trial; Lord Ellenborough at the second and third. Lord Ellenborough felt his defeat so sensibly, that on the following day he sent to Lord Sidmouth the draft of a letter of resignation. Pellew's Life of Lord Sidmouth, iii. 236; Hone's Printed Trials; Mr. Charles Knight's Narrative in Martineau's Hist., i. 144.

[2] Lord Dudley's Letters, 199.

period. Alexander M'Laren, a weaver, and Thomas Baird, a grocer,[1] were tried for sedition before the High Court of Justiciary at Edinburgh. The weaver had made an intemperate speech at Kilmarnoch, in favour of parliamentary reform, which the grocer had been concerned in printing. It was shown that petitions had been received by Parliament, expressed in language at least as strong: but the accused, though defended by the admirable arguments and eloquence of Francis Jeffrey, were found guilty of sedition.[2]

M'Laren and Baird, March 5th, 1817.

Neil Douglas, 'Universalist Preacher,' had sought to enliven his prayers and sermons with political lucubrations; and spies being sent to observe him, reported that the fervid preacher, with rapid utterance and in a strong Highland dialect, had drawn a seditious parallel between our afflicted king and Nebuchadnezzar, King of Babylon; and between the prince regent and King Belshazzar. The crown witnesses, unused to the eccentricities of the preacher, had evidently failed to comprehend him; while others, more familiar with Neil Douglas, his dialect, opinions, and preaching, proved him to be as innocent of sedition, as he probably was of religious edification. He was ably defended by Mr. Jeffrey, and acquitted by the jury.[3]

Neil Douglas, 1817.

But the year 1819 was the culminating point of the protracted contest between the state and liberty of opinion. Distress still

Public meetings in 1819.

---

[1] So stated in evidence, St. Tr., xxxiii. 22, though called in the indictment 'a merchant.'
[2] St. Tr., xxxiii. 1.   [3] *Ibid.*, 634.

weighed heavily upon the working classes. They assembled at Carlisle, at Leeds, at Glasgow, at Ashton-under-Line, at Stockport, and in London, to discuss their wants, and to devise remedies for their destitution. Demagogues were prompt in giving a political direction to their deliberations; and universal suffrage and annual parliaments were soon accepted as the sovereign remedy for the social ills of which they complained. It was affirmed that the constitutional right to return members belonged to all communities. Unrepresented towns were invited to exercise that right, in anticipation of its more formal acknowledgment; and accordingly, at a large meeting at Birmingham, Sir Charles Wolseley was elected 'legislatorial attorney and representative' of that populous place.[1]

<small>State of the manufacturing population.</small> Other circumstances contributed to invest these large assemblages with a character of peculiar insecurity. A great social change had been rapidly developed. The extraordinary growth of manufactures had suddenly brought together vast populations, severed from those ties which usually connect the members of a healthy society. They were strangers,—deprived of the associations of home and kindred,—without affection or traditional respect for their employers, — and baffling, by their numbers, the ministrations of the church and the softening influence of charity. Distressed and discontented, they were readily exposed to the influence of the most mischievous por-

[1] Ann. Reg., 1819, p. 104. Sir Charles was afterwards arrested, while attending a meeting at Smithfield, for seditious words spoken by him at Stockport.

tion of the press, and to the lowest demagogues; while so great were their numbers, and so densely massed together, that their assemblages assumed proportions previously unknown; and became alarming to the inhabitants and magistracy, and dangerous to the public peace.

These crowded meetings, though addressed in language of excitement and extravagance, had hitherto been held without disturbance. The government had watched them, and taken precautions to repress disorder: but had not attempted any interference with their proceedings. On the 30th of July, however, a proclamation was issued against seditious meetings; and large assemblages of men were viewed with increased alarm by the government and magistracy. *Proclamation, July 30th, 1819.*

Following the example of Birmingham,[1] the reformers of Manchester appointed a meeting for the 9th of August, for the election of a 'legislatorial attorney:' but the magistrates having issued a notice declaring an assemblage for such a purpose illegal, another meeting was advertised for the 16th, to petition for parliamentary reform. Great preparations were made for this occasion; and in various parts of Lancashire large bodies of operatives were drilled, in the night time, and practised in military training. It was the avowed object of this drilling to enable the men to march in an orderly manner to the meeting: but the *Meeting at Manchester dispersed, Aug. 16th, 1819.*

---

[1] At the Leeds meeting it had been resolved that a similar election should take place, when a suitable candidate had been found: but no representative had been chosen.—*Ann. Reg.*, 1819, p. 105.

magistrates were, not unnaturally, alarmed at demonstrations so threatening.

On the 16th, St. Peter's Field, in Manchester, became the scene of a deplorable catastrophe. Forty thousand men[1] and two clubs of female reformers, marched in to the meeting, bearing flags, on which were inscribed the objects of their political faith,—'Universal Suffrage,' 'Equal Representation or Death,' and 'No Corn Laws.' However menacing their numbers, their conduct was orderly and peaceful. Mr. Hunt having taken the chair, had just commenced his address, when he was interrupted by the advance of cavalry upon the people. The Manchester Yeomanry, having been sent by the magistrates to aid the chief constable in arresting Mr. Hunt, and other reform leaders, on the platform, executed their instructions so awkwardly as to find themselves surrounded and hemmed in by the dense crowd,—and utterly powerless. The 15th Hussars, now summoned to their rescue, charged the people sword in hand; and in ten minutes the meeting was dispersed, the leaders were arrested, and the terrified crowd driven like sheep through the streets. Many were cut down by sabres, or trampled upon by the horses; but more were crushed and wounded in their frantic struggles to escape from the military. Between 300 and 400 persons were injured: but happily no more than five or six lives were lost.

This grievous event brought to a sudden crisis

---

[1] It was variously estimated at from 20,000 to 60,000. Lord Liverpool said 20,000; Lord Castlereagh, 40,000. In the indictment against Hunt and others it was laid at 60,000.

the antagonism between the government, and the popular right of meeting to discuss griev- ances. The magistrates complimented the military upon their forbearance: and the government immediately thanked both the magistrates and the military, for their zeal and discretion in maintaining the public peace. But it was indignantly asked,—not by demagogues and men ignorant of the law, but by statesmen and lawyers of eminence, —by whom the public tranquillity had been disturbed? Other meetings had been held without molestation: why then was this meeting singled out for the inopportune vigour of the magistrates? If it threatened danger, why was it not prevented by a timely exercise of authority? If Hunt and his associates had violated the law, why were they not arrested before or after the meeting? Or if arrested on the hustings, why not by the civil power? The people were peaceable and orderly,—they had threatened no one,—they had offered no resistance. Then why had they been charged and routed by the cavalry? It was even doubted if the Riot Act had been duly read. It had certainly not been heard; and the crowd, without notice or warning, found themselves under the flashing swords of the soldiery.[1]

*State of public feeling.*

[1] The evidence on this point was very confused. Earl Grey, after reading all the documents, affirmed that the Riot Act had not been read. Lord Liverpool said it had been completely read once, and partly read a second time. Lord Castlereagh said the Riot Act had been read from the window of the house in which the magistrates were assembled. This not being deemed sufficient, another magistrate went out into the crowd to read it, and was trampled under foot. Another vainly endeavoured to read it at the hustings after the arrest of Mr. Hunt.

Throughout the country, 'the Manchester Massacre,' as it was termed, aroused feelings of anger and indignation. Influential meetings were held in many of the chief counties and cities, denouncing the conduct of the magistrates and the government, and demanding inquiry. In the manufacturing districts, the working classes assembled, in large numbers, to express their sympathy with the sufferers, and their bitter spirit of resentment against the authorities. Dangerous discontents were inflamed into sedition. Yet all these excited meetings were held peaceably, except one at Paisley, where the magistrates having caused the colours to be seized, riots and outrages ensued.[1] But ministers were hard and defiant. The Common Council of the city of London addressed the prince regent, praying for an inquiry, and were sternly rebuked in his reply. Earl Fitzwilliam, a nobleman of the highest character, who had zealously assisted the government in the repression of disorders in his own county, joined the Duke of Norfolk and several other noblemen and gentlemen of the first importance, in a requisition to the high sheriff of the county of York, to call a meeting for the same purpose. At this meeting he attended and spoke; and was dismissed from his lord lieutenancy.[2] Hitherto

*Meetings and petitions for inquiry.*

---

Hans. Deb., 1st Ser., xli. 4, 51, &c.; Pellew's Life of Lord Sidmouth, iii. 249, *et seq.*; Ann. Reg., 1819, p. 106; Trial of Mr. Hunt and others, 1820; Ann. Reg., 1820; Chron., 41; Barn. and Ald. Rep., iii. 566; Papers laid before Parliament, Nov. 1819; Hans. Deb., 1st Ser., xli. 230 (Mr. Hay's statement); Bamford's Passages from the Life of a Radical, i. 176-213; Prentice's Manchester, 160.

[1] Ann. Reg., 1819, p. 109.

[2] Pellew's Life of Lord Sidmouth, iii. 263-272; Ann. Reg., 1819, p. 113, and Lord Grey's observations; Hans. Deb., 1st Ser., xli. 11-15.

the Whigs had discountenanced the radical reformers: but now the rigours of the government forced them to make common cause with that party, in opposing the measures of the executive.[1]

In the midst of this perilous excitement, Parliament was assembled, in November; and the Manchester meeting was naturally the first object of discussion. Amendments were moved to the Address, in the Lords, by Earl Grey, and in the Commons by Mr. Tierney, reprobating all dangerous schemes: but urging the duty of giving just attention to the complaints of the people, and the propriety of inquiring into the events at Manchester.[2] It was the object of the opposition to respond to the numerous meetings, petitions, and addresses, which had prayed for inquiry; and to evince a spirit of sympathy and conciliation on the part of Parliament, which had been signally wanting in the government. Earl Grey said, 'there was no attempt at conciliation, no concession to the people; nothing was attended to but a resort to coercion, as the only remedy which could be adopted.' 'The natural consequences of such a system, when once begun, was that it could not be stopped: discontents begot the necessity of force: the employment of force increased discontents:

*Meeting of Parliament, Nov. 23rd, 1819.*

The resolutions of this meeting, without condemning the magistrates, merely demanded inquiry.

[1] Lord Liverpool, writing to Lord Sidmouth, Sept. 30th, 1819, said: 'As far as the Manchester business goes, it will identify even the respectable part of the opposition with Hunt and the radical reformers.'—*Pellew's Life of Lord Sidmouth*, iii. 270.

[2] Hans. Deb., 1st Ser., xli. 4, 51; Lord Sidmouth's Life, iii. 297, *et seq.*

these would demand the exercise of new powers, till by degrees they would depart from all the principles of the constitution.' It was urged, in the language of Burke, that, 'a House of Commons who, in all disputes between the people and administration, presume against the people,—who punish their disorders, but refuse even to inquire into the provocations to them,—this is an unnatural, a monstrous state of things, in such a constitution.'

*Inquiry refused.* But conciliation formed no part of the hard policy of ministers. Sedition was to be trampled out. The executive had endeavoured to maintain the peace of the country: but its hands must now be strengthened. In both Houses the amendments were defeated by large majorities;[1] and a similar fate awaited distinct motions for inquiry, proposed, a few days afterwards, by Lord Lansdowne in the Lords, and Lord Althorp in the Commons.[2]

*The Six Acts.* Papers were laid before Parliament containing evidence of the state of the country, which were immediately followed by the introduction of further measures of repression,—then designated, and since familiarly known as, the 'Six Acts.' The first deprived defendants in cases of misdemeanour of the right of traversing: to which Lord Holland induced the chancellor to add a clause, obliging the attorney-general to bring defendants to

---

[1] In the Lords there were 159 for the Address, and 34 for the amendment. In the Commons, 381 for the Address, and 150 for the amendment.—*Hans. Deb.*, 1st Ser., xli. 50, 228.

[2] Nov. 30th. Contents, 47; Non-contents, 178. Ayes, 150; Noes, 323.—*Ibid.*, 418, 517.

trial within twelve months. By a second it was proposed to enable the court, on the conviction of a publisher of a seditious libel, to order the seizure of all copies of the libel in his possession, and to punish him, on a second conviction, with fine, imprisonment, banishment, or transportation. By a third, the newspaper stamp duty was imposed upon pamphlets and other papers containing news, or observations on public affairs; and recognizances were required from the publishers of newspapers and pamphlets for the payment of any penalty. By a fourth, no meeting of more than fifty persons was permitted to be held without six days' notice being given by seven householders to a resident justice of the peace; and all but freeholders or inhabitants of the county, parish or township, were prohibited from attending, under penalty of fine and imprisonment. The justice could change the proposed time and place of meeting: but no meeting was permitted to adjourn itself. Every meeting tending to incite the people to hatred and contempt of the king's person, or the government and constitution of the realm, was declared an unlawful assembly; and extraordinary powers were given to justices for the dispersion of such meetings, and the capture of persons addressing them. If any persons should be killed or injured in the dispersion of an unlawful meeting, the justice was indemnified. Attending a meeting with arms, or with flags, banners, or other ensigns or emblems, was an offence punishable with two years' imprisonment. Lecture and debating rooms were to be licensed, and open to inspection.

By a fifth, the training of persons in the use of arms was prohibited; and by a sixth, the magistrates, in the disturbed counties, were empowered to search for and seize arms.

All these measures, except that for prohibiting military training, were strenuously opposed in both Houses. They were justified by the government on the ground of the dangers which threatened society. It was argued by Lord Castlereagh, 'that unless we could reconcile the exercise of our liberties with the preservation of the public peace, our liberties would inevitably perish.' It was said that blasphemous and seditious libels were undermining the very foundations of society, while public meetings, under pretence of discussing grievances, were assembled for purposes of intimidation, and the display of physical force. Even the example of the French Revolution was not yet considered out of date: but was still relied on, in justification of these measures.[1] On the other side, it was contended that the libel laws were already sufficiently severe, and always liable to be capriciously administered. Writings, which at one time would be adjudged innocent and laudable, at another, would be punished as subversive of the laws and constitution. Zealous juries would be too ready to confound invectives against ministers with incitements to hatred and contempt of established institutions. The punishments proposed were excessive. Transportation had hitherto been confined to felonious

<small>*The bills opposed in Parliament.*</small>

---

[1] See especially Speech of Lord Grenville, Nov. 30th, 1819, on Lord Lansdowne's motion for inquiry.—*Hans. Deb.*, 1st Ser., xli. 448.

offences; and banishment was unknown to the laws of England. Such punishments would either deter juries from finding persons guilty of libel: or, if inflicted, would be out of all proportion to the offence. The extent of the mischief was also denied. It was an unjust reproach to the religion of the country to suppose that blasphemy would be generally tolerated, and to its loyalty, that sedition would be encouraged.

To the Seditious Meetings Bill it was objected that the constitutional right of assembling to discuss grievances was to be limited to the narrow bounds of a parish, and exercised at the pleasure of a magistrate,—probably a stanch supporter of ministers, jealous of popular rights, and full of prejudice against radicals and mob orators.[1]

These discussions were not without advantage. The monstrous punishment of transportation was withdrawn from the Seditious Libels Bill; and modifications were admitted into the bill for restraining seditious meetings: but these severe measures were eventually passed with little change.[2]

In presence of a novel development of popular meetings in crowded districts, ministers sought to prevent the assemblage of vast numbers from different parts, and to localise political discussion. Nor can it be denied that the unsettled condition and ignorance of the manufacturing

*Distrust of the people.*

---

[1] Hans. Deb., 1st Ser., xli. 343, 378, 594, &c.
[2] 60 Geo. III. and 1 Geo. IV. c. 1, 2, 4, 6, 8, 9. All these were permanent, except the Seditious Meetings Act, which, introduced as a permanent measure, was afterwards limited to five years, and the Seizure of Arms Act, which expired on the 25th March, 1822.

population justified apprehensions and precaution. The policy, however, which dictated these measures was not limited to the correction of a special danger: but was marked, as before, by settled distrust of the press and popular privileges. Ten years before it had been finely said by Mr. Brougham, 'Let the public discuss! So much the better. Even uproar is wholesome in England, while a whisper is fatal in France.'[1] But this truth had not yet been accepted by the rulers of that period.[2] They had not yet learned to rely upon the loyalty and good sense of the people, and upon the support of the middle classes, in upholding order and repressing outrage. On the other hand, we cannot but recognise in the language of the opposition leaders a bold confidence in their countrymen, and a prescient statesmanship, —destined in a few years to be accepted as the policy of the state.

Disaffection, however, still prevailed; and the evil passions of this distempered period soon afterwards exploded in the atrocious conspiracy of Thistlewood, and his miscreant gang. To the honour of Englishmen, few were guilty of plotting this bloody and insensate crime, the discovery

*Cato Street conspiracy, Feb., 1820.*

---

[1] In defence of the Stamford News.

[2] Stringent as were the measures of the government, they fell short of the views of the old Tory party. Mr. Bankes wrote to Lord Colchester, Dec. 31st, 1819:—'My only doubt is whether we have gone far enough in our endeavour to restrain and correct the licentiousness and abuse of the press.'—*Lord Colchester's Diary*, iii. 104.

Lord Redesdale, another type of the same school, wrote: 'I doubt whether it would not have been fortunate for the country, if half Manchester had been burned, and Glasgow had endured a little singeing.'—To Lord Colchester, Jan. 4th, 1820.—*Ibid.*, iii. 107.

of which filled all classes of men with horror and disgust.[1]

While the country was still excited by this startling event, Hunt and his associates were convicted, with five others, of unlawfully meeting together, with divers other persons unknown, for the purpose of creating discontent and disaffection, and of exciting the king's subjects to hatred of the government and constitution. Hunt was sentenced to two years and six months' imprisonment, and the others to one year's imprisonment. Sir Charles Wolseley and Harrison, a dissenting preacher, were also tried and sentenced to eighteen months' imprisonment for their participation in the Stockport meeting.[2]  *Trials of Hunt and Sir C. Wolseley, 1820.*

Let us now examine the general results of the long contest which had been maintained between the ill-regulated, mischievous, and often criminal struggles of the people for freedom, on the one hand, and the harsh policy of repression maintained by the government, on the other. The last twenty-eight years of the reign of George III. formed a period of perilous transition for liberty of opinion. While the right of free discussion had been discredited by factious license, by wild and dangerous theories, by turbulence and sedition,—the government and legisla- *Review of the contest between authority and liberty of opinion.*

---

[1] Ann. Reg., 1820, p. 34, and Chron. 29; St. Tr., xxxiii. 681; Pellew's Life of Lord Sidmouth, iii. 311–325. Lord Sidmouth himself says (p. 320): 'Party feelings appeared to be absorbed in those of indignation, which the lower orders had also evinced very strikingly upon the occasion.'

[2] Ann. Reg., 1820; Chron. 41; Barn. and Ald. Rep., iii. 566; Bamford's Life of a Radical, ii. 56–103, 162.

ture, in guarding against these excesses, had discountenanced and repressed legitimate agitation. The advocates of parliamentary reform had been confounded with Jacobins, and fomenters of revolution. Men who boldly impeached the conduct of their rulers, had been punished for sedition. The discussion of grievances,—the highest privilege of freemen,—had been checked and menaced. The assertion of popular rights had been denounced by ministers, and frowned upon by society, until low demagogues were able to supplant the natural leaders of the people, in the confidence of those classes who most needed safe guidance. Authority was placed in constant antagonism to large masses of people, who had no voice in the government of their country. Mutual distrust and alienation grew up between them. The people lost confidence in rulers whom they knew only by oppressive taxes, and harsh laws severely administered. The government, harassed by suspicions of disaffection, detected conspiracy and treason in every murmur of popular discontent.[1]

Hitherto the government had prevailed over every adverse influence. It had defied parliamentary opposition by never-failing majorities: it had trampled upon the press; it had stifled public discussion. In quelling sedition,

*Final domination of opinion over authority.*

[1] On May 12th, 1817, Earl Grey truly said: 'It is no longer the encroachments of power, of which we are jealous, but the too great extension of freedom. Every symptom of popular uneasiness, every ill-regulated effort of that spirit, without which liberty cannot exist, but which, whilst it exists, will break out into occasional excesses, affords a pretence which we seem emulous to seize, for imposing on it new restraints.'—*Hans. Deb.*, 1st Ser., xxxvi. 446.

it had forgotten to respect liberty. But henceforward, we shall find its supremacy gradually declining, and yielding to the advancing power and intelligence of the people. The working classes were making rapid advances in numbers, industrial resources, and knowledge. Commerce and manufactures, bringing them together in large masses, had given them coherence and force. Education had been widely extended; and discontent had quickened political inquiry. The press had contributed to the enlightenment of the people. Even demagogues who had misled them, yet stirred up their minds to covet knowledge, and to love freedom, The numbers, wealth, and influence of the middle classes had been extended, to a degree unknown at any former period. A new society had sprung up, outnumbering the limited class by whom the state was governed; and rapidly gaining upon them, in enlightenment and social influence. Superior to the arts of demagogues, and with every incitement to loyalty and patriotism,—their extended interests and important position led them to watch, with earnestness and sober judgment, the course of public affairs. Their views were represented by the best public writers of the time, whose cultivated taste and intellectual resources received encouragement from their patronage. Hence was formed a public opinion of greater moral force and authority. The middle classes were with ministers in quelling sedition: but against them when they menaced freedom. During the war they had generally sided with the government: but after the peace, the unconciliatory policy of ministers, a too rigorous repression of the press, and restraints upon public liberty, tended to estrange those who found their own temperate opinions expressed by the leaders of the Parliamentary opposition. Their adhesion to the Whigs was the commencement of a new political era,[1]—fruitful of constitutional growth and renovation. Confidence was established between constitutional statesmen in Parliament, and the most active and inquiring minds of the country. Agitation, no longer left to demagogues and operatives, but uniting the influence of all classes under eminent leaders, became an instrument for influencing the deliberations of Parliament,—as legitimate as it was powerful.

From this time, public opinion became a power which ministers were unable to subdue, and to which statesmen of all parties learned, more and more, to defer. In the worst of times, it had never been without its influence: but from the accession of George IV. it gathered strength until it was able, as we shall see, to dominate over ministers and parliaments.

Meanwhile, the severities of the law failed to suppress libels,[2] or to appease discontents. Complaints of both evils were as rife as ever. A portion of the press still abounded in libels

*The press not purified by rigour.*

---

[1] See *supra*, p. 186.
[2] Mr. Fremantle, writing to the Marquess of Buckingham, Aug. 30th, 1820, says: 'The press is completely open to treason, sedition, blasphemy, and falsehood, with impunity.' 'I don't know whether you see *Cobbett's Independent Whig*, and many other papers now circulating most extensively, and which are dangerous much beyond anything I can describe. I have an opportunity of seeing them, and can speak, therefore, from knowledge.'—*Court and Cabinets of Geo. IV.*, i. 68; Cockburn's Mem., 308.

upon public and private character, which the moral tone of its readers did not yet discourage. It was not in default of legal repression that such libels were published: but because they were acceptable to the vitiated taste of the lower classes of that day. If severity could have suppressed them, the unthankful efforts of the attorney-general, the secretary of state, and the magistrates, would have long since been crowned with success. But in 1821, the Constitutional Association officiously tendered its intervention, in the execution of the law. The dangers of such a scheme had been exposed nearly thirty years before;[1] and were at once acknowledged in a more enlightened and dispassionate age. This association even ventured to address a circular to every justice of the peace, expounding the law of libel. An irresponsible combination, embracing magistrates and jurymen throughout the country, and almost exclusively of one political party, threatened the liberty of the press, and the impartial administration of justice. The Court of King's Bench, sensible of these dangers, allowed members of the association to be challenged as jurors; and discussions in Parliament, opportunely raised by Mr. Brougham and Mr. Whitbread, completed the discomfiture of those zealous gentlemen, whom the vigilance of Lord Sidmouth, the activity of the attorney-general, and the zeal of country justices had failed to satisfy.[2] Had ministers

*The Constitutional Society, 1821.*

---

[1] See *supra*, p. 291.
[2] Ann. Reg., 1821, p. 205; Edinb. Rev., vol. xxxvii. (1821) 114-131; Hans. Deb., 2nd Ser., v. 891, 1046, 1487-1491.

needed any incitement to vigour, they would have received it from the king himself, who took the deepest personal interest in prosecutions of the press;[1] and from men of rank and influence, who were oversensitive to every political danger.[2]

The government had soon to deal with a political organisation more formidable than any which had hitherto needed its vigilance,— the Catholic Association in Ireland. The objects, constitution, and proceedings of this body demand especial notice, as exemplifying the bounds within which political agitation may be lawfully practised. To obtain the repeal of statutes imposing civil disabilities upon five-sixths of the population of Ireland, was a legitimate object of association. It was no visionary scheme, tending to the subversion of the state: but a practical measure of relief, which had been urged upon the legislature by the first statesmen of the time. To attain this end, it was lawful to instruct and arouse the people, by speeches and tracts, and by appeals to their reason and feelings. It was also lawful to demonstrate to Parliament the unanimity and earnestness of the people, in demanding a redress of grievances; and to influence its deliberations by the moral force of a

*Catholic Association.*

---

[1] On January 9th, 1821, His Majesty wrote to Lord Eldon: 'As the courts of law will now be open within a few days, I am desirous to know the decision that has been taken by the attorney-general upon the mode in which all the vendors of treason, and libellers, such as Benbow, &c. &c., are to be prosecuted. This is a measure so vitally indispensable to my feelings, as well as to the country, that I must insist that no further loss of time should be suffered to elapse before proceedings be instituted.'—*Court and Cabinets of Geo. IV.*, i. 107.

[2] *Ibid.*, 121, &c.; Lord Colchester's Mem., iii. 87, &c.

great popular movement. With these objects, organisation, in various forms, had been at work for many years.[1] In 1809, a Catholic Committee had been formed in Dublin, of which Mr. O'Connell,—destined to become a prominent figure in the history of his country,—was a leading member. Active in the preparation of petitions, and holding weekly meetings, it endeavoured, by discussion and association, to arouse the Catholics to a sense of their wrongs.[2] In 1811, it proposed to enlarge its constitution by assembling managers of petitions, from all parts of Ireland: but this project was arrested by the government, as a contravention of the Irish Convention Act, which prohibited the appointment of delegates or representatives.[3] The movement now languished for several years;[4] and it was not until 1823 that the Catholic Association was formed on a wider basis.[5] It embraced Catholic nobles, gentry, priesthood, peasantry;[6] and though disclaiming a delegated authority, its constitution and objects made it, in effect, the representative of the Catholic body. Exclusively Catholic, its organisation embraced the whole of Ireland. Constantly increasing in numbers and influence, it at length assumed all

---

[1] The first association or committee was formed so far back as 1760.—*Wyse's Cath. Asso.*, i. 69; *O'Conor's Hist. of the Irish Catholics*, i. 262. Another committee was arranged in 1773.—*Wyse*, i. 91; and a more general committee or association in 1790.—*Ibid.*, 104.

[2] Wyse, i. 142-165.

[3] 33 Geo. III. c. 29 (Ireland); See Debates, Feb. 22nd, March 7th, and April 4th, 1811.—*Hans. Deb.*, 1st Ser., xix. 1-18, 269-321, 700; Wyse, i. 174-178.

[4] A Catholic board was formed, but soon dissolved.—*Wyse*, i. 179.

[5] *Ibid.*, 199.     [6] *Ibid.*, 205.

the attributes of a national parliament. It held its 'sessions' in Dublin, appointed committees, received petitions, directed a census of the population of Ireland to be taken; and, above all, levied contributions, in the form of a Catholic rent, upon every parish in Ireland.[1] Its stirring addresses were read from the altars of all Catholic chapels. Its debates,—abounding in appeals to the passions of the people,—were published in every newspaper. The speeches of such orators as O'Connell and Sheil could not fail to command attention: but additional publicity was secured to all the proceedings of the Association, by contributions from the Catholic rent.

In 1825, its power had become too great to be borne, if the authority of the state was to be upheld. Either the Parliament at Westminster, or its rival in Dublin, must give way. The one must grant the demands of the Catholics, or the other must be silenced. Ministers were not yet prepared for the former alternative; and determined to suppress the Catholic Association. This, however, was a measure of no ordinary difficulty. The association was not unlawful; and was engaged in forwarding a legitimate cause. It could not be directly put down, without a glaring violation of the right of discussion and association. Agitation was not to be treated as lawful, so long as it was impotent; and condemned when it was beginning to be assured of success.

---

[1] Hans. Deb., 2nd Ser., xi. 944 (May 31st, 1824); *Ibid.*, xii. 171, *et seq.* (Feb. 10–15); Wyse, i. 208–217. Mr. Wyse assigns a later date to this census, i. 247; *Ibid.*, ii. App. xxxvii.

This embarrassment was avoided by embracing in the same measure, Orange Societies and other similar bodies, by which political and religious animosities were fomented.

The king, on opening Parliament, adverted to 'associations which have adopted proceed&shy;ings irreconcilable with the spirit of the constitution;' and a bill was immediately brought in to amend the laws relating to unlawful societies in Ireland. This bill prohibited the permanent sittings of political societies,—the appointment of committees to continue more than fourteen days,—the levying of money for the redress of grievances,—the affiliation and correspondence of societies,—the exclusion of persons on the ground of religion,—and the administration of oaths.[1] It was strenuously resisted. Ministers were counselled to stay agitation by redressing grievances, rather than by vain attempts to prevent their free discussion. But so perilous was the state of Ireland,—so fierce the hatred of her parties, and so full of warning her history,—that a measure, otherwise open to grave constitutional objections, found justification in the declared necessity of ensuring the public peace.[2] Its operation, however, was limited to three years.

*Suppressed by Parliament, 1825.*

*Feb. 10th, 1825.*

The Catholic Association was dissolved in obedience to this act: but was immediately replaced by a new association, constituted so as to evade the provisions of the recent law. This society professed to be established for

*But continued in another form.*

[1] 6 Geo. IV. c. 4.
[2] Hans. Deb., 2nd Ser., xii. 2-122, 128-522, &c.

promoting education, and other charitable objects; and every week, a separate meeting was convened, purporting to be unconnected with the association. 'Fourteen days' meetings,' and aggregate meetings were also held; and at all these assemblies the same violent language was used, and the same measures adopted, as in the time of the original society. While thus eluding the recent statute, this astute body was beyond the reach of the common law, being associated neither for the purpose of doing any unlawful act, nor of doing any lawful act in an unlawful manner. It was equally unscathed by the Convention Act of 1793, as not professing a representative character. In other respects the new association openly defied the law. Permanent committees were appointed, and the Catholic rent was collected by their own 'churchwardens' in every parish.[1] The government watched these proceedings with jealousy and alarm: but perceived no means of restraining them. The act was about to expire at the end of the session of 1828; and, after very anxious consideration, ministers determined not to propose its renewal. It could not have been made effectual without such restraints upon the liberty of speech, and public meetings, as they could not venture to recommend, and which Parliament would, perhaps, have declined to sanction.[2]

No sooner had the act expired, than the old Catholic Association, with all its organisation and

---

[1] Opinion of Mr. Joy, 1828; Sir R. Peel's Mem., i. 45; Wyse, i. 222-246; *Ibid.*, ii. App. xxxix.

[2] Memorandum and Correspondence of Mr. Peel, the Marquess of Anglesey, and Mr. Lamb.—*Peel's Mem.*, i. 22-58, 150.

offensive tactics, was revived. At the same time, the Orange Societies were resuscitated; and other Protestant associations, called Brunswick Clubs, were established on the model of the Catholic Association, and collected a Protestant rent.[1] Catholic Association revived, 1828.

Meanwhile, the agitation fomented by the Catholic Association was most threatening. Meetings were assembled to which large bodies of Catholics marched in military array, bearing flags and music, dressed in uniforms, and disciplined to word of command. Such assemblages were obviously dangerous to the public peace. Ministers and the Irish executive watched them with solicitude: and long balanced between the evils of permitting such demonstrations, on the one side, and precipitating a bloody collision with excited masses of the people, on the other. They were further embarrassed by counter demonstrations of the Protestants, and by the hot zeal of the Orange Societies, which represented their cautious vigilance as timidity, and their inaction as an abandonment of the functions of government. They were advised that such meetings, having no definite object sanctioned by law, and being assembled in such numbers and with such organisation as to strike a well-grounded fear into peaceable inhabitants, were illegal by the common law, even when accompanied by no act of violence.[2] And at Dangerous meetings, Sept., 1828. Proclamation against them, Oct. 1st, 1828.

---

[1] Wyse, i. 347-359.
[2] Opinion of attorney and solicitor-general of England.—*Sir R. Peel's Mem.*, i. 225; Queen *v.* Soley, 11 Modern Reports, and King *v.* Hunt and others.

length they determined to prevent such meetings, and to concert measures for their dispersion by force.¹ A proclamation being issued for that purpose, met with a ready obedience. It formed no part of the scheme of the Catholic leaders to risk a collision with military force, or with their Protestant rivals; and the association had already begun to discourage these dangerous assemblages, in anticipation of disorders injurious to their cause. The immediate object of the government was secured: but the association,—while it avoided a contest with authority,—adroitly assumed all the credit of restoring tranquillity to the country.²

But the proceedings of the association itself became more violent and offensive than ever. Its leaders were insolent and defiant to the government, and exercised an absolute sway over the Catholic population. In vain the government took counsel with its law officers.³ Neither the Convention Act of 1793, nor the common law could be relied on, for restraining the proceedings of an association which the legislature itself had interposed, three years before, to condemn. Peace was maintained, as the Catholics were unwilling to disturb it: but the country was virtually under the dominion of the association.

In the following year, however, the suppression of

---

[1] The correspondence of Mr. Peel with Lord Anglesey and the Irish executive, discloses all the considerations by which the government was influenced, under circumstances of great embarrassment.—*Sir R. Peel's Mem.*, i. 207–231.
[2] Ann. Reg., 1828, p. 140–146; Peel's Mem., i. 232.
[3] Peel's Mem., i. 243–264.

this and other societies in Ireland formed part of the general scheme of Catholic Emancipation.[1] The Catholic Association was, at length, extinguished: but not until its objects had been fully accomplished. It was the first time a measure had been forced upon a hostile court and reluctant Parliament, a dominant party and an unwilling people, by the pressure of a political organisation. The abolition of the slave trade was due to the conviction which had been wrought by facts, arguments, and appeals to the moral and religious feelings of the people. But the Catholic cause owed its triumph to no such moral conversion. The government was overawed by the hostile demonstrations of a formidable confederacy, supported by the Irish people and priesthood, and menacing authority with their physical force. It was, in truth, a dangerous example; and threatened the future independence of Parliament. But however powerful this association, its efforts would have been paralysed without a good cause, espoused by eminent statesmen, and an influential party in Parliament. The state would have known how to repel irrational demands, however urged: but was unable to resist the combined pressure of parliamentary and popular force, the sympathies of many liberal Protestants in Ireland, and the steady convictions of an enlightened minority in England. In our balanced constitution, political agitation, to be successful, must be based

*Suppression of the association in 1829.*

*A good cause necessary for successful agitation.*

---

[1] See Chap. XIII.; 10 Geo. IV. c. 1.

on a real grievance, adequately represented in Parliament, and in the press,—and supported by the rational approval of enlightened men. But though the independence of Parliament remained intact, the triumph of the Catholic Association marked the increased force of political agitation, as an element in our constitution. It was becoming superior to authorities and party combinations, by which the state had hitherto been governed.

During the short reign of George IV., the influence of public opinion made steady advances. The press obtained a wider extension; and the people advanced in education, intelligence, and self-reliance. There was also a marked improvement in political literature, corresponding with the national progress. And thus the very causes which were increasing the power of the people, were qualifying them to use it wisely.

<small>Increased influence of public opinion in reign of George IV.</small>

<small>Improvement of the press.</small>

It was not by the severities of the law that the inferior press was destined to be improved, and its mischievous tendencies corrected. These expedients, —after a trial of two centuries,—had failed. But moral causes were in operation by which the general standard of society was elevated. The church and other religious bodies had become more zealous in their sacred mission:[1] society was awakening to the duty of educating the people; and the material progress of the country was developing a more general and active intelligence. The classes most needing elevation had begun to desire sound and

[1] See Chap. XIV.

wholesome instruction; and this inestimable benefit was gradually extended to them. Improved publications successfully competed for popular favour with writings of a lower character; and, in cultivating the public taste, at the same time raised the general standard of periodical literature. A large share of the credit of this important work is due to the Society for the Diffusion of Useful Knowledge, established in 1826, and to the exertions of its chief promoters, Lord Brougham, Mr. Matthew Davenport Hill, and Mr. Charles Knight.[1] The publications of this society were followed by those of the Society for promoting Christian Knowledge, and by the admirable serials of Messrs. Chambers. By these and other periodical papers,—as well political as literary,—an extraordinary impulse was given to general education. Public writers promptly responded to the general spirit of the time; and the aberrations of the press were, in great measure, corrected.

The government, however,—while it viewed with alarm the growing force of public opinion, which controlled its own authority,—failed to observe its true spirit and tendency. Still holding to the traditions of a polity, then on the very point of exhaustion, it was unable to reconcile the rough energies of popular discussion with respect for the law, and obedience to constituted authority. It regarded the press as an obstacle to good government, instead of conciliating its support by a bold confidence in public approbation.

[1] Edinb. Rev., xlvi. 225, &c.; Knight's Passages of a Working Life, ii. chap. 2-6, &c.

This spirit dictated to the Duke of Wellington's administration, its ill-advised prosecutions of the press, in 1830. By passing the Roman Catholic Relief Act, ministers had provoked the resentment of the Tory press; and foremost among their assailants was the 'Morning Journal.' One article, appearing to impute personal corruption to Lord Chancellor Lyndhurst, could not be overlooked; but the editor having sworn that his lordship was not the person alluded to, an information against him was abandoned. The attorney-general, however, now filed no less than three *ex-officio* informations against the editor and proprietors, for this and two other articles, as libels upon the king, the ministers, and Parliament. A fourth prosecution was also instituted, for a separate libel upon the Duke of Wellington. So soon as the personal character of a member of the administration had been cleared, ministers might have allowed animadversions upon their public conduct to pass with impunity. If the right of free discussion was not respected, the excitement of the times might have claimed indulgence. Again, the accumulation of charges against the same persons, betrayed a spirit of persecution. It was not justice that was sought, but vengeance, and the ruin of an obnoxious journal. So far as the punishment of their political foes was concerned, ministers prevailed.[1] But their success

[1] Verdicts were obtained in three out of the four prosecutions. In the second a partial verdict only was given (guilty of libel on the king, but not on his ministers), with a recommendation to mercy,— Mr. Alexander, the editor, being sentenced to a year's imprisonment, a fine of 300*l.*, and to give security for good behaviour during three

was gained at the expense of much unpopularity. Tories, sympathising with writers of their own party, united with the opposition in condemning this assault upon the liberty of the press. Nor was the temper of the people such as to bear, any longer, with complacency, a harsh execution of the libel laws. The unsuccessful prosecution of Cobbett, in the following year, by a Whig attorney-general, nearly brought to a close the long series of contests between the government and the press.¹ *Failure of prosecution of Cobbett, 1831.*

Since that time, the utmost latitude of criticism and invective has been permitted to the press, in discussing public men and measures. The law has rarely been appealed to, even for the exposure of malignity and falsehood.² Prosecutions for libel, like the censorship, have fallen out of our constitutional system. When the press errs, it is by the press itself that its errors are left to be corrected. Repression has ceased to be the policy of rulers; and statesmen have at length fully realised the wise maxim of Lord Bacon, that 'the punishing of wits enhances their authority; and a forbidden writing is thought to be a certain spark of truth, that flies up in the faces of them that seek to tread it out.' *Complete freedom of the press established.*

years; and the proprietors to lesser punishments.—Ann. Reg., 1830, p. 3, 119; Hans. Deb., 2nd Ser., xxii. 1167.

¹ He was charged with no libel on ministers, but with inciting labourers to burn ricks; Ann. Reg. 1831, Chron., p. 95. In the same year Carlile and Haley were indicted; and in 1833, Reeve, Ager, Grant, Bell, Hetherington, Russell, and Stevens.—Hunt's Fourth Est., ii. 67; Roebuck's Hist. of the Whig Ministry, ii. 219, *n.*

² The law was also greatly improved by Lord Campbell's Libel Act, 6 and 7 Vict. c. 96

Henceforth the freedom of the press was assured; and nothing was now wanting to its full expansion, but a revision of the fiscal laws, by which its utmost development was restrained. These were the stamp, advertisement, and paper duties. It was not until after a struggle of thirty years, that all these duties were repealed: but in order to complete our survey of the press, their history may, at once, be briefly told.

*Fiscal laws affecting the press.*

The newspaper stamp of Queen Anne had risen, by successive additions, to fourpence. Originating in jealousy of the press, its extension was due, partly to the same policy, and partly to the exigencies of finance. So high a tax, while it discouraged cheap newspapers, was naturally liable to evasion. Tracts, and other unstamped papers, containing news and comments upon public affairs, were widely circulated among the poor; and it was to restrain this practice, that the stamp laws had been extended to that class of papers by one of the Six Acts.[1] They were denounced as seditious and blasphemous, and were to be extinguished. But the passion for news and political discussion was not to be repressed; and unstamped publications were more rife than ever. Such papers occupied the same place in the periodical press, as tracts printed, at a former period, in evasion of the licenser. All concerned in such papers were violating the law, and braving its terrors: the gaol was ever before their eyes. This was no honourable calling; and none but the meanest would engage in it. Hence

*Newspaper stamps.*

---

[1] 60 Geo. III. c. 9; *supra*, p. 243.

the poor, who most needed wholesome instruction, received the very worst, from a contraband press. During the Reform agitation, a new class of publishers, of higher character and purpose, set up unstamped newspapers for the working classes, and defied the government in the spirit of Prynne and Lilburne. Their sentiments, already democratic, were further embittered by their hard wrestling with the law. They suffered imprisonment, but their papers continued in large circulation; they were fined, but their fines were paid by subscription. Prosecutions against publishers and vendors of such papers were becoming a serious aggravation of the criminal law. Prisons were filled with offenders;[1] and the state was again at war with the press, in a new form.

If the law could not overcome the unstamped press, it was clear that the law itself must give way. Mr. Lytton Bulwer[2] and Mr. Hume exposed the growing evils of the newspaper stamp; ministers were too painfully sensible of its embarrassments; and in 1836, it was reduced to one penny, and the unstamped press was put down. At the same time, a portion of the paper duty was remitted. Already, in 1833, the advertisement duty had been reduced; and newspapers now laboured under a lighter weight. *Unstamped newspapers.*

Meanwhile, efforts had been made to provide an antidote for the poison circulated in the lowest of the unstamped papers, by a cheap *Taxes on knowledge.*

---

[1] From 1831 to 1835 there were no less than 728 prosecutions and about 500 cases of imprisonment.—Mr. Hume's Return Sept., 1836, No. 21; Hunt's Fourth Estate, 69–87.

[2] June 14th, 1832; Hans. Deb., 3rd Ser., xiii. 619.

and popular literature without news:[1] but the progress of this beneficent work disclosed the pressure of the paper duty upon all cheap publications, the cost of which was to be repaid by extensive circulation. Cheapness and expansion were evidently becoming the characteristics of the periodical press; to which every tax, however light, was an impediment. Hence a new movement for the repeal of all 'taxes on knowledge,' led by Mr. Milner Gibson, with admirable ability, address, and persistence. In 1853, the advertisement duty was swept away; and in 1855, the last penny of the newspaper stamp was relinquished. Nothing was now left but the duty on paper; and this was assailed with no less vigour. Denounced by penny newspapers, which the repeal of the stamp duty had called into existence: complained of by publishers of cheap books; and deplored by the friends of popular education, it fell, six years later, after a parliamentary contest, memorable in history.[2] And now the press was free alike from legal oppression, and fiscal impediments. It stands responsible to society for the wise use of its unlimited franchises; and learning from the history of our liberties, that public virtue owes more to freedom, than to jealousy and restraint,—may we not have faith in the moderation of the press, and the temperate judgment of the people?

*Public jealousies of the press.* The influence of the press has extended with its liberty; but it has not been suffered to dominate over the independent opinion of

[1] *Supra*, p. 376.
[2] Hans. Deb., 3rd Series, cxxv. 118; cxxviii. 1128; cxxxvii. 1110, &c. *Supra*, p. 108.

the country. The people love freedom too well to bow the knee to any dictator, whether in the council, the senate, or the press. And no sooner has the dictation of any journal, conscious of its power, become too pronounced, than its influence has sensibly declined. Free itself, the press has been taught to respect, with decency and moderation, the freedom of others.

Opinion,—free in the press,—free in every form of public discussion,—has become not less free in society. It is never coerced into silence or conformity, as in America, by the tyrannous force of a majority.[1] However small a minority: however unpopular, irrational, eccentric, perverse, or unpatriotic its sentiments : however despised or pitied ; it may speak out fearlessly, in full confidence of toleration. The majority, conscious of right, and assured of its proper influence in the state, neither fears nor resents opposition.[2]

*General freedom of opinion.*

The freedom of the press was fully assured before the passing of the Reform Act ; and political organisation,—more potent than the press,—was now about to advance suddenly to its extreme development. The agitation for Parliamentary Reform in 1831–32 exceeded that of any previous time, in its wide-spread organisation, in

*Political unions, 1831.*

---

[1] 'Tant que la majorité est douteuse, on parle ; mais dès qu'elle s'est irrévocablement prononcée, chacun se tait, et amis comme ennemis semblent alors s'attacher de concert à son char.'—*De Tocqueville, Democr. en Amer.*, i. 307.

[2] In politics this is true nearly to the extent of Mr. Mill's axiom : 'If all mankind, minus one, were of one opinion, and only one person were of the contrary opinion, mankind would be no more justified in silencing that one person, than he, if he had the power, would be justified in silencing mankind.'—*On Liberty*, 33.

the numbers associated, in earnestness, and faith in the cause. In this agitation there were also notable circumstances, wholly unprecedented. The middle and the working classes were, for the first time, cordially united in a common cause: they were led by a great constitutional party; and,—more remarkable still,—instead of opposing the government, they were the ardent supporters of the king's ministers. To these circumstances is mainly due the safe passage of the country through a most perilous crisis. The violence of the masses was moderated by their more instructed associates,—who, again, were admitted to the friendly counsels of many eminent members of the ministerial party. Popular combination assumed the form of 'Political Unions,' which were established in the metropolis, and in all the large towns throughout the country. Of the provincial unions, that of Birmingham took the lead. Founded for another purpose so early as January, 1830,[1] it became the type of most other unions throughout the country. Its original design was 'to form a general political union between the lower and middle classes of the people;'[2] and it 'called, with confidence, upon the ancient aristocracy of the land to come forward, and take their proper station at the head of the people, in this great crisis of the national affairs.'[3] In this spirit, when the Reform agitation

<small>The Birmingham Political Union.</small>

[1] Curiously enough, it was founded by Mr. Thomas Attwood, a Tory, to advance his currency doctrines, and to denounce the resumption of cash payments in 1819.—Report of Proceedings, Jan. 25th, 1830 (Hodgett's Birmingham).
[2] Requisition to High Bailiff of Birmingham, Jan., 1830.
[3] Report of Proceedings, Jan. 25th, 1830, p. 12.

commenced, the council thought it prudent not to 'claim universal suffrage, vote by ballot, or annual parliaments, because all the upper classes of the community, and the great majority of the middle classes, deem them dangerous, and the council cannot find that they have the sanction of experience to prove them safe.'[1] And throughout the resolutions and speeches of the society, the same desire was shown to propitiate the aristocracy, and to unite the middle and working classes.[2]

Before the fate of the first Reform Bill was ascertained, the political unions confined their exertions to debates and resolutions in favour of reform, and the preparation of numerous petitions to Parliament. Already, indeed, they boasted of their numbers and physical force. The chairman of the Birmingham Union vaunted that they could find two armies,—each as numerous and brave as that which conquered at Waterloo,—if the king and his ministers required them.[3] But however strong the language sometimes used, discussion and popular association were, as yet, the sole objects of these unions. No sooner, however, was the bill lost, and Parliament dissolved, than they were aroused to a more formidable activity. Their first object was to influence the elections, and to secure the return of a majority of reformers. Electors and

*Activity of the unions.*

---

[1] Report of Council, May 17th, 1830.
[2] Proceedings of Union, *passim.* 'You have the flower of the nobility with you; you have the sons of the heroes of Runnymede with you: the best and the noblest blood of England is on your side.'
—*Birmingham Journal,* May 14th, 1832.
[3] Ann. Reg., 1831, p. 80.

non-electors, co-operating in these unions, were equally eager in the cause of reform: but with the restricted franchises of that time, the former would have been unequal to contend against the great territorial interests opposed to them. The unions, however, threw themselves hotly into the contest; and their demonstrations, exceeding the license of electioneering, and too often amounting to intimidation, overpowered the dispirited anti-reformers. There were election riots at Wigan, at Lanark, at Ayr, and at Edinburgh.[1] The interposition of the unions, and the popular excitement which they encouraged, brought some discredit upon the cause of reform: but contributed to the ministerial majority in the new Parliament.

As the parliamentary struggle proceeded, upon the second Reform Bill, the demonstrations of the political unions became more threatening. Meetings were held and petitions presented, which, in expressing the excited feelings of vast bodies of men, were, at the same time, alarming demonstrations of physical force. When the measure was about to be discussed in the House of Lords, a meeting of 150,000 men assembled at Birmingham, declared by acclamation that if all other constitutional means of ensuring the success of the Reform Bill should fail, they would refuse the payment of taxes, as John Hampden had refused to pay ship-money, except by a levy upon their goods.[2]

*Meetings and petitions.*

Oct. 3rd, 1831.

[1] Ann. Reg., 1831, p. 152.
[2] Ann. Reg., 1831, p. 282. See Hans. Deb., 3rd Ser., vii. 1323; Report of Proceedings of Meeting at Newhall Hill, Oct. 3rd, 1831;

It was the first time, in our history, that the aristocracy had singly confronted the people. Hitherto the people had contended with the crown,—supported by the aristocracy and large classes of the community: now the aristocracy stood alone, in presence of a popular force, almost revolutionary. If they continued the contest too long for the safety of the state, they at least met its dangers with the high courage which befits a noble race. Unawed by numbers, clamour, and threats, the Lords rejected the second Reform Bill. The excitement of the time now led to disorders disgraceful to the popular cause. Mobs paraded the streets of London, hooting, pelting, and even assaulting distinguished peers, and breaking their windows.[1] There were riots at Derby: when, some rioters being seized, the mob stormed the gaol and set the prisoners free. At Nottingham, the Castle was burned by the populace, as an act of vengeance against the Duke of Newcastle. In both these places, the riots were not repressed without the aid of a military force.[2] For two nights and days, Bristol was the prey of a turbulent and drunken rabble. They broke into the prisons, and having let loose the prisoners, deliberately set on fire the buildings. They rifled and burned down the Mansion House, the Bishop's Palace, the Custom House, the Excise

*Conflict between the nobles and the people.*

*Riots on rejection of second Reform Bill.*

Oct. 29th, 1831.

Speech of Mr. Edmonds, &c.; Roebuck's Hist. of the Whig Ministry, ii. 218.

[1] Ann. Reg., 1831, p. 280; Twiss's Life of Lord Eldon, iii. 153; Courts and Cabinets of Will. IV. and Queen Vict., i. 364.

[2] Ann. Reg., 1831, p. 280.

Office, and many private houses. The irresolution and incapacity of magistrates and military commanders left a populous and wealthy city, at the mercy of thieves and incendiaries: nor was order at length restored without military force and loss of life, which a more timely and vigorous interposition might have averted.[1] These painful events were deplored by reformers, as a disgrace and hindrance to their cause; and watched by their opponents, as probable inducements to reaction.

Hitherto the political unions had been locally organised, and independent of one another, while forwarding an object common to all.

*Political unions invited to send delegates.*

They were daily growing more dangerous; and the scheme of an armed national guard was even projected. But however threatening their demonstrations, they had been conducted within the bounds of law. In November, 1831, however, they assumed a different character. A National Union was formed in London, to which the several provincial unions throughout the country were invited to send delegates. From that time, the limits of lawful agitation were exceeded; and the entire organisation became illegal.[2]

At the same time, meetings assembled in connection with the unions, were assuming a character more violent and unlawful. The Metropolitan Union,—an association independent of the London Political Union, and advocating extreme

*Alarming meetings held.*

---

[1] Ann. Reg., 1831, p. 291. Twelve persons were killed, and ninety-four wounded and injured.
[2] 39 Geo. III. c. 79; 57 Geo. III. c. 19; *supra*, p. 329, 343.

measures of democratic reform,—gave notice, in a seditious advertisement, of a meeting for the 7th of November, at White Conduit House. The magistrates of Hatton Garden issued a notice declaring the proposed meeting seditious and illegal; and enjoining loyal and well-disposed persons not to attend it. Whereupon a deputation of working men waited upon Lord Melbourne, at the Home Office, and were convinced by his lordship, of the illegality of their proceedings. The meeting was at once abandoned.[1] Danger to the public peace was averted, by confidence in the government. Some exception was taken to an act of official courtesy towards men compromised by sedition: but who can doubt the wisdom of preventing, rather than punishing, a breach of the law?

Lawful agitation could not be stayed: but when associations, otherwise dangerous, had begun to transgress the law, Ministers were constrained to interfere; and accordingly, on the 22nd of November, 1831, a proclamation was issued for the repression of political unions. It pointed out that such associations, 'composed of separate bodies, with various divisions and subdivisions, under leaders with a gradation of ranks and authority, and distinguished by certain badges, and subject to the general control and direction of a superior council,' were 'unconstitutional and illegal,' and commanded all loyal subjects to refrain from joining them. The 'National Political Union' denied that this proclamation applied to itself, or to

*Proclamation against political unions.*

[1] Ann. Reg., 1831, p. 297.

the majority of existing unions. But the Birmingham Union modified an extensive organisation of unions, in the Midland Counties, which had been projected; and the system of delegation, correspondence, and affiliation was generally checked and discouraged.[1]

*Unions discountenanced in Parliament.* On the meeting of Parliament on the 6th of December, political unions were further discountenanced in the speech from the throne, in which His Majesty declared that such combinations were incompatible with regular government, and signified his determination to repress all illegal proceedings.[2]

*Unions more threatening than ever.* But an organisation directed to the attainment of Parliamentary Reform, could not be abandoned until that object was accomplished. The unions continued in full activity; their numbers were increased by a more general adhesion of the middle classes; and if ostensibly conforming to the law, in their rules and regulations, their proceedings were characterised, more than ever, by menace and intimidation. When the third Reform Bill was awaiting the committee in the Lords, immense meetings were assembled at Birmingham, Manchester, Edinburgh, Glasgow, and other populous places, which by their numbers, combination, and resolute purpose, as well as by the speeches made and petitions agreed to, proclaimed a determination to overawe the Peers, who were still opposed to the bill. The withholding of taxes was again threatened,

[1] Ann. Reg., 1831, p. 297; Twiss' Life of Lord Eldon, iii. 163.
[2] Hans. Deb., 3rd Ser., ix. 5.

and even the extinction of the peerage itself, if the bill should be rejected. On the 7th of May, 1832, all the unions of the counties of Warwick, Worcester, and Stafford, assembled at Newhall Hill, Birmingham, to the number of nearly 150,000. A petition to the Commons was there agreed to, praying them to withhold the supplies, in order to ensure the safety of the Reform Bill; and declaring that the people would think it necessary to have arms for their defence. Other petitions from Manchester and elsewhere, praying that the supplies might be withheld, were brought to London by excited deputations.[1]

The adverse vote of the Lords in Committee, and the resignation of the Reform ministry, was succeeded by demonstrations of still greater violence. Revolutionary sentiments, and appeals to force and coercion, succeeded to reasoning and political agitation. The immediate creation of peers was demanded. 'More lords, or none:' to this had it come, said the clamorous leaders of the unions. A general refusal of taxes was counselled. The Commons having declared themselves not to be the representatives of the people, had no right to vote taxes. Then why should the people pay them? The National Political Union called upon the Commons to withhold supplies from the Treasury, and entrust them to commissioners named by themselves. The metropolis was covered with placards inviting *Dangerous excitement during the Reform crisis.*

[1] Ann. Reg., 1832, p. 172; Hans. Deb., 3rd Ser., xii. 876, 1032, 1274; Roebuck's Hist. of the Whig Ministry, ii. 295; Prentice's Recollections of Manchester, 408–415.

the people to union, and a general resistance to the payment of taxes. A run upon the Bank for gold was counselled, 'to stop the Duke.' The extinction of the privileged orders,—and even of the monarchy itself,—general confusion and anarchy, were threatened. Prodigious crowds of people marched to open-air meetings, with banners and revolutionary mottoes, to listen to the frantic addresses of demagogues, by whom these sentiments were delivered.[1] The refusal to pay taxes was even encouraged by men of station and influence,—by Lord Milton, Mr. Duncombe, and Mr. William Brougham.[2] The press also, responding to the prevailing excitement, preached resistance and force.[3]

*Considerations upon the popular triumph.*

The limits of constitutional agitation and pressure had long been exceeded; and the country seemed to be on the very verge of revolution, when the political tempest was calmed, by the final surrender of the Lords to the popular will. An imminent danger was averted: but the triumph of an agitation conducted with so much violence, and marked by so many of the characteristics of revolution, portended serious perils to the even course of constitutional government. The Lords alone had now been coerced: but might not the executive, and the entire legislature, at some future period, be forced to submit to the like coercion? Such apprehensions were not without justifi-

[1] Ann. Reg., 1832, p. 169, *et seq.*; Roebuck's Hist. of the Whig Ministry, ii. 288–297.
[2] Roebuck's Hist. of the Whig Ministry, ii. 291, 297; Hans. Deb., 3rd Ser., xiii. 430, June 5th, 1832.
[3] Courts and Cabinets of Will. IV. and Victoria, i. 303–331.

cation from the immediate aspect of the times : but further experience has proved that the success of this popular measure was due, not only to the dangerous pressure of democracy, but to other causes not less material to successful agitation,—the inherent justice of the measure itself,—the union of the middle and working classes, under the guidance of their natural leaders,—and the support of a strong parliamentary party, embracing the majority of one house, and a considerable minority in the other.

At the very time when this popular excitement was raging in England, an agitation of a different kind, and followed by results widely dissimilar, had been commenced in Ireland. Mr. O'Connell, emboldened by his successful advocacy of the Catholic claims, resumed the exciting and profitable arts of the demagogue ; and urged the repeal of the legislative union of England and Ireland. But his new cause was one to which no agitation promised success. Not a statesman could be found to counsel the dismemberment of the empire. All political parties alike repudiated it : the press denounced it : the sense of the nation revolted against it. Those who most deplored the wrongs and misgovernment of Ireland, foresaw nothing but an aggravation of those evils, in the idle and factious cry for repeal. But Mr. O'Connell hoped, by demonstrations of physical force, to advance a cause which met with none of that moral support which is essential to success. On the 27th of December, 1830, a procession of trades' unions through the streets of
<small>Agitation for the repeal of the Union, 1830-31.</small>

<small>Mr. O'Connell's contests with the Irish executive, 1830-31.</small>

Dublin was prevented by a proclamation of the lord-lieutenant, under the Act for the suppression of dangerous assemblies and associations in Ireland,[1] as threatening to the public peace. An association was then formed 'for the prevention of unlawful meetings:' but again, the meeting of this body was prohibited by proclamation. Mr. O'Connell's subtle and crafty mind quickly planned fresh devices to evade the act. First, to escape the meshes of the law against societies, he constituted himself the 'Pacificator of Ireland,' and met his friends once a-week at a public breakfast, at Home's hotel. These meetings were also proclaimed illegal, under the act. Next, a number of societies were formed, with various names, but all having a common object. All these,—whatever their pretexts and devices,—were prohibited.

Mr. O'Connell now resorted to public meetings, by which the acts of the lord-lieutenant were denounced as tyrannical and unlawful: but he was soon to quail before the law. On the 18th of January, 1831, he was apprehended and held to bail, with some of his associates, on informations charging him with having held various meetings, in violation of the lord-lieutenant's proclamation. True bills having been found against him, he pleaded not guilty to the first fourteen counts, and put in demurrers to the others. But not being prepared to argue the demurrers, he was permitted to

*Mr. O'Connell submits to the law, 1831.*

---

[1] 10 Geo. IV. c. 1, by which the Catholic Association had been suppressed (*supra*, p. 213). It was in force for one year from March 5th, 1829, and until the end of the then next session of Parliament.

withdraw them, and enter a plea of not guilty. This plea, again, he soon afterwards withdrew, and pleaded guilty to the first fourteen counts in the indictment; when the attorney-general entered a *nolle prosequi* on the remaining counts, which charged him with a conspiracy. So tame a submission to the law, after intemperate defiance and denunciations, went far to discredit the character of the great agitator. He was, however, suffered to escape without punishment. He was never brought up for judgment; and the act of 1829, not having been renewed, expired at the end of the short session, in April 1831.[1] The repeal agitation was for a time repressed. Had its objects and means been worthier, it would have met with more support. But the government, relying upon public opinion, had not shrunk from a prompt vindication of the law; and men of every class and party, except the followers of Mr. O'Connell himself, condemned the vain political delusions, by which the Irish people had been disturbed.

This baneful agitation, however, was renewed in 1840, and continued, for some time, in forms more dangerous and mischievous than ever. A Repeal Association was formed with an extensive organisation of members, associates, and volunteers, and of officers designated as inspectors, repeal-wardens, and collectors. By the agency of these officers, the repeal rent was collected, and repeal newspapers, tracts, poems, songs, cards, and other devices disseminated among

*Renewal of repeal agitation, in 1840.*

---

[1] Ann. Reg., 1831, ch. x.; Hans. Deb. (14th and 16th Feb., 1831), 3rd Ser., ii. 490, 609.

the people. In 1843, many 'monster meetings,' assembled by Mr. O'Connell, were of the most threatening character. At Mullingar, upwards of 100,000 people were collected to listen to inflammatory speeches from the liberator.[1] On the Hill of Tara, where the rebels had been defeated in 1798, 250,000 people were said to have assembled[2] for the same purpose. These meetings, by their numbers and organisation, and by the order and discipline with which they were assembled and marshalled, assumed the form of military demonstrations. Menace and intimidation were plainly their object,—not political discussion. The language of the liberator and his friends was designed to alienate the minds of the people from the English government and nation. Englishmen were designated as 'Saxons:' their laws and rulers were denounced: Irishmen who submitted to the yoke were slaves and cowards. Justice was to be sought in arbitration courts, appointed by themselves, and not in the constituted tribunals. To give battle to the English, was no uncommon theme of repeal oratory. 'If he had to go to battle,' said O'Connell, at Roscommon, 'he should have the strong and steady tee-totallers with him: the tee-total bands would play before them, and animate them in the time of peril: their wives and daughters, thanking God for their sobriety, would be praying for their safety; and he told them

*May 14th, 1843.*

*Aug. 15th, 1843.*

*Aug. 20th, 1843.*

---

[1] Ann. Reg., 1843, p. 228, 231.
[2] Ann. Reg., 1843, p. 231. Some said even a million; Speech of attorney-general, *Ibid.*, 1844, p. 310.

there was not an army in the world that he would not fight, with his tee-totallers. Yes, tee-totalism was the first sure ground on which rested their hope of sweeping away Saxon domination, and giving Ireland to the Irish.'[1] This was not constitutional agitation, but disaffection and revolt. At length, a monster meeting having been announced to take place at Clontarf, near Dublin, the government issued a proclamation[2] to prevent it; and by necessary military precautions, effectually arrested the dangerous demonstration. The exertions of the government were seconded by Mr. O'Connell himself, who issued a notice abandoning the meeting, and used all his influence to prevent the assembling of the repealers. *Oct. 8th, 1843.*

This immediate danger having been averted, the government resolved to bring Mr. O'Connell and his confederates to justice, for their defiance of the law; and on the 14th of October, Mr. O'Connell, his son, and eight of his friends were arrested and held to bail on charges of conspiracy, sedition, and the unlawful assembling of large numbers of persons for the purpose of obtaining a repeal of the Union, by intimidation and the exhibition of physical force.[3] *Trial of Mr. O'Connell and the repeal leaders.* *Nov. 2nd, 1843.*

[1] Ann. Reg., 1843, p. 234; Ibid., 1844, p. 335, *et seq*. Trial of Mr. O'Connell; summing up of chief justice, &c.

[2] The proclamation stated 'that the motives and objects of the persons to be assembled thereat, are not the fair legal exercise of constitutional rights and privileges, but to bring into hatred and contempt the government and constitution of the United Kingdom, as by law established, and to accomplish alterations in the laws and constitution of the realm, by intimidation, and the demonstration of physical force.'

[3] Ann. Reg., 1843, p. 237.

From this moment, Mr. O'Connell moderated his language,—abjured the use of the irritating term of 'Saxon,'—exhorted his followers to tranquillity and submission; and gave tokens of his readiness even to abandon the cause of repeal itself.[1] At length the trial was commenced: but, at the outset, a painful incident, due to the peculiar condition of Ireland, deprived it of much of its moral weight, and raised imputations of unfairness. The old feud between Catholic and Protestant was the foundation of the repeal movement: it embittered every political struggle; and notoriously interfered with the administration of justice. Neither party expected justice from the other. And in this trial, eleven Catholics having been challenged by the crown, the jury was composed exclusively of Protestants. The leader of the Catholic party,—the man who had triumphed over Protestant ascendency, was to be tried by his foes.[2] After a trial of twenty-five days, in which the proceedings of the agitators were fully disclosed, Mr. O'Connell was found guilty upon all, or parts of all, the counts of the indictment; and the other defendants (except Father Tierney) on nearly all.

*Trial commenced, Jan 15th, 1844.*

*May 30th, 1844.* Mr. O'Connell was sentenced to a year's imprisonment, to pay a fine of 2,000*l.*, and to give security for good behaviour for seven years. The other defendants were sentenced to somewhat lighter punishments; and Mr. Tierney was not called up for judgment.

---

[1] Ann. Reg., 1843, p. 238.
[2] Hans. Deb., 3rd Ser., lxxiii. 435; lxxvi. 1956, &c.

Mr. O'Connell was now old, and in prison. Who can wonder that he met with compassion and sympathy? His friends complained that he had been unfairly tried; and the lawfulness of his conviction was immediately questioned by a writ of error. Many who condemned the dangerous excesses of the repeal agitation, remembered his former services to his country,—his towering genius, and rare endowments; and grieved that such a man should be laid low. After four months' imprisonment, however, the judgment of the court below was reversed by the House of Lords, on the writ of error, and the repealers were once more at liberty. The liberator was borne from his prison, in triumph, through the streets of Dublin. He was received with tumultuous applause at meetings, where he still promised a repeal of the Union: his rent continued to be collected: but the agitation no longer threatened danger to the state. Even the miscarriage of the prosecution favoured the cause of order. If one who had defied the government of England could yet rely upon the impartial equity of its highest court, where was the injustice of the hated Saxon? And having escaped by technical errors in the indictment, and not by any shortcomings of the law itself, O'Connell was sensible that he could not again venture to transgress the bounds of lawful agitation. *The writ of error.*

Henceforth the cause of repeal gradually languished and died out. Having no support but factious violence, working upon general discontent, and many social maladies,—it might, indeed, *Failure of the repeal agitation.*

have led to tumults, bloodshed, and civil war,—but never to the coercion of the government and legislature of England. Revived a few years later, by Mr. Smith O'Brien, it again perished in an abortive and ridiculous insurrection.[1]

<small>Conclusion of repeal agitation, 1848.</small>

<small>Mr. Smith O'Brien.</small>

During the repeal agitation in Ireland, other combinations, in both countries, were not without peril to the peace of society. In Ireland, Catholics and Protestants had long been opposed, like two hostile races;[2] and while the former had been struggling to throw off their civil disabilities, to lessen the burthen of tithes, to humble the Protestant Church, to enlarge their own influence, and lastly, to secure an absolute domination by casting off the Protestant legislature of the United Kingdom,—the latter had combined, with not less earnestness, to maintain that Protestant ascendency, which was assailed and endangered. So far back as 1795, Orange societies had been established in Ireland, and particularly in the north, where the population was chiefly Protestant. Early in the present century they were extended to England, and an active correspondence was maintained between the societies of the two kingdoms. As the agitation of the Catholics increased, the confederation expanded. Checked, for a time, in Ireland, together with the Catholic Association, by the Act of 1825, it assumed, in 1828, the imposing character of a national institution. The Duke of Cumberland was inaugurated,

<small>Orange lodges.</small>

---

[1] Ann. Reg., 1848, p. 95; Chron., p. 95.
[2] *Infra*, Chap. XVI. (Ireland).

in London, as grand master: commissions and warrants were made out under the great seal of the order: office-bearers were designated, in the language of royalty, as 'trusty and well-beloved:' large subscriptions were collected; and lodges founded in every part of the empire, whence delegates were sent to the grand lodge. Peers, members of the House of Commons, country gentlemen, magistrates, clergy, and officers in the army and navy, were the patrons and promoters of this organisation. The members were exclusively Protestants: they were admitted with a religious ceremony, and taught secret signs and pass-words.[1] In the following year, all the hopes of Orangemen were suddenly dashed, and the objects of the institution frustrated, by the surrender of the Protestant citadel, by the ministers of the crown. Hitherto their loyalty had scarcely been exceeded by their Protestant zeal: but now the violence and folly of some of their most active, but least discreet members, brought imputations even upon their fidelity to the crown. Such men were possessed by the most extravagant illusions. It was pretended that the Duke of Wellington was preparing to seize upon the crown, as military dictator; and idle plots were even fomented to set aside the succession of the Duke of Clarence, as insane, and the prospective claims of the infant Princess Victoria, as a female and a minor, in order that the Duke of Cumberland might reign, as a Protestant monarch, over a Protestant people.[2] Treason lurked amid

---

[1] Commons' Report, 1835, p. vi.–x.
[2] Hans. Deb., xxxi. 797, 807; Ann. Reg., 1836, p. 11.

their follies. Meanwhile, the organisation was extended until it numbered 1,500 lodges comprising 220,000 Orangemen in Ireland; and 381 lodges in Great Britain, with 140,000 members. There were thirty Orange lodges in the army at home, and many others in the colonies,[1] which had been held without the knowledge of the commanding officers of regiments.

*Parliamentary inquiries, 1835.* Secret as were the proceedings of the Grand Orange Society, the processions of its lodges in Ireland, and its extensive ramifications elsewhere, could not fail to arouse suspicion and alarm; and at length, in 1835, the magnitude and dangerous character of the organisation were fully exposed by a committee of the House of Commons. It was shown to provoke animosities, to interfere with the administration of justice, and to endanger military discipline.[2] Mr. Hume urged the *Orange lodges in the army condemned, 1835.* necessity of prompt measures for suppressing Orange and other secret associations among the soldiery; and so fully was the case established, that the House concurred in an address to the king, praying him to suppress political societies in the army, and calling attention to the conduct of the Duke of Cumberland.[3] His Majesty promised his ready compliance.[4] The most indefensible part of the organisation was now condemned.

---

[1] Commons' Report, 1835, xi.–xv., xxvii.; Ann. Reg., 1835, chap. xii.: Martineau's Hist., ii. 266–275.
[2] Report, p. xviii.
[3] Hans. Deb., 3rd Ser., xxx. 58, 95, 266; Ann. Reg., 1835, chap. xii.; Comm. Journ., xc. 533.
[4] *Ibid.*, 552.

Early in the ensuing session, the disclosures of the committee being then complete, another address was unanimously agreed to, praying the king to take measures for the effectual discouragement of Orange lodges, and generally of all political societies, excluding persons of different religions, and using secret signs and symbols, and acting by means of associated branches. Again the King assured the House of his compliance.[1] His Majesty's answer having been communicated to the Duke of Cumberland by the Home Secretary, his Royal Highness announced that he had already recommended the dissolution of Orange societies in Ireland, and would take measures to dissolve them in England.[2]

*Address against Orange lodges, Feb. 23rd, 1836.*

Other societies have endeavoured to advance their cause by public discussions, and appeals to their numbers and resolution. The Orange Association laboured secretly to augment its numbers, and stimulate the ardour of its associates, by private intercourse and correspondence. Publicity is the very life of constitutional agitation: but secrecy and covert action distinguished this anomalous institution. Such peculiarities raised suspicions that men who shrank from appealing to public opinion, meditated a resort to force. It was too late to repel Catholic aggression and democracy by argument: but might they not, even yet, be resisted by the sword?[3] That such designs were entertained by

*Peculiarity of Orange societies.*

---

[1] Hans. Deb., 3rd Ser., xxxi. 779, 870.
[2] Ann. Reg., 1836, p. 19.
[3] See Letters of Col. Fairman, Report of Committee, 1835, No. 605, p. xvi.

the leading Orangemen, few but their most rancorous enemies affected to believe: but it was plain that a prince of the blood, and the proudest nobles, —inflamed by political discontents, and associated with reckless and foolish men,—might become not less dangerous to the state, than the most vulgar tribunes of the people.

Such were the failures of two great combinations, Anti-Slavery Association. respectively representing the Catholics and Protestants of Ireland, and their ancient feuds. While they were in dangerous conflict, another movement,—essentially differing from these in the sentiments from which it sprang, and the means by which it was forwarded,—was brought to a successful issue. In 1833 the generous labours of the Anti-Slavery Association were consummated. The venerable leaders of the movement which had condemned the slave-trade,[1] together with Mr. Fowell Buxton, and other younger associates, had revived the same agency, for attaining the abolition of slavery itself. Again were the moral and religious feelings of the people successfully appealed to: again did the press, the pulpit, the platform, —petitions, addresses, and debates, stimulate and instruct the people. Again was public opinion persuaded and convinced; and again a noble cause was won, without violence, menace, or dictation.[2]

Let us now turn to other combinations of this Trades' unions, 1834. period, formed by working men alone, with scarcely a leader from another class. In

[1] *Supra*, p. 128.
[2] Life of Wilberforce, v. 122–127, 163–171, &c.; Life of Sir Fowell Buxton, 125, 256, 311, &c.; Ann. Reg. 1833, ch. vii.

1834, the trades' unions which had hitherto restricted their action to matters affecting the interests of operatives and their employers, were suddenly impelled to a strong political demonstration. Six labourers had been tried at Dorchester for adminis- *The Dorchester labourers.* tering unlawful oaths, and were sentenced to transportation.[1] The unionists were persuaded that these men had been punished as an example to themselves: they had administered similar oaths, and were amenable to the same terrible law. Their leaders, therefore, resolved to demand the *Procession of trades' unions, April 21st, 1834.* recall of the Dorchester labourers; and to support their representations by an exhibition of physical force. A petition to the king was accordingly prepared; and a meeting of trades' unions was summoned to assemble at Copenhagen Fields on the 21st of April, and escort a deputation, by whom it was to be presented, to the Home Office. About 30,000 men assembled on that day, marshalled in their respective unions, and bearing emblems of their several trades. After the meeting, they formed a procession and marched, in orderly array, past Whitehall, to Kennington Common, while the deputation was left to its mission, at the Home Office. The leaders hoped to overawe the government by their numbers and union: but were quickly undeceived. The deputation presented themselves at the Home Office, and solicited the interview which Lord Melbourne had appointed:

---

[1] Courts and Cabinets of Will. IV., &c., ii. 82. The Duke of Buckingham says that two out of the six 'Dorchester labourers' were dissenting ministers.

but they were met by Mr. Phillips, the under-secretary, and acquainted that Lord Melbourne could not receive the petition presented in such a manner, nor admit them to his presence, attended, as they were, by 30,000 men. They retired, humbled and crestfallen,—and half afraid to announce their discomfiture at Kennington: they had failed in their mission, by reason of the very demonstration upon which they had rested their hopes of success.

Meanwhile the procession passed onwards, without disturbance. The people gazed upon them as they passed, with mingled feelings of interest and pity, but with little apprehension. The streets were quiet: there were no signs of preparation to quell disorder: not a soldier was to be seen: even the police were in the background. Yet, during the previous night, the metropolis had been prepared as for a siege. The streets were commanded by unseen artillery: the barracks and public offices were filled with soldiers under arms: large numbers of police and special constables were close at hand. Riot and outrage could have been crushed at a blow: but neither sight nor sound was there, to betray distrust of the people, or provoke them to a collision with authority. To a government thus prepared, numbers were no menace: they were peaceable, and were unmolested. The vast assemblage dispersed; and a few days afterwards, a deputation, with the petition, was courteously received by Lord Melbourne.[1] It was a noble example of moderation and firmness on

[1] Ann. Reg., 1834, Chron., p. 58; Court and Cabinets of Will. IV., ii. 82; Personal observation.

the part of the executive,—worthy of imitation in all times.

Soon after these events, a wider combination of working men was commenced,—the history of which is pregnant with political instruc- *The Chartists, 1837-48.* tion. The origin of Chartism was due to distress and social discontents, rather than to political causes. Operatives were jealous of their employers, and discontented with their wages, and the high price of food; and between 1835 and 1839, many were working short time in the factories, or were wholly out of employment. The recent introduction of the new poor law was also represented as an aggravation of their wrongs. Their discontents were fomented, but their distresses not alleviated, by trades' unions.

In 1838, they held vast torch-light meetings throughout Lancashire. They were addressed in language of frantic violence: *Torch-light meetings.* they were known to be collecting arms: factories were burned: tumults and insurrection were threatened. In November, the government desired the magistrates to give notice of the illegality of such meetings, and of their intention to *Nov. 22nd, 1838.* prevent them; and in December, a proclamation was issued for that purpose.[1]

Hitherto the Chartists had been little better than the Luddites of a former period. Whatever their political objects, they were obscured by turbulence and a wild spirit of *The National Petition, 1839.*

---

[1] Ann. Reg., 1839, p. 304; Carlyle's Tract on Chartism; Life of Sir C. Napier, ii. 1-150.

discontent,—to which hatred of capitalists seemed to be the chief incitement. But in 1838, the 'People's Charter' was agreed upon; and a national petition read at numerous meetings, in support of it.[1] Early in 1839, a national convention of delegates from the working classes was established in London, whose views were explained in the monster national petition, signed by 1,280,000 persons, and presented to the House of Commons on the 14th of June.[2] It prayed for universal suffrage, vote by ballot, annual parliaments, the payment of members, and the abolition of their property qualification,—such being the five points of the people's charter. The members of the convention deprecated appeals to physical force; and separated themselves, as far as possible, from those turbulent chartists who had preached, and sometimes even practised, a different doctrine. The petition was discussed with temper and moderation: but certainly with no signs of submission to the numbers and organisation of the petitioners.[3]

While the political section of Chartists were appealing to Parliament for democratic reform, their lawless associates, in the country, were making the name of Chartists hateful to all classes of society. There were Chartist riots at Birmingham, at Sheffield, at Newcastle: contributions were extorted from house to house by threats

*Chartist riots and turbulence.*

[1] Ann. Reg., 1838, Chron., p. 120.
[2] Hans. Deb., 3rd Ser., xlviii. 222; Ann. Reg., 1839, p. 304.
[3] June 14th, July 12th, Hans. Deb., 3rd Ser., xlviii. 222, xlix. 220. A motion for referring it to a committee was negatived by a majority of 189—Ayes, 46; Noes, 235.

and violence: the services of the church were invaded by the intrusion of large bodies of Chartists. At some of their meetings, the proceedings bore a remarkable resemblance to those of 1819. At a great meeting at Kersal Moor, near Manchester, there were several female associations; and in imitation of the election of legislatorial attorneys, Chartists were desired to attend every election; when the members returned by show of hands, being the true representatives of the people, would meet in London at a time to be appointed. Thousands of armed men attacked the town of Newport: but were repulsed with loss by the spirit of Mr. Phillipps, the mayor, and his brother magistrates, and the well-directed fire of a small file of troops. Three of their leaders, Frost, Williams, and Jones, were tried and transported for their share in this rebellious outrage.[1] Such excesses were clearly due to social disorganisation among the operatives,—to be met by commercial and social remedies,—rather than to political discontents,—to be cured by constitutional changes; but being associated with political agitation, they disgraced a cause which,—even if unstained by crimes and outrage,—would have been utterly hopeless. *Riot at Newport.*

The Chartists occupied the position of the democrats and radical reformers of 1793, 1817, and 1819. Prior to 1830, reformers among the working classes had always demanded universal suffrage and annual parliaments. No scheme less comprehensive embraced their own *Weakness of working classes alone, in agitation.*

[1] Ann. Reg., 1839, p. 393; Chron., 73, 132-164.

claims to a share in the government of the country. But measures so democratic having been repudiated by the Whig party and the middle classes, the cause of reform had languished.[1] In 1830 the working classes, powerless alone, had formed an alliance with the reform party and the middle classes ; and, waiving their own claims, had contributed to the passing of a measure which enfranchised every class but themselves.[2] Now they were again alone in their agitation. Their numbers were greater, their knowledge advanced, and their organisation more extended : but their hopes of forcing democracy upon Parliament were not less desperate. Their predecessors in the cause had been met by repression and coercion. Free from such restraints, the Chartists had to encounter the moral force of public opinion, and the strength of a Parliament resting upon a wider basis of representation, and popular confidence.

*Chartist meeting of April 10th, 1848.* This agitation, however hopeless, was continued for several years ; and in 1848, the Revolution in France inspired the Chartists with new life. Relying upon the public excitement, and their own numbers, they now hoped to extort from the fears of Parliament, what they had failed to obtain from its sympathies. A meeting was accordingly summoned to assemble on the 10th of April, at Kennington Common, and carry a Chartist petition, pretending to bear the signatures of 5,000,000 persons, to the very doors of the House of Commons. The Chartist leaders seemed to have

[1] *Supra*, Vol. I. 402 ; Vol. II. 357.    [2] *Supra*, p. 305.

forgotten the discomfiture of the trades' unions in 1835: but the government, profiting by the experience of that memorable occasion, prepared to protect Parliament from intimidation, and the public peace from disturbance.

On the 6th, a notice was issued declaring the proposed meeting criminal and illegal,—as tending to excite terror and alarm; and the intention of repairing to Parliament, on pretence of presenting a petition, with excessive numbers, unlawful,—and calling upon well-disposed persons not to attend. At the same time, it was announced that the constitutional right of meeting to petition, and of presenting the petition, would be respected.[1]  *Preparations of the government.*

On the 10th, the bridges, the Bank, the Tower, and the neighbourhood of Kennington Common, were guarded by horse, foot, and artillery. Westminster Bridge, and the streets and approaches to the Houses of Parliament and public offices, were commanded by unseen ordnance. An overpowering military force,—vigilant, yet out of sight,—was ready for immediate action. The Houses of Parliament were filled with police; and the streets guarded by 170,000 special constables. The assembling of this latter force was the noblest example of the strength of a constitutional government, to be found in history. The maintenance of peace and order was confided to the people themselves. All classes of society vied with one another  *The special constables.*

[1] Ann. Reg. 1848; Chron, p. 51.

in loyalty and courage. Nobles and gentlemen of fashion, lawyers, merchants, scholars, clergymen, tradesmen, and operatives, hastened together to be sworn, and claim the privilege of bearing the constable's staff, on this day of peril. The Chartists found themselves opposed not to their rulers only, but to the vast moral and material force of English society. They might, indeed, be guilty of outrage: but intimidation was beyond their power.

*Failure of the meeting.* The Chartists, proceeding from various parts of the town, at length assembled at Kennington Common. A body of 150,000 men had been expected: not more than 25,000 attended,— to whom may be added about 10,000 spectators, attracted by curiosity. Mr. Feargus O'Connor, their leader, being summoned to confer with Mr. Mayne, the Police Commissioner, was informed that the meeting would not be interfered with, if Mr. O'Connor would engage for its peaceable character: but that the procession to Westminster would be prevented by force. The disconcerted Chartists found all their proceedings a mockery. The meeting, having been assembled for the sake of the procession, was now without an object, and soon broke up in confusion. To attempt a procession was wholly out of the question. The Chartists were on the wrong side of the river, and completely entrapped. Even the departing crowds were intercepted and dispersed on their arrival at the bridges, so as to prevent a dangerous re-union on the other side. Torrents of rain opportunely completed their dispersion; and in the afternoon the streets were deserted. Not a trace was left of the recent excitement.[1]

Discomfiture pursued this petition, even into the House of Commons. It was numerously signed, beyond all example: but Mr. O'Connor, in presenting it, affirmed that it bore 5,706,000 signatures. A few days afterwards, the real number was ascertained to be 1,900,000,—of which many were in the same handwriting, and others fictitious, jocose, and impertinent. The vast numbers who had signed this petition, earnestly and in good faith, entitled it to respect: but the exaggeration, levity, and carelessness of its promoters brought upon it discredit and ridicule.[2] The failure of the Chartist agitation was another example of the hopelessness of a cause not supported by a parliamentary party,—by enlightened opinion,—and by the co-operation of several classes of society. *Signatures to the petition.*

The last political agitation which remains to be described was essentially different in its objects, incidents, character, and result. The 'Anti-Corn-Law League' affords the most remarkable example in our history, of a great cause won against powerful interests and prejudice, by the overpowering force of reason and public opinion. When the League was formed in 1838, both Houses of Parliament, the first statesmen of all parties, and the landlords and farmers throughout the country, *Anti-Corn-Law League.*

---

[1] Ann. Reg., 1848; Chron., p. 50; Newspapers, 9th, 10th, and 11th April, 1848; Personal observation.

[2] The Queen, the Duke of Wellington, Sir R. Peel, and others, were represented as having signed it several times.—Hans. Deb., 3rd Series, xcviii. 285; Report of Public Petitions Committee.

firmly upheld the protective duties upon corn; while merchants, manufacturers, traders, and the inhabitants of towns, were generally indifferent to the cause of free trade. The parliamentary advocates of free trade in corn, led by Mr. Poulett Thomson and Mr. Charles Villiers, had already exhausted the resources of political science, in support and illustration of this measure. Their party was respectable in numbers, in talent, and political influence; and was slowly gathering strength. It was supported, in the country, by many political philosophers, by thoughtful writers in the press, and by a few far-seeing merchants and manufacturers: but the impulse of a popular movement, and public conviction, was wanting. This it became the mission of the Anti-Corn-Law League to create.

*Its organisation.* This association at once seized upon all the means by which, in a free country, public opinion may be acted upon. Free-trade newspapers, pamphlets, and tracts were circulated with extraordinary industry and perseverance. The leaders of the League, and, above all, Mr. Cobden, addressed meetings, in every part of the country, in language calculated at once to instruct the public mind in the true principles of free trade, and to impress upon the people the vital importance of those principles to the interests of the whole community. Delegates, from all parts of England, were assembled at Westminster,[1] Manchester, and elsewhere, who conferred with ministers, and members of Parliament.[2]

[1] Prentice's History of the Anti-Corn-Law League, i. 101, 107, 125.     [2] *Ibid.*, 150, 200.

In 1842, they numbered nearly 1,600.[1] In London, Drury Lane and Covent Garden theatres were borrowed from the drama, and converted into arenas for political discussion, where crowded audiences listened with earnest, and often passionate, attention, to the stirring oratory of the corn-law repealers. In country towns, these intrepid advocates even undertook to convert farmers to the doctrines of free trade; and were ready to break a lance with all comers, in the town-hall or corn exchange. The whole country was awakened by the masterly logic and illustration of Mr. Cobden, and the vigorous eloquence of Mr. Bright. Religion was pressed into the service of this wide-spread agitation. Conferences of ministers were held at Manchester, Carnarvon, and Edinburgh, where the corn laws were denounced as sinful restraints upon the bounty of the Almighty; and the clergy of all denominations were exhorted to use the persuasions of the pulpit, and every influence of their sacred calling, in the cause.[2] Even the sympathies of the fair sex were enlisted in the agitation, by the gaieties and excitement of free-trade bazaars.[3] Large subscriptions were raised, which enabled the League to support a numerous staff of agents, who everywhere collected and disseminated information upon the operation of the corn laws; and encouraged the preparation of petitions.

By these means public opinion was rapidly instructed, and won over to the cause of free trade in corn. But Parliament and the constituencies were

[1] Prentice's History of the Anti-Corn-Law League, i. 306.
[2] *Ibid.*, i. 234, 252, 290.      [3] *Ibid.*, i. 296.

still to be overcome. Parliament was addressed in petitions from nearly every parish; and nothing was left undone, that debates and divisions could accomplish within its walls. The constituencies were ap-

1844.  pealed to, at every election, on behalf of free-trade candidates: the registration was diligently watched; and no pains were spared to add free-trade voters to the register. Nor did the League stop here: but finding that, with all their efforts, the constituencies were still opposed to them, they resorted to an extensive creation of votes by means of 40s. freeholds, purchased by the working classes.[1]

Never had political organisation been so complete.
Its success. The circumstances of the time favoured its efforts; and in 1846, the protective corn law,—with which the most powerful interests in the state were connected,—was unconditionally, and for ever abandoned. There had been great pressure from without, but no turbulence. Strong feelings had been aroused in the exciting struggle: landlords had been denounced: class exasperated against class: Parliament approached in a spirit of dictation. Impetuous orators, heated in the cause, had breathed words of fire: promises of cheap bread to hungry men, and complaints that it was denied them, were full of peril: but this vast organisation was never discredited by acts of violence or lawlessness. The leaders had triumphed in a great popular cause, without the least taint of sedition.

[1] Prentice's Hist., *passim*, and particularly i. 64, 90, 126, 137, 225, 410; ii. 168, 236, &c.; M. Bastiat, Cobden et la Ligue; Ann. Reg., 1843, 1844.

'This movement had enjoyed every condition of success. The cause itself appealed alike to the reason and judgment of thinking men, and to the interests and passions of the multitude: it had the essential basis of Parliamentary support; and it united, for a common object, the employers of labour and the working classes. The latter condition mainly ensured its success. Manufacturers foresaw, in free trade, an indefinite extension of the productive energies of the country; operatives hoped for cheap bread, higher wages, and more constant employment. These two classes, while suffering from the commercial stagnation of past years, had been estranged and hostile. Trades' unions and chartism had widened the breach between them: but they now worked heartily together, in advancing a measure which promised advantage to them all. *Causes of success.*

The history of the League yet furnishes another lesson. It was permitted to survive its triumph;[1] and such is the love of freedom which animates Englishmen, that no sooner had its mission been accomplished, than men who had laboured with it, became jealous of its power, and dreaded its dictation. Its influence rapidly declined; and at length it became unpopular, even in its own strongholds. *The Corn-law League, after 1846.*

In reviewing the history of political agitation, we cannot be blind to the perils which have sometimes threatened the state. We have observed fierce antagonism between the people and their rulers,—evil passions and turbulence,—class divided against class,—associations overbearing the *Review of political agitation.*

[1] It was suspended in July 1846: see Cobden's Speeches, i. 387; but its organisation was maintained for other purposes.

councils of Parliament,—and large bodies of subjects exalting themselves into the very seat of government. Such have been the storms of the political atmosphere, which, in a free state, alternate with the calms and light breezes of public opinion; and statesmen have learned to calculate their force and direction. There have been fears and dangers: but popular discontents have been dissipated; wrongs have been redressed; and public liberties established, without revolution: while popular violence and intimidation have been overborne, by the combined force of government and society. And what have been the results of agitation upon the legislation of the country? Not a measure has been forced upon Parliament, which the calm judgment of a later time has not since approved: not an agitation has failed, which posterity has not condemned. The abolition of the slave trade and slavery, Catholic emancipation, parliamentary reform, and the repeal of the corn laws, were the fruits of successful agitation,—the repeal of the Union, and chartism, conspicuous examples of failure.

But it may be asked, is agitation to be the normal condition of the state? Are the people to be ever combining, and the government now resisting, and now yielding to, their pressure? Is constitutional government to be worked with this perpetual wear and tear,—this straining and wrenching of its very framework? We fervently hope not. The struggles we have narrated, marked the transition from old to new principles of government,—from exclusion, repression, and distrust, to comprehension, sympathy, and confidence. Parliament, yielding slowly to the expansive energies of society, was stirred and shaken by their upheavings. But with a free and instructed press, a wider representation, and a Parliament enjoying the general confidence of the people,—agitation has nearly lost its fulcrum. Should Parliament, however, oppose itself to the progressive impulses of another generation, let it study well the history of the past; and discern the signs of a pressure from without, which may not wisely be resisted. Let it reflect upon the wise maxim of Macaulay: 'the true secret of the power of agitators is the obstinacy of rulers; and liberal governments make a moderate people.'[1]

The development of free institutions, and the entire recognition of liberty of opinion, have wrought an essential change in the relations of the government and the people. *Altered relations of government to the people.* Mutual confidence has succeeded to mutual distrust. They act in concert, instead of opposition; and share, with one another, the cares and responsibility of state affairs. If the power and independence of ministers are sometimes impaired by the necessity of admitting the whole people to their councils,—their position is more often fortified by public approbation. Free discussion aids them in all their deliberations: the first intellects of the country counsel them: the good sense of the people strengthens their convictions. If they judge rightly, they may rely with confidence on public opinion;

[1] Speech on Reform Bill, 5th July, 1831; Hans. Deb., 3rd Ser., iv. 118.

and even if they err, so prompt is popular criticism, that they may yet have time to repair their error. The people having advanced in enlightenment as well as in freedom, their judgment has become more discriminating, and less capricious, than in former times. To wise rulers, therefore, government has become less difficult. It has been their aim to satisfy the enlightened judgment of the whole community, freely expressed, and readily interpreted. To read it rightly,—to cherish sentiments in advance of it, rather than to halt and falter behind it,—has become the first office of a successful statesman.

*Concurrent increase of power and intelligence in the people.* What theory of a free state can transcend this gradual development of freedom,—in which the power of the people has increased with their capacity for self-government? It is this remarkable condition that has distinguished English freedom from democracy. Public opinion is expressed, not by the clamorous chorus of the multitude: but by the measured voices of all classes, parties, and interests. It is declared by the press, the exchange, the market, the club, and society at large. It is subject to as many checks and balances as the constitution itself; and represents the national intelligence, rather than the popular will.

END OF THE SECOND VOLUME.

*Spottiswoode & Co., Printers, London and Westminster.*

www.ingramcontent.com/pod-product-compliance
Lightning Source LLC
Chambersburg PA
CBHW020739020526
44115CB00030B/607